JAMES R. WALKER

Lakota Belief
and Ritual

EDITED BY

Raymond J. DeMallie and Elaine A. Jahner

UNIVERSITY OF NEBRASKA PRESS
LINCOLN AND LONDON

Published in cooperation with
the Colorado Historical Society

First Bison Book printing: 1991
Most recent printing indicated by the last digit below:
10   9   8   7   6   5

Library of Congress Cataloging-in-Publication Data
Walker, J. R. (James R.). b. 1849.
Lakota belief and ritual / James R. Walker: edited by Raymond J. DeMallie and
Elaine A. Jahner.
p.   cm.
Includes bibliographical references and index.
ISBN 0-8032-9731-9 (paper).—ISBN 0-8032-2551-2 (cloth)
1. Oglala Indians—Religion and mythology.   2. Oglala Indians—Rites and cere-
monies.   I. DeMallie, Raymond J., 1946–   .   II. Jahner, Elaine, 1942–   .   III.
Title.
E99.O3W17   1991
299'.785—dc20
91-15037   CIP

Contents

List of Illustrations

Black and white photographs

following p. 66
James Riley Walker
James R. Walker and Red Cloud
Red Cloud
Little Wound
George Sword
Afraid of Bear
American Horse
Thunder Bear

following p. 130
Rocky Bear
Red Hawk
Thomas Tyon
No Flesh
Short Bull and Joseph Horn Cloud
William Garnett, Charles Ash Bates, and American Horse
Group from Pine Ridge at Rodman Wanamaker's "Last Great
    Indian Council"
Blue Horse

following p. 194
Pine Ridge Agency, ca. 1900
Pine Ridge Agency, co. 1909
Dancing at Pine Ridge

Preface

Today more than ever before, people are trying to understand both their own and others' traditions; they are learning to appreciate that each way of life has its own value and particular capacity to tap the creative resources of human consciousness. As people the world over seek to learn about the many ways in which others have related to their immediate and to their cosmic environment, they are turning toward American Indian tribal traditions. They are listening to tribal wisdom that has survived in oral tradition and are seeking those documents that record accurately past ways of thinking and relating. Part of the world's heritage of authentic documents is the famous but until now almost inaccessible James R. Walker collection of traditional Lakota knowledge. The collection records teachings by men whose statements of belief show the energy, depth, and imaginative intensity characteristic of the Lakota response to specific cultural, social, and ecological challenges.

James R. Walker spent eighteen years in South Dakota as agency physician on the Pine Ridge Reservation, the home of the Oglala Sioux. From 1896 until 1914, he collected material relating to almost every facet of the old Lakota way of life. He also arranged to have Lakota people write for him and conduct interviews. The creation of a record of the spiritual and philosophical bases of the buffalo-hunting way of life became a quest for Walker. Beginning as a total outsider to the Oglalas, through his medical work and his expression of interest in the traditional ways he eventually became a trusted friend.

The old men at Pine Ridge instructed Walker in their traditional religion, first of all, because, in the words of George Sword, "the Gods of the Oglala would be more pleased if the holy men told of them so that they might be kept in remembrance and all the world might know of them." The collective decision to instruct Walker as a Lakota holy man was not made without consulting the gods themselves; Walker recorded that first Little Wound sought a vision and then the other holy men agreed to abide by his decision. Only after this did they begin to instruct Walker in the sacred things that were not common knowledge.

The holy men who instructed Walker included some of the most famous and influential old men of the reservation. Besides Sword and Little Wound (who claimed the position of head chief of the Oglalas) there were American Horse, Red Cloud, Bad Wound, and No Flesh, all important leaders. There were also shamans like Ringing Shield, Finger, and Red Hawk. Particularly important was Thomas Tyon, a mixed-blood whom the holy men trusted and who frequently served as Walker's interpreter.

In his studies with the old men, Walker attempted to reach into the past to describe Lakota religion before the introduction of Christian religions to the Oglalas. He himself published a summary of his studies in his 1917 monograph *The Sun Dance and Other Ceremonies of the Oglala Division of the Teton Dakota,* the distillation of two decades' work. But today much of our interest is in the actual statements by individual Lakotas upon which Walker based his own interpretations. We can learn facts from Walker's summaries, but we need the actual statements of individuals to help us understand how influential members of the tribe understood those facts and related them to changing circumstances.

This volume is the first of four that will present the best and most important portions of the hundreds of pages of notes, interviews, texts, and essays that James R. Walker amassed during his eighteen years at Pine Ridge Reservation. Among them, these books will present the previously unpublished interview notes taken by Walker in his work with the Oglalas. Each volume is unique. The first, after giving biographical details on Walker, is concerned with beliefs that form the foundation for the Lakota way of life. It includes material on religion, ritual, and warfare. The second volume will concern Lakota myth, in which the fundamental moral concepts of the culture are embodied. The third volume will deal with Lakota social organization, concepts of time and history, and winter counts. The fourth volume

will present a translation of the writings of George Sword, Oglala warrior, later agency policeman and judge of the Court of
Indian Offenses at Pine Ridge. At Walker's request, Sword
wrote an extensive record of all aspects of the traditional way of
life, from religion and myth to ritual, warfare, and even games.
And to introduce himself, he wrote an autobiography. Thus the
first three volumes are thematic, while the fourth examines the
totality of Lakota life from the perspective of a single individual.
It must be stressed that these publications supplement Walker's
Sun Dance rather than supersede it. In addition to providing his
own synthesis of Oglala religion, that work is important because
it reproduces verbatim some valuable texts and interviews,
which are not reprinted in the present volumes.

Over the years, Walker's *Sun Dance* has become a classic, a
key work for understanding the traditional Lakota way of life. In
preparing his monograph, Walker did not approach the sun
dance ceremony in isolation, but used it as the focus around
which to synthesize the fundamentals of Lakota religion. He
wrote and published under the rubric of anthropology even
though he himself had no formal training in that discipline. At
the turn of the century it was only among anthropologists and
folklorists that there was serious scholarly interest in recording
the religions of native American groups. Walker clearly felt that
he was making a contribution to the "science" of anthropology,
not to the field of religion, philosophy, or literature. His interest
was in describing the religion of the Lakotas as though it were
written by a Lakota who was at home in the English language
and versed in scholarship. He strove for objectivity, attempting
to get each statement verified by several of the old men, synthesizing their information, and seeking their final approval of
his work.

Although in Walker's time there were few anthropological
studies of the various Sioux tribes, nevertheless there was a considerable body of data already recorded when he began his
work. Walker might have checked each detail from every available source with the holy men who had agreed to instruct him.
But he chose, instead, to ignore the previous written record.
Walker was not a scholar, contributing to the scholarly literature
as an end in itself. He was rather a recorder of what the holy
men knew and would tell him, a reporter of a religious tradition
still alive but which he and the old men who instructed him

believed would soon pass away, supplanted by Christianity and non-Indian culture. It would thus have been pointless for Walker to have turned to the literature; he was not trying to write a history of Lakota religion or to place it in any comparative perspective. Rather, he was describing it as an integral system, a philosophy and religion alive in the minds of the handful of old men at Pine Ridge who had chosen to instruct him so that he might record their traditions for posterity.

That Walker ignored the previous literature on the Lakotas is both a strength and a weakness. It is a strength, obviously, because it did not prejudice his own investigations. It is a weakness because the literature might have given Walker insights into directions for his own investigations.

Walker's continuing and deepening relationship with the people he was interviewing was one determining factor in the kinds of information he was able to record. His instructions from Clark Wissler, an anthropologist from the American Museum of Natural History who first suggested and provided financial support for Walker's studies, also have to be considered. They shaped both the form and content of Walker's published work. It was Wissler who directed Walker to focus his description on the sun dance and other ceremonies. The introduction to Walker and his work given in Part I of this volume will enable readers to understand something of Walker's own attitudes toward the material and the ways in which he tried to organize, systematize, and prepare certain portions of what he collected for publication.

Some of Walker's information is unique; much of it is more detailed than other published accounts of the same subjects, both before and since. Yet without the basic data from which it was written—the interviews and Lakota texts that Walker collected during his long study—the information presented in *The Sun Dance* remained suspect. The very style, written as though it were a manual for the instruction of a sun dance candidate and a sun dance priest, struck a literary chord that made scholars wary. There has been no question about the few very excellent and important texts published as an appendix to the monograph, including Sword's accounts of the concepts of *wakan*, *Wakan Tanka*, and *šicun*; Finger's conception of *Škan*; Tyon's discussions of the symbolism of the number four and of the circle; and No Flesh's account of the causes of disease. These are basic and have been cited time and again in later studies. But there has always been the latent question, If Walker had so much original data, why did he not publish more of it?

Searching through the doctor's papers, we can easily find the answer. Walker was a modest man; he did not feel that the notes he took on rambling interviews jumping from topic to topic were worthy of publication. The material was, to use his own term, "too fragmentary." He assumed that the only efficient use of his material to the science of anthropology was through the systematic summaries that he composed of it.

Now it is another story. In Walker's time, closer to the buffalo days when plains Indian cultures were lived out in the old ways, it seemed a relatively easy task to amass rather quickly a large collection of interview notes from older Indians. For us today, every recorded fragment is part of a precious legacy, never to be replaced. The publication at last of Walker's primary materials allows his work to be reassessed in the light of other scholarly evidence and makes available for the first time the direct words of some of the old men of Pine Ridge, his instructors.

Today we cherish this direct evidence because we realize that the scholar's syntheses and reworkings are complementary to the believer's own words but we need both as we try to approach as nearly as possible the believer's attitude. We have developed respect for oral traditions, which convey many levels of meaning simultaneously. A corollary to this more appreciative attentiveness to surviving oral traditions is our concern for exact records of past oral traditions. The information presented in the documents in this book is such a record.

A comment George Sword made to Walker may serve as a guide to the contents of the present volume. In discussing Lakota religion, Sword said that the "ceremonies of the Lakota are the ceremonies of the people, the ceremonies of the warriors, and the ceremonies of the shamans." Each part of this book presents details about these three types of ceremonies while the emphasis on belief in relation to ritual provides the general framework for understanding why the holy men stressed the role of ceremony in all acquisition of knowledge. This book presents for the first time the raw materials from which Walker fashioned his reconstruction of Lakota religion on the basis of ceremony.

The documents included here show the diversity of religious responses on the part of Oglala leaders at a critical time in Lakota history. The years of warfare, the Ghost Dance, and the Wounded Knee massacre were still fresh and vital memories. The Lakotas appeared to be defeated. Conversion to Christianity seemed inevitable and the conflict between Lakota religion and Christianity seemed an either-or choice. Reflection upon the nature of Lakota belief was inevitable for the holy men, forced as they were by historical circumstances to consider and weigh their beliefs. Seldom is the religious thought of particular individuals facing critical historical junctures so well documented as is that of Walker's key informants.

Part I, "James R. Walker: His Life and Work," provides the background necessary to appreciate Walker's work both in the context of his time and from the perspective of today. Beginning with biographical data based largely on the work of Maurice Frink, Part I provides a sketch of Walker's life and presents an account of his studies at Pine Ridge. As much as possible the story is told in Walker's own words, using extracts from his lengthy correspondence with Clark Wissler. The biography of Walker is followed by his autobiographical account of studying Oglala religion and by his brief synthesis of the fundamentals of Oglala mythology. The latter is presented here because it is a secondary document, not a primary one. It is based on information provided by his informants, but it is Walker's own systematization and synthesis of that information. It provides important background knowledge for the reader to appreciate the variation in details among the holy men's accounts and the extent to which Walker's synthesis—well known from his *Sun Dance*—is, in fact, a product of his drive to create a single continuous narrative out of the fragmentary and often conflicting accounts given by his informants. Part I ends with a brief review of other materials, both published and unpublished, that relate to the religion of the Sioux peoples. It is intended to point the reader beyond Walker to information with which to place his work in comparative perspective.

Parts II–V present the primary documents, either direct accounts of Walker's informants or syntheses by Walker of data collected from the old men. Part II, "Belief," deals especially with the abstract concepts that provide the basis for Lakota religion—concepts such as *wakan, Wakan Tanka, Škan*—and with the foundations for all Lakota ritual, the pipe, purification lodge, vision seeking, spirits. These forty-three documents contain information given by many different Lakotas, reflecting different perspectives and emphases. Study of the variations among them is essential for an appreciation of the dimensions of individuality in Lakota religion.

Part III, "Narratives by Thomas Tyon," consists of nineteen documents originally written in Lakota, translated by the editors. Tyon frequently served as Walker's interpreter and was familiar with the kinds of information Walker wished to record. These narratives were not written by Tyon from his own knowledge, but from information provided to him by some of the shamans at Pine Ridge. All deal with aspects of religious life, centering around the quality of *wakan.* They consider the fundamental beliefs and rituals as well as the role of animals and other natural phenomena in Lakota religion. These documents differ from those in Part II because they are translations of original Lakota texts. They all undoubtedly reflect to some degree Tyon's personal perspective, and as far as we know, they were never translated by Walker. That he was apparently unfamiliar with their content makes them a valuable independent check on the documents in Part II. Comparison between these two parts is essential for an understanding of the extent to which Walker shaped and influenced his material merely in the process of setting it down in writing.

Part IV, "Ritual," consists of twenty-four documents relating to the sun dance, *Hunka,* and buffalo ceremony. They provide many of the details from which Walker composed his accounts of those ceremonies in his *Sun Dance.* These documents are best appreciated in comparison with Walker's earlier account, but they are on the whole more primary sources and may be cited with greater authority. Document 63 is an account of the sun dance by Tyon, translated by the editors from the original Lakota text. Of special importance are the two previously unpublished paintings by Short Bull depicting the sun dance (see documents 68 and 69). These masterful compositions represent virtually hundreds of details from which Walker developed to a considerable extent his understanding of the visual aspects of the performance of the ceremony.

Part V, "Warfare," consists of six documents and fourteen drawings relating to the ritual and religious aspects of warfare, and particularly to the men's societies. Documents 89 and 90 are again translations from Lakota texts by Tyon. Document 92 reproduces drawings by Thunder Bear that present an unparalleled visual picture of Lakota war insignia and regalia of the warrior societies.

Walker's manuscripts, notes, and letters have not previously been generally accessible. He sent to Wissler portions of his materials, which remain in the archives of the Department of Anthropology of the American Museum of Natural History in New York. A listing of them was published in Raymond J. DeMallie, "A Partial Bibliography of Archival Manuscript Material Relating to the Dakota Indians" (1970). A copy of Walker's manuscript on Oglala mythology was sent to Franz Boas at Columbia University (perhaps by Wissler). Boas sent it to Ella C. Deloria to take back to the Lakotas for study. Today a typescript of the manuscript, with notes by Deloria, is in the Boas Collection in the American Philosophical Society in Philadelphia. The bulk of Walker's papers remained with his family in Colorado. The story of the rediscovery of these papers by Maurice Frink and their acquisition by the Colorado Historical Society in Denver provides the background for the present publication.

In 1913, Frink, newly graduated from high school in Elkhart, Indiana, was permitted by his physician father to visit Walker for the summer at Pine Ridge in order to learn about Indians at first hand. Frink's visit to the reservation proved to be a central experience in his life. Years later he recalled how the doctor took him around in his Model T Ford on visits to patients and told him about his efforts to record Lakota religion and culture. When it was time to return home, Walker invited young Frink to choose something from a trunk filled with Oglala artifacts as a remembrance. He selected an eagle-bone sun dance whistle with a down feather attached.

During the years that followed, Frink served in the army in World War I and then embarked on a career in journalism, spending three decades on the staff of the *Elkhart Truth*. In 1951 he and his wife, Edith, their family grown, moved west and settled in Boulder, Colorado, where he lectured in the University of Colorado School of Journalism. He also served as executive director of the Colorado Historical Society from 1954 to 1962.

In 1958 Frink received a letter from Frank H. H. Roberts, Jr., of the Smithsonian Institution, forwarding a request from Karl A. Nowotny of the Museum für Völkerkunde in Vienna. Nowotny, an anthropologist, had read Walker's *Sun Dance* and wanted to learn the whereabouts of Walker's papers. Upon receipt of Roberts's letter, Frink attempted to locate Walker's descendants. He found Walker's granddaughter, Mrs. Emeline Wensley Hughes, was living in Denver and possessed the written and printed material that Walker had when he died. In September 1958, Mrs. Hughes made the initial gift of her grandfather's papers to the society, adding to the collection on several later occasions. Included were finished and unfinished manuscripts, notes, lists, interviews, photographs, statistics, drawings, and phonograph recordings of Oglala sun dance songs.

Following his retirement from the society in 1962, Frink concentrated on various research and writing projects, interrupted by a year of service with his wife at Fort Defiance, Arizona, in the VISTA program. Throughout this period he dreamed of writing a biography of Walker and publishing some of the material in the Colorado Historical Society that the doctor had recorded at Pine Ridge. The work would be called "Pine Ridge Medicine Man."

Frink completed the manuscript in 1970 and delivered it to the Colorado Historical Society, which held an option to publish it. Unfortunately, he died in 1972 and the society was unable to realize the publication of the book. Increasingly, however, the society received requests from the Oglala community at Pine Ridge for copies of the material collected by Walker for use in Oglala history classes. Mimeographed notebooks of the myth cycle have been widely circulated among the Lakotas, fulfilling a deeply felt need for materials relating to their traditional religion and culture.

Responding to this demand, we proposed a publication that would combine Walker's materials from the Colorado Historical Society, the American Museum of Natural History, and the American Philosophical Society. We have built on Frink's work and have relied on his manuscript particularly for biographical details about Walker. During the spring of 1978, we assembled the totality of Walker's papers and selected from them the materials for the three volumes of which *Lakota Belief and Ritual* is the first. All the primary interview materials and all the Lakota texts were selected for publication. The manuscript materials omitted were those already published in Walker's *Sun Dance*, incomplete and repetitive drafts of Walker's syntheses of data, popular lectures by Walker that summarize well-known materials, and medical and anthropometric data on the Oglalas. When the three volumes are published, virtually all the primary data collected by Walker on Lakota religion, mythology, and other aspects of culture will be available in print. Together these materials form a unique and valuable source, available for the benefit of the Lakotas themselves and for all others interested in learning from the tribal knowledge of a traditional people.

Note on the editing

While editing the documents in English for inclusion in this volume, we have changed only obvious errors in spelling and punctuation. In some cases we have broken up long sentences and improved awkward grammar. In any case in which we have actually added a word or possibly changed a meaning, we have made our addition in brackets. In some cases, particularly in the descriptions of drawings in Part V, Walker's commentary was obviously written very hurriedly and was in places ungrammatical. We have been freer in these instances in editing the text. Walker intended everything he wrote to be edited stylistically by Clark Wissler and the staff of the American Museum. In the interests of time, Walker made no effort to deal with the mechanics of writing. For example, he wrote to Wissler regarding the publication of his 1914 paper "Oglala Kinship": "I am greatly indebted to you and your assistants for this paper, for I cannot spell the English language, and for this reason my productions appear ridiculous" (AMNH correspondence files). In a few cases words and phrases have been stricken from the typewritten manuscripts, evidently by the American Museum staff, apparently for editorial purposes. We have restored those to the documents printed here on the grounds that we are looking for the original text. All ellipses in the documents are Walker's. Editorial deletions are indicated by three asterisks (* * *). Italicized sentences in documents dictated by Indians indicate comments by Walker. The titles for the documents have for the most part been supplied by us. The names of informants and dates of the documents are given whenever known. The source for each document is indicated after the title by "CHS"

(Colorado Historical Society) or "AMNH" (American Museum of Natural History).

Our editorial policy has been to make the documents readable, but at the same time our primary concern has been to safeguard the integrity of the text. This is particularly important in Walker's interviews with Indians, where we wish to come as near as possible to the original words of the Lakota narrator, as Walker understood them. We have made every effort to provide context for the documents so that in those instances in which style can indeed show the organizational predispositions of the narrators, the reader has access to all available information about the document. Significant historical data and references to comparative sources in Walker's published writings and in the literature generally are given in footnotes to each document.

Biographical information on each of Walker's informants and interpreters is presented in Appendix I, "The Authorities."

Walker used no diacritical marks in writing Lakota words. Thus in his writing he confused *s* and *š*, *g* and *ġ*, *h* and *ḣ*, and *n* and *ŋ*. To the reader knowledgeable in Lakota, this does not ordinarily affect intelligibility. In cases in which Lakota words are not to be found, or not to be found easily, in the standard Lakota dictionaries, we have provided footnotes. See Appendix II, "Phonetic Key," for further commentary on Lakota phonetics. We have corrected misspellings of common Lakota words, but in any case in which the variant spelling might be significant, we have let it stand. All Lakota words are printed in italics to emphasize that they represent Lakota concepts, not English ones.

In some of his writings Walker used the suffix *-pi* as the Lakota equivalent of the English plural *-s*, e.g., *Lakotapi*, "Sioux Indians." The Lakota suffix *-pi* does indicate plurality (see document 14). However, it is added only to verbal forms; when it occurs with nouns it verbalizes them, e.g., *Lakota*, "Sioux Indian"; *Lakotapi*, "they are Sioux Indians." We have let Walker's use of *-pi* stand in the documents printed in this book but elsewhere we use Lakota nouns as both singular and plural. (For further discussion see Franz Boas and Ella C. Deloria, *Dakota Grammar*, p. 157.) Tribal names, e.g., Lakota, Oglala, are the only exceptions. Throughout, we have used their standard plural forms—Lakotas, Oglalas—both in our text and in the documents.

In translating the Lakota texts of Thomas Tyon (documents 44–63 and 89–90) we have remained as close as possible to the originals, presenting here English versions that closely reflect Lakota oral narrative style. For example, we have retained the Lakota quotatives in English, translating *ške* as "it is said" and *keyapi* as "they say," every time they occur, in order to maintain any possible distinction in meaning between the two terms. The quotatives indicate that the narrator is repeating someone else's statements and they are an integral part of oral style. We have also chosen to allow our English translations to reflect the Lakota ambiguity of pronoun reference rather than risk the chance that our sense of the exact referent might be wrong. Some adaptations have been made to English word and sentence order to improve intelligibility, although in any case in which adaptation to English threatened a possible loss of Lakota meaning, we have not adapted.

Some sentences and phrases were especially difficult to translate either because the available resources did not permit any obvious translation or because the semantic domain of the Lakota terms was significantly different from that of the English. In such cases we have included the Lakota words in parentheses, reproducing Tyon's orthography and word boundaries. He used *x* for *š*, *r* for *ġ* and sometimes *ḣ*, *n* for *ŋ*, and *k* for *g* (see Appendix II, "Phonetic Key"). Tyon was very inconsistent in the use of *n* to indicate nasalization of the preceding vowel; he also used it in many places in which it does not ordinarily occur in modern Lakota pronunciation.

We have consulted the three major dictionaries of Dakota and Lakota in editing this work and cite them only where there seems to be some particular value in doing so. Walker himself seems to have relied primarily on John P. Williamson, *An English-Dakota Dictionary* (1902) and secondarily on Stephen R. Riggs, *A Dakota-English Dictionary* (1890). We have also used Eugene Buechel, *Lakota-English Dictionary* (1970), which includes an English-Lakota index. Buechel's work incorporated Riggs's fairly completely, although there are many forms in Williamson that do not appear in Buechel. For grammatical reference we have relied on Boas and Deloria, *Dakota Grammar* (1941).

It is important for the reader to understand that the Sioux, in traditional times, formed three major geographical groups.

The Santees, largely in Minnesota; the Yanktons (including the Yanktonais), on the prairies of western Minnesota and eastern North and South Dakota; and the Tetons, west of the Missouri River on the plains of North and South Dakota and Nebraska. These locations are only approximate, for there was much travel and movement, and bands from any of the three major groups might at any given time be living with another of the major groups.

Each of these three major groups represented a distinctive dialect of the Sioux language, though they were all mutually intelligible. The Santees and Yanktons called themselves Dakota, whereas the Tetons called themselves Lakota. We use *Sioux* as the designation for all these groups, *Lakota* for the Teton or Western Sioux (divided into seven tribes: Oglala, Brulé *(Sicangu)*, Minneconjou, Sans Arc *(Itazipco)*, Two Kettles, Hunkpapa, and Blackfeet Lakota) and *Dakota* to refer generally to the Santee and Yankton groups. The reader should note that this is an English convention only; the Sioux themselves used the terms *Dakota* or *Lakota*, depending on the dialect of the speaker, to refer to *all* the Sioux groups. To differentiate the three groups, the terms *Titonwan*, "Teton"; *Isanati*, "Santee"; and *Ihanktonwan*, "Yankton," were used.

For historical reference the reader should see especially George E. Hyde, *Red Cloud's Folk* (1937) and *A Sioux Chronicle* (1956), histories of the Oglalas; Hyde's *Spotted Tail's Folk: A History of the Brulé Sioux* (1961); James C. Olson, *Red Cloud and the Sioux Problem* (1965), a reexamination of Oglala history, focusing particularly on military affairs; and Roy W. Meyer, *History of the Santee Sioux* (1967).

Acknowledgments

Our debts in preparing this volume are unusually complicated. We are indebted in the first place to Maurice Frink for his work in preserving and organizing the Colorado Historical Society's collection of Walker material and for tracing the doctor's biography. Though neither of us ever met him, his previous work has shaped and guided our own. We hope that he would approve of our efforts.

Over the years Frink was aided by many correspondents and friends in his attempt to prepare the collection for publication. In the acknowledgments to his manuscript "Pine Ridge Medicine Man" he specially expressed his thanks to the following: John C. Ewers, senior ethnologist, Smithsonian Institution; Karl A. Nowotny, Institute of Folk Art, University of Cologne, Germany; Ben Reifel of the Sioux tribe, former congressman from South Dakota and former superintendent of the Pine Ridge Reservation; the Reverend G. R. Welschons, S. J., Holy Rosary Indian Mission; Bob Lee, editor of the *Sturgis Tribune and Black Hills Press,* Sturgis, South Dakota; Charles Trimble, Pine Ridge and Denver; Robert Savage, Omaha; John L. Smith, Des Moines; Will H. Spindler, Chadron, Nebraska; Dr. Walker's granddaughter, Emeline Wensley Hughes, Denver; Ella C. Deloria, Vermillion, South Dakota; Marvin F. Kivett and the staff of the Nebraska State Historical Society; Kristine Haglund, curator, Buffalo Bill Memorial Museum, Golden, Colorado; Howard Higman, Robert M. Hunter, Bryan P. Michener, and Gottfried Lang of the University of Colorado; photographer David W. Zimmerly; the Reverend Fathers S. J. Gentle, Paul B. Steinmetz, and William M. Fay; and Gerald and Vivian One Feather and Joe Cress of Pine Ridge. And to this list Frink added, "If I have omitted someone, I am sorry (even George

Sword, recounting forty war coups, said he might have over-looked one)."

On our part, we gratefully express our appreciation to Mrs. Hughes for her encouragement of the project. We owe a special debt to the Colorado Historical Society for its strong support in all phases of this project and for sharing in the costs of publication. We also wish to express our thanks to the Department of Anthropology, American Museum of Natural History, New York, for allowing us to reproduce the Walker material in their collections. We are also indebted to the American Museum of Natural History, the Colorado Historical Society, the Denver Art Museum, Indiana University Museum, and the National Anthropological Archives at the Smithsonian Institution for allowing us to reproduce photographs from their collections.

It is a delight to acknowledge our indebtedness to Anne Keller, a Lakota woman from Rosebud Reservation, who worked through the translations of Thomas Tyon's writings with us. We all learned from the experience, but we, especially, benefited from her insight into her native language and her ability to express that insight in English.

We are also indebted to the Center for Great Plains Studies and the Research Council at the University of Nebraska–Lincoln for sponsoring the project and for providing Elaine Jahner with financial assistance during its first phases. For her the effort would not have begun when it did, nor maintained its momentum, without the support of Roberta Wilson, a member of the American Indian Higher Education Consortium staff in Denver. Jahner knows that for her the real beginning of the project was many years ago when friends and coworkers at Standing Rock Reservation asked if she could help them find materials related to their culture. She thanks them as the search continues.

For Ray DeMallie the genesis of the project was over a decade ago when he obtained access to the Walker manuscripts for purposes of study. For this he gratefully acknowledges the help of Margaret C. Blaker, former archivist of the National Anthropological Archives, Smithsonian Institution; Enid Thompson, former archivist of the Colorado Historical Society; Stanley F. Freed and David Hurst Thomas, of the Department of Anthropology, American Museum of Natural History; and John L. Smith, of Des Moines, Iowa. DeMallie also wishes to thank the

American Philosophical Society for a small grant from the Phillips Fund that provided crucial support during the initial stages in the preparation of this manuscript, and the Center for the History of the American Indian, Newberry Library, Chicago, where, during a year's residence as a fellow, the final work on the manuscript was completed.

We also wish to give special thanks to Maxine Benson, Curator of Documentary Resources, Colorado Historical Society, for providing the biographical material on Maurice Frink and his involvement with the Walker Collection incorporated in the Preface; to Cathryne Johnson, also of the Colorado Historical Society, for her steadfast support throughout the project; to Father Peter J. Powell, Newberry Library, for providing information on Cheyenne warrior societies; to Terry Anderson, who generously checked details from Walker's official correspondence in the records of the Office of Indian Affairs, National Archives and Records Service; and to Susan Applegate, Indiana University Museum, for providing high-quality prints from negatives in the Wanamaker photograph collection.

Preface to the Bison Book Edition

A decade of continued study of James R. Walker's documents on Oglala religion since the original publication of *Lakota Belief and Ritual* in 1980 has reinforced their significance as unique sources for the understanding of late-nineteenth- and early-twentieth-century Lakota thought. The availability of this book in a paperback edition will broaden its audience and pose new opportunities for interpretation. A few additional words of explanation may help to contextualize Walker's contribution and further an understanding of its strengths and weaknesses.

During his lifetime, Walker published only one major study based on the voluminous material he collected during eighteen years as agency physician on the Pine Ridge Reservation, *The Sun Dance and Other Ceremonies of the Oglala Division of the Teton Dakota* (1917). It includes his reconstructions of the sun dance, *huŋká*, and buffalo ceremonies; a short series of documents from Oglala narrators on fundamental religious topics; and some myths and tales. Taken as a whole, it offers a range of information unique in the literature on the Lakotas, and presents challenges for scholars to interpret and integrate with the work of other writers. Ethnographers writing about the Lakotas have used Walker's data as an authoritative source, but such reference was rarely critical because Walker published information found nowhere else in ethnographic accounts.

The uniqueness of Walker's data, particularly in regard to such concepts as the names and relationships of what he termed the gods (*Wak'áŋ T'áŋka*, the great spirits, the totality of all that is sacred) as well as the sacred myths told about their doings, lies in Walker's close affiliation with a number of holy men (*wic'áša wak'áŋ*). These holy men, he said, entrusted him with shared, secret information about the religion of the past that they wanted

preserved but that they chose not to pass down to their own people because such knowledge was no longer useful in dealing with
the changed life on the reservation. In this manner, Walker suggested, a major religious disjunction occurred.

There is disagreement about the extent to which such a system of shared, secret knowledge ever existed among the holy men
of the Oglalas. Perhaps it was created in part by the collective decision of a group of them, sanctioned by the vision sought by Short
Bull (see below, pp. 47–48), to honor Walker's request for information about religion and ceremonies so that a record would be
preserved for the future. Study of the documents that Walker collected substantiates the existence of a body of shared knowledge
but with considerable personal differences in interpretation. The
system of religious knowledge, as presented in Walker's *Sun
Dance,* resulted from his own synthesis of information provided
by many holy men. Through his work and developing knowledge
of the sacred, Walker in effect became a holy man himself, began
to systematize the information recorded by each of the Oglala
holy men, and synthesized it much as every individual holy man
must have done. But rather than relying on visions, the traditional Lakota way, Walker turned to logic and consistency as the
checks on his interpretation of Lakota religion. This approach
was misunderstood by many who relied on the monograph he
published in 1917. Only critical study of Walker's original sources
can allow us to judge that approach constructively.

In order to understand Walker's own interpretations, and to
make available the original materials from which he worked, we
undertook to collate, edit, and publish his manuscripts. *Lakota Belief and Ritual* was the first portion of that material to appear, followed by *Lakota Society,* under Raymond J. DeMallie's editorship
(1982) and *Lakota Myth,* under Elaine A. Jahner's editorship
(1983). The very valuable material written in Lakota by George
Sword for Walker is still being translated and edited by DeMallie.
Since the project was originally conceived, more of Sword's writings have come to light, but, unfortunately, the myth texts believed to have been written by Sword have not been found.

When we began editing Walker's manuscripts we had a
strong sense that they form a body of primary materials open to a
variety of interpretations and that sense strengthened our determination to present them with as little editorial interference as

possible, given constraints of readability. Therefore, our primary editorial task was to try to identify the sources of Walker's data and the conditions under which they were gathered, insofar as that is possible in a collection of manuscript fragments. An outstanding feature of Walker's work was his regular reference to the individual Lakotas who gave him information or who translated for him. He named his sources because it seemed the natural thing to do, not because he understood the scholarly importance of attributing information. As a consequence, he was sometimes careless, but the collection as a whole includes more attribution than we find elsewhere in ethnographic literature on the Lakotas. In the decade since the original publication of *Lakota Belief and Ritual,* this facet of the collection has proven to be a major reason for the scholarly attention the book has attracted. Virtually every academic discipline has been affected by a "call to context" as issues of culture, ethnicity, and nationalism have taken on increasing international political significance; and the Walker collection provides an example of how specific individuals interpreted beliefs during a time of extreme cultural stress.

When scholarly analysis takes individuals into account, details can often prove an important part of the historical puzzle if enough of them accumulate. That accounts for our most problematical editorial decision. We let stand some points in Walker's writings that, from an objective scholarly perspective, we judged to be incorrect. Yet, in the context we tried to establish with each volume of Walker's materials, they reflect elements in someone's interpretation—often Walker's own, in other cases that of the various Lakotas who served as his consultants. Although they represent only minor details, they are significant. As the Walker material is used more and more for religious and cultural interpretation, the potential for such errors to mislead grows if readers are inclined to see an individual's interpretation as evidence of broad-based cultural belief.

The primary cause for most of these errors was Walker's lack of understanding of linguistics and Clark Wissler's failure to seek out the linguistic advice that could have helped Walker. In terms of linguistics, Walker fell into two fundamental errors, both of which reflected opinions held by various of the holy men, both of which have cultural but not linguistic validity, and both of which frequently led him astray.

The first was to have confused the sounds of the Lakota language with letters in the English alphabet. Thus he failed to recognize that aspiration and glottalization were linguistically significant in diffentiating stops (i.e., that *c, k, p, t* are historically different sounds from *c', k', p', t'* and *c', k', p', t'*) and that the oral vowels (*a, i, u*) are historically different sounds from their nasalized counterparts (*aŋ, iŋ, uŋ*). Thus, for example, when Sword explained that the word *wak'áŋ* ("holy") was derived from the word *kaŋ* (meaning "old"), he was expressing a folk etymology, that is, a culturally valid statement, in this case that anything old was considered to be sacred. This, however, is not a historically correct etymology, for in terms of the development of the Lakota language, *kaŋ* and *k'aŋ* come from different sources. Similarly, Walker (or his interpreter) translated Red Cloud's "*Iyotan Wakantu*" as "Supreme Mystery" (p. 140), when the form Red Cloud used most certainly was *Iyótaŋ Waŋkátu*, "Great Above." The transposition of nasalization between syllables (*wakaŋtu/waŋkatu*), a common scriptographic error, together with the systematic failure to indicate aspiration, incorrectly convinced Walker that the second word had *wak'áŋ* at its root. That misunderstanding led us as editors into error as well, mistranslating the name as "Great Mystery Above" in note 43, page 297 (an error corrected in the Bison Book edition).

The second of Walker's linguistic errors came in assuming that every syllable represented a separate word with a distinct meaning and that all multisyllable words were composed of these basic one-syllable words, which were assumed to be older. Again, this was an opinion expressed by various of his Lakota consultants, including Sword, and as such has undeniable cultural interest, but it does not accurately reflect the development of the Lakota language. Thus, returning to an example above, Walker accepted as linguistically true Sword's statement that *wak'áŋ* was a composite of two words, *wa* "something" and *kaŋ* "old." Applying the theory to other words frequently proved less satisfactory, however. For example, in analyzing the word *Wakíŋyaŋ*, the spirit of thunder and lightning, Walker suggested the etymology "flashing white" (see p. 120), yet historically the word is clearly *wa* "something" and *kiŋyáŋ* "flying," i.e., "flying thing." Walker apparently found no way of reducing *kiŋyáŋ* to two component words.

Specific linguistic issues will be addressed in the publication of Sword's writings, to be presented bilingually; these texts will provide a major check on the quality and nuances of Walker's translations.

Walker himself repeatedly acknowledged the difficulty of obtaining valid translations and of the potential that mistranslation had for leading him into error. But good translation is always more an art than a science, and translations, by their very nature, demand continuing critique. No single version can suffice. Our translations of the writings of Tyon and Thunder Bear in this volume, for example, represent a process of negotiation between us as well as a conscious attempt to remain as close as possible to Walker's style. In retrospect, we would revise details of the translations. For example, in the captions on the drawings by Thunder Bear, the word *ohítika* has been translated as "furious" or "furiously," following Walker's preference; yet the simpler, usual translation "brave" would likely be more satisfactory. Whenever we had any question about the validity of a translation, however, we included the Lakota words so that others could evaluate the adequacy of our translations. In some instances we have later judged our translations of such questionable material to be incorrect. For example, Tyon's phrase *"mni wakanta najin kin"* (p. 154), which we translated "Water, standing in a *wakan* manner," now seems quite obviously to be *mní waŋkáta nájiŋ kiŋ*, "the water standing above," a ritual phrase referring to the steam caused by pouring water on hot rocks in the sweat lodge. (The key in this instance was once again recognizing Tyon's scriptographic transposition of nasalization in the first two syllables of the word *waŋkáta*.)

Beyond problems related to linguistics and translation, there are other problems that have to do with Walker's personal limitations and inclinations. Walker, by his own admission, was an atrocious speller who sometimes sacrificed elegance and precision to get information recorded quickly on the typewriter during the brief periods he could spare for his research. He rewrote and retyped his own writings time and again, finally sending them to Clark Wissler and his staff at the American Museum of Natural History in New York, where they underwent further stylistic revision and another retyping. Thus sometimes the editorial question had to be faced: Which is truer to Walker's intention, an earlier, less polished draft or a later, edited revision? We tried to be guided by principles of comprehensibility, while always preferring an original from Walker's own typewriter when such was available.

We edited the contents of the documents only minimally, correcting obvious spelling and grammatical errors, as Walker originally intended his editors in New York to do, but when correcting an infelicity of phrasing or spelling would jeopardize meaning, we let the original stand. Similarly, even when we sensed that Walker had mistyped Lakota words, we let his original stand, for there is now no way to differentiate true errors from variant forms. This was particularly annoying in the shortened forms of Lakota names by which the four winds are designated. Odd variations occur that seem to be incorrect, perhaps relating to Walker's developing understanding of these concepts but possibly only typographical errors, and the temptation to systematize them—to avoid confusion on a reader's part—was strong. We nonetheless resisted, fearful of standardizing a consensus that might obscure some historically or culturally significant variation, and restricted our observations of such variations to notes.

Another editorial issue of consequence was the decision to let Walker's transcriptions of Lakota words stand as he wrote them, without adding diacritical marks and other special symbols (see Appendix II). As a result, for example, readers not familiar with the language pronounce "Skan" as though it were English, whereas the Lakota form is actually *Škáŋ*, pronounced with an initial *sh* and a nasalized *a*. Thus the way in which Walker wrote Lakota words is not helpful in determining their pronunciation. On the other hand, the attempt to add special symbols to Walker's transcriptions would have required decisions for which no basis could be found in the Walker corpus; for example, did he intend the word "sicun," meaning a kind of spirit, to be pronounced "*šic'úŋ* or *sic'úŋ*? Although our sense is that the former is correct, there are no valid grounds for ruling out the latter, and both forms may be acceptable variants. Similarly, when Walker wrote "Iya" and "Iyo," both as designations for the giant, an evil being (*Íya*), the second form seems simply to be an error, yet it is repeated in various of Walker's documents. The same is true for the shortened name of the West Wind (*Eyá*), which Walker usually wrote "Eya" but sometimes "Iya," a seeming confusion with the evil being. Both these instances seem to reflect Walker's habitual poor spelling, yet to have corrected and systematized them, even though making the documents easier to read, ran the risk of obscuring some fundamental understanding (or misunderstanding) that may prove a clue in the analysis of the material. Whether our refusal to systematize such matters editorially will in the long run cause more confusion than enlightenment is unknowable. Yet it is consistent with out goal of serving to present Walker's primary material, without interpreting it.

In this Bison Book edition we have corrected typographical errors in the hardcover edition and made other minor corrections but have not attempted any fundamental revision of our editorial apparatus or Lakota translations. "Further Comparative Materials for the Study of Sioux Religion," below, serves as an addendum to the bibliographic survey included in the original publication. It lists major sources (books and monographs) published since 1978 that provide material directly useful for comparison with Walker's. The bibliography at the end of the volume has been expanded to include these additional titles.

Further Comparative Materials for the Study of Sioux Religion

From 1978—when "Comparative Materials for the Study of Sioux Religion" (pp. 54–61) was written—through 1990, there has been a steady increase in the literature on Sioux religion. Two important historical sources have appeared. The first is Walker's own *Lakota Myth*, edited by Elaine A. Jahner (1983), which brings together all of the myths found in his unpublished papers together with his retelling of them in epic form, on the model of classical Greek and Roman mythology. *The Sons of the Wind*, edited by D. M. Dooling (1984), freely reworks Walker's myth epics for a popular audience. The second important historical source is *The Sixth Grandfather: Black Elk's Teachings Given to John G. Neihardt*, edited by Raymond J. DeMallie (1984), which presents the transcripts of Neihardt's conversations with the Oglala holy man Black Elk in 1931 and 1944. They convey the religious experiences and traditions of a man a generation younger than most of Walker's consultants and, like most of them, also a practicing Christian. Representing the next period in Oglala religious history, Black Elk's material bears careful comparison with Walker's record.

Thomas H. Lewis's *The Medicine Men: Oglala Sioux Ceremony and Healing* (1990) preserves a record of Lakota religious practices on Pine Ridge from 1967 to 1972. It is a valuable description of the revitalization of tradition during this period, particularly the sun dance, *yuwípi*, and the *heyók'a*, documented by observation and by long quotations from religious leaders. The author's perspective is that of a psychiatrist who worked with the reservation mental health program, providing a point of view from Western medicine that is unique in the literature.

The Canadian Sioux by James H. Howard (1984) includes important material on religious belief and ceremony among the Sioux of Canada, most of whom are descendants of the Santees who fled there from Minnesota in 1862.

In 1982 a symposium was convened at Mary College (now the University of Mary) in Bismarck, North Dakota, to bring together scholars and practitioners of Sioux religion to present their views and search for common ground. The resulting volume, *Sioux Indian Religion: Tradition and Innovation*, edited by Raymond J. DeMallie and Douglas R. Parks (1987), includes chapters by DeMallie and Jahner summarizing Walker's material on religion and myth, as well as important contributions by Sioux authors on the sacred pipe, sun dance, role of women in traditional religious revitalization, *yuwípi*, and the Native American Church. The book also explores the relationship of Christianity and native religion, from both Indian and non-Indian perspectives.

Lakota Ceremonial Songs (1983), by John Around Him and translated by Albert White Hat, accompanied by a cassette tape, records the words and music of contemporary Oglala ritual.

William K. Powers's *Yuwipi: Vision and Experience in Oglala Ritual* (1982) is an excellent presentation of the *yuwípi* ritual, vision questing, and twentieth-century Oglala holy men. The same author's *Sacred Language: The Nature of Supernatural Discourse in Lakota* (1986) touches on a wide selection of topics in Lakota religion from a variety of anthropological viewpoints and makes considerable use of Walker's material while attempting some critical evaluation.

Julian Rice's *Lakota Storytelling: Black Elk, Ella Deloria, and Frank Fools Crow* (1989) is a literary interpretation of Lakota narrative style that explores symbolic patterns and relates them to published ethnography. Many of the narratives are related directly to mythic and religious material recorded by Walker.

Three recent books dealing with Lakota religion are addressed to a broad reading public. Joseph Epes Brown's *The Spiritual Legacy of the American Indian* (1982) draws together a selection of his popular essays, most of which focus on Lakota spirituality and are rooted in his earlier work with Black Elk (Brown 1953). *I Become Part of It: Sacred Dimensions in Native American Life*, edited by D. M. Dooling and Paul Jordan-Smith (1989), is a collection of articles reprinted from the journal *Parabola* that includes essays by Brown and Jahner as well as by Arthur Amiotte, a Lakota scholar and religious leader. *The Good Red Road: Passages into Native America,* by Kenneth Lincoln with Al Logan Slagle (1987), records the experiences of a group of students and their professor who came from UCLA to study in Lakota country and developed an understanding of traditional religion as a vehicle used by the Lakota people to achieve cultural revitalization in the face of the enormous social problems posed by reservation life.

Three recent works examine the dialogue between Lakota religion and Roman Catholicism. The most descriptive and analytical is *Pipe, Bible, and Peyote among the Oglala Lakota,* by Paul B. Steinmetz, S.J. (1980; rev. ed. 1990). Written from the perspective of a missionary priest who worked among the Lakotas from 1961 to 1981 to bring native and Christian beliefs and practices together, and who has a personal understanding of contemporary Lakota spiritual life, the book includes an overview of traditional religion and the Native American Church, and investigates the diversity of religious life on the modern Pine Ridge Reservation. *The Pipe and Christ: A Christian–Sioux Dialogue* by William Stolzman, S.J. (1986), based on discussions between Jesuits and the Lakota religious leaders of Rosebud Reservation, takes a more actively pastoral view in using fulfillment theology to bring Lakota tradition together with Christianity. *The Sacred Vision: Native American Religion and Its Practice Today* by Michael F. Steltenkamp (1982) is a personal record of one Jesuit priest's experiences with contemporary Lakota religion.

Finally, two books by Lakota authors offer contemporary commentaries on the future direction of Sioux religion. *Black Elk: The Sacred Ways of a Lakota* by Wallace Black Elk and William S. Lyon (1990) is a valuable life story of an Oglala religious leader who is active in extending Lakota beliefs and ritual practices to a wide audience of Indians and non-Indians alike. *Mother Earth Spirituality: Native American Paths to Healing Ourselves and Our World* by Ed McGaa (Eagle Man) (1990) serves as a practical guide for connecting Lakota religion with the New Age and environmental movements as a spiritual means for dealing with global problems of the late twentieth century.

I

James R. Walker:
His Life and Work

Physician and Anthropologist[1]

James R. Walker is an intriguing figure for many reasons. His service in the Civil War, his experiences as a physician on three Indian reservations, his scientific studies of tuberculosis and his anthropological studies of the Lakotas are public aspects of a long and active life. His personal life is now little known; he seems to have been much alone, devoting his time to his work, while his family lived physically separated from him. He had a scientific mind, was always inquiring into the whys and hows of the world around him, and was a tinkerer with at least one invention to his credit—an early automobile steering device. After retirement, he settled on a small ranch at the foot of the Colorado Rockies and seems to have developed a personally satisfying philosophy through contemplation of nature and of Lakota religious and philosophical beliefs. Never famous or flamboyant, he lived always with modest dignity.

Walker's life and work are a fit subject for a full-scale biographical study. But no attempt to write a biography of the man is intended here. The following sketch of his life presents only enough to place his ethnographic studies of the Lakotas in context so that the reader can evaluate them intelligently. Whenever possible, we have quoted from Walker's reports and correspondence to allow him to tell of his work in his own words. We feel that this is important because Walker remains even yet an enigmatic figure; through his own words, the reader can evaluate Walker on his own terms.

Early Career

James Riley Walker was born March 4, 1849, in a log cabin near Richview, Illinois, the oldest of William Henry and Mary A. E. Walker's ten children. His father, a farmer and merchant, entered the Union Army in 1863 and became captain of Company B, 111th Illinois Volunteer Infantry. He was wounded at the battle of Kenesaw Mountain and was discharged in 1865. After the war, William H. Walker rode a Methodist circuit in Kansas; in 1900 he retired to Pasadena, California.[2]

James R. Walker later wrote in an official document, "At a very early age I ran away from home and lost my people, and my own age." On January 29, 1864, at only fourteen years and ten months of age—but claiming to be sixteen—Walker enlisted as a private in the Union Army, Company D, Thirteenth Regiment of Illinois Cavalry Volunteers. He was discharged August 31, 1865, at Pine Bluff, Arkansas. According to his discharge papers, Walker was five feet two, with light hair, by occupation a farmer.[3]

In June 1864, only five months after he had enlisted, Walker was hospitalized for dysentery. It left him with a debilitating ailment that plagued him the rest of his life and prevented him from undertaking manual labor. Late in life he told a newspaper reporter that while in the Union Army he had been assigned to duty with the United States Sanitary Commission, a semigovernmental organization that ministered to soldiers in camp, on battlefields, and in hospitals.[4]

After his discharge Walker finished school in Richview and attended Northwestern University Medical School, where he received the degree of Doctor of Medicine in 1873. The next year he began practice in Richview and on June 4, 1877, he married Annie Amelia Cox at Tamaroa, Illinois.[5]

That same year the doctor, for reasons of health, decided to leave the Midwest for a job that would take him outdoors in a more invigorating climate. He heard that doctors were needed on Indian reservations and, on inquiring, was offered a post with the Chippewas in northern Minnesota. Walker closed his office in Richview and headed for the north woods. At first he intended it to be only a temporary move until his health improved. The rigors of reservation life did not appeal to Mrs. Walker, and she never came to understand Indians as he did. Part of the time he was in Minnesota and later when he was stationed on other reservations, she lived in surroundings more congenial to her, even though it meant being apart from him. They had one child, Maude, born in Richview before they left for Minnesota.[6]

Walker's papers record little about his years with the Chippewas. The administration of the eight Chippewa reservations was centered at the White Earth Agency, which had some six thousand Indians under its charge. Walker himself was stationed at Leech Lake, where he served not only as physician but as overseer of the subagency.[7]

During the winter of 1882–83 a major smallpox epidemic swept through the area, with disastrous consequences for the Chippewas. A lengthy account of the event is preserved in Walker's papers. According to this report the epidemic began January 6 and ended February 27, when the last death occurred. Walker reported that of the 109 Indians exposed to the disease, 84 contracted it and 72 died. Walker quarantined the afflicted Indians in log cabins and as soon as he could obtain some of the virus, he vaccinated all of the Indians in the vicinity of Lake Winnibigoshish. Extremely cold temperatures, as low as 52 degrees below zero, checked the progress of the epidemic. The smallpox was both preceded and accompanied by chicken pox, measles, and a "peculiar sweating malarious fever." Agency personnel lauded Walker's diligence, skill, and personal sacrifice in treating the sick, and he was credited with preventing an epidemic of major proportions that might have swept through the entire region. In 1906, President Roosevelt decorated Walker for his heroism in preventing the spread of the disease.[8]

Walker's duties, according to official instructions from the commissioner of Indian Affairs, included the suppression of dancing, gambling, and drinking of alcoholic beverages among the Chippewas. He reported strict enforcement of these orders and wrote that the White Earth Reservation "came to have the best reputation for law abiding and the prompt suppression of crimes or misdemeanors."[9]

In 1893 a series of monetary payments to the Chippewas for lands lost through the construction of a reservoir triggered an influx of whiskey on the reservation. In attempting to confiscate some of the contraband, Walker was threatened by an Indian. Walker drew a gun to defend himself and accidentally shot the man, inflicting a minor wound. A crowd of Indians surrounded the doctor's house and threatened to kill him. Walker later reported: "The wounded man, and his father, after they were in my house, used their influence to quiet the mob and prevent violence . . . I mention this to show that the animosity of the rioters was caused by my trying to stop drinking and gambling, and that the shooting of the Indian only precipitated a conflict which was inevitable in the near future."[10]

Unable to quiet the Indians, Walker telegraphed to the U. S. marshal at St. Paul. Company D of the Third Infantry arrived at White Earth, and C. A. Ruffee, the Indian agent in charge of all the Chippewa subagencies, allowed the troopers to march to Leech Lake. Their arrival quieted the situation, but Ruffee blamed Walker for the incident. He wrote, "Dr. Walker was greatly to blame by his rashness, almost creating an outbreak and bringing obloquy upon many innocent persons."[11]

As a result of the incident Walker was reassigned to the Colville Agency in northeastern Washington on September 30, 1893. There is nothing about Dr. Walker's tour of duty at Colville in his papers. He remained there until February 12, 1896, when he was transferred to the United States Indian school at Carlisle, Pennsylvania. He was at Carlisle only five months. On July 15, 1896, he was once again reassigned, this time as agency physician on the Pine Ridge Reservation. Pine Ridge was the second largest Indian reservation in the country. Only five years past the Ghost Dance and Wounded Knee massacre, it was still considered the "wildest" of the Sioux reservations by many people. Here for the next eighteen years Dr. Walker worked as full-time physician and part-time anthropologist.[12]

Medical Work at Pine Ridge

Health care at Pine Ridge had been inadequate from the establishment of the agency in 1878. The U. S. Indian Office did not supervise its agency doctors, and not until 1891 were physicians placed in a classified service and required to pass examinations in addition to having a medical degree. Their efficiency depended upon their individual character and ability and their personal sense of duty.[13]

Charles Alexander Eastman, a Santee Sioux Indian educated in the East, served as agency physician at Pine Ridge from 1890 until 1892. He later wrote:

> The doctors who were in the service in those days had an easy time of it. They scarcely ever went outside of the agency enclosure, and issued their pills and compounds after the most casual inquiry. As late as 1890, when the Government sent me out as physician to ten thousand Ogallalla Sioux and Northern Cheyennes at Pine Ridge

Agency, I found my predecessor still practicing his profession through a small hole in the wall between his office and the general assembly room of the Indians. One of the first things I did was to close that hole; and I allowed no man to diagnose his own trouble or choose his pills.

Dr. Eastman added that, like other physicians then in the Indian Service, he had to use his own funds and gifts of money from friends to buy medicines and surgical instruments. Drugs supplied to the Indians by contractors were "often obsolete in kind, and either stale or of the poorest quality." Eastman wrote, "The old-time 'medicine-man' was really better than the average white doctor in those days for although his treatment was largely suggestive, his herbs were harmless and he did allay some distress which the other aggravated, because he used powerful drugs almost at random and did not attend to his cases intelligently."[14]

When the government opened a hospital at Pine Ridge on November 22, 1892, it met a long-felt need. Connected with the boarding school, the hospital had two wards that could give proper accommodations to only five patients each, although more were crowded in during cold weather. In February 1893, Dr. Z. T. Daniel became the reservation physician. He recommended that the government's periodic and scattered instructions to Indian Service doctors be reappraised, modernized, and compiled in serviceable form. He also recommended that an agency physician be sent annually as a representative of the medical department of the Indian Service to meetings of the American Medical Association, and he urged that Indian Service doctors be supplied with textbooks and medical journals. Daniel wrote, "The sole medical work at this agency belonging to the Government is an edition of the United States Dispensatory of the date of 1871. It is hardly necessary to say that this work is now a pharmaceutical fossil."[15]

After Walker's arrival in 1896, the medical work at Pine Ridge progressed significantly. During the first few years of Walker's tenure as physician at Pine Ridge, there was a considerable improvement in the health situation, particularly in regard to tuberculosis. He attributed the change to his continual supervision of the Indians. As he later told a newspaper reporter, he saw his first eighteen years' experience with Indians as a foundation for his work with the Oglalas. He said, "I determined to know the Indian from the Indian point of view."[16]

Walker's determination was at one with his firm intent to combat tuberculosis. In 1897, a year after his arrival, he was able to persuade the Indian Office to hire an additional doctor to care for the routine work of health care, leaving Walker free to focus on the problem of tuberculosis. He decided from the outset to work with the traditional Indian medicine men rather than against them, and it was undoubtedly that decision that gained him the Oglalas' respect and cooperation. Walker studied the traditional Indian ways of treating the sick, investigated the native concepts of disease, and taught the medicine men his secrets in exchange for theirs. These actions were the first steps in his study of Lakota culture. His reports to the Commissioner of Indian Affairs show the success of his efforts.

In 1899, Acting Agent Clapp, introducing Walker's report, spoke of "the advancement that has been made under his wise and judicious methods." The report showed the reservation population to be 7,150, which included 6,788 full-blood and mixed-blood Indians, 360 whites, and 2 Negroes. The highest birth rate was among the mixed-bloods, the highest death rate among children under four. During the year Walker and the other reservation doctor had treated 1,215 full-blood Indians, 447 mixed-bloods, 143 whites, and both Negroes—a total of 1,807 patients. In the same report Walker mentions the high incidence of tuberculosis at Pine Ridge and the need for more physicians. The report also alludes to the role of the traditional holy men in treating the sick. The cautious phrasing of this allusion is especially interesting in light of the fact that he had begun to study the shamans' methods three years earlier. Walker wrote:

> The prevailing disease among the Ogalalla Sioux Indians is tuberculosis, almost one-half of whom appear to be affected by it. The larger percentage is among the children, and it appears to be increasing. * * *
> During the year there were a large number of cases of grippe, but the only epidemic on the reservation was one of measles in the remoter districts, from which there died 34 children and 2 adults.
> These Indians will ask the agency physicians to see their sick if they be conveniently near, but the most of them will not make much exertion to call the physician, and usually if the sick person considers his case hopeless he will resort to the customs of his forefathers, which appear to combine medical and religious ceremonies that soothe his dying hours.
> The demands by the Indians for the services of the physicians have

more than doubled in the last three years, and at times there are more calls than the two physicians now at this agency can possibly attend to; for the Indians on the remoter parts of the reservation live two days' travel from the agency, and at times it takes the physician eight to ten days to make a single trip for the purpose of visiting the sick, and if a sick person on the remoter parts of the reservation sends for the physician it will be at least four days before he can see the patient, and it may be longer.[17]

Walker ended his report with a request for a third doctor to be stationed at Kyle, forty-five miles northeast of the agency.

In his 1900 report Walker commented that tuberculosis was still increasing but that more Indians were aware that cleanliness and better housing helped combat it. This report is more explicit than the previous one about the role of the medicine men.

These Indians still call upon their "medicine men," and probably will continue to do so until the older generation passes away, for this is their inherited religion, and in this they are not blamable. On the contrary, they are to be commended for the fact that if the Government physicians appear during their most sacred ceremonies, they suspend them and respectfully listen to the doctors and, what is better, are willing to try their methods.[18]

Unfortunately, in 1903 Walker lost his assistant and had to take on routine medical work in addition to his studies of traditional ways and his supervision of tubercular patients. Nevertheless, both of these closely related projects escalated in the next few years. Clark Wissler engaged him as an anthropological collaborator and he established a sanitary camp for the control of tuberculosis. In 1907 he wrote to Wissler, "I have been doing about three men's work, and every moment from the time I rise in the morning until I go to bed at night has been fully occupied."[19]

The medical needs at Pine Ridge Reservation motivated Walker's efforts to learn the ways of the traditional holy men. Because his studies of Oglala religion arose out of a desire to become a more effective physician to the Lakota people, they are unique. What began as a professional medical interest grew into a personal passion, and by the end of his life, Walker's dedication to recording Oglala religion became all-consuming.

On February 5, 1906, Walker wrote a lengthy letter that outlined both the development of his medical work at Pine Ridge and his growth in understanding the role of the medicine men. This letter is an essential document for all who want to understand the man and his work.

When I came to Pine Ridge in 1896, I had eighteen years of experience with tuberculosis among the Indians, and had learned that the greatest difficulty in the management of the disease on an Indian reservation is the lack of control of the cases, arising principally from the antagonism of the Indian medicine men.

At that time I planned to get control of the sick among these Indians, which was approved by the Hon. Commissioner of Indian Affairs, and pursuant to this plan, a physician was appointed in 1897 to assist me.

This plan was to get the cooperation of the medicine men, and is best explained as follows.

In my first relations with the medicine men I considered them arrant humbugs whose practices should be suppressed by every means. But I found that if an attempt were made to do this, they continued their practices, only in secret, and that a feeling of resentment was aroused among the Indians against those whom they considered responsible for such action, and for that reason they more stubbornly rejected that which was offered instead of the things attempted to be suppressed.

I then studied their methods of treating the sick, and the results.

I found that they have little knowledge of disease, that the most of their medicines are inert, and that their practices consist mostly of mysticism and trickery.

But I also learned that the Indians have faith in the power of the medicine men to relieve suffering, and that most of the medicine men have a sincere confidence in their power to do so; that the sick believe the mystical forms and ceremonies of the medicine men to be solemn rites that propitiate malignant powers; that these ceremonies beget an expectation of relief so that when the medicine man suggests that there is relief the patient declares that he feels it; that in minor ailments, this relief is real and permanent; that in serious illness it sooths the patient and consoles the friends; that because of these results the medicine men maintain a powerful influence among the Indians in all matters pertaining to the sick.

These facts I could neither refute nor ignore, so therefore I determined to enlist the cooperation of the medicine men in getting a control of the sick, trusting to circumstances to do away with their conjuring.

I cultivated amicable relations with them to gain their freindship, praising the good they did, supplying them with simple remedies and instructing them in their uses. But privately I charged them with their trickery and persuaded them to abandon such methods.

To gain their confidence I used such methods as the following.

The Indians believed that consumption is caused by a worm that eats away the lung, and the medicine men supported this belief by pretending to take a worm from the chest of a consumptive, and exhibiting it to the patient and friends.

In the presence of their people I agreed with them that consumption is caused by something destroying the lung, but privately I convicted them of their trick with the worm and promised them that if the sputa of a consumptive were brought to me I would show them the things which caused the disease.

When the sputa was brought, I stained and mounted the specimen in the presence of the medicine men and succeeded in showing the bacilli to some.

Such processes were repeated until a confidence in my understanding of diseases was established. To gain their faith, the history of every case of sickness that came to my knowledge was recorded, whether treated by myself or by the medicine men, and these records were used to demonstrate the superior benefits of a rational treatment of the sick.

By such methods I got a practical control of tuberculosis among these Indians.

The process was tedious and there was much annoyance and discouragement, but the Indians became willing to obey my instructions.

To maintain this control required constant personal supervision, and as my assistant did the ordinary medical work demanded at this agency, I was free to visit the Indians at their homes, to superintend sanitary measures, and to do the microscopical work essential to the early diagnosis of pulmonary tuberculosis.

The tuberculosis received medical treatment according to the needs of each case, but the main dependence in the treatment of the disease was upon cleanliness and regularity of habits, protection and nourishment of the body, and an abundance of free air at all times and of sunshine when possible.

To prevent new cases an effort was made to give the Indians an effective understanding that the disease is communicated by material contained in the waste products of the disease, and they were urgently instructed to carefully collect and quickly destroy all sputa from consumptives and all discharges from scrofulous sores.

I had no means of enforcing my directions. I could only persuade the Indians to obey them. This was more easy to do when I was able to show them by the records the benefits they were receiving, for these records showed a continuous decrease of the disease while this plan was in effect. They show that from 1897 to 1903 the annual number of new cases was reduced 49 per cent, and the annual number of deaths from this disease was reduced 44 per cent.

In 1903 my assistant was taken from me and the medical supervision of nearly one-third of the population of the reservation was placed in his charge.

The conditions of the duties that devolve upon each of us by this arrangement of the medical service make it impossible for either of us to personally supervise the sanitary work at the homes of the Indians.

I still have a nominal supervision of something over two-thirds of the population of the reservation, but because I cannot visit them as I formerly did, they think that I have lost interest in their welfare and

slight them, and they have somewhat resentfully disregarded my
instructions and have been reverting to their old ways of caring for
the sick and carelessness of the dangers of infection.

Consequently, since 1903 the annual number of new cases has
increased over 30 per cent and the annual number of deaths from
tuberculosis has increased more than 62 per cent.

This great increase enables me to show to the Indians the results of
their folly, and they are beginning again to give some heed to the
danger of infection so that they are now checking the rapid increase
of the disease. * * *[20]

Walker continued his efforts to combat tuberculosis at Pine
Ridge. In May 1906 he read a paper entitled "Tuberculosis
among the Oglala Sioux Indians" to the annual meeting of the
National Association for the Study and Prevention of Tuberculosis held in Washington, D. C. The paper, published in the
American Journal of Medical Science, was reprinted in the *Southern
Workman* the same year and attracted considerable attention.
After describing the epidemic proportions of the disease among
the Oglalas, he traced the cause to inadequate sanitation resulting from the change from movable tipis to immovable wooden
houses. The unsanitary conditions, he argued, caused the disease to increase dramatically because people had increased contact with infected material, which in turn lowered their resist-
ance to the disease. He concluded his paper by suggesting the
practicality of establishing a sanitary camp for the control of the
disease, moving the infected persons into tents that could more
easily be kept clean, seeing that they had plenty of fresh air and
sunshine, and supervising their diet.[21]

Earlier, on February 14, 1906, Walker had written to the
commissioner of Indian affairs to recommend the establishment
of such a camp at Pine Ridge. He pointed out the additional
advantage that it would be cheaper than a conventional
sanitarium, and because the tents could be moved it would ob-
viate the Indians' fear of entering a structure in which a death
had occurred.[22]

Throughout 1906, 1907, and 1908 Walker continued to
write letters concerning the proposed camp. On December 13,
1907, the commissioner of Indian affairs authorized that one
and one-half sections of suitable land be reserved for the camp.
On May 4, 1908, Walker reported that there were six hundred
cases of tuberculosis on the reservation, and on July 18 and
September 12 he sent estimates to Washington for the costs of

construction of the camp. But the planning did not bear fruit.[23]

Walker seems to have been in continual altercation with the Indian agent and the boarding school personnel over the establishment of the sanitary camp. Despite the strife, Agent John R. Brennan had high regard for Walker's capabilities. He wrote to the commissioner of Indian affairs on November 11, 1909, stating that Walker was "eminently fitted" for the position of superintendent of the national asylum for Indians at Canton, South Dakota, and that he deserved the promotion. However, nothing came of this recommendation either.[24]

Judging from the available records, Walker appears to have spent his remaining years at Pine Ridge going about the everyday business of a reservation physician, driving vast distances by buggy, later by car, to visit patients in outlying communities. He became more and more engrossed in the study of traditional Oglala culture and evidently ceased to argue for reform in the medical service on the reservation.

Anthropological Studies at Pine Ridge

The mutual trust and respect that developed between Walker and the traditional Oglalas at Pine Ridge, combined with Walker's ever growing interest in understanding the religious and philosophical foundations of Lakota culture and his year-round residence on the reservation, put him in an incomparable position to undertake formal anthropological study. There is no evidence that during the first years of his study he had any intention of doing such work. Nor is there any evidence one way or the other that he was familiar with previous anthropological studies of the Sioux. But a chance encounter with an anthropologist led him to realize the value of the information he was learning and set him off on what was in all respects a second career.

In 1902 anthropologist Clark Wissler from the American Museum of Natural History in New York visited Pine Ridge in order to collect specimens for the museum and to investigate the possibilities for more extended fieldwork there. Following the lead of Alfred L. Kroeber's work on the Arapahoes of Wyoming, the museum staff was engaged in an effort to make representative collections from the plains tribes and to gather information on a variety of topics of scientific interest. Although Wissler later wrote that the museum did not commit itself to a thorough comparative study of the plains cultures until 1907, the basic concepts were clearly evolving as early as 1903. Following Kroeber's example, museum investigators studied mythology, religion, ceremonies, symbolism, and men's and women's social, religious, and military societies and associations.[25]

As the plan developed, its intent was more than simply descriptive. By comparing the ritual details of the sun dance and of the military societies from tribe to tribe, investigators hoped to come to an understanding of historical dimensions, such as where these social phenomena had originated, how they had spread from tribe to tribe, and which details were contributed by which tribe. Ethnologists believed the sun dance and the military societies to be the central and most important institutions of the plains tribes; through comparison of the historical development of each they hoped to reconstruct a more general history of the dynamics of cultural development on the plains.[26]

The method and probably the plan originated with Franz Boas, the head of the anthropology department at the American Museum. Boas at the time was the undisputed leader of American anthropology, and most of the men who carried out the plains research through the American Museum had been his students. In 1905 Boas quit the museum for full-time teaching at Columbia University, leaving Wissler as head of the anthropology department and director of the research.[27]

From their first meeting Wissler recognized in Walker a man of similar interests in Indian customs; he immediately proposed to the doctor that he carry out investigations for the museum. Wissler used this method successfully on other reservations, enlisting the aid of literate and interested whites and Indians alike to carry out investigations in the field and to send their notes, manuscripts, and texts in Indian languages to New York, where he and his staff could edit them for publication. The method was not unique to Wissler. It was a standard one at the time and was used with notable success by Boas in his studies of the Northwest Coast.

Through the correspondence between Walker and Wissler it is possible to get a fairly complete picture of the types of work that Walker undertook for the museum. However, it is not always possible to determine which facets of the work reflect Walker's original thinking and which represent Wissler's stimulation. The basic research problems seem to have been worked out in person, during Wissler's visits to Pine Ridge. For parts of two or three summers Wissler stayed at Pine Ridge, living in Walker's house and collaborating closely with him. He also worked with Charles and Richard Nines, Indian traders at Pine Ridge who helped Walker translate the texts that were written for him by George Sword, Thomas Tyon, and Thunder Bear. The Nines brothers also carried out fieldwork on their own for Wissler on the subject of the societies and ceremonial associations, sending their notes to Wissler in New York. This material was incorporated in Wissler's 1912 paper on the subject, and forms the bulk of the data included in it.

In the introduction to *Societies and Ceremonial Associations in the Oglala Division of the Teton-Dakota* Wissler outlined his view of the study of the Oglalas then in progress. Referring to his first visit in 1902 he wrote:

> At the outset he [Wissler] made the acquaintance of Dr. J. R. Walker who took up certain phases of the work, especially games, the sun dance, the hunka and related ceremonies. Later, Messrs. Charles and Richard Nines joined in the work with their thorough knowledge of the Oglala language. Through the combined efforts of these gentlemen, there has been gathered the data for the comprehensive treatment of Oglala culture, of which the present paper is a part.[28]

Thus Wissler intended to use the assistance of Walker and the Nines brothers to put into print a complete record of all aspects of Lakota life. This effort paralleled the work with the Blackfeet which he was carrying on simultaneously.

Wissler began by authorizing Walker to collect various specimens for the museum, to record music (a museum graphophone and blank wax cylinders were sent to him late in 1904), and to record games the Oglalas played. On March 31, 1904, Wissler wrote to Walker that he was pleased with his progress and suggested that he attempt to collect a series of specimens illustrating the various steps in the preparation of a shield.[29]

On March 1, 1905, Wissler wrote Walker a rather triumphant note:

> My dear Doctor:
> We have just completed a reorganization of our department and I have taken charge of American Ethnology. Now I shall be in a position to arrange for your work in a definite way.
> Will you consider the question and write me as to what you would prefer to take up. * * * It is not necessary that you choose such work

as will add to our collections in the Museum for we are interested in research.[30]

Walker wasted no time in replying, and his letter of March 8, 1905, outlines his personal reasons for undertaking the work as well as his own plan to record anthropometric data on the Oglalas in conjunction with his role as a physician:

> I have never made a systematic study of any particular thing in regard to these Indians. All I have done has been from a love for the knowledge of the race, and a desire to compare their peculiarities and their likenesses to the white race with what I know of our own people.
> I have never been in a position to do thorough work on any branch of work pertaining to the ethnology of these Indians, but should be delighted to do so. * * *
> Is there some line of work that you think it would be desirable for me to do? * * *
> You perhaps will remember that I have been somewhat interested in taking the measurements, height, weight, chest measure, &c. of this people.
> Would a systematic work in this line be of use to you?
> By taking it up systematically it would cost me about 10¢ per capita, and would probably take two years to get the measurements of the 3051 adult Indians and the 708 adult Mixed bloods.
> I merely suggest this. Probably you may suggest something that will be of much more value to the Museum.
> I have about 36 records of Indian music, more especially ceremonial, and will at an early date sort it, sending you the better records, and with them a catalogue, giving the name of the song, who sung by, the words in Indian and a translation, and the relations of the songs to a ceremony, if it has such.

In a letter dated May 10, 1905 (now missing), Wissler evidently authorized Walker to begin the collection of anthropometric data on children and encouraged him to take up the study of the *Hunka* ceremony, the "fraternal lodge" of the Oglalas. The *Hunka* was a topic of considerable interest in anthropology because Alice C. Fletcher had published in 1904 an extensive description of the corresponding Pawnee ceremony, the *Hako,* complete with all the ritual prayers in both Pawnee and English.[31]

Walker replied on May 12, 1905:

> I note what you say in regard to the Fraternal Lodge of the Sioux and I think that I shall take that matter up, in compliance with your former suggestion that I select some work to do for the American Museum. * * *

I will try and learn just what the music is that I have already gotten, and will send it to you, if you think this is best.

Some of it is quite good and typical Indian music, but after it was recorded I learned that it was not exactly what the persons who sang it claimed that it was.

These Indians are very apt to do this sort of thing, just to get the pay, and because they think that the white people will not know the difference.

Walker's expression of distrust in this letter must be understood in the context of the times. Far too much of what then passed for anthropology was based on brief visits to reservations, where information was collected from virtually anyone who would agree to talk to the visitor. Since language was a barrier, this practice meant that many early investigators gathered their data from informants who might be mixed-bloods, missionaries, or white men married into Indian tribes. Brief visits did not allow for development of trust and understanding between Indians and investigators, so traditional Indians were frequently uncooperative toward what appeared to them as overcurious outsiders whose motives were suspect. Frequently these contacts degenerated to a mere exchange of money for artifacts and information, and the whites were sometimes duped by being told false or only partially correct information. That Walker was aware of these problems and sensitive to them put him a long step ahead in enabling him to carry out significant studies, especially since his interests took him into esoteric areas of the culture.

Walker, like other anthropologists of his day, invariably used the term informant to refer to those people who gave him information. It was in no way a pejorative term from Walker's perspective, but was used as a shorthand expression to identify those individuals who contributed to his studies and whose word was judged to be authoritative because of age, ability, or social status.

During the first half of 1905 Walker completed his work on Oglala games and sent a manuscript to Wissler for his editorial revisions. Wissler sent the paper on to the *Journal of American Folk-Lore*, where it was printed in two parts in 1905 and 1906.[32] The letter to Wissler of June 25, 1905, that accompanied the manuscript, made clear Walker's own feelings of humility about contributing to a field in which he had no training. He wrote of his frustration caused by the limited amount of time that his duties as agency physician permitted him to spend on the anthropological work, and he outlined more clearly his method of gathering information:

> Enclosed herewith find description of the games played by the Sioux Indians from olden times. I have been a long time in getting this ready for you. This is partly due to my lack of experience in doing such work by reason of which, often when I would write up the notes I had taken, I would find a woeful lack of detail which would necessitate further investigation.
>
> You understand that I have been able to give but fragments of time, here and there, to this work, never having but a short time to work at it uninterruptedly. But I have preferred to take the time to make the work correct rather than send it to you incorrect. * * *
>
> It is very tedious work to get information from them regarding their rites, ceremonies, for they will tell something and declare that there is no more to tell and when questioned in regard to things that they allude to there is a great deal more to tell. Then after one has told it, another will tell a great deal that the first one has not mentioned, and so on.
>
> And when brought together they will all agree that all that has been told is right and should have been all told together.
>
> Thus the information must be picked up in fragments, here and there, and pieced together, and amended, and gone over and over, before it is full and accurate.

It is important to understand Walker's method of working. In all his studies he attempted to compile an authoritative, composite picture of Oglala culture. He did not seek to present the individual personalities of his informants or the disagreements among them, nor was he interested in recording the process by which his informants revealed information to him. His final goal was to present descriptions of Oglala culture as though they were written by an Oglala attempting to compile a consensus account of his people's aboriginal lifeway. It must be understood in connection with his belief—and the belief that was expressed time and time again by the old men who were his informants— that the native features of Oglala culture were fast disappearing and would not be preserved through oral tradition, but only through the medium of writing. This was the guiding principle for all of Walker's studies.

During 1905 and 1906 Walker was concerned largely with his medical work at Pine Ridge. It gave him the opportunity to collect anthropometric data, however, and by December 6, 1905, he wrote to Wissler that he had measured the height, chest, and weight, and recorded the age, of over one thousand children from five to eighteen years of age, counting each child separately each year he or she was measured. On January 7, 1907, Walker sent Wissler his final measurement data on both full-and mixed-blood children, amounting to 1,000 original measurements and 457 remeasurements. The biological relationship of each child to others was also recorded.

In sending these data Walker did not undertake any analysis, assuming that Wissler would prefer to do it himself. Wissler was very enthusiastic about the data, and on February 11, 1908, wrote to Walker, at his request, to assure him of the scientific value of his work. Wissler later published an article based on these data, showing that, compared with available statistics for white children, Oglala children were taller and heavier, and that mixed-blood Oglala children fell between the values for Indians and whites. The data also suggested that the Oglalas matured more rapidly than whites during the fifteenth and sixteenth years, and that the variability among Indian children was less than among white children.[33]

The anthropometric study completed, Walker returned to his notes on the *Hunka* ceremony and on religion. He seemed discouraged with his progress, perhaps preferring the scientific concreteness of numerical measurements to the puzzling intricacy of cultural systems. On January 30, 1907, he wrote to Wissler:

> I have been trying to work on the *Hunka* ceremony lately, but am so interrupted that I cannot work satisfactorily. I am continually getting more light on the subject. Have had an old man recently give me such instructions as were given in ancient times to the one who was being initiated into the order.
> I had this in an imperfect form but I consider the information I got from him as valuable, as they show the old Indians' ideas, and indicate their morality. The instructions relative to stealing horses from other tribes of Indians, taking women and children, the torture of prisoners, and taking of game were very interesting to me. * * *
> I find that after I have straightened out a part and gotten it into a consistent shape, that long afterwards something will turn up that relates to the part already worked over and that requires fresh inquiry and a readjustment of everything.

During much of 1907 and 1908, although Walker was busy with his attempts to establish a sanitary camp for tuberculars at Pine Ridge, he seems to have continued to collect information on religion whenever possible. Then in the fall of 1908 Wissler sent him an offprint of some Sioux myths that he had collected in English at Pine Ridge and published in the *Journal of American Folk-Lore*.[34] In response Walker wrote an enthusiastic letter to Wissler on November 17, 1908, offering to send him myths. He wrote:

> The elaborateness and detail of stories told by these Indians depends much on the teller just as among the white people.
> I have the story of the Stone Boy as told by a professional Story Teller, a Sioux, and it is much more elaborate than yours.

Walker's anthropological work seems to have been something of a mystery to other agency personnel. Major John R. Brennan, the Pine Ridge Indian agent, wrote of him in December 1908: "Dr. Walker is curing several thousand Indians annually and working on his [reservation] statistics, and to fill in the time, I understand he is writing a novel or book of Indian legends."[35]

The next year, on June 8, 1909, Walker again wrote to Wissler indicating the importance that he placed on a full recording of Oglala myths: "In some of their legends there are allusions to customs, forms, ceremonies, and observances of which nothing appears to have been given by any authority I have seen and which can be known of only by the most intimate association with the older Indians." The significance of this discovery cannot be overestimated. The anthropologists at the American Museum had long been recording mythology from plains tribes, both in English and in texts in native languages, but little use had been made of any of this arcane material. It remained an essentially isolated aspect of culture and little attempt was made to relate it to religious ceremonies or other areas of belief.

In the same letter Walker expressed his ever growing concern with the difficulties of translation from Lakota to English. He himself was not fluent in the language and relied largely on interpreters to translate for him. He wrote:

> Another serious difficulty I have encountered is to get a correct interpretation of the narrations of the older Indians, for interpreters give their ideas instead of translating what the Indians say. As for instance, in the *Hunka* Ceremony, interpreter after interpreter has given their invocations as made to "good spirits" and "evil spirits" and "spirits of the earth" &c., and I have found that these invocations were addressed to particular superhuman or supernatural beings, as for instance, *Inyan, Iktomi, Tate* &c.

Walker's greatest difficulties were with the problems of translating from Lakota to English, and it was in this regard that his ideas and attitudes were farthest from those of anthropologists.

Walker's understanding of the nature of Lakota language seems to have come largely from George Sword. Sword, although a traditionalist, was literate in the Lakota language and agreed to write accounts of Lakota culture and religion, as well as an autobiography. He insisted that a great change had come over the Lakota language since it had been reduced to writing by white missionaries. Sword felt that as the language was formerly spoken—and as it was still spoken in ceremonies and formal speeches—each syllable was a distinct unit of meaning. Sequences of syllables that missionaries accepted as equivalents for English words were really phrases, according to Sword. But the younger Oglalas had come to accept the newer view and the language had changed to the extent that younger men could no longer understand the old formal speech.[36]

Walker coupled this in his mind with a belief that the Lakotas were evolving from a primitive to a civilized state, and that their language was similarly evolving. It was a common belief about the nature of languages, and was characteristic of the thought of nineteenth-century evolutionary theorists. It was one of the most damaging misconceptions of evolutionary theory because it suggested that uncivilized people were incapable of the same levels of abstract thought and precise expression as civilized people. Boas's fundamental theoretical contribution was to demonstrate the independence of race, language, and culture and to point out the fallacy of assuming a progressive development of complexity on each of these levels.[37]

Why Wissler did not attempt to educate Walker on the thinking of modern anthropology about the nature of language remains a mystery. In the 1905 paper on Oglala games that Wissler had edited for publication, Walker wrote the following, which seems to have characterized his thinking about the Lakota language throughout his life:

> Owing to the paucity of their language it is difficult for these Indians to give a differential description [of the various games]. * * * Apparently the original Sioux language was composed entirely of words of a single syllable, and the vocabulary was very limited. Things, conditions, and actions, not named in the original language, were described by phrases composed of the original words. These

phrases became agglutinated, and formed compound words, and the language as spoken at the present time is largely composed of these compound or phrase words. Because of the primitive ideas expressed by the elements of these compound words it is difficult to make an exact translation of them into English.[38]

Thus Walker assumed that the Lakota language was incapable of the same precision of expression as English. This attitude was very damaging to the progress of his studies. In the first place, it blinded him to the deeper significance of the kinds of linguistic changes about which Sword was speaking. Second, it placed Walker in an antiquated nineteenth-century theoretical mold and made his work suspect to modern anthropologists, who would be inclined to doubt the validity of all of it. The modern anthropological view is that all languages are essentially perfect means of communication, none more or less capable of precise expression.[39]

By the fall of 1909 Walker had already collected a large amount of information on Oglala religion, probably the bulk of all that he was to gather. At this time he had his earlier notes on becoming a buffalo medicine man, his notes taken in the course of his studies for the museum, and the texts by Sword. Early in October he took a leave of absence and went to New York, where he stayed with Wissler for over a month, working daily at the museum. He seems to have been very disturbed by the fragmentary nature of his notes and was still undecided on the best method for compiling them. As always, translation was problematical. He had the manuscripts as written by Sword, but was unable to perfect translations of them. Back at Pine Ridge, he wrote to Wissler on November 27, 1909:

> I began the paper on the Oglala Dakotas while there [in New York] but I found my notes so mixed up in ethnology, enthnography, phylology, mythology, legends and stories that I thought it best to bring the whole here and work it out where I could get at the Indians when puzzled on some questions.
>
> Now, Doctor, I will write this paper in my own way and submit it to you and then correct it at your suggestion so as to give it any value it may have. It may be full of errors because of my lack of research among authorities and of training, and I would be thankful if I can have these errors pointed out to me. * * *
>
> I should be pleased to get more [phonograph] records for you. They would probably come in good in the matter of the Sun Dance that we spoke of. * * *
>
> I do not know of anything that would give me greater pleasure than to do ethnological work, for itself.

During the winter of 1909 Walker continued his efforts to get the Sword texts translated. He wrote to Wissler on February 11, 1910:

> I have had Clarence Three-stars translate each of the manuscripts by Sword, but his work is not at all satisfactory to me for he has given so liberal a translation that it has destroyed the ethnological value of the work.
>
> He first rewrote the work adding what he thought Sword had left out, and then he gave in his translation what he thought Sword should have said.
>
> Thus the original spirit and meaning was not only lost, but perverted.
>
> I think the only way is to have him or some one as capable to make a literal copy with an interlinear translation and then from this get a liberal translation. * * *
>
> To me the manuscripts appear to be of ethnic value and that this value is all destroyed by Clarence's faulty translation. * * *
>
> I have now, in addition to the manuscript by Sword which I showed you, about 250 pages additional, all relative to the customs and ceremonies of the Oglala Sioux, written by Sword, without suggestion by white influence.
>
> I do not yet know just what the matters are, but judging by the work he has done, if a good translation can be gotten this will, by a critical study, throw a flood of light on the ethics of this people.

The following winter Walker hired Charles Nines to translate Sword's text on the Kit Fox society for publication in Wissler's forthcoming monograph on Oglala societies. Nines completed the work, as well as a translation of Sword's text on the sun dance, but he did so under protest. He found the work very difficult, although he continued to help Walker with it from time to time, even after Walker had retired and moved to Denver. But if Walker ever managed to translate the larger portion of the Sword material, there is no evidence of it left in his papers.[40]

By the summer of 1910 Walker was beginning to write his monograph on the sun dance. On July 15 of that year he wrote a long letter to Wissler outlining his thinking on the subject:

> Following your instructions, I have made an especial effort to get the sun-dance ceremony from these Indians.
>
> It appears to me that there was no fixed form for the ceremony, but that it was performed in a similar way each time, and that each performance embraced some features, but that some were much more elaborate than others, and in the more elaborate adjunct ceremonies were permitted.
>
> In these adjuncts several societies appear with their peculiar performances, but they become a recognised part of the *Wi-wanyank-wacipi* or Sun-dance.

In looking over authoritative descriptions of the sun-dance I have observed the same discrepencies that occur in the descriptions given me by the Indians, and they probably arise from the same cause.

In giving to one Indian the description of another which differs from his, the latter agrees that the description not his is right as well as his own, and usually says that either way is right.

I have seen no description of the ceremony which gives the symbolism of the various things done, or the full intent of the performance.

Would it be well to compose a complete sun-dance ceremony, embracing all that might be performed, provided every thing mentioned can be established by information from the Indians as having been performed as a part of the dance.

Or would it be best to confine the description to show how the dance could have been performed, giving the variations.

I have collected the 25 songs that were essential to the whole ceremony (on phonograph records, named and numbered in the order they were sung when the ceremony was performed after a certain order), but there are other songs that could be sung on the occasion, and these I have not yet collected.[41]

I have been without an assistant since I returned from New York nearly all the time so that I have had little time to give to the work I wish to do for you. * * *

I have tried to have Sword prepare the regalia of the societies but so far have succeeded in getting that of only one. He seems reluctant to make them, whether because he does not know how, or whether there was no specific regalia, I cannot determine. * * *

The most difficult part of the work I have undertaken is to get the significance or symbolism of forms, ceremonies, and things done.

This will soon be lost if it is not gotten before long.

I should like to have your opinion about the manner of the description of the things I shall write of.

Of course much of it cannot be from personal observation and must be from such information as I can gather.

They would be more succinct and readable if they gave an ideal description, but they would have the appearance of greater scientifc accuracy if the various manners of doing things were told; but the latter method would be much more verbose.

In either case it appears to me that the source of the information should be given for reference, perhaps as an appendix.

You fully understand how the decision of a small but vital point may require much time and research and will therefore understand why I have so little to offer you now.

The key here is Walker's commitment to an attempt to understand the symbolism behind each ritual act or object. In the whole literature on plains Indian sun dances, both before and since Walker's work, there is no account that attempts so systematically this symbolic level of analysis. It is this that makes Walker's study so valuable.

Clearly Walker was familiar with other works on the sun dance. He must have seen George A. Dorsey's monographs on the Arapahoe and Cheyenne sun dances that were published by the Field Columbian Museum in Chicago in 1903 and 1905. These studies focus entirely on minute descriptions of ritual action rather than on the meaning behind the ritual behavior. Dorsey witnessed several Cheyenne and Arapahoe sun dances and photographed them in incredible detail, and minutely described each action. He interviewed sun dance priests, gained permission to sit with them during the ceremony, and even brought them to Chicago during the winter to help him write his studies. Yet the investigation of meaning behind the ritual is entirely lacking.[42]

There are four main reasons that might account for this lack. The first is that Dorsey, and most other plains anthropologists at the time, collected data in English. Interpreters could deal easily with descriptions of action but could not so easily translate prayers and sacred concepts into English. Second, the Cheyenne and Arapahoe sun dances were still living traditions, being publicly performed almost every year. Very likely the holy men would simply have refused to tell the esoteric symbolism of the ceremony for fear of offending the spirits and weakening or destroying the efficacy of the ceremony. Walker's informants, on the other hand, made it clear to him that their reason for relating the sacred concepts to him was in order to preserve them, since they felt the Lakota sun dance to be dead. An interesting possibility is that since Walker never saw a sun dance, his attention was never drawn by the spectacular pageantry of the ritual occasion. Since he was dealing only with remembered accounts of the past, abstract meanings had more significance to him than actual behavior. Third, anthropologists were on the whole not studying the sun dance as an end in itself, but, as mentioned earlier, were more concerned with studying sun dance traits so that differences from tribe to tribe could be plotted as a means of reconstructing plains Indian history. A fourth reason, more tentative, involves the greater freedom and variation that characterized the Lakota sun dance as opposed to the more structured ceremonies of many other tribes. The Lakota religion was not embodied in long series of memorized prayer texts like the Pawnee, Omaha, or Blackfeet, and even the details of ritual behavior varied from ceremony to ceremony. What was esoteric knowledge was not standardized as it was in many other tribes, but was individual. Each man possessed certain types of esoteric knowledge based on his own visions and sacred experiences. These might or might not be shared with other shamans in the sweat lodge. Thus there was no single tightly structured body of sacred knowledge to be carefully guarded, and anthropologists could begin to understand some details of the ritual symbolism more easily than with many other plains tribes.

In the end Walker chose to present the esoteric knowledge of ritual symbolism as though it were a coherent and structured body of knowledge. This approach emphasized his role as the collector and organizer of the material and his feeling that there should be a single consensus account reconstructible for all aspects of culture. Thus he began to write his sun dance monograph as a description of an ideal type of sun dance, combining all the possibilities and potentialities of the ceremony. This approach did not develop out of Walker's interaction with Wissler and with anthropology, but rather in spite of it. It seems to have evolved out of a deep-rooted desire on Walker's part actually to become an Oglala shaman so that he might authoritatively interpret Lakota religion for posterity. Wissler wrote to Walker on August 4, 1910, warning him of the importance of keeping the behavioral or objective facts and ideological or symbolic ones distinct:

> I believe that your manuscript should be so ordered as to show exactly what you find the sun dance to be. I infer that you find certain procedures absolutely essential to a performance of the ceremony. Why can not this be taken as the fundamental element and so presented? Then you can go ahead with the various things that may be performed. This will not only organize your treatise on a logical consistent basis but will resolve it into definite units easily treated and understood. In treating these units you seem to recognize two aspects—the objective movements or appearances and the symbolism or ideas underlying them. I need not remind you that each is important and that neither should be confused with the other. Your account of the sun dance should certainly give all the recognized possible adjunct ceremonies reflecting all the degrees of importance and uncertainty the statements of your informants imply; but I do not favor the presentation of what may be called an ideal sun dance. You have a concise way of expressing yourself that appeals to me. I am sure the method of treating by units and speaking straight out as to what you believe to be the actual status of each ceremony will be most effective. You need not worry as to the number of words, let that go as it will.

It seems to me that we should publish all the useful accounts, written by Indians, as annotations to your direct concise statement of the ceremony as you understand it.[43]

On February 9, 1911, Walker sent Wissler a progress report:

Writing up the Sun-dance as it was practiced among the Oglala Titons is something like writing a system of Christian Theology from talking with ordinary laymen, only the Sun-dance is the more difficult.

As this people practiced the Sun-dance it was a religious ceremony from their point of view in all its bearings.

I have talked with a number of persons who have witnessed the dance, and some of whom have taken a part in it, and with some who have been leaders and I have a written description, in the native language, by one who has danced the dance.

So there is no difficulty in giving a plain description of the performance.

While I had little trouble in getting a description of the performance, I have found almost insurmountable difficulty in getting the underlying principles that governed the forms and rites, for there are few now alive who understood them; and these few have almost forgotten their former customs and beliefs.

By getting what I can from one and then from another and so on, and then piecing these bits of information together, it appears to me that I am making progress in securing a comprehensive description of the ceremony.

One source of great help is the old legends, in many of which are explained reasons for beliefs and rites.

While the native men probably could not formally classify the Sun-dance, or rather give it the proper sequence in telling of it, yet they invariably tell of it as:

First: The period of preparation of the candidates for the dance, which may be of an indefinite time.

Second: The preparation for the dance, which is an indefinite time lasting from when they start from their camps to the time when the tipis are placed in the circle of the ceremonial camp.

Third: The ceremony proper, lasting from the time when the tipis are placed in the ceremonial circle, forming the Sun-dance camp, until this circle is broken at the close of the dance.

Fourth: The time of returning from the dance.

Customary rites governed each of these periods, and, apparently, there was a reason for each rite.

During the gathering for the Sun-dance, a number of correlative ceremonies could be and often were performed.

So, a thorough description of the Sun-dance would be an almost complete mythology of the Oglala Titons.

I quickly wrote of the gathering of the clans [i.e., bands], up to the time they would be about the place where the ceremonial camp was to be made, and up to the beginning of the preliminary ceremonies, the evening before the spot whereon the mysterious pole was to be erected was to be chosen and the enclosure of the circle of the ceremonial camp was to be cleared of the evil spirits.

But then the difficult part began, as, for instance, "Why was a maiden chosen to officiate in the ceremony?" and "How did she establish her virginity?"

And numerous other similar questions.

And similar questions arose regarding all the things done during each day of the ceremony.

Among other things was the question of "Why was the camp arranged in one particular way relative to the gentes and subgentes of the people?"

This does not pertain to this ceremony alone but the custom was more strictly observed at the gatherings for the Sun-dance than on any other occasions, unless it was at a war-council camp.

To answer this question requires much research.

Then the ceremony of "Biting the Snake" was very obscure, and while it is independent of the Sun-dance it is an essential part of it.

Many who could tell me of the Sun-dance could tell nothing of the "Biting of the Snake" and most of them did not know that it was an essential part of the performance of the Sun-dance, though all knew there was such a ceremony.

The ceremony is a performance before a Shaman whereby a woman establishes her virginity.

Now, Doctor, I am trying to gather these things and put them in their proper sequence, with succinct reasons for them.

In doing this I am subject to such criticisms as this:

A white man married to an Indian woman, who has spent a large part of his life among the Oglalas, said of my work:

"He is writing things I never heard of, and I think the Indians don't know anything about them either." "They do these things just because they happen to do them that way. They have no reason for it. You ask one of them and see if he can give you any reason for doing things in a certain way."

This criticism, in more extended and better form, has been made by others; and the younger generation of these Indians would probably make the same criticism. A superficial investigation of the subject would uphold the criticism.

But in my investigations I have carefully avoided leading questions or suggestions, and all the information I have accepted has been given without suggestion on my part.

Such investigation accumulates a great amount of immaterial matter in which there are, here and there, given relevant facts on which to base further inquiry.

So, Doctor, my progress is slow, and were one to occupy oneself with such an investigation only, it would be very expensive.

But, as it is only an avocation of mine, the expenses have been small.

I have paid some story tellers and for some translations and that is all the outlay of money I have made.

Wissler replied on February 14, 1911, attempting to steer Walker out of the path of writing an entirely ideal or synthetic account of the sun dance, and stressing the importance of mentioning informants' disagreements in his work:

> There can be little doubt that the sun dance was the one great unifying ceremony of the Plains Indians toward which all other ceremonial activities converged. I often feel that it was more in the nature of an occasion for demonstration of all formal ceremonial obligations rather than a distinct ceremony itself. Though it is true that it was inaugurated by a ceremonial almost peculiar to it, this may be little more than the sign that the hour has arrived. * * * In the statement of procedure you are entirely dependent on your informants and should endeavor to render the statements of Indians with fidelity. When there are important disagreements it may be well to give each side a place in your narrative. Thus, a student will feel that he is himself weighing the evidence rather than simply taking your word for it. I often feel that the ideal thing would be to publish all the statements of informants together with an estimate and summary by the investigator. I like your grouping of the various parts of the sun dance, as the period of preparation, the time of returning, etc., for under these heads you can treat each ceremony as seems convenient. It is not necessary to follow the order of a sequence because that can be stated in a table once for all.
>
> We come now to the second part of the problem; the interpretation and the philosophy of these ceremonies. Here is where the personal equation of the investigator comes in. The result in the end will be a complete interpretation: yours and those of your informants. You are right in that mythology furnishes the best basis for such interpretations it being to these practices what the Bible is to those of the Christian religion. * * * In our work it is of the utmost importance to reflect the most intelligent Indian interpretation. The investigator owes us his last word as the case appears to his practised vision.[44]

But Walker found it impossible to minimize the "personal equation." On May 28, 1911, he wrote to Wissler to inform him that he was following exactly the course that Wissler had asked him not to take, and was writing an account of an ideal sun dance:

> I am writing The Sun Dance just as I would for my own information and will submit this to you for your criticism and suggestion as to the form you wish, which I think will be something entirely different, in that you want the evidence upon which the statements are made.
>
> As you understand this evidence is contained in a vast mass of material, the most of which is irrelevant.
>
> In my study of the mythology of the Oglalas, I have been compelled to learn something of their language as it was spoken in

what may be called the prescriptorial period. This language differs much in form and meaning to the language as it is written today. The written Dakota is in the Santee dialect, which differs much from the Titon, and especially from the dialect of the Oglala Titons. But the younger Oglalas have been so much influenced by the written language that they write and speak much like it, and they cannot understand a formal address or ceremonial address given by one of the older Indians who speaks the prescriptorial language.

I have also had to learn something of the esoteric language of the shamans which was taught only to those who danced the *Wacipi Wakan.*

In this way I think I have cleared up much confusion that existed in the descriptions of other writers on this mythology.

While no Indian has been able to give me the complete mythology in a systematic way, I have gotten a quite complete system of it in piece-meal, which I am attempting to systematize in a manner approved by older Indians who are probably as good authority on it as exists.

I still lack some details but hope to get them from some older Indians.

My plan is to give an ideal ceremony of the Sun Dance so as to bring in all the forms and ceremonies that the most elaborate performance would have had in former times.

I know that you do not approve of this plan but it is the only method I have for bringing together all the information I have gathered on the matter in a comprehensive way.

I will submit my work to you and then you may criticize it in the most severe way, and suggest what you would wish, for this will be what I most desire. * * *

If you visit me this summer this matter can then be discussed and it may be you can show me a better way to do the work.

If Wissler made any strenuous objection to Walker's decision, there is no record of it. He probably felt that the ideal account would not be misleading as long as Walker published significant interviews and texts as an appendix that would provide the reader with the primary data on which the synthetic account was based. The following extracts from their correspondence of 1911 and 1912 clarify the way in which the published work evolved.

Walker to Wissler, November 13, 1911:

Not until since you were here did I realize the close connection of the Buffalo (real and mythical) with the Sun Dance, and I am now trying to get the concepts of the older Indians on this point.

Walker to Wissler, December 18, 1911:

Here is the first installment of the Sun Dance. Is it acceptable? Give your criticism freely, for it will be helpful to me. * * *

Did you ever attempt one of those puzzles made by cutting a picture into irregular bits and try to restore each bit to its place so as to restore the picture?

Well, giving the Sun Dance from the data I have is something like mixing the bits of several pictures and then trying to restore each to its proper place. Only more so.

Wissler to Walker, February 5, 1912:

I have gone over the manuscript you sent me and find it very interesting indeed. We shall edit it and make a revised copy, a duplicate of which I shall send you in the course of a week or two. I have very little to suggest. * * *

I believe we should make progress if you send us the first draft of your manuscript and let us try our hand in revising it. Judging from the way you have handled this portion, I believe you will do just as well if you simply drive ahead and write as the spirit moves you, leaving the corrections and refining to us. We can then return to you the refined copy which you can approve or disapprove as the case may be.

Walker to Wissler, February 7, 1912:

I have completed the Sun Dance up to the Fourth Day of the formal camp which is the last day of the dance.

I have written this paper as if it were by one who believes and practices as did the old Oglalas, because I can express the concepts [of] those people better in this manner than if I were to give a description of their forms and ceremonies.

If this style is not suitable for your purposes do not hesitate to let me know and if I can I will prepare a paper suitable.

Walker to Wissler, March 20, 1912:

Now in my paper on the Sun Dance I am very liberal in giving the concepts of the Indians, but to get this liberality I required very accurate literal translations, and much cross examination.

Take for instance the term *Wakan Tanka*. I have not yet asked an interpreter for the meaning of it but what he replied instantly "The Great Spirit." Today if any Lakota is speaking to a white man he will use this term to mean Jehova, or the Christian God, and by common consent it has come to mean The Great Spirit. This was a stumbling block to me for many years, and very confusing when trying to get the concepts of the older Indians expressed by it. Most of them would confuse the words and the concepts. I now find that at the present time, to the younger generation, this term expresses a concept of Jehova while to the older Indians it expresses a concept of the being that in former times they titled *Taku Skanskan,* and in still older times, in the language of the shamans, was simply *Skan;* except that the modern conception attributes to *Wakan Tanka,* who is *Taku Skanskan,* all his potency as *Skan,* and some of the attributes of Jehova; or with some *Wakan Tanka* is all their former gods who were *wakan tanka* combined into one and that one is *Skan.* * * *

I have been waiting some months to clear up the matter of the different orders of the sun dance. It was made clear to me that there were the four kinds, but now, during the last day of the dance, I find that I have not sufficient data to give, specifically, the different classes in their order. Several of the older Indians whom I have questioned about this professed to know nothing of there being four kinds, but on cross examination they declared that there were different kinds, and in each instance they gave then four kinds. But apparently they had never before thought of classifying them.

The same difficulty has arisen in regard to the mythology. Some to whom I have referred the matter have said they did not know of the order of mythology as I give it, but they would voluntarily give as much of the mythology as they could remember, and then it was found that it agreed exactly with that arranged by myself. Some would give one portion of the mythology, and others other parts, which, if I had not known something of the matter would have been very confusing, and this did confuse me for many years. There are some contradictions in the mythology, especially in the appellations, as for instance, the Rock is "The Grandfather," while the Sun is often addressed as Grandfather.

From this correspondence it would seem that the sun dance study was nearly complete by the end of 1912, yet that was not the case. The more he wrote, the more concerned Walker became about his lack of understanding of details of the general belief foundations of Lakota religion.

During the winter of 1911 Thomas Tyon wrote a series of texts for Walker based on interviews that he had had with older Oglala shamans. Tyon was a mixed-blood, and was the government farmer for White Clay district. Although a Christian, he was oriented primarily toward Lakota culture. He did not speak English very well, but was entirely literate in Lakota. One of his texts was an account of the sun dance, with recordings of the songs sung by Sword. The text was translated by John Monroe and revised by Walker with the intention of printing it bilingually. There is no evidence, however, that Walker ever translated the remainder of Tyon's writings on Lakota religion.[45]

As an example of Walker's confusion regarding even basic details, he wrote to Wissler on February 13, 1912: "I have some information that there is a legend relative to the origin of the pipe, but have not yet heard it." Walker was unaware that he had two versions of the story in Lakota, one by Sword and one by Tyon, and he was equally unaware that a version of the story had been published in 1906.[46]

On May 13, 1912, Walker again wrote to inform Wissler that he had hired Short Bull to paint two large pictures of the sun dance to help fill in the visual aspects of the ceremony.

Walker continued to work on the sun dance manuscript, writing and rewriting, and attempting to incorporate more and more of what he had learned so as to create a holistic picture of the ceremony as representative of Lakota religion. Finally, on December 22, 1913, he wrote to Wissler to announce that he would have to rewrite the entirety of what he had so far produced:

> I think I have about all the information I shall be able to get in regard to the sun dance. It is a mass of material. I have just measured it, and the MSS lying flat is five and a half inches thick. It makes me tired to look at it. All that I sent to you I will have to rewrite because of important items omitted from it. * * *
>
> Much of the stuff I have relative to the sun dance is rubbish, but in a thing that is largely rubbish there may be one item that is of importance. To fully appreciate the correctness of my work, according to the information that I have received, such items must be known. But it would hardly pay to reproduce a lengthy paper that is nearly all repetition of that given elsewhere, only to give one point.

In the midst of his work on the sun dance, Walker found time to write, at Wissler's request, a paper on the Lakota kinship system. It was based on an excellent text on the subject by Tyon, and is a classic paper of its kind. Published in the *American Anthropologist* in 1914, together with the text itself, it attracted considerable attention, even though it is marred by dozens of printer's errors. The work clearly shows Walker's grasp of the structure of Oglala kinship, but, in contrast to his control of religious data, he does not seem to have appreciated fully the way in which the kinship system interrelated with other parts of the culture.[47]

Retirement and Writing

Walker retired from the Indian Service in 1914. The last year at Pine Ridge was a trying one. During February and March of 1913 a younger doctor, who remained at Pine Ridge for only about eight weeks, filed a complaint against Walker, charging him with incompetence and dereliction of duty. On June 15, 1913, Walker sent a lengthy and very convincing defense of his medical policies to the commissioner of Indian affairs.[48]

In April 1914 Walker took at six-month leave of absence.

He learned only later that he had been officially retired on May 5, two months following his sixty-fifth birthday.[49] Evidently he never returned to Pine Ridge for any further ethnographic work.

Before leaving the reservation, Walker quite fortuitously had a very important interview with Finger, a shaman, who filled in for him an important link in the Oglala religious system—the position of the god Škan. He also heard from Finger, evidently for the first time, the story of the bringing of the pipe to the Lakota people.[50] Walker wrote to Wissler from Fort Lupton, Colorado, on January 13, 1915:

> When I left the Pine Ridge Agency I expected to return there on about the first of November last, but it is probable that the Department is letting me out, for while they granted me six months' leave of absence they have not notified me to return to duty, and they have appointed a man as physician to fill the place I occupied.
>
> I came to Colorado to care for a small ranch and some bees that I own, as I could not get a suitable person to take charge of them last spring. These have kept me very busy indeed, and I have worked hard but I have enjoyed excellent health, and like the occupation so much that probably I shall continue on the place caring for bees principally. * * *
>
> A few days before leaving the Pine Ridge Agency I had an interview with Finger, an old and conservative Oglala, which was of much interest to me, and of much value relative to the mythology of the Oglala.
>
> It came about in this way: I was at the house of Finger in the evening, and when starting for the agency, all were outside in the gloaming, and a very brilliant meteor fell. Finger exclaimed in a loud voice, "Wohpa. Wohpe-e-e-e." He then harangued for a short time and the women built a fire, and when it had burned to coals Finger burned a quantity of sweet grass on it, evidently with forms and ceremonial mutterings.
>
> I asked him the meaning of this, but he would tell me nothing. I then offered him pay, and he agreed to come to my office and tell me what he knew of the mythology relative to his performance. About thirty days afterwards, on the 25th of March, he came for this purpose, and I secured an interpreter of unusual ability for grasping the concept of the Lakota language and translating it. The interview lasted nearly all night, and I believe the old man tried honestly to give the concepts of the shamans relative to the matters discussed. The most of the matter discussed was relative to Taku Skanskan, or Skan, to Wohpe, and to the immortality of the Wakan. I left the Agency on the first of April, so had no opportunity of reviewing the matter with Finger, or of submitting it to others of the Oglala for their discussion.
>
> The information I got from Finger clears up much that was obscure, especially relative to Taku Skanskan. Perhaps you will

remember that I said that I could not give a translation of *Skan*, which is the shamanistic term for *Taku Skanskan*, and that according to the best information I had, *Skan* meant the sky. I so translated it, with the approval of several old Indians, including George Sword, though each and all declaring that *Skan* was the sky, and was also a spirit that was everywhere, and that gave life and motion to everything that lives or moves. Every interpreter interpreted *Taku Skanskan* as "What Moves-moves," or that which gives motion to everything that moves. From the information given by Finger it is evident that his concept of *Taku Skanskan*, or *Skan*, is a vague, or nebulous idea of force or energy. Recalling attempts of other Oglala to define the word I am sure that they had the same kind of a concept of *Skan*. I am now surprised that this did not appear to me before talking with Finger.

Another proposition that Finger gave utterance to is that "Anything that has a birth must have a death. The *Wakan* has no birth and it has no death." "The spirit, the ghost, and the familiar of man are not born with him but are given to him at the time of his birth. They are *Wakan* and therefore will never die."

He cleared other things that were obscure to me. I should have very much liked to have talked with him about the sun dance, but did not have the opportunity.

My interpreter was an educated man, and well informed, but he had never before this interview heard the words *Skan*, *Wohpe*, *sicun*, or *ton*, used to convey the concepts as given by Finger, though he recalled having heard them used with an allusive sense.

Finger's discussion of *Wakan Tanka* agreed with that given in that part of my paper on the sun dance submitted to you, except relative to *Skan* and the relative existence of the four superior Gods. For instance he gave *Inyan*, The Rock, as the first in existence, and the grandfather of all things; *Maka*, The Earth as the next in existence, and the grandmother of all things; *Skan* next in existence after the Earth, because He gave life and motion to all things; *Wi*, The Sun as the last in existence, but also the most powerful and august of *Wakan Tanka*, being *Wakan Tanka Kin*, The *Wakan Tanka*. He also said that the Associate *Wakan Tanka*, *Wi Han*, The Moon; *Tate*, The Wind; *Wakinyan*, The Winged; and *Wohpe* were as the other self of the four Superior Gods; that is, that *Wi* and *Wihan* are as one; *Skan* and The Wind are as one; The Rock and The Winged are as one; and that The Earth and *Wohpe* are as one. That while there are eight personalities that are *Wakan Tanka*, four Superior and four Associate, they are all as one and there is but one *Wakan Tanka*. This is The Great Mystery known only to the wisest shamans.

Discussing *Wi* and *Skan* Finger said that while The Sun was the Superior and most powerful of the Gods, yet He derived His power from *Skan*. That many of the Lakota believed *Wi* and *Skan* to be one and the same personalities; but that *Wi* was a *Wakan Tanka* visible in the sky only half the time, while *Skan* was the *Nagi Tanka*, the great Spirit, everywhere at all times, and invisible, except His color which was the blue seen in the sky at all times.

Because of this interview I think I should translate *Taku Skanskan*, or *Skan,* as either Force or Energy. And that I should express in my paper the doctrine of the immortality of the spirit of man.

One of your papers led me to make inquiries relative to the social arrangements of an Oglala camp, and I learned an important matter pertaining to the government of the camp, and of the camp's movements. Much as I had talked to the Oglala about this they had not mentioned it to me, but when I inquired about it each gave information agreeing with every other, and all gave it the importance properly belonging to it. This was relative to the *Mihunka* who were chosen or accepted as magistrates for the camp. This should be employed in the preface relative to the government of the camp, as it takes an important part in the movement of a camp to the place chosen for holding the sun dance.

Maybe these details are not of much interest to you, but it is a relief to write of them for they have been hard to get, and it seems to me that they are necessary in order to give a clear concept of why as well as how the Lakota danced the sun dance.

I am fully alive to the sense that my paper is based entirely upon information given by others, and that it is in part constructive: that I may have been misinformed, either intentionally or because of the difficulty in getting correct translations of the language of my informants. But the intention of the paper is to give such information as I have received. This last is written because of a criticism of one to whom I submitted some of my information for his judgment upon it.

I have all my manuscripts stored in a fireproof vault because of your suggestion relative to their safety. I have not had the time to make copies of them as you suggested and when I work on the paper I need them at hand for reference.

Walker completed the writing of his sun dance study in 1915 and 1916. Extracts from his letters to Wissler give a sense of his frustration in having to work alone, a feeling for the intense dedication he felt to completing the project in the best manner possible, and also an indication of the quality of his life in retirement.

August 8, 1915:

I think I have finished what I have to write on the Sun Dance, except getting the significance of the dried buffalo penis and of the burning buffalo chips. It may be that you can give me some light on these points. My most valued informants are all now dead, the two I most depended upon, George Sword and Thomas Tyon, have gone the way of all flesh. Sword intimated that the dried buffalo penis was used in the dance to give increased virility to the dancers, or as he put it, "So that the dancers could get more children." Tyon, after consulting with some of the older men, said that they differed, but all thought it was to have something to do with having wives and children. Tyon also consulted with others in regard to the burning of buffalo chips and it appeared that the idea was that these chips have a *wakanla,* or spirit-like of themselves, independent of the buffalo, and that this spirit-like is released by burning, as the smoke, and this ascended to the Buffalo God as an intermediary. However, some with whom I talked denied this and said chips were used simply because it was the most convenient fuel to burn on the altar. But as buffalo chips were used for the fire on the altar in other ceremonies, and at places where other fuel was more convenient, I am inclined to think that burning them in this way had some significance.

I have completed the text of my paper which makes about 100 pages like this that this letter is written on [8″ × 10″, typed double-spaced]. If I add such footnotes as appear to me necessary to give a good understanding of the matter this will nearly double that number of pages. I undertook to write these notes in while writing the text, but soon found I could not do so without confusion. If the interviews, papers, and notes that the text is based on are added there will be over three hundred pages, for I have much material gotten since that for which you paid me.

In the text I have used the translation "Force" for the word *"Skan"* or "The Great Spirit." On reading the paper "Force" appears to me to be too bald or raw a term. While it is clear to me that in using the term *"Skan"* the shamans' conception was of a force, that is, the power that moves everything that moves, but it was also of a distinct being, a supreme spirit. So now it appears to me that the better plan would be to distinctly and fully define the Lakota concept of *Skan* in the teachings of the Mentor to the Candidate, and by a footnote, and then use the word *"Skan"* where a Lakota would use it. The shamans when speaking to the people used the term *"Taku Skanskan,"* and the people used this term also when speaking of this being; but in their ceremonies the shamans used the terms *"Skan"* and "The Great Spirit" interchangeably. *Wohpe* or the Intermediator and *Wasicun* will both require distinct definition, and footnotes to give a correct idea concerning them; especially *Wasicun,* for this has so often been mistranslated as medicine-bag.

I have translated *Wakinyan* as the Winged-One, but it now appears to me that Winged-God is a more accurate translation. This is the being that is usually translated as The Thunder Bird. The word *Wakinyan* is derived from the two words *wakan,* here meaning a God, and *kinyan,* a flying or winged thing.

These little differences take much time to be reconciled, but I think it worthwhile. Don't you?

I have been fully occupied in my new vocation, but am much pleased in following it. * * *

If the addenda are to be the accumulation of material that the paper is based on, numerous references to them should be given as footnotes, and some of the material should be referred to in widely separated parts of the text. Further, much of this material would have to be corrected because when beginning the investigation I accepted the interpreters' version as correct, and afterwards found it to be erroneous, as, for instance, they invariably interpreted *"Wakan Tanka"* as "The Great Spirit," which is an error that confuses the entire mythology of the Lakota.

February 25, 1916:

I have completed the paper as it will go into your hands and am trying to get into shape the information it is based on. In doing this I am taking only the pertinent parts of such interviews and notes as I have and arranging them so that all the information gotten from one source will be together. Perhaps you will remember that I had numerous notes and scraps of information, sometimes a number gotten from the same person at different times. Some of these relate to entirely different matters from the sun dance but have in them parts that throw light on either the rites or reason for the rites in that ceremony. In such cases I am trying to get such light in shape so as to substantiate the paper.

I have arranged the paper entirely differently from the draft of the first part I sent to you. I have tried to make the whole paper as if it were instructions given by an Oglala for the performance of all that pertains to the sun dance. As I progressed in formulating the paper this almost forced itself upon me.

I would send the paper to you were it not for the fact that I have to refer to it very frequently in selecting the appendix. I have not yet numbered the paragraphs for reference for I could not yet do so until I have the information arranged for reference. I will enter the number on the paper with a pen, arranging the evidence as an appendix.

I am having the hardest work with retranslating articles written in Lakota. A number of times I have had to correspond with some Oglala to get the correct concept of some words. But I believe that I can make a better translation than any one who I have tried to have translate for me. The Nines brothers were very good but they lacked a sufficient knowledge of English to give the word that would express the correct concept. And besides, they had become conventional in interpreting. They gave me invaluable aid and put me on the track of correct translation.

Another difficulty is a misconception of the Lakota language which is held by men who are authorities in Phylology. This is a very interesting subject that I would like to give some attention to.

I shall give several papers written originally in Lakota as sources of information. These I will translate and interpret as I did the paper on relationship of the Lakota.

I have several long legends that give much information that I would not have gotten otherwise. This information was confirmed upon inquiry of the Holy Men or Shamans.

By the way, I became a Shaman before leaving the reservation and was instructed in much of the esoteric lore of the shamans. I was saluted by the older Oglala as the Holy Man. Before this I was *Wasicu Wakan* ["holy white man"] and I became *Wicasa Wakan* ["holy man"].

You perhaps think I wish to accumulate an unnecessary amount of information to accompany my paper. But it gives matters in such radically different light from anything I have seen upon the subjects that I wish to have all the proof I can to sustain what I give. I have often set down things as so and so but have found that such views were not accepted by all the Oglala and so have dropped them. * * *

The fact though is that I feel ashamed of the product of all the time I spent on this thing. You probably could have done as much in a few weeks as I have done in a number of years. I am reminded of the mountain bringing forth the mouse. However, I do not think of myself as a mountain, it is only the amount of work that is that big.

I do hope you will be able to call on me on some of your trips to the west. I have not much of a place. Only a shack, four acres of land, some bees and hens. But I can give you a place to sleep, something to eat, and acres of good air while you view the snowy tops of the Rockies.

I have quit the practice of medicine and banished the telephone. Go to bed when I wish, get up when I like, work at times, and go to the movies for amusement. Have a garden and cook by electricity. Wear old clothes and sometimes shave. Have shade trees and pick fruit from my own trees and vines. Raise pumpkins and things. Last year produced four and a half tons of honey. Sold most of it in New York and maybe you ate some of it. It was good honey. You see I live high, about a mile high, where the air is rare and the women vote. That is, some of them do, and some are just plain ladies. I believe in preparedness for I am too old to fight.

March 14, 1916:

In translating the legends of "When the People Laughed at The Moon" and "When The Directions Were Made on the World" as written by Sword, I came upon what appears to me to be valuable information relative to the relation of the Supernatural beings *Inyan*, The Rock; *Wakinyan*, The Winged God; *Iktomi*, The Imp of mischief; *Wazi*, The Old Man, The Wizard; *Wakanka*, The Old Woman, The Witch; *Tate*, The Wind; *Tate Tob*, The Four Winds; *Yum*, The Whirlwind; and *Anog Ite*, Face on Both Sides, or The Double Woman.[51] Also the relation of *Skan*, The Great Spirit, and *Wohpe*, The Mediator or The Feminine.

There is also in these legends information relative to the establishment of the time, a moon, and a year and its seasons. The mythology as I have written it leaves much to be explained, and the information above mentioned explains some of this. * * *

The legends are quite long, they in fact being of the kind told by the professional story tellers of the Lakota who tell their stories at the winter camp, usually prolonging the story during the entire occupancy of the camp.

It appears to me that this information, received in this way, is sufficient for accepting it relative to the mythology of the Lakota, for it harmonizes with much that was only alluded to in all other information I had received regarding the matters referred to.

December 29, 1916:

Under separate cover I am sending you the MS I have written relative to the Sun Dance, *Hunka*, and Buffalo ceremonies. Accompanying them are a number of other papers for your inspection, and if they can be used, for your use. I send these because of your saying in one of your letters that you should like to see the matter I have on hand, and you might use the most of it. The most of the material is in the form of notes which cover much more than the ceremonials of the Oglala. I have made excerpts from these notes and send them to you. I have in addition about twenty pages of notes taken while Sword and others were instructing me as a Shaman. But these are simply a repetition of much that is in the paper on the Sun Dance, and are so confusedly intermingled that they would be difficult to understand in references.

I have made no footnotes or explanatory notes because, as you may perceive, to make them in full would make them so numerous that they would be tedious and further, in many instances a simple statement would require reference to several notes. It appears to me that the accompanying papers cover most of that which requires explanation, and give that which may be required in a more connected manner than could be given by annotation. I would like it if there are inclosed papers that you cannot use you would return them to me.

I wish to reserve the right to use the legends in another manner, for I have been told that the legends I have would, if properly arranged, be of literary value. My personal equation enters largely into all of the MS, for it is all either liberal translation or my arrangement of hastily taken notes. * * *

Now as to expenses. You have paid me for all the expenses I have incurred that can be distinctly separated as pertaining to the subjects of the papers, except the paintings by Short Bull. I gathered the information relative to the aboriginal state of the Oglala for my personal satisfaction and had no plan or principal object in view. I got information when, where, and how I could get it, consequently notes gathered are so jumbled that it is almost impossible to separate them in such a manner to apportion the expenses that should be chargeable to the paper.

The expenses incurred in getting information varied from nothing to giving a feast. The most expensive items were those relative to the symbolism of the Lakota. But, while one must know something of the symbolism in order to understand the ceremonial, these items should not be chargeable against the MS sent to you. The only notes you have not already paid me for and that should be chargeable to the MS are those taken during the interview with Finger. He was reluctant to give the information and I had to bring him to my office, keep him, and return him to his home, and pay him for the interview. The notes on this interview accompany the MS.

The feast I gave when becoming a shaman might be properly

chargeable to the MS but fortunately the ox for beef, the flour, sugar, coffee, pork and lard cost me nothing, and the only expense to me was for two 25 pound boxes of crackers and one-half dozen cans of tomatoes. Since I have been at Fort Lupton my only expense has been a few postage stamps on letters of inquiry relative to obscure points in the ceremonies. If you so desire I will send you an itemized account of these expenses which will amount to less than $35, I think. If you can use the MS pay me what you think it is worth.

Maybe that I should explain to you regarding some matters in the MS which appear to give tedious detail, as for instance, the expression often occurs that "He filled and lighted the pipe and smoked it." You can see by the notes accompanying that filling the pipe is a rite, lighting it is another rite and smoking the pipe is still another rite; that either one or more of these rites may be done without either of the others, and the significance of the rite depends on how it is done. The intention is to give no details that have no signification, and in that part given as instruction to the Shaman to explain that which is relative to the ceremony. In rewriting the *Hunka* and Buffalo ceremonies I have left out that which is explained in the Sun Dance.

I will shortly mail to you the pictures by Short-bull, but I would like to keep the book written by Sword for a time as it contains some things that have not yet been translated and I should like to learn what they are. It appears to me that the "Young Man's Vision" would be a good accompaniment to the Buffalo Ceremony as it bears the same relation to the young man as the Buffalo Ceremony does to the young woman.

The symbolism of the Lakota is an interesting subject. I do not know whether it has been written of or not.

Wissler seems to have been satisfied with the manuscript despite the lack of precise footnoting to informants' statements. As finally written, the accounts of the instructions given to the sun dance candidates and the shamans participating in the ceremony incorporated Walker's complete syntheses of Lakota social organization and religion in addition to the information relating particularly to the sun dance. As Walker wrote in the introduction, the information is given "as it was received, as nearly as may be, when irrelevant material is eliminated and it is systematized."[52]

System is the key word in understanding Walker's approach to the monograph. Inconsistencies at all levels were eliminated. This is a doctrinal account, written as though with the intention of standardizing ritual form and belief for all time.

The material on the sun dance is followed by briefer accounts of the *Hunka* and Buffalo ceremonies (both descriptions of specific occurrences of the ceremonies as witnessed by Walker), a series of interviews, notes, and texts dealing with important religious and philosophical concepts, and a substantial series of myths.

On the whole the only portion of the work relatively untouched by Walker's drive to systematize is the myth section. He arranged the myths to form as closely as possible a sequence. Yet he was clearly unsatisfied, at least esthetically, with the myth portion. He wished to systematize the whole, to make a continuous mythic epic comparable to the Greek that would memorialize the Lakota mythologic world. To this end he devoted the rest of his intellectual endeavors.[53]

After his retirement to Colorado Walker was invited from time to time to deliver speeches on various aspects of Indian culture. He seems to have become part of the intellectual circles of Denver. When his health worsened in 1918 he was forced to give up his ranch and reluctantly moved to Denver, finally settling in Wheatridge, a Denver suburb. There he continued his literary work.[54]

On November 8, 1919, Walker wrote to Wissler that he was still "pegging away at the MSS of Sword" and finding significant details for his mythology; "it makes a connected story of the creation of the world, and all on it, and the beginning of the various Gods." By 1921 Walker had finished a draft of the mythology. On April 9 he wrote to Wissler: "I have deduced from various Oglala stories, legends and writings an almost complete Oglala mythology. I would be glad to submit it to you. Quite all of it has been approved by the older of the Oglala." The many partial drafts of this material that Walker left among his papers attest to the great amount of effort he put into it.[55]

The Oglala mythology represents the culmination of Walker's studies, the ultimate synthesis and systematization of the Oglala world view. That no Oglala had likely ever produced such a synthesis did not seem to trouble Walker. To him it had become a duty to preserve for the Lakotas and for the world the sacred and secret knowledge that had been entrusted to him by Little Wound, Ringing Shield, Sword, Tyon, Finger, and others. Since none of these men had been able to do this literary work themselves—though Sword had tried, writing in Lakota— Walker had taken it on for them, and by becoming a shaman he doubtless felt that he was, in a way at least, authorized to do the work. Moreover, Walker experienced more and more as he lived on after all his informants had died the feeling that he was the last person alive with this knowledge.

On July 30, 1925, Walker wrote a final letter to Wissler:

> I have worked in trying to arrange the Oglala myths as they might have been arranged by an Oglala had he understood the concepts of the narrators and been able to express them in the English language. This requires much disentangling them from the legends told by the Oglala story tellers and instructions given me by Oglala Shamans or Holy Men. My former instructors are now all dead, so I have not the assistance I had when in doubt as to my interpretation of Oglala manuscript.
>
> I want to finish this work before I join the Great Majority for I believe none other has quite as thorough information from the old Indians relative to their ancient traditions as was given to me.

Walker died December 11, 1926, at age seventy-seven. He had managed to complete the mythology.[56]

Walker's Contribution

This is not the place to attempt to write an assessment of the value of Walker's achievements. His works have both strengths and weaknesses. In the end his total contribution may be judged as the single most significant one to the recording of nineteenth-century Lakota religion. Yet his work must be understood within the limitations of its time.

Walker was educated during the middle of the nineteenth century, at a time when the Western World had just discovered the power of the idea of progress. Concepts of social and biological evolution gained general acceptance. Eventually the developmental scheme of human culture and society became understood as the triumph of the strong over the weak, the more developed over the less, and the civilized over the primitive. Walker's outlook was entirely within this nineteenth-century mode. He believed the Lakotas to be one of the last groups of primitive man in America, fast vanishing into civilization. For him, the notion that Lakota culture was primitive was not a pejorative one, for there is no doubt that he valued the traditional Lakota way especially because he understood it to be closer to nature than was civilization. The stereotype of the noble savage colored Walker's attempts to reconstruct systematically the fundamentals of Lakota belief.[57]

Just as the man must not be unfairly condemned because his thought reflected the times in which he lived, so his work must not be judged invalid because it springs from an outdated view of human history. Both the man and his work have something in them that transcends the time and makes them worthy of study yet today.

Because some of the material Walker gathered was secret, because he was bound not to reveal it until after his informants were all dead, and because most of the original interviews, notes, and texts have not been published, the very authenticity of his material has sometimes been questioned. Thus Ella C. Deloria, the Lakota linguist, was asked by Franz Boas in 1937 to try to authenticate Walker's material by interviewing old Lakotas at Rosebud and Pine Ridge. Boas, who had been familiar at least at second hand with Walker's anthropological work from its inception, was very certain of its great value, but was equally certain that some corroborating data were needed before any of Walker's material could be unhesitatingly accepted. Deloria read the interviews, texts, and myths as printed in *The Sun Dance* to her informants but obtained little by way of results. By this time she could find no one who remembered the symbolic significance of the ritual actions recorded in such detail by Walker. Discouraged, she wrote to Boas, "The 'why' of all these things seems to have gone with the medicine men." Most of her informants expressed doubt about the authenticity of the material, and they were particularly incensed at the suggestion that the shamans might have held back from the people secret knowledge that they as shamans shared in common.[58]

That so much could have been lost in the twenty-four years since Walker left Pine Ridge is explainable only if some of the key parts of the information—particularly the data on gods and their interrelationships embodied largely in the myths, and some of the shared ideas of the sacred, like the concept of *Skan,* that were the property of shamans—were indeed secret. If this was really so, it places a truly enormous value on Walker's work—in fact, the value that he insisted that it had. With the publication at last of all the original material that has survived in the Walker papers it is now possible to evaluate the primary sources independently of Walker's syntheses. Here is rich material for study, by Indians and non-Indians alike. It is the legacy of the only white man ever to be saluted by the traditional Oglalas, the men of the buffalo-hunting days, as *Wicasa Wakan,* "Holy Man." Like him, we are engaged in the same intellectual activity, a search for the bases of Lakota culture, and through this some more fundamental insights into the nature of the human person in relation to the universe.

Walker's Autobiographical Statement

For twenty years my vocation brought me into intimate contact with the Oglalas as they lived their daily lives and practiced their customs.[59] When I first went among them [in 1896] Christian missionaries had labored among them for many years. The U.S. Department of Indian Affairs had established a sufficient number of primary schools to accommodate all their children of school age and was compelling such children to attend these schools where all were required to speak English while under the supervision of the teachers. A boarding school was established to further educate those who could be induced to attend it. A large number of those above school age had attended non-reservation schools. So quite all under forty years of age knew something of the requirements of civilization. And quite all the older people lived in accord with their tribal customs, as nearly as their environment would permit. I observed that those who attended the schools made little practical use of the education they had received there, and preferred to live according to the ideals of their kinspeople; that they adopted only such requirements of civilization as added to their physical comfort with the least physical effort. The older Oglalas recognized no absolute personal rights other than self-preservation and rather loose kindred ties. * * *

The Oglalas were very religious, but not at all pious. They did not worship any thing. By sacrifices and ceremonies they propitiated their Gods to secure their aid, or placated them to appease their anger. * * * One or more of the Oglala Gods is ever present, therefore it behooves an Oglala to avoid offense by conduct in accord with the ceremonies prescribed by the shamans.

In order to understand them and the motives that actuated

them, I undertook a study of them as a people and sought from them information such as they would give to a child when rearing it according to their tribal methods.

Usually the common people told all they knew of their traits, customs and ceremonies. There were many inconsistencies in the information acquired in this manner. When asked to explain such inconsistencies, the informants usually said that these were mysteries that only the holy men could explain.

To get the desired information, I became an Oglala medicine man, complying with the requirements of their order. Among the Oglalas there were several cults of medicine men and I applied for admission to their ranks. Their requirements were that I should choose as instructor a Buffalo medicine man. He instructed me in their classification of diseases, their remedies and the methods of procedure and the equipment I must have as a Buffalo medicine man. This equipment was a skull of a buffalo, a medicine bag made potent by proper ceremony, a ceremonial pipe and stem, a medicine rattle, and a drum. As an insignia I was given a small buffalo horn and told that it should be worn attached to a belt around my waist when I ministered to the sick or suffering. I was informed that if I became proficient as a medicine man I would be entitled to wear the Buffalo medicine man's insignia, which was a strip from the back of a tanned buffalo skin with the tail attached so that it would hang down my back to below my knees and the other end of the strip fashioned into a cap fitting my head, having two small buffalo horns attached so that they would stand out like when on the buffalo.

These medicine men had material medicines of actual medicinal qualities and some that were not so effective. Their ministrations were most effective by suggestion. I learned the twelve ritual songs that may be incanted either aloud or in whispers while treating a patient. Their method of procedure is to first smoke the pipe while gazing at the patient; then to blow smoke from the pipe into the nostril cavities of the buffalo skull to arouse the favor of the Buffalo God, the deity of the Buffalo medicine men; then to prepare the medicine to be administered, incanting while doing so a song describing the effect that the medicine will cause; then to administer the medicine by portions, singing while each portion is administered a song that suggests progressive relief and rattling the medicine rattle to frighten away the cause of the illness; and finally to sing a song of triumph declaring the disease conquered. The entire procedure is psychological and very successful because of its power of suggestion.

In some cases the procedure alone was given without any material medicine. Their success in relieving undoubted suffering, even lowering the temperature of fever and relieving pain in such diseases as inflammatory rheumatism was a matter of much interest to me. As a medicine man I practiced some of their methods, sometimes with success, but not such as the Oglala medicine men had.

I inquired of my instructor why the formula of the procedure was necessary and his reply was that that was a mystery known only by the Gods and could be explained only by the holy men. I sought information from the holy men and was told that they taught their mystic lore only to candidates for admission to their order who were acceptable to the Gods and that no other than a full-blooded Oglala had ever been ordained as a holy man. At this time there were but five holy men among the Oglalas and three of these were very old. The progress of civilization had extinguished the belief in their traditions and for some years none had sought to be ordained by them.

Long Knife [George Sword], who had been a renowned holy man but had renounced the traditions of the order to become a consistent deacon of a Christian denomination, then argued to the holy men that soon they would go from the world and all their sacred lore would pass with them unless they revealed it so that it could be preserved in writing; that future generations of the Oglalas should be informed as to all that their ancestors believed and practiced; that the Gods of the Oglalas would be more pleased if the holy men told of them so that they might be kept in remembrance and that all the world might know of them.

Short Bull, a holy man, the apostle of the Ghost Dance among the Sioux, proposed to seek a vision from the Oglala deities relative to the matter and the other holy men agreed to abide by Short Bull's interpretation of such vision as he might receive. I never learned what vision Short Bull received, but he must have interpreted it favorably, for some time later Long Knife informed me that if I would comply with the requirements of a candidate for ordination, the holy men would reveal to me the mysteries of their order and tell me their sacred lore. I was asked to pledge my word that I would not divulge what I learned until after there were no longer any holy men among the Oglalas so that their Great Judge of Spirits would not hold against them that they had done wrong to make the sacred things common.

I readily agreed to these terms. Then good men connected with missionary work among the Oglalas complained that I encouraged the people in their heathenish customs. A U.S. Inspector, Colonel James McLaughlin, was sent to investigate this complaint.[60] Upon his recommendation the secretary of the interior notified the complainants that my activities were not opposed to the policy of the Department of Indian Affairs in its efforts to civilize the Indians under its jurisdiction.

But there was the question of an interpreter. I had employed members of mixed-blood families who had been educated in English as interpreters, but none of these understood the mystic language as spoken by the holy men and the holy men would not explain it to them. Fortunately, Long Knife, though he did not speak English, understood it sufficiently well to correct misinterpretations of the Oglala dialect. Gray Goose [Thomas Tyon] spoke English indifferently and when he could not express an idea in English he would, with the help of Long Knife, explain so that the idea could be grasped. These two, Gray Goose and Long Knife, did the interpreting that was necessary when my informants were instructing me in the sacred lore of the Oglala holy men. The process of giving and receiving this information was long, tedious and costly. When it was deemed that I was sufficiently instructed relative to the customs, usages, and ceremonies of the Oglalas I was required to dance the Holy Dance with the holy men. This was considered as obligating me to hold as sacred the mystic lore of the holy men and then they taught it to me. Then they taught me their sacred lore. This was of their deities and their relation to each other and to other creatures. These formulas were of mystic words in the ceremonial language of the holy men and were meaningless to the common people. There was a formula addressed to all their deities, a formula addressed to each deity, and a special formula addressed to *Wohpe*, the Mediator. Then each holy man had a formula that he alone used when invoking the potency of the God that was his special patron. It was required of each candidate to seek a vision to have revealed to him which deity he should choose for his patron. It was considered that I was incompetent to receive such a vision, so Short Bull chose for me as my patron the Buffalo God. Then, that I might give to my patron due reverence and comprehend communications from the Gods, a *sicun*, that is, a ceremonial bundle regarded as a fetish, was ceremonially prepared for me in this manner: Short Bull chose the material, which consisted of a soft-tanned fawn skin as the container, the tusk of a bear, the claw of an eagle, the rattle of a rattlesnake, a wisp of human hair, and a wisp of sweetgrass. The holy men consecrated the container by each invoking the potency of his *sicun* to make the container sacred. Then I was required to smear a little of my blood on each of the things to be enclosed in the container. When this was done I was required to hold them all in my hands while the holy men placed their hands on my head and implored the Gods to give me their aid when I should need it. Then the articles were carefully enclosed in the container and it was folded about them and bound with cords made of sinews, each holy man tying a knot in the cords, muttering his special formula while doing so.

When finished, the bundle was given to me and I was informed that it was my personal possession to be held by me only and that its potency could be made effective only by my repeating the formula that was taught to me; and that if I failed to give to my *sicun* the reverential care due it, its potency would bring upon me disaster of some kind; that if I regarded my *sicun* with due reverence I would understand the sacred lore of the Oglalas, but until I professed a faith in their Gods, powers to do supernatural things or receive communications from the Gods would not be granted to me. I was then pronounced a holy man and was so addressed by all the Oglalas.

The holy men required me to comply with the rites and ceremonies which they prescribed. I did so sincerely, for I recognized in their traditions that universal equality of mankind which sees in nature mysteries beyond human understanding and deifies that which causes them. The sacred mysteries of the Oglala holy men were certain rites to be done which would impart to them superhuman powers and enable them to hold communion with their deities and speak their will and by the aid of consecrated fetishes to do miraculous things.

When I was pronounced a holy man and worthy, then the holy men instructed me relative to their lore. This they did by telling me their legends. They could not tell these in a consecutive manner, neither did any legend give all the attributes of any of their mythologic characters. One legend would give to one or more of their deities certain attributes and another legend give other attributes to these deities so that the different legends must be considered in order to understand the lore sufficiently to account for the motives that actuated the Oglalas in their peculiar traditional traits. The legends as I give them are not translations of those as they were told in their language by my informants for such would be tedious repetitions of ideas and allusions. The intent is to give the legends as a holy man could have given them had he been able to express his ideas in the English language. Most of the legends I give were submitted to my informants and approved by them. I could not thus submit all for the holy men ceased to exist before I had prepared the legends. The last of the order of holy men among the Oglalas has gone before his final judge and the progress of civilization has extinguished the order. * * *

Walker's Outline of Oglala Mythology[61]

* * * The category of the Gods as held by the shamans place them in four ranks with four in each rank, having prestige and precedence according to rank and place in rank.

The first rank is of the Superior Gods who are *Wi* (the Sun), the chief of the Gods; *Skan* (the Sky), the Great All-powerful Spirit; *Maka* (the Earth), the ancestress of all upon the world and provider for all; and *Inyan* (the Rock), the primal source of all things.

The second rank is of the Associate Gods who are *Hanwi* (the Moon), created by *Wi* to be his companion; *Tate* (the Wind), created by *Skan* to be his companion; *Unk* (Contention), created by *Maka* to be her companion, but who was cast into the waters and is the Goddess of the Waters and ancestress of all evil beings; and *Wakinyan* (Winged One), created by *Inyan* to be his active associate.

The third rank is of the four Subordinate Gods who are *Ta Tanka* (The Buffalo God), the patron of ceremonies, of health, and of provision; *Hu Nonp* (the Bear God), the patron of wisdom; *Wani* (the Four Winds), the vitalizer and weather; and *Yum* (the Whirlwind), the God of chance, of games, and of love.

The fourth rank is of the Inferior Gods who are *Nagi* (the Spirit); *Niya* (the Ghost); *Sicun* (the Intellect); and *Nagila* (the immaterial self of irrational things).

These sixteen Gods are each but a personal manifestation of one Supreme Being and that being is *Wakan Tanka*, the Great Mystery.

Skan created of his essence a daughter to be the Mediator and named her *Wohpe*. He endowed her with God-like attributes and made her the patron of harmony, beauty, and pleasure. She is more beautiful than any other being.

Inyan has two offspring. The older was brought forth full-grown from an egg in an antinatural manner by *Wakinyan*. His name was *Ksa* and he was the God of wisdom but he become the imp of mischief and his name is *Iktomi*.

The second son of *Inyan* is *Iya*, who is utterly evil and the chief of all evil beings. He committed incest with his mother *Unk* and their offspring is a very beautiful, very enticing, and very deceitful demon whose name is *Gnaski*.

These are the characters that appear most often in Oglala mythology. The mythic legends give the genesis of the Gods and of all creation. A brief of those relative to the four Superior Gods is this:

Before there was any other thing, or any time, *Inyan* was, and his spirit was *Wakan Tanka*. *Han* was then but she is not a thing for she is only the black of darkness. *Inyan* was soft and shapeless but he had all powers. The powers were in his blood and his blood was blue. He longed for another that he might exercise his powers upon it. There could be no other unless he would create it of that which he must take from himself. If he did so he must impart to it a spirit and give to it a portion of his blood. As much of his blood as would go from him, so much of his powers would go with it.

He concluded to create another as a part of himself so that he could retain control of the powers. So he took from himself that which he spread over and around himself in the shape of a great disk whose edge is where there is no beyond. He named this disk *Maka* and imparted to it a spirit which is *Maka-akan* (the Earth God).

To create *Maka* he took so much from himself that he opened all his veins and all his blood flowed from him and he shrank and became hard and powerless. As his blood flowed it became waters and it is the waters.

But powers cannot abide in waters, so they separated themselves and became a being in the shape of a great blue dome whose edge is at but not upon the edge of *Maka*. The powers are a spirit and the blue dome, the sky, the Great Spirit *Skan*. *Inyan*, *Maka*, and the waters are the world and *Skan* is the sky above the world.

Maka was contentious and upbraided *Inyan* because he did not create her a separate being and demanded that he banish *Han*. He replied that he was powerless and then she taunted him with his impotency and nagged him until he agreed to appeal to *Skan*. *Skan* heard the complaint of *Maka* and the plea of *Inyan* that she be appeased. Thus *Skan* was created a judge and is the final and supreme judge of all things.

He decreed that *Maka* must remain forever attached to *Inyan* as she was created. To appease her he created *Anp*, who is not a thing for he is only the red of light. *Skan* banished *Han* to the regions under the world and placed *Anp* on the world. Then there was light everywhere on the world but there was no heat nor any shadow.

Maka saw herself, that she was naked and cold, and complained to *Skan* of this. *Skan* then took from *Inyan* and from *Maka* and from the waters and from himself that with which he created a shining disk. This disk he named *Wi* and imparted to it a spirit which is *Wi-akan* (the Sun God). He placed *Wi* above the blue dome and commanded him to shine on all the world, giving heat to everything, and to make a shadow for each thing. *Wi* did as he was commanded and all on the world was hot.

Maka had no comfort except in shadow and she implored *Skan* to return *Han* upon the world. Then *Skan* commanded *Anp* and *Han* to follow each other and remain for a space upon the world. He commanded *Wi* to go before *Anp* to the regions under the world and follow him above the world. All did as they were commanded.

Thus there were the four Superior Gods and there was established *Anp-etu* and *Han-yetu*, the first [two] of the four times, the daytime and the nighttime.

There are several legends that together give the genesis of the third of the four times, the Moon time. A brief of them is this:

The Gods had their feasts in the regions under the world. There *Skan* created mankind to be servants of the Gods. Mankind increased and became many, so *Skan* named them the *Pte* people. The chief of the *Pte, Wa,* and his wife, *Ka,* had a daughter whose name was *Ite.* She was more beautiful than any other being except *Wohpe. Tate* took her for his wife and she bore to him four sons at one birth and was again with child. *Ite* was vain of her beauty, so *Ksa* and *Gnaski* plotted to have her usurp the place of *Hanwi* as the companion of *Wi.* Her mother, *Ka,* was a seer and foretold that if *Ite* sat with *Wi* she and her parents would exist forever. So *Wa* and *Ka* abetted *Ksa* and *Gnaski* in their scheming. At the feast of the Gods *Ite* sat on the seat of *Hanwi* beside *Wi* and he smiled upon her. *Hanwi* hid her face in shame and *Tate* bowed his head in grief.

Because of this *Skan* condemned *Ite* that her unborn son should leave her and she should exist forever on the world with two faces, one enticingly beautiful, the other terrifyingly horrid. So she is the Two Faced Woman, *Anog Ite,* who incites dissension, temptation, and gossip.

Skan condemned *Wa* and *Ka* that they should exist forever on the world separate, one as a wizard and the other as a witch, and he named them *Wazi* and *Kanka.* So they are the Wizard and the Witch that help or hinder as they are pleased or displeased.

Because *Ksa* had used his wisdom to cause a Goddess to hide her face in shame and a God to bow his head in grief, *Skan* condemned him that he should sit at the feasts of the Gods no more, and should exist forever on the world without a friend, and his wisdom should be only cunning that would entrap him in his own schemes. He named him *Iktomi.* So *Iktomi* is the imp of mischief whose delight it is to make others ridiculous.

Because *Wi* had submitted to the wiles of a woman, *Skan* decreed that *Hanwi* should be his companion no more, and he should journey alone. To compensate *Hanwi, Skan* gave her a time, and that time is from when she comes nearest to *Wi* until she returns there again. Thus was established *Hanwi-yetu,* the third of the four times, the Moon time.

There are a number of legends which together give the genesis of the fourth of the four times, the year time. A brief of them is:

Tate so loved *Ite* that he plead with *Skan* that he and his four sons and his little unborn son might abide on the world so that they would be near their mother. *Skan* granted this plea and decreed that the four brothers should establish the four directions on the world. *Tate* placed his lodge at the center of the world and his four sons went forth to do the task assigned to them. They traveled around on the edge of the world and on it established four directions so as to divide the circle into four equal parts.

In doing so they had many adventures and underwent many hardships, for *Ibom, Gnaski,* and *Iktomi* opposed them, while *Wohpe, Wazi,* and *Kanka* aided them. These legends tell of plots, schemes, and combats, of intrigues, jealousies, and loves, and of wonderful deeds done.

Wohpe dwelt with *Tate* while his sons were absent and kept count of the Moon times from when they left their father's lodge until they returned to it. There she loved *Tate's* little unborn son, *Yum,* as though he were her child. She taught him to dance and all the games and he loved her.

When the four brothers had completed their task, *Skan* gave to each one of the directions they had established and made a season for each direction. He commanded them to each bring his season upon the world and during it to control the weather. He then bestowed upon them God-like attributes so that the four are one God and his name is *Wani* (Vigor) and he made them messengers of the Gods.

Wohpe showed her father that the four brothers were absent from their father's lodge twelve moon times, so *Skan* decreed that twelve moons should constitute one *Wani-yetu,* the fourth of the four times, a year time.

Wohpe pled for little *Yum,* so *Skan* bestowed upon him God-like attributes and made him the God of dancing, of games, and of love. But he is a very fickle God.

Comparative Materials for the Study of Sioux Religion

In order to place Walker's material on Lakota religion in comparative perspective, and especially to appreciate the unique contribution he was able to make because of his close relationship to the holy men of the Oglalas, a brief review of the history of the study of Sioux religion is presented here. It is not intended to be exhaustive, but to lead the reader to the major sources that provide substantive information on Sioux religion, ritual, mythology, and philosophy.

Aside from the superficial observations of early white travelers, the first substantial body of data on Sioux religion was recorded by the geographer Joseph N. Nicollet in 1838 and 1839, mainly from interviews with Santee and Yankton Sioux. Nicollet was studying the Dakota language, and in the process he recorded basic concepts associated with religion, including *wakan* and *wašicun*, names for types of medicine men and holy men, as well as accounts of the sun dance, *Hunka* ceremony, ceremonies of swearing oaths, and the vision quest. Though brief, his work is insightful and serves as an important independent check on later data because, even though his was among the first to be recorded, it was not published until 1976.[62]

The earliest published data come from Mary Eastman's *Dahcotah* (1849), collected from the Santees living near Fort Snelling, Minnesota. Most important, she recorded information on the various gods and ceremonies of the Dakotas, as well as a number of myths. Following Eastman were two fur traders, both of whom died in the 1862 Minnesota uprising. One was James W. Lynd, whose manuscript, "The Religion of the Dakota," was published posthumously in 1864. His work covers the same material as Eastman's but more systematically and in greater detail. The second of the fur traders was Philander Prescott, also an interpreter, who served as the U. S. superintendent of Indian farming among the eastern Sioux from 1849 to 1856. Some of his writings were included in Henry R. Schoolcraft's compendium, *Information Respecting the History, Condition and Prospects of the Indian Tribes of the United States* (vols. 2–4, 1852–54). The remainder of his work, including his memoirs, was not published until 1966.[63]

Three important missionary sources, also from the Santees, date from this time. The first is Stephen R. Riggs, *Tah-koo Wahkaṅ; or, The Gospel among the Dakotas* (1869), a history of the missionization of the Santees that discusses Dakota concepts of religion, the gods, and ceremonies. The second source is Gideon H. Pond, who as a missionary was opposed to the Dakota medicine men and holy men. Nonetheless, he published two informative articles, "Power and Influence of Dakota Medicine Men" (1854, in the Schoolcraft compendium), and a summary of Dakota religion, "Dakota Superstitions" (1867). The long description of Dakota life written by his brother, Samuel Pond, the third missionary source, was not published until 1908 under the title "The Dakotas or Sioux in Minnesota as They Were in 1834." In addition, the Pond brothers recorded a long series of myths and legends in Dakota, which have never been published.[64]

Taken together, these early sources provide a firm foundation on which to base an understanding of the fundamental features of Dakota religion. They are important, in a comparative sense, for understanding Lakota religion and for reconstructing a general history of Sioux religion.

Chronologically the next sources are anthropological. They are all brief. Captain John G. Bourke, a military officer and an amateur anthropologist, wrote an account of the 1881 sun dance at Pine Ridge, and Alice C. Fletcher, a professional anthropologist, described the same ceremony at Rosebud in 1882. In addition, Fletcher, in 1884, published under the title *Indian Ceremonies* substantial accounts of the White Buffalo ceremony among the Hunkpapas, the Elk ceremony and ghost keeping ceremony of the Oglalas, and the Four Winds ceremony of the Santees.

In 1887 George Bushotter wrote a long series of texts, giving for the first time an account of Sioux religion by a Lakota written in the Lakota language. In addition to a long description of the sun dance he wrote about other ceremonies, myths, and beliefs. His was a child's understanding of these matters, though, for he left home at age fifteen to be educated at Hampton Institute in Virginia. Bushotter's manuscripts have never been published in full, but in 1894, J. Owen Dorsey published an encyclopedic survey of available information on the religions of each of the Siouan tribes and included in it the relevant material from Bushotter's writings.[65]

Immediately after the Wounded Knee massacre, James Mooney, also from the Bureau of American Ethnology, visited Pine Ridge and recorded the songs and ceremony of the Lakota Ghost Dance; he also wrote an important history of the events leading up to the Wounded Knee tragedy. He included much basic information on Lakota religion in his account and published all the songs in both Lakota and English.[66]

In the early years of this century Clark Wissler published

some data on Lakota religion and mythology based on his brief fieldwork at Pine Ridge and Crow Creek reservations (1905 and 1907). In 1906 George A. Dorsey published, for the first time, a version of the story of the bringing of the pipe to the Lakota people, a cornerstone of Lakota religion. Edward S. Curtis, the famous photographer, wrote substantial accounts concerning the pipe, the sun dance, vision quest, *Hunka,* and ghost keeping ceremonies, including some Lakota texts of prayers and ceremonial songs (1908). At the same time Natalie Curtis, recording music at Pine Ridge and Rosebud, collected briefer accounts of the Ghost Dance and some valuable data on medicine men and religion. Part of her work, including the songs, was published in both Lakota and English (1907). Frederick Weygold, writing in German, published a full description of the *Hunka* ceremony based on information given by an Oglala named Tschanchacha ("Kinnikinic"), including songs and a long text printed in Lakota with German interlinear translation. Weygold's analysis of the ceremony stresses the role of the pipe as a means of achieving mediation between men and the gods.

Chronologically, the next source is Walker's own monograph, *The Sun Dance* (1917), a synthesis of Lakota religion based on accounts of ceremonies and followed by a valuable series of texts and myths printed in English only.

Perhaps the most significant publication on Sioux religion since Walker's is Frances Densmore's *Teton Sioux Music* (1918), the only source to include musical notation of ceremonial songs. She collected her information primarily on the Standing Rock Reservation, where she made hundreds of recordings. The book includes lengthy accounts of major ceremonies and the longest recorded version of the story of the bringing of the sacred pipe. Particularly valuable in Densmore's work are the extensive verbatim transcripts of the words of her informants and the many personal accounts of visions and other religious experiences. The songs, published in both Lakota and English, include valuable data on the sacred language and poetic idioms.

Also in 1918, Sarah Emilia Olden published *The People of Tipi Sapa,* which contains a considerable amount of material on religion, including song texts in the Yankton dialect. All of the ethnographic material in the book was dictated by Philip Deloria, an Episcopal priest, the son of a Yankton chief.

The writings of Aaron McGaffey Beede, Episcopal missionary to the Standing Rock Sioux and later county judge, provide another important perspective on the traditional Lakota religion. Beede's work, dating about 1900–1930, is highly philosophical and emphasizes the most general concepts underlying Lakota thought. It remains unpublished.[67]

In 1919 Alanson Skinner described the sun dance of the Sisseton Dakotas and in 1920 the medicine ceremony of the Wahpeton Dakotas. In 1919 Wilson D. Wallis described the sun dance of the Canadian Dakotas and in 1923 published an article, "Beliefs and Tales of the Canadian Dakota." Long after, in 1947, Wallis finally published the remainder of his material as *The Canadian Dakota*, a valuable account giving information on medicine men and women and extensive data on the *heyoka*. These sources provide an excellent comparative perspective on the large body of earlier sources on Santee religion.

Five Sioux Indians recorded extensive data on traditional religion, each in a different way. The first was a medical doctor, Charles Alexander Eastman, a Santee Sioux who explored the foundations of Dakota philosophy and religion and counterposed it to civilization as an example to be emulated. His synthesis was *The Soul of the Indian* (1911), but to follow the development of his thought it is essential to read his autobiographical works, *Indian Boyhood* (1902) and *From the Deep Woods to Civilization* (1916).[68]

The second was Joseph White Bull, a Minneconjou whose major interest during his youth had been in traditional warfare. A renowned warrior, a nephew of Sitting Bull and a participant in the Custer fight, he dictated his autobiography to Stanley Vestal, who published it as *Warpath* (1934). The book is insightful and gives a valuable perspective on the role of religion, spirits, and visions in the life of an eminently worldly man, a man of action. His pictorial autobiography, *The Warrior Who Killed Custer*, translated and edited by James H. Howard (1968) is also helpful in understanding White Bull.

The third was an Oglala, Luther Standing Bear. He was educated at the Carlisle Indian school in Pennsylvania and was a movie actor living in Hollywood when he wrote his masterful *Land of the Spotted Eagle* (1933), a personal synthesis of Lakota culture and an insightful criticism of contemporary American civilization. His autobiography, *My People the Sioux* (1928), allows us to understand something of the development of his philosophy.

The fourth was Black Elk, the Oglala holy man and visionary whose life story was empathetically recorded by another visionary, John G. Neihardt, and published as *Black Elk Speaks* (1932). Through Black Elk's story we see the introduction of the Ghost Dance religion and its integration with traditional Lakota religion. Black Elk's recounting of a series of Lakota myths was published in Neihardt's *When the Tree Flowered* (1952). The original interviews of Black Elk by Neihardt in 1931 and 1944 contain many details that do not appear in the published works.[69] These are as yet unpublished. Black Elk's synthesis of the ceremonies of the old religion was dictated to Joseph Epes Brown, who recorded it in *The Sacred Pipe* (1953). Black Elk, more than any other native American, has captured the imagination of the white man, and his philosophy and religious system have been read with a kind of religious fervor by many. The essential religiousness of the man has transcended the problems of translation and cross-cultural communication.

The fifth, and most prolific, was Ella C. Deloria (daughter of Philip Deloria), a linguist and a collaborator with anthropologists Franz Boas and Ruth Benedict. She recorded thousands of pages of material in both Lakota and English on all aspects of traditional life.[70] Her *Dakota Texts,* an important collection of myths and legends, was published in 1932. Part of her efforts were directed to an attempt, beginning in 1937, to validate Walker's materials by interviewing older Lakota people. In addition, she made translations of the Pond brothers' Santee myths, the Bushotter texts, and a portion of George Sword's writings. The editorial notes that she prepared for these translations provide invaluable data on Lakota semantics. In collaboration with Franz Boas, Deloria also published the most useful grammar of the language, *Dakota Grammar* (1941). Her brief summary of Lakota life and an appeal for equitable treatment of the American Indian was published as *Speaking of Indians* (1944). It is probably the best summary of the Lakota way of life to be found in the printed literature. Her major work on Sioux religion (which was not quite finished before her death in 1971) has not yet been published.

In recent years a minor flood of material has been published on Lakota religion. Two studies have relied very heavily on Walker's published work. The first is Royal B. Hassrick's *The Sioux: Life and Customs of a Warrior Society* (1964). It provides a readable general survey of Lakota life, written from a psychological perspective. The second is William K. Powers' *Oglala Religion* (1977), which is written from the perspective of structural anthropology.

Much of the recent work has been devoted to recording modern Lakota religion. The list is long, but the following must be included among the more significant publications. Stephen E. Feraca's *Wakinyan: Contemporary Teton Dakota Religion* (1963) is an excellent and very readable survey based on field studies at Pine Ridge. Robert Ruby's *The Oglala Sioux* (1955), though it must be read with caution, includes some good material on the *Yuwipi* ceremony. Eugene Fugle's "The Nature and Function of the Lakota Night Cults" (1966) and Luis Kemnitzer's "The Cultural Provenience of Artifacts Used in Yuwipi" (1970) and "Structure, Content, and Cultural Meaning of *Yuwipi*" (1976) (both based on a dissertation on *Yuwipi*), continue the study of this aspect of modern Lakota religion. Powers's *Oglala Religion* also makes original contributions to the study of the *Yuwipi* ceremony.

John L. Smith published two summary articles on the history and present meaning of the sacred calf pipe bundle (1967 and 1970), and Paul Steinmetz, S. J., published an informative article on the incorporation of the pipe into Roman Catholic ritual at Pine Ridge (1969).

Richard Erdoes's excellent editing of John Fire's autobiography, *Lame Deer, Seeker of Visions* (1972), provides a personal and in-depth understanding of the role of traditional religion in the life of a present-day holy man. The short but very informative interview with holy man Pete Catches, "On Being An Ascetic," published by David Zimmerly (1969), is also important.

Two other personal statements are recorded on phonograph records. *Crow Dog's Paradise* (1971, Elektra EKS 74091) is concerned largely with music of the Native American Church, but also includes a verbal account by Leonard Crow Dog of the place of peyote in Lakota life. *Fools Crow* (1977, Tatanka Records) gives Frank Fools Crow's personal account of Lakota religion, including the story of the bringing of the pipe. Fools Crow speaks in Lakota on one side and Matthew King provides an English translation on the other; the record is accompanied by a complete transcript of both the Lakota and the English.

Two significant works appeared in 1978. The first is

Thomas E. Mails, *Sundancing at Rosebud and Pine Ridge,* which provides data about the sun dance in recent years. It includes in-depth interviews with Bill Schweigman (Chief Eagle Feather), a sun dance leader at Rosebud, and with Fools Crow at Pine Ridge. The work also provides an extensive photographic documentary of sun dances at Rosebud in 1974 and 1975. The second, a work of major importance, is the posthumous publication of Eugene Buechel's *Lakota Tales and Texts,* edited by Paul Manhart, S. J. The book consists of transcriptions of stories recorded by Buechel himself and by Ivan Stars and Peter Iron Shell between 1904 and 1923 from dictation by Lakotas at Rosebud and Pine Ridge. They are reproduced only in the original Lakota, without English translations. The texts include accounts of the bringing of the pipe, ghost keeping, sun dance, *Hunka,* purfication lodge, vision quest, *Yuwipi, heyoka,* Double Women, Deer Women, bear medicine, and buffalo medicine, as well as a number of accounts of warfare and of the Omaha and Crow Owners societies. In addition the volume includes valuable texts on social and political organization and kinship, and a series of myths. It will be a major resource for the comparative study of Lakota religion.

II

Belief

The documents that Walker gathered explaining the foundations of Lakota religious beliefs are presented in Part II. In arranging and editing the material we have tried to enable the reader to follow various kinds of unity integral both to the texts themselves and to the context in which the information was shared. Each document represents a particular kind of synthesis influenced by personal and social factors that affect the interpretation of statements. Therefore, as our first editorial principle we have stressed the unity of each individual Lakota's own contribution. Fortunately, we know the names of most of the men who gave information to Walker, so we have been able to bring together enough documents to enable the reader to gain a sense of the subjective awareness that characterized men like Little Wound, George Sword, Red Cloud, and others. The Lakotas traditionally recognized the importance of a personal component in any formal presentation by beginning public performances with conventional autobiographical statements in which a speaker could give his status and right to knowledge. Because Walker's documents retain many of these autobiographical elements, we can follow the Lakota custom of weighing evidence against our knowledge of the person giving it.

Sometimes the testimony of one informant reinforces that of others. Often though, they disagree on details. Walker concentrated on finding the points of agreement, but the documents show that a few concepts constituted the nuclei of meaning in Lakota religious belief. These traditional elements formed a kind of middle ground between the known and the unknown, the defined and the indefinable. Individual holy men employed traditional concepts to help them search the mysterious unknown, and then they articulated new insights by expanding the meaning of traditional images.

Within the context of each person's contribution, we have employed a chronological guide for ordering the material whenever we could ascertain the date of a document. This not only facilitates historical research but also permits the reader to gain some sense of the order in which Walker himself learned the material and to trace any progression that exists in the kinds of information that the holy men presented from 1896 to 1914.

Our organization of these documents is contrary to what Walker himself intended. He chose to organize his material thematically, on the assumption that he was reconstructing an integrated religious system, and therefore the specific person who gave the information was not as important as the information itself. We have occasionally been able to develop a theme without disrupting other kinds of unity, as in the case of the documents about *wakan* and *Wakan Tanka* (documents 3–5). However, most of the documents touch upon many themes and show how narrators integrated many levels of meaning by relating them to fundamental beliefs. There is a natural progression of emphasis in this part from fundamental concepts and ceremonies to the nature and role of specific spirits in Lakota religion and then to documents of a primarily historical nature. In spite of the regular thematic recurrence there is no exact repetition. Each new presentation of a topic shows how associations among fundamental concepts gradually reveal the dominant categories of Lakota religious thought and the ways in which those categories are intimately related to the social and historical conditions that affected the narrators of the documents.

In addition to the major focus on belief, this part contains important historical data as well. Four documents by Short Bull (40–43) record beliefs related to the Ghost Dance as well as some of the hopes aroused by it. Red Cloud's abdication speech (document 38) is of major historical importance. It is deeply moving and articulates the basic issues in Indian relations with non-Indians: "They tell us that we are Indians and they are white men and that we must be treated different from the white man. This is true. But the white man should say how he should be treated and the Indian should say how he should be treated. It is not so." In the same speech, Red Cloud reveals his disagreement with Bull Bear, a subject that is further illuminated by document 72 in Part IV, where Little Wound confirms that he is the son of Bull Bear and that his father "was murdered by Red Cloud." These statements clear up historical issues that have long been debated in the literature and also show that Walker had the cooperation of both the traditional Oglala political factions.

James Riley Walker, ca. 1909. Courtesy Amon Carter Museum, Fort Worth.

James R. Walker visiting Red Cloud at the chief's home near the Pine Ridge Agency. Undated. Courtesy Amon Carter Museum, Forth Worth

Red Cloud, 1898. Photograph by Jesse Hastings Bratley. Crane Collection, Denver Museum of Natural History, negative number BR 61-258

Little Wound. Undated. Walker Collection, Colorado Historical
Society

George Sword, 1909. Photograph by Joseph Kossuth Dixon, taken at the Crow Agency, Montana. Wanamaker Collection, Indiana University Museum

Afraid of Bear, 1909. Photograph by Joseph Kossuth Dixon, taken at the Crow Agency, Montana. Wanamaker Collection, Indiana University Museum

American Horse, 1907. Photograph by J. Throssel. Wanamaker Collection, Indiana University Museum

Thunder Bear, 1896. Photograph by William Dinwiddie, taken in Washington, D.C. Smithsonian Institution National Anthropological Archives

1. Foundations. Little Wound, September 3, 1896 (Antoine Herman, interpreter). (AMNH)

I am the head chief of the Oglalas and my father was the head chief.[1] In a camp of all the Oglalas I am entitled to place my tipi at the chief place opposite to the entrance to the camp circle. I am a shaman and I have danced the Sun Dance, so if I show my scars no Oglala will dispute my word. . . .

The Oglalas have many dances and they are all ceremonies and must be done according to the form adopted by the shamans. . . . They have dances for war and for peace; for victory and defeat; for chase and for ripe fruits; for enjoyment and for mourning; for going away and for returning; for warriors and for all the people; for the societies and for individuals; for men and for women; for widows and for maidens; for shamans. . . . The sacred dances are the Dance for the Dead, the Scalp Dance, the Holy Dance, and the Sun Dance. . . . Each dance has its songs so that when the songs are heard, it may be known what dance is danced. The music of the songs is different for each dance. . . . The Sun Dance has twenty-four songs. Four of these must be sung each time the Sun Dance is danced. . . .

If the other shamans will agree to it, I will tell you what I know of the secrets of the shamans. . . . In my boy vision, the Buffalo came to me and when I sought the shaman's vision, the Wind spoke to me. . . . I can tell you of the Buffalo but I cannot tell you of the Wind for that is my secret as a shaman. . . .

The Buffalo is the *kola* (comrade) of the Sun. At night they are familiar and counsel together about all things. The Buffalo gives all game to the Lakotas. He is pleased with those who are generous and hates those who are stingy.

An industrious woman pleases him. He gives many children to the women he likes. He protects maidens. . . . He controls all affairs of love, but the Crazy Buffalo[2] may deceive the young people in their love affairs. Then they do wrong. He cares for pregnant women. A young woman should have his mark on her head. A shaman should paint a red mark at the parting of her hair. He should perform a ceremony when doing this. A woman who wears this mark will be industrious. She will bear many children. She will not quarrel. . . .

If a man sees the Buffalo in his boy vision, he should paint the picture of a buffalo on his shield and on his tipi. He will be a successful hunter. . . . He will get the woman he wishes for his wife.

---

2. Instructing Walker as a Medicine Man. Little Wound, American Horse, and Lone Star, September 12, 1896 (Antoine Herman, interpreter). (AMNH)

We have decided to tell you of the ceremonies of the Oglalas if you will provide a feast. We will do this so you may know how to be the medicine man for the people. . . . (*Feast was promised and afterwards a beef, ten pounds of coffee, a box of crackers, and one hundred pounds of flour were given for the feast.*)

The Oglalas do ceremonies because this pleases the Gods. Some ceremonies please some of the Gods and other ceremonies please other Gods. A shaman has authority over all ceremonies. A shaman should conduct all the greater ceremonies. . . . A simple ceremony may affect only the one who does it. . . . Some ceremonies affect all the people. In such ceremonies all the people have a part to do. If the people do not do their part in such ceremonies, the Gods will be angry. . . .

We will tell you of the ceremonies as if you were an Oglala who wished to take your part in them. We will not tell you of the parts of them that the shamans do secretly. . . .

---

3. *Wakan.* Little Wound. (AMNH)

As the Oglalas speak, this is two words. It is *wa* and it is *kan*. *Wa* means anything which is something. It also means anything with which something can be done. When one says *wakan*, this means anything which is *kan*. *Wakan* is something which is *kan*.[3]

A *wakan* man is one who is wise. It is one who knows the spirits. It is one who has power with the spirits. It is one who communicates with the spirits. It is one who can do strange things. A *wakan* man knows things that the people do not know. He knows the ceremonies and the songs. He can tell the people what their visions mean. He can tell the people what the spirits wish them to do. He can tell what is to be in the future. He can talk with animals and with trees and with stones. He can talk with everything on earth.

The *Wakan Tanka* are those which made everything. They are *Wakanpi*. *Wakanpi* are all things that are above mankind. There are many kinds of the *Wakanpi*. The *Wakan Tanka* are *Wakanpi*. The spirits are *Wakanpi*. The beings that govern things are *Wakanpi*.

The *Wakanpi* have power over everything on earth. They watch mankind all the time. They control everything that mankind does. Mankind should please them in all things. If mankind does not please them, they will do harm to them. They should be pleased by songs and ceremonies. Gifts should be made to them. Mankind should ask them for what they wish. They may be like a father to mankind. But the evil *Wakanpi* are to be feared. They do evil to mankind. There are many of these. The greatest of these is *Iya*. He is *Wakan Tanka*.

Mankind should think about the *Wakanpi* and do what will please them. They should think of them as they think of their fathers and their mothers. But the evil *Wakanpi* they should think of as an enemy.

Animals may be *wakan*. When an animal is *wakan*, then mankind should treat it as if it were one of the *Wakanpi*. Things that do not live may be *wakan*. When anything is food, it is *wakan* because it makes life. When anything is medicine, it is *wakan* for it keeps life in the body. When anything is hard to understand, it is *wakan* because mankind does not know what it is. Anything that is used in the ceremony and songs to the *Wakanpi* is *wakan* because it should not be used for anything else. Little children are *wakan* because they do not speak. Crazy people are *wakan* because the *Wakanpi* are in them. Anything that is very old is *wakan* because no one knows when it was made. Anyone with great power is *wakan* because the *Wakanpi* helps them. Anything that is very dangerous is *wakan* because *Iya*[4] helps it. Anything that is poison or anything that intoxicates is *wakan* because the Sky helps it.

The songs and the ceremonies of the Oglalas are *wakan* because they belong to the *Wakanpi*. A very old man or a very old woman is *wakan* because they know many things. But an old man is not like a *wakan* man. If he has learned the *wakan* things, then he is a *wakan* man. The spirit of every man is *wakan* and the ghost is *wakan*.

Wakan Tanka are many. But they are all the same as one. The evil *Wakan Tanka* is not one of The *Wakan Tanka*.[5] The *Wakan Tanka* are above all the other *Wakanpi*. The Sun is *Wakan Tanka*, and the Sky and the Earth and the Rock. They are *Wakan Tanka*. *Wakinyan*, this is *Wakan Tanka* but it is different from The *Wakan Tanka*. The Thunderbird and the Wind are *Wakan Tanka* with the Sun and the Sky. The stars are *Wakan Tanka*, but they have nothing to do with the people on the earth. Mankind need pay no attention to the stars.

---

4. *Wakan Tanka*. Good Seat. (AMNH)

I am an old man. I know what my father said. I know what his father said. In the old times, the Indians knew many things. Now they have forgotten many things. The white men have made them forget that which their fathers told them.

Wakan was anything that was hard to understand. A rock was sometimes *wakan*. Anything might be *wakan*. When anyone did something that no one understood, this was *wakan*. If the thing done was what no one could understand, it was *Wakan Tanka*. How the world was made is *Wakan Tanka*. How the sun was made is *Wakan Tanka*. How men used to talk to the animals and birds was *Wakan Tanka*. Where the spirits and ghosts are is *Wakan Tanka*. How the spirits act is *wakan*. A spirit is *wakan*.

In old times, the Indians did not know of a Great Spirit. There are two kinds of spirits. *Wanagi,* that is the spirit *(nagi)* that has once been in a man. *Nagi* (a spirit) has never been in a man. When *wanagi* is in a man, it is *woniya* (the life). When a man dies, his *woniya* is then *wanagi*. When a man is alive, he has his *woniya* (breath of life) and his *nagi* (spirit). His *nagi* is not a part of himself. His *nagi* cares for him and warns him of danger and helps him out of difficulties. When he dies, it goes with his *wanagi* to the spirit world *(wanagi makoce)*. The spirit world is far beyond the pines.

There is no *Nagi Tanka.* How the spirits live in the spirit land and what they do, that is *Wakan Tanka.* The *nagi* are in the world all the time. They do things and talk to men. Then they are *wakan.* The *wica nagi* (the spirit of a man) may come back to the world to see its people.

When a man dies, his *wanagi* leaves his body. It stays near it for a short time. It is well to please it while it lingers near the body. If it is not pleased, it may do some harm to someone. After a time, it goes on the journey to the spirit world. Its *nagi* goes with it to show it the way. It is happy if it has company. If another *wica nagi* goes with it, it is better. It is happy if it can take the *wamaka nagi* (animal spirit) of his horse and his dog. It is happy if it can take *wo nagi* (spirit of food) with it. His gun and food.

The journey is *wakan.* It is *Wakan Tanka.* He must cross a river on a very narrow tree. If he is afraid to cross the river, he returns to the world and wanders about forever. If he crosses the river, he goes to the spirit world.

The spirits live in spirit tipis. They do only what gives them pleasure. There are women in the spirit world. They do not bear children. If a man conquers an enemy, the enemy must serve him in the spirit world. If a man is killed by an enemy, he must serve the one who kills him in the spirit world. A spirit who is serving another in the spirit world may come back to this world and do something that will give him his freedom. Some wise men can call the spirits.

There are good spirits *(nagi)* and bad spirits *(nagi).* The bad spirits are in this world all the time. They only do mischief. They were driven out of the spirit world by the good spirits. A man's spirit *(wica nagi)* may become a bad spirit. The spirit of animals *(wamaka nagi)* may go to the spirit world. Only the spirits of good animals go to the spirit world. The spirits of bad animals like the wolf and the snake do not go to the spirit world.

A spirit is like a shadow. It is nothing. There are other beings. But they are not spirits. They belong to the world. They are *wakan.* They have power over men and things. They are *wo wakan* (belong to the mysterious). They are *taku wakan* (things mysterious).

The *Wakinyan* (Thunderbird) is one. The *Tatanka* (Great Beast)[6] is one; the *Unktehi* (One Who Kills), *Taku Skanskan* (Changes Things), *Tunkan* (Venerable One), *Inyan* (Stone), *Heyoka* (Opposite to Nature), *Waziya* (Of the North), *Iya*,[7] *Tate* (Wind), *Yate*[8] (North Wind), *Yanpa* (East Wind), *Okaga* (South Wind), *Iktomi* (Spider-like). These are all *wakan*. The sun, the moon, the morning star, the evening star, the north star, the seven stars, the six stars, the rainbow—these are all *wakan*.

Anything that moves or does anything has a spirit. Men give the spirits things to get their help or they give them things to keep them from doing them harm. If the spirits would stay away from men, then the men would care nothing for them, only for the spirits of their friends. The spirits often do things against each other. The strongest or the cunningest spirit wins.

A man may be *wakan* and then the spirits are afraid of him. This is the way the white men have driven the spirits away. The white man's spirits are very far away. They will not come when called. They can not be bought with gifts. They do not care for men who are alive. The white man's spirit land is no where.

---

5. *Wakan.* James R. Walker.[9] (CHS)

Long ago, the Lakotas believed that there were marvelous beings whose existence, powers or doings they could not understand. These beings they called *Wakan Kin* (The *Wakan*). There were many of the *Wakan*, some good and some bad. Of the *Wakan* who were good, some were greater than others. The greater were called *Wakan Wankantu* (Superior *Wakan*). The others were called *Taku Wakan* (*Wakan* Relatives). They were not relatives the same as a father or a brother but like the Lakota are all relatives to each [other]. The bad *Wakan* were not relative either to the good or to each other.

The Lakotas also believed that each of mankind has a *nagi* (spirit), a *niya* (ghost), and a *sicun* (guardian). The Lakota concept of *sicun* is very complex. That of the *sicun* pertaining to mankind is that it is an influence that forewarns of danger, admonishes for right against wrong, and controls others of mankind. According to their doctrine, one may acquire other *sicunpi (sicuns)*. Their concepts relative to acquired *sicuns* are that such *sicuns* are the potencies of the *Wakan* or of a *Wakanla* imparted to inanimate substance. The spirit, the ghost and the guardian are not *wakan*. But because no man can understand them, the old Lakotas call them *wakanla* (*wakan*-ish; the Lakota *la* is equivalent to the English *ish* in that it makes adjectives of nouns meaning of the nature of or a diminutive of).

The old Lakotas also believed that each thing except the *Wakan* and mankind had something like a spirit. This something they called a *nagila* (spiritish). These *nagipila* (spirits-ish) were *wakanpila* (*wakans*-ish). Ordinarily, the people call a *wakanla*, *wakan*. *Wakan Tanka* (Great *Wakan*) and *Wakan Kin* mean the same. In former times the term *Wakan Tanka* was seldom used but now it is used more often than *Wakan Kin*. The younger Oglalas mean the God of the Christians when they say *Wakan Tanka*. When a shaman says *Wakan Tanka*, he means the same as *Wakan Kin* as used in former times. This means all the *Wakan* and the *Wakanpila,* both of mankind and of other things, for the old Oglalas believed that these were all the same as one. This is *kan* (incomprehensible, an incomprehensible fact that cannot be demonstrated).

Things other than the *Wakan* are called *wakan* by the Lakotas because they amaze as the *Wakan* do. A *wicasa wakan* (*wakan* man, shaman) is so called because he has marvelous power and wisdom so that he can speak and do as the *Wakan* do. *Mini wakan* (*wakan* water, intoxicating liquor) is so called because its effects are like those of the *Wakan*. *Maza wakan* (*wakan* iron, a gun) is called *wakan* because a shot from it is like the act of the *Wakan*.

If a man does a mysterious thing, it is called *wakan* because it is done as the *Wakan* do. *Wasica wakan* (white citizen of the United States) is called *wakan* because he is able to do marvelous things as the *Wakan* would do them. This differs from other authoritative interpretations of the term *wasica wakan,* but according to Sword, *wasica* is the same as the word *wasicun,* the name of the ceremonial bag of the Lakotas and of its mythical potency which by elision changes the *un* to *a* before *w*. He held that the first white men seen by the Lakotas were supposed to have ceremonial bags which gave them power to do as the *Wakan* do and so they were called *wasica wakan* or *wakan* potency.

When an Oglala is amazed by anything he may say that it is *wakan* meaning that it is *wakanla* (like *wakan*). It appears from the above information that "divine" is the proper interpretation of *wakan*.

---

6. Foundations. George Sword, September 5, 1896 (Bruce Means, interpreter). (CHS)

I know the old customs of the Lakotas, and all their ceremonies, for I was a *wicasa wakan* (holy man, or shaman), and I have conducted all the ceremonies. I have conducted the Sun Dance, which is the greatest ceremony of the Lakotas. The scars on my body show that I have danced the Sun Dance, and no Lakota will dispute my word. I was also a *pejuta wicasa* (medicine man), and belonged with the Bear medicine people. The Bear medicine men have all the medicine ceremonies that other kinds of medicine men have and much more. So I can tell all the medicine ceremonies. I was a *wakiconze* (magistrate) and so I know all the customs of the camp and of the march. I was also a *blota hunka* (commander of war parties) and have led many war parties against the enemy, both of Indians and white men. The scars on my body show the wounds I have received in battle. So I know the ceremonies of war. I have been on the tribal chase of the buffalo, and know all the ceremonies of the chase.

When I served the Lakota *Wakan Tanka*, I did so with all my power. When I went on the warpath I always did all the ceremonies to gain the favor of the Lakota *Wakan Tanka*. But when the Lakotas fought with the white soldiers, the white people always won the victory. I went to Washington and to other large cities, and that showed me that the white people dug in the ground and built houses that could not be moved. Then I knew that when they came they could not be driven away. For this reason I took a new name, the name of Sword, because the leaders of the white soldiers wore swords. I determined to adopt the customs of the white people, and to persuade my people to do so.

I became the first leader of the U.S. Indian Police among the Oglalas, and was their captain until the Oglalas ceased to think of fighting the white people. Then I became a deacon in the Christian church, and am so now, and will be until my death. I cannot speak English, but I understand it so that I know when it is interpreted wrong. I have learned to write in Lakota, but I write as the old Lakota spoke when they talked in a formal manner. The young Oglalas do not understand a formal talk by an old Lakota, because the white people have changed the Lakota language, and the young people speak it as the white people have written it. I will write of the old customs and ceremonies for you. I will write that which all the people knew. But the secrets of the shamans I am afraid to write, for I have my old outfit as a shaman, and I am afraid to offend it. If a shaman offends his ceremonial outfit, it will bring disaster upon him.

In old times the Lakotas believed that *Wakan Tanka* was everywhere all the time and observed everything that each one of mankind did and even knew what anyone thought, that he might be pleased or displeased because of something that one did. So the shamans taught the people ceremonies that would please the *Wakan Tanka* and gain their favor. They taught ceremonies regarding everything a man does. These ceremonies must be done exactly as they are taught. Every word and every motion said or done in the ceremony must be right. If a ceremony is not done right it does no good, and may do much harm. The ceremonies of the Lakotas are the ceremonies of the people, the ceremonies of the warriors, and the ceremonies of the shamans. I can tell you of the ceremonies of the people and the warriors, but I am afraid to tell you the ceremonies of the shamans.

When a Lakota does anything in a formal manner he should first smoke the pipe. This is because the spirit in the pipe smoke is pleasing to *Wakan Tanka* and to all spirits. In any ceremony this should be the first thing that is done. To do this right the smoking material should be carefully prepared and mixed. If one is to smoke for another ceremony, he should sing a song or pray to a God while preparing the smoking material. Then he should take the pipe in his left hand, holding the bowl so that the stem does not point away from himself, and fill the bowl slowly, carefully tamping the material with a smoking stick or the first finger of his right hand. When the bowl is filled, the pipe should be lighted with a coal of fire and not with a blaze. This is because the spirit in the fire is in the burning coals and the spirit in the blaze is going away from the fire. A man may smoke alone, and if he is doing so as a ceremony he should smoke the pipe until its contents are all consumed and then he should empty the ashes into the fire so that all may be consumed. This is because if the contents of a pipe that is smoked as a ceremony are emptied on the ground someone may step on them, or spit on them, and this would make *Wakan Tanka* angry. But if more than one is to smoke they do so because the spirit in the pipe will make their spirits all agree. Then when the pipe is lighted it must be passed from one to another each smoking only a few whiffs, until the contents are consumed, and then the pipe should be emptied in the fire. If there is no fire burning, the contents should be emptied on the ground and carefully covered with earth.

The smoke of the pipe may be made an offering by pointing the stem of a lighted pipe toward the one to whom the smoke is offered. A Lakota may smoke the pipe as only an enjoyment, and then as many pipes may be lighted as wished, but if it is done as a ceremony only one pipe should be smoked. The shamans have ceremonial pipes that are never smoked except during a ceremony.

There is a pipe that belongs to all the Lakotas.[10] This is held by a keeper and kept from view except on important occasions when it is unwrapped with much ceremony and is only lighted when there are matters of interest to all the Lakotas. When it is smoked, what is then done is binding on all the Lakotas.

In their ceremonies the Lakotas make smoke with the pipe, and also of sweetgrass, and of sage, and of cedar leaves, and of buffalo chips. Making smoke with these things is *wazilya* (incensing).

In all ceremonies that have to do with *Wakan Tanka,* after smoking the pipe an incense of sweetgrass should be made. This is because that spirit that is in the smoke of sweetgrass is pleasing to the *Wakan Tanka,* and will incline him to hear the ceremony with favor. The incense is also distasteful to all evil beings and thwarts their powers. The incense should be made in the following manner: there should be provided dried sweetgrass and dried cottonwood. The cottonwood should be burned until it is burning coals, and then the sweetgrass should be sprinkled on these coals slowly so as to make a smoke. The one who sprinkles the sweetgrass on the coals should either sing a song or pray to a God while doing so. If such an incense is not made, *Wakan Tanka* may not heed the ceremony.

After an incense of sweetgrass, there may be made an incense of sage in the same manner as that of sweetgrass. This should be done because the spirit in the smoke of the sage is very offensive to all evil beings and they will fly from it. They even fear the herb of sage and will not stay where it is. So if anyone carries sage, or keeps it near, the evil beings fear to come near such a one.

If a Lakota is doing a ceremony relative to *Wakinyan* (Winged-One, often translated the Thunderbird), he should make an incense of the leaves of the cedar tree. This is because the cedar tree is the favorite of *Wakinyan,* and he never strikes it with lightning. The smell of the smoke of the cedar is pleasing to him. When a thunderstorm is coming, one should make an incense of cedar leaves to propitiate *Wakinyan.*

In any ceremony that pertains to hunting, or the Buffalo, a Lakota should make incense with buffalo chips in this manner. He should make a fire of anything that will burn easily, and when there are burning coals he should put dried buffalo chips on them so as to make a smoke. This is because the spirit of a buffalo remains in dried buffalo chips and it is in the smoke from them. This spirit goes to *Wakan Tanka,* and pleases him so that he will help in the chase. In the tribal chase this incense should be made by a shaman when the scouts report a herd of buffalo located. In the Sun Dance the shaman should make an incense of buffalo chips.

These are all the smokes that are customary in the ceremonies of the Lakotas, but the spirit of anything is released in the smoke of it. So *wosnapi* (offering to a spirit or to God) may be made by burning the thing with a ceremony making it an offering.

A Lakota can secure the favor of *Wakan Tanka,* or of any spirit, if he will make a suitable offering. The offering may be made in either one of three ways. It may be abandoned in the name of the one to whom it is offered, or it may be given to one whose hands are painted red to show that they are sacred. Or it may be burned in the name of one to whom the offering is made.

If it is abandoned, the spirit of the offering goes to the one to whom the offering is made, but the thing itself remains as it was before it was offered. It is the same with things given to red hands. But if the offering is burned, its spirit goes away forever in the smoke, and the thing offered is destroyed. Most often offerings are made by abandoning them because the things offered belong to the first who takes possession of them.

In this manner the needy may be helped. Most offerings that are made by giving are given to shamans, but they may be given to anyone whose hands are painted red. An offering is always *wotehila*[11] (taboo) to the one who makes it, except offerings of food or drink. One may make an offering of these by throwing on the ground a bit, and then eat or drink the remainder.

A Lakota may be forbidden to do anything. The thing he is forbidden to do is *tehila* (taboo) to him. To secure the favor of *Wakan Tanka* a man may vow to taboo something. Or to placate *Wakan Tanka* or a spirit he may make such a vow. Or a shaman may forbid one to do something and then that is a taboo to the one forbidden. Or *Wakan Tanka* may in a vision forbid one to do something, and then that is taboo to that one. Anything offered as an offering is taboo to the one who offers it, except food or drink. If the taboo is the part of game animals it must be taboo to everyone, and must be left as food for the spirits. If one does that which is taboo for him *Wakan Tanka* will be displeased, and will bring some misfortune on such a one. The only manner of freedom from a taboo is by *Inipi* and *Hanblapi.*

Before a Lakota undertakes anything of importance he should strengthen his life by *Inipi* (taking a vapor bath). This may be done to refresh one, or as a medicine to cure the sick, or as a part of any ceremony. It must always be done in an *Ini ti* (sweat lodge), which must be made of slender saplings thrust into the ground in a circle so that their tops can be bent and fastened together so as to form a dome, which must be covered so the smoke can not pass through the covering. The door must be large enough for a man to creep through and so that it can be closed tightly. The vapor is made by pouring water or other things on hot stones inside the lodge. To take the bath one must go inside the lodge and when it is closed tightly he must make the vapor. He must be naked and while pouring the water he must sing or pray. When he has made the vapor, he should come out and wash himself with cold water. As many may *Inipi* as can get inside the lodge together. If this is done for an important ceremony a shaman should conduct the *Inipi*, and he may perform as much ceremony while doing so as he wishes. Nothing should be permitted in an *Ini ti* but that which is necessary for the ceremony. An *Ini ti* should never have its door toward the north. *Wakan Tanka* is pleased by *Inipi*, for it strengthens the life and purifies the body.

No Lakota should undertake anything of great importance without first seeking a vision relative to it. *Hanble* (a vision) is a communication from *Wakan Tanka* or a spirit to one of mankind. It may come at any time or in any manner to anyone. It may be relative to the one who receives it, or to another. It may be communicated in Lakota, or *hanbloglaka* (language of the spirits). Or it may be only by sight or sounds not of a language. It may come directly from the one giving it, or it may be sent by an *akicita* (messenger). It may come unsought for or it may come by seeking it. To seek a vision one should *Inipi*, and then remain alone as much as possible, thinking continually of that about which he desires a vision. While doing this he should eat no food nor take any drink, but he may smoke the pipe. It is best to have the instruction of a shaman and do according to this. If the vision desired is concerning a matter of much importance, a shaman should supervise all the ceremony relative to it. If it is a small matter, there need be but little ceremony, but if it is of very great importance there should be much ceremony. The greatest ceremony is the Sun Dance in order to receive a communication from the Sun. When one receives a communication in a vision he should be governed by it, for otherwise *Wakan Tanka* will bring misfortune upon him. If the communication is in Lakota he will understand it, but if it is in the language of the spirits a shaman should interpret it.

When a boy's voice is changing he should seek a vision to govern his life. A girl may seek a vision by wrapping her first menstrual flow and placing it in a tree. Visions frequently come without seeking to very old men or women and to shamans.

Wicasa wakan (holy man, or shaman) is made by other shamans by ceremony and teaching that which a shaman should know. He is made holy by the ceremony so that he can communicate with *Wakan Tanka,* and the ceremony also prepares his outfit and gives to it supernatural powers. This outfit may be anything that has a spirit imparted to it so that it will have all the powers of the spirit and all that are used to cover and keep it in. This outfit is his *wasicun* (ceremonial implement) and it is very holy, and should be considered as a God. It must be prayed [over] for its power. A shaman governs all the ceremonies of the Lakota, so he must know them. He must know *iye wakan* (holy language, or the language of the shamans), and *hanbloglaka* (spirit language). He must know all the laws and customs of the Lakotas, for he may prohibit or change any of them. But if he does this it must be because it is the will of *Wakan Tanka.* He is entitled to sit in any council, but he should not speak on any subject, except to tell the will of *Wakan Tanka.* He is feared by all the people, but if it is found that he deceives the people he may be punished by the *akicita* (marshals) in any manner they see fit, even to killing him.

When a shaman has been punished by the marshals he is no longer regarded as a holy man. Maybe he will then become *wicasa hmunga* (wizard). The oldest or wisest shamans are the most respected. A shaman should conduct the larger ceremonies, but anyone may perform the smaller. A shaman may prohibit anyone from performing any one or more of the ceremonies. A shaman can make anything taboo to anyone, or he can lift any taboo. There are many diseases that only a shaman can cure. He does this with his *wasicun* and not with medicines.

The common people of the Lakotas call that which is the wrapping of a *wasicun, wopiye.* Most of the interpreters interpret this *wopiye* as medicine bag. That is wrong, for the word neither means a bag nor medicine. It means a thing to do good with. A good interpretation would be that it is the thing of power.

Ozuha pejuta is a medicine bag. *Ozuha* means a bag, and *pejuta* means a medicine. *Ozuha pejuta* means simply a bag to keep medicines in. It is the same as any other bag, and it has no more power than a bag to keep corn in.

Often when a shaman is performing a ceremony with his *wasicun* the interpreters say he is a medicine man making medicine. This is very foolish. It is the same as if when the minister is giving communion it was said he is a physician making medicine for the communicants.

These things must all be understood before one can understand the old customs and ceremonies of the Lakotas.

7. On Ceremonies. George Sword, September 9, 1896 (Bruce Means, interpreter). (AMNH)

In former times the Lakotas had customs and ceremonies that governed almost everything they did. The shamans governed the ceremonies. The *akicita* governed the other customs. The council appointed the *akicita* and considered all matters concerning the band. The *wakiconze* heard all disputes if it was agreed to submit them to him. He was the *mihunka* (godfather) to all, and he was the chief when a band was moving. The medicine men governed all ceremonies of medicine. But a shaman could change any custom or ceremony . . .

I can tell all the customs and ceremonies the Oglalas practiced before they knew the white people. But I can not tell the secret things of the shamans because they should be told only to one who is to become a shaman . . . There are some ceremonies that must be understood before one can understand other ceremonies. These are soothing the spirit, strengthening the ghost, pleasing the God, and learning the will of the God . . .

The spirit is soothed by smoking the pipe. Anyone may smoke a pipe for pleasure. It is a ceremony when it is done formally. The ghost is strengthened by doing what the white people call a sweat bath. Anyone may do this for refreshment but if it is done right it is a ceremony. The God is pleased by making a smoke with sweetgrass. Anyone can make this smoke but it should not be done except as a ceremony and then in a particular way.

Anyone may learn the will of the God in this manner: he should strengthen his ghost; he should be alone; he should wear no clothing except a robe; he should neither eat nor drink; he should soothe his spirit; he should think continually concerning that which he wishes; no living thing should be near him. Doing this in this manner is seeking a vision. If it is the will of the God, he will receive a communication . . . These ceremonies are a part of all the important ceremonies of the Oglalas.

8. The Pipe. George Sword, September 20, 1896 (Bruce Means, interpreter). (AMNH)

The pipe was first given to the Lakotas by the God. The spirit of the God is in the smoke from the pipe. The pipe that was given by the God is kept by a keeper. The keeper was appointed by the shamans. When the keeper dies, his kinspeople keep it. Usually this is his oldest son. This is the ceremonial pipe of all the Lakotas.

Each band of the Lakotas may have a ceremonial pipe. It is kept by a keeper appointed by a shaman. Each shaman may have a ceremonial pipe. He keeps it and uses it only when he is performing an important ceremony.

Anyone may have a pipe and may smoke it for pleasure. The spirit of the God is in the smoke of any pipe if the pipe is smoked in the proper manner. Any pipe may be smoked ceremoniously in this manner. The smoking material should be carefully prepared on a block or board. While preparing it, one may pray or sing. Then the bowl of the pipe should be held in the left hand with the stem held toward the body. The smoking material should be carefully put into the bowl with the right hand and tamped down with a pipe stick. The filling of the pipe is an important part of the ceremony. One may pray or sing while filling it. The pipe should be lighted with a burning coal and not with a flame. If the pipe is not filled and lighted in this manner, the spirit of the God will not be in the smoke from the pipe. The pipe should be smoked until the contents are all consumed. If it stops burning before all the contents are consumed, it should be emptied and filled before smoking again. The remains in the pipe thus smoked should be emptied into a fire, for if it is emptied on the ground it may be stepped on and this would offend the God.

When a pipe is smoked in this manner, the spirit that is in the smoke goes with it into the mouth and body and then it comes out and goes upward. When this spirit is in the body, it soothes the spirit of the smoker. When it goes upward, it soothes the God. So the God and the spirit are as friends.

When a man smokes a pipe as a ceremony, he should think of that for which he is smoking and then the God will think of the same thing. If at one time more than one man smokes as a ceremony, it should be done in this manner. The pipe should be filled and lighted and then it should be passed from one to another, each smoking a whiff or two. It should be thus passed until all the contents are consumed and then emptied in a fire. The spirit in the smoke will soothe the spirits of all who thus smoke together and all will be as friends and all think alike. When the Lakotas smoke in this manner, it is like when the Christians take communion. It is smoking in communion . . .

The Lakota should smoke the pipe first when considering any matter of importance . . . The first rite in any ceremony of the Lakotas should be to smoke the pipe . . . When anyone performs a ceremony after he has smoked the pipe, he should please the God so that the God will give attention to the ceremony . . .

The God is pleased by making a smoke with sweetgrass in the proper manner. The sweetgrass should be sprinkled on burning coals so that it will make a smoke. If one sings or prays while making the smoke, it will be more pleasing to the God . . . The smoke of the sage will drive away all evil if it is made in this manner: the sage should be put on burning coals of fire so that it will smoke and while making the smoke, one should pray to the evil to go away . . . Evil beings hate the smoke of the sage.

---

9. Life and Visions. George Sword, October 2, 1896 (Elmore Red Eyes, interpreter).[12] (AMNH)

A man's *ni* is his life. It is the same as his breath. It gives him his strength. All that is inside a man's body it keeps clean. If it is weak it cannot clean the inside of the body. If it goes away from a man he is dead . . . *Niya* is that which causes the *ni*. It is given at the time of the birth. It is the ghost. . . . The white people call *ini kaga* taking a sweat bath. The Lakotas mean all the ceremony when they [say] *ini kaga* ["to make *ini*"] or *inipi*. When they say *ini* or *inipi* they mean that it is to make the ghost strong . . . *Inipi* makes clean everything inside the body . . . *Inipi* cause a man's *ni* to put out of his body all that makes him tired, or all that causes disease, or all that causes him to think wrong . . . *Ini kaga* must be done according to the customs of Lakotas. It must be done in an *ini ti*. This is what the white people call a sweat lodge.

The *ini ti* must be made according to Lakota custom. If it is made in any other shape the ceremony will do no good . . . *Ini kaga* may be with only a little ceremony, but there may be much ceremony in performing it.

Wowihanble is something told to a man by something that is not a man. It is what the white people call a holy dream (vision). God tells his will to man by *wowihanble* . . . In former times if a man wished to know the will of his God he sought a vision. *Inhanblapi* in Lakota means seeking a vision. This is a ceremony that must be done as the Lakotas do it.

To seek a vision a Lakota must think about it all the time. He must first strengthen his ghost. Then he must wear no clothing except a robe. He must be alone. He must neither eat nor drink. He must smoke the pipe and sing and pray. The language of the vision is *hanblogagia [hanbloglagia]*. Only the shamans understand this language. If a Lakota wished to do something important he should seek a vision about it. A shaman may perform this ceremony with many rites.

---

10. Seeking a Vision. George Sword (translated by Bert Means). (CHS)

It is the custom of all the Lakotas to seek a vision when they are to undertake some important thing or wish for something very earnestly. A vision is something told by a *wakan* being and it is told as if in a dream. The *wakan* beings are the superior beings, that is, they are superior to ordinary mankind. They know what is past and present and what will be. They can speak Lakota or any other language and they can use the sign language. Nearly all the superior beings have *akicita* and they send their communications by them. If one of these messengers gives a communication, it will be known from whom it comes because no two of the *Wakan* use the same *akicita*. There are four kinds of superior beings and each kind may give a communication. It may be known which kind it is that gives the communication by the kind of vision it is and by the messenger that gives it. When one seeks a vision and receives a communication he must obey as he is told to do. If he does not, all the superior beings will be against him.

If a boy or a young man wishes to know what he should do all his life, he should seek a vision. He may pray to a superior being to give it to him. Maybe that being will do so but maybe another will give him a vision and tell him what he should do and how he should live. There are many kinds of preparation for seeking a vision. If the vision is for something of little importance, there is not much to do before seeking it. The most important vision is of the sun. The preparation for that is made by dancing the Sun Dance.

Sometimes a vision is given without seeking it. Usually this is done only to the shamans and to old men or old women. If a man is alone and speaks to no one and neither eats nor drinks anything and thinks continually about the superior beings, he may have a vision. The usual way to seek a vision is to purify the body in an *Initi* by pouring water on hot stones and then go naked, only wrapped in a robe, to the top of a hill, and stay there without speaking to anyone of mankind or eating, or drinking, and thinking continually about the vision he wishes.

If one goes to [a] hill in this manner, he should remain there until he receives a vision or until he is nearly perished. His people should sing songs and pray to the superior being to give him a vision. They should give gifts and do nothing that would offend the superior being he is asking for a vision. When he comes to where he is to stay while fasting, he should prepare a place about as long as a man and about half as wide. He should take from this place all vegetation of every kind and all bugs and worms and everything that lives. He should have four charms made by a shaman and tied in little bundles about as big as the end of a finger. These should be fastened to the small ends of sprouts of the plum tree. These are spirit banners.

He should put a banner, first at the west side of the place he has prepared; then one at the north side; then one at the east side; then one at the south side. He should have a pipe and plenty of *cansasa*[13] and tobacco mixed. He should then light his pipe and point the mouthpiece first toward the west and then toward the north and then toward the east and then toward the south. Then he should point it toward the sky and then toward the earth and then toward the sun. He should have some sweetgrass and very often he should burn some of this and some sage. If he does these things in the right way, he will surely receive a vision. If a little boy is seeking a vision, a man may stand far from him and do these things for him.

If he seeks a vision about a very important thing, he should have a shaman help him get ready for it and advise him about when he has had a communication. The shaman should make the *Initi* and do a ceremony while they are in it. When he comes from the hill, he and the shaman and as many others as he may invite should *ini* in the *Initi* and the shaman should do another ceremony. These things are all done to please the superior beings.

If one has a vision, he sees something. It may be like a man or it may be like an animal or a bird or an insect or anything that breathes, or it may be like a light of some kind or a cloud. He may see it come to him. Maybe it will come and he will not see it coming. It may speak to him or it may not speak. If it speaks to him, it may speak so that he will understand what it says, but maybe it will speak as the shamans speak. Maybe it will make only a noise. He should remember what it says and how it speaks. Maybe it will speak without his having a vision. If he sees something it is a vision, if he hears something it is a communication.

When a Lakota seeks a vision, he should remain on the place he prepares until he receives either a vision or has a communication. He should stay there awaiting this as long as he is able and can live, if it need be for him to do so. If he concludes he is not to have a vision from the one he has asked, he may ask *Taku Skanskan* for a vision. If he does this, he should stand and offer smoke to *Wakan Tanka*. Then he should look toward the sky and offer smoke to *Nagi Tanka*. He should then bow with his face to the ground and look at nothing until he has a vision or a communication. When he can endure no longer to wait, he may go to his people.

When he goes to his people, if he has had a vision, he should go singing. If he has not had a vision, he should go silently and with his face covered.

11. Consecrating a Pipe. George Sword. (AMNH)

In the incantation ceremonies over a spirit pipe, the shaman is usually assisted by several others. Before undertaking this ceremony, the shaman usually seeks a vision and if he sees one, he is governed by its communication. If this is that he should not undertake the ceremony, he abandons his intentions of doing so. But if it is not against his consecrating a pipe, he calls those whom he expects to assist him in the ceremony and together they consider the result of his quest for a vision. If he has not seen one, they will probably abandon the intention of consecrating the pipe, or the shaman may again seek the vision or they may decide that the incantation ceremonies may proceed by making such additions to them as they think may be required by the conditions of the failure to see a vision.

If he has seen a vision and it has not been adverse to the ceremony, he and his friends who assist him will consider what the vision indicates shall be done during the ceremony and having agreed upon this, they proceed with incantation as follows with the addition of that which they have agreed that the vision indicates.

A quantity of *cansasa* and of sweetgrass is provided. Those who are to take part in the ceremony, all of whom must be shamans, assemble and build a fire in a tipi which they must occupy alone. When the fire has burned down to coals, they sit in a circle about it. The pipe that is to be consecrated is filled with *cansasa*. Sweetgrass is then sprinkled on the coals so as to fill the tipi with sweet-smelling smoke. Then the shaman hands the pipe to one of his assistants who calls upon some one or more of the subordinate spirits and says in substance:

"Oh Spirits of the Earth, the Air, the Clouds, the Thunder and Lightning, and of the Water. We offer you this smoke. This pipestem is to be used only when offering smoke to the spirits. Give it power to overcome the malignant influences of all the evil spirits or powers which you can control."

He then lights the pipe and smokes a few whiffs and hands it to another assistant, who calls upon one or more of the subordinate spirits, and he may call upon the same as those invoked by one of the assistants who has preceded him. He says in substance:

"Oh Spirit of the West, the East, of the North, of the South, etc. We offer you this smoke. This pipestem is to be used only when offering smoke to the spirits. Give it power to overcome the malignant influences of all the evil spirits or powers which you can control."

He then smokes a few whiffs and hands it to another assistant, who invokes the spirits in a like manner, saying in substance:

"Oh Spirits of War and Peace, of Food, of Medicine, of Sunshine etc. We offer you smoke. This pipestem is to be used only when offering smoke to the spirits. Give it power to overcome the malignant influences of all the evil spirits or powers which you can control."

This process is continued until all the assistants have taken a part like this in the ceremony, and an assistant may smoke one or more times and call one or more times upon the same spirit or call upon different spirits each time he smokes until all the subordinate spirits with which they are familiar have been called upon and their aid invoked.

Then the entire process is repeated with each ornament upon the stem, as for instance, one of the assistants upon receiving the pipe says in substance:

"Oh Spirit of the Earth, the Air, the Water, and the Spirit that cares for the Eagle! We offer you this smoke. The eagle feathers that are on this pipestem will be used only when offering smoke to the spirits. Give them power to overcome the malignant influences of all the evil spirits which you can control."

Another may say: "Oh Spirit of the Thunder and Lightning and of the Fire with which this stem has been ornamented, we offer you smoke. This pipestem is marked in this way by the fire and will be used only when offering smoke to the spirits. Give it power to overcome the malignant influences of all the spirits you can control."

The principal shaman takes no part in the incantation over the stem and only sits present until the consecration of the stem is complete. When the incantation is over, [and] the stem and its ornaments have been completed, the principal shaman takes the pipe and carefully cleans the bowl and fills it with *cansasa*. A new fire is built, and while it is burning, a song addressed to the Great Spirit is sung and the principal shaman makes an address and he may be followed by one or more of the others. The song and the address are extemporaneous. When the fire has burned to coals, the principal shaman takes the pipe and, sprinkling sweetgrass upon the coals, moves the pipe in a circle in the smoke of the grass. While moving the pipe, he says in substance:

"Oh Spirits of the Earth, the Air (naming each spirit that has been called upon), smoke has been offered to you. My friends have asked each of you to give power to this pipestem and its ornaments to overcome the malignant influence of all the evil spirits or powers which you can control. I ask you to listen to their requests and give this pipestem and its ornaments the powers they have asked of you. I am now about to offer smoke to the Great Spirit, *Taku Wakan*, and to ask him to give to this pipe power to overcome all evil influences. I ask you to listen to my prayer to him."

He then lights the pipe and they all rise to their feet and stand with bowed heads. After a short pause, the principal shaman lifts the pipe as high above his head as he can reach, holding it with both hands with the stem pointing upwards. He then says in substance:

"Oh Great Spirit! *Taku Wakan*, you have heard my friends ask the spirits to give to this pipestem power to overcome all malignant influences of the evil spirits or powers which they can control. All the *cansasa* in this pipe shall be smoked as an offering to you. In all time to come, whenever this pipe is smoked in any other manner, it shall be broken and the pieces destroyed, or if it shall pass into strange hands and [be] smoked in an irreverent manner then let it be as a common pipe. We ask that whenever this pipe is smoked to you, that you will command the spirits that have been invoked to do as they have been asked to do."

The pipe is then considered *wakan*, that is, mysterious or holy, and it must remain intact as it is at the time of its consecration. The pipe and stem must always be used together and no ornament must be removed from it, for if the pipe is not kept inviolate the Great Spirit might be offended and if any ornament is removed, the spirit who was invoked in the consecration of that ornament might be offended and refuse to aid in overcoming the particular evil influence that it governs.

A shaman is always the custodian of a spirit pipe and jealously guards it from profane use or even exposure to the merely curious and in fact will deny having such a pipe to those whom he considers unworthy of using it. The custody passes from father to son if the son becomes a shaman. Or if the son is not a shaman then when the shaman begins to fear death he calls another shaman and secretly confides to him the pipe, which in such cases can be used only after the death of the shaman and the period of mourning for him has passed. If a shaman dies while holding such a pipe in custody, his family or friends call together other shamans and they decide who shall have the custody of the pipe.

It is considered almost sacrilegious to speak of such a pipe in a spirit of levity and in ordinary conversation it is referred to in an indirect way and not mentioned directly as such a pipe. This pipe is used only on the most solemn occasions and generally for ceremonial purposes. It may pass from the hands of its custodian to any other person entitled to use it but in such cases the most solemn guarantees must be given that it will not be profaned in any way.

If the pipe is lost or stolen or in any manner passes into the keeping of an unauthorized person, it is the duty of any shaman who knows of the fact to annul its potency and sacred character by incantation. Generally more than one shaman associates in this ceremony, each performing such rites as he deems best for his purpose. Some pipes are considered much more efficacious than others and an ancient pipe is held in peculiar veneration.

A recently consecrated pipe or one that is believed to have but little potency may be deprived of its mysterious power by the agreement of its custodian and by the proper incantation of a shaman. In such cases the pipe becomes an ordinary pipe and may be disposed of as its owner sees fit. Usually the owner gives it away for fear that the evil powers that it formerly controlled will be exercised upon him because he no longer has the protection of the pipe as a spirit pipe. When two or more persons smoke such a pipe together, its influences are supposed to bind them together forever in amicable relationship.

12. Treating the Sick. George Sword, August 5, 1901. (CHS)

Disease is caused by the *wakan* (mysterious), or it may be caused by the mysterious-like *(wakanla)*. The evil mysteries may impart their potencies to the body and this will cause disease. Poisons and snakes and water creatures cause disease in this way. A magician can cause disease by his mysterious powers. A holy man can cause disease by his songs and ceremonies.

A medicine man can treat a disease with his medicines. He must know the song appropriate to his medicine. There are many kinds of medicine men. Some kinds of medicine men belong to an order such as the Bear medicine. Bear medicine men are like a brotherhood.

Some medicine men have only one medicine. They may discover this in some way or it may be revealed to them in a vision. The Bear medicine men teach each other the songs and ceremonies and the medicines they must use and what they are good for. If a man has a medicine that he has discovered, he does not teach this to anyone.

When one has a medicine, he must have a song for it and he must know something to say every time he uses it. If the wrong song or invocation is used, the medicine will do no good. Then another medicine man should try his medicines.

Everyone who treats the sick should have a drum and rattles. The drum and the rattles please the *wakan* and they will help. A medicine is called *pejuta* in Lakota. This may be anything that will cure the sick. A medicine man is called *pejuta wicasa* in Lakota. He keeps his medicines in a receptacle called *wozuha pejuta* in Lakota. This is his medicine bag. He may have only one kind of medicine in it or he may have a great many kinds. If he is a Bear medicine man, he should have all of the Bear medicines in his medicine bag. There are ten kinds of Bear medicines. A Bear medicine man may have other kinds of medicines also. He may keep these in his Bear medicine bag if he wishes to do so. The medicine bag may be of anything that will hold the medicines. Usually it is made of the skin of something.

A Bear medicine man should have something in his medicine bag to cut with. He should cut inflamed places and places about wounds that are not healing properly. This should be a sharp flint. If a magician has made one sick, then medicines will not cure such a one. The magician or a holy man should treat such a person.

A magician is called *wapiya wicasa* in Lakota when he makes one well, and when he makes one ill, he is called *wakan skan wicasa*. He treats the sick secretly and no one knows what he does. He makes charms and philters and he may make very deadly potions. He is in league with the great evil one. He can do mysterious things to anyone, either present or far away. The things he does or makes are not medicines. He makes charms to win games or to kill enemies, or to win the love of men and women.

The holy man is the most potent in treating the sick. He can speak with the Great Mystery and they will help him. He does not treat the sick with medicines. He has a ceremonial bag. It is called *wopiye* in Lakota. This does not have medicines in it. It has a mystery in it and this mystery makes the bag very potent. It has all the potency of the mystery. The holy man invokes his ceremonial bundle or bag. It may be like a bag or it may be like a bundle. Or it may be anything that is revealed to him in a vision. This bag is prepared with much ceremony by other holy men and the thing in it is made holy by ceremony. It may represent the Bear or the Buffalo, or the *wakan* of the sky, or anything. Then it is like a part of himself. It is like his ghost only it has more power than a man's ghost has.

The holy man prays to his ceremonial bag. He must know the song that belongs to it and the right words to say in praying to it. Then when he sings this song and says these words, the bag will do as he bids. It is not the bag which does this but that which is in the bag. This is called *sicun* in Lakota. The bag is called *wasicun*. A holy man does not give medicine to the sick unless he is a medicine man also. If he is a medicine man, he may give medicines and invoke his ceremonial bag also, and the bag will compel the medicine to do as he wishes it.

A holy man may be a magician also. But such men are to be feared and the people will not patronize them. A holy man is more potent than a medicine man or a magician. He can cause his ceremonial bag to overcome the medicines and charms of the others.

When the medicine man treats the sick, his medicines must be swallowed or smoked or steamed. When the magician treats the sick, no one knows what he does for he does it secretly. When the holy man treats the sick, he performs a ceremony and invokes his ceremonial bag and the familiar *(sicun)* in it does what he asks it to do. The medicine bag has in it ten medicines:

1. *Taopi Pejuta:* used for wounds; powder, stirred in a cup of water and drink it all.

2. *Keya Ta Cante* (turtle's heart dried and powdered): used for wounds; stirred up with water and drink it.

3. *Canli Wakan* (holy tobacco): used for wounds; smoked in a pipe by all present and the pipe pointed towards the wound.

4. *Hante Pejuta* (cedar medicine): used to disinfect. Burn it on a fire in the room; burn it in the sweat house; chew it and put it on the scalp lock.

5. *Icahpahu Pejuta* (the pith of soap weed): used for swelling; powder and mix with water and rub it on the swelling.

6. *Pejuta To* (blue medicine): used in anemia; powder and make an infusion and drink it.

7. *Sinkpe-tawote Pejuta* (calamus root): used for delirium and trouble about the head; the patient chews it, or the doctor chews it and spits it in the face and over the head of the patient or rubs it on the head and face of the patient.

8. *Pejuta Skuya* (sweet medicine): used for failure of the menses; powder it and make an infusion of it and drink it.

9. *Wahpezizila Pejuta* (yellow leaves medicine): used for swellings with pains; powdered and mixed with either water or grease and rubbed on.

10. *Tazi-yazan Pejuta* (yucca): powder and drink for stomach ache.[14]

---

13. The Secret Knowledge of Shamans. George Sword, Bad Wound, No Flesh, and Thomas Tyon, July 2–3, 1905 (Thomas Tyon, interpreter). (AMNH)

We will tell you of things that were known only to the shamans. . . .[15] *Wakan Tanka* is above everything and he governs everything. . . . When *Wakan Tanka* wishes one of mankind to do something in some manner he makes his wishes known, either in a vision or through a shaman. . . .

A *wicasa wakan* (holy man or shaman) represents *Wakan Tanka* and speaks for him. . . . The shamans address *Wakan Tanka* as *Tobtob Kin.* This is in the speech that only the shamans know. The shamans speak this speech in all their ceremonies and songs so that the people may not learn those things that only the shamans should know. . . . *Tobtob Kin* are Four-times-four Gods while *Tob Kin* is only the Four Winds. The Four Winds is a God and is the *akicita* (messenger) of all the other Gods. The Four-times-four are *Wikan* [Sun] and *Hanwikan* [Moon]; *Taku Skanskan* [That which moves (Sky)] and *Tatekan* [Wind]; *Tob Kin* [The Four (Winds)] and *Yumnikan* [Whirlwind]; *Makakan* [Earth] and *Wohpe* [the Beautiful Woman]; *Inyankan* [Rock] and *Wakinyan* [Thunder Being]; *Tatankakan* [Buffalo Bull] and *Hunonpakan* [Two Legged (Grizzly Bear)]; *Wanagi* [Human Spirit] and *Woniya* [Human Life]; and *Nagila* [Nonhuman Spirit] and *Wasicunpi* [Guardian Spirits]. These are the names of the Good Gods as they are known to the people.

The Bad Gods are *Iyo*[16] or *Ibom,* and *Gnaskinyan* [Crazy Buffalo] and *Anog Ite* [Double Face] and *Untehi* [Water Monsters] and *Mini Watu* [Water Spirits] and *Can Oti* [Tree Dwellers] and *Ungla* [Goblins] and *Gica* [Dwarfs] and *Nagila Sica* [Evil Nonhuman Spirit]. *Iyo* is the chief of the Evil Gods and he is the evil *Wakan Tanka.* When he is like a giant he is *Iyo,* and when he is like a cyclone he is *Ibom.* . . .

Gnaskinyan is the most to be feared of the Evil Gods. He appears like the good Buffalo God and persuades the people to do all kinds of evil things. The *Hmugma Wicasa* (wizards) do his ceremonies. . . . When a shaman is to perform a ceremony, he should first smoke the pipe and then make an incense with sweetgrass and then with sage. He should then pray to the Four and then to the Four-times-four. But if he is to do the ceremony for only one of the Gods, he should pray to that God instead of to *Wakan Tanka.* . . .

A shaman should have a drum and two rattles; these should be made sacred by a ceremony. . . . He should always sound his drum and rattles when he is performing a ceremony. . . . He may have some other person sound his drum and rattles while he does other things.

A shaman must always have his *wasicun* and must always use it in a ceremony. It is a God. . . . The *wasicun* is like the God whose power it has. . . . If one dances the Sun Dance to become a shaman he must understand all these things. . . . A shaman has his songs and his formulae. He has a song and formula for each God. Other shamans may have different songs and formulae for the same Gods. . . . These songs and formulae are in the speech of the shamans. . . . When a shaman prays, he first sings his song or he repeats his formula and then he tells the God what he wishes. . . . Then he tells the people what the God wishes. . . . Maybe he will pray to his *wasicun* and tell it what he wishes. . . . He must pray to his *wasicun* in the same manner as he prays to a God. . . .

Wakan Tanka is like sixteen different persons. But each person is *kan*. Therefore they are all only the same as one. . . . All the God persons have *ton*. The *ton* is the power to do supernatural things. . . . Half of the Good Gods have *tan ton*[17] (have physical properties), and half are *tan ton sni* (have no physical properties). Half of those who are *tan ton* are *tan ton yan* (visible) and half of those who are *tan ton sni* are *tan ton yan sni* (invisible). All the other Gods are visible or invisible as they choose to be. . . . All the Evil Gods are visible or invisible as they choose to be. . . . The invisible Gods never appear in a vision except to a shaman. . . . The ceremonies for the visible and the invisible Gods differ except the Sun Dance. The Sun Dance is a ceremony the same as if *Wikan* were both visible and invisible. This is because *Wi* is the chief of the Gods. . . .

The *ton* of *Wi* is in fire and it can not be imparted to anything. *Wi* comes in a vision only to those who dance the Sun Dance. . . . The *ton* of *Wohpe* is in the smoke from the pipe and in incense from sweetgrass and it can not be imparted to any other thing. The *ton* of *Skan* is the most powerful and it can be imparted only by very wise shamans and with a great deal of ceremony. No one but a very wise shaman should have a *sicun* with the *ton* of *Skan*. . . . *Hanwi, Wakinyan, Nagi*, and *Niya* each have a *ton* but they can not be imparted to anything. The *ton* of *Tate, Tatob* and *Yumni* is the same as that of *Skan*. These four always go together. The *ton* of all the other Gods each can be imparted to anything that is suitable. . . .

A shaman must impart a *ton* with the right ceremony done in the right manner. . . . When a shaman imparts a *ton* to anything the thing is made a *sicun*. A *sicun* is like the God. ... A shaman must put the container on a *sicun* and this makes it a *wasicun*. ... A God may tell anyone in a vision how to make a *wasicun*. This is the way the medicine men learn how to make their medicines. ...

Anyone may invoke his *wasicun* by repeating the correct formula or singing the right song. ... When one invokes his *wasicun*, it will do as he wishes. ... A *wasicun* can do only what the God can do. ... A more powerful *wasicun* will prevail against a less powerful. ... If a shaman deceives the people, the *akicita* should punish him. They may make him pay the one deceived or they may take his *wasicun* from him or they may kill him. ... If the *akicita* punish a shaman wrongfully, he can bring a curse upon them.

---

14. *Kan* and Its Derivitives. George Sword. (CHS)

Kan means anything that is old or that has existed for a long time or that should be accepted because it has been so in former times, or it may mean a strange or wonderful thing or that which can not be comprehended, or that which should not be questioned or it may mean a sacred or supernatural thing. Other words are used before or after the word *kan* to give it particular meaning. The words that may be used before it are *a, wa, wo, ya,* and *yu*. The words that may be used after it are *la* and *pi*.

When the word *a* is used before *kan*, it makes the word *akan*. This means that the thing spoken of is *kan*.

The word *wa* means that something or someone is something or does something. When it is used before *kan*, it makes the word *wakan*. This means that which is *kan*, or does *kan*; or one who is or does *kan*. If one says *wa ma kan*, this means what I do is *kan*. The younger Oglalas do not understand this for they speak Lakota in a new way.

The word *wo* is made of two words which are *wa* and *on*. *On* means relative to or of that kind. If one should say *on kan*, or *onkan*, this would mean that the thing spoken of related to something *kan*. *Onkan* is a good Lakota word but the young people would not understand it. The old people would say *wa on kan* if they used all the words. But instead of saying *wa on*, they say *wo* and when using this before *kan* they say *wo kan* or *wokan*. If an old Oglala were speaking of himself he would say *wo ma kan*. This would mean that what I do is relative to *kan*.

The word *ya* means to change a thing or person and make it different from what it was before the change or a thing that has been made thus different. When one says *ya kan*, it means that the thing spoken of has been made *kan* by changing it, or if one says *ya ma kan*, he means that he is changed so that he is now *kan*. If I now say *ya ma kan*, the young people laugh at me and say I talk foolish. They say *ma wakan*. When an old Oglala would say *ya wa wica kan*, the young people would say *wicasa yawakan*. When one speaks Lakota as it was spoken in former times, the young Lakotas do not understand it.

The word *yu* means nearly the same as *ya*. *Ya* means that a thing is caused by action done for the purpose of causing it, while *yu* means that a thing is caused indirectly. If it is said that a thing is *ya kan*, it is understood that action was done for the purpose of making it *kan*, but if it is said that it is *yu kan*, it is understood that it became *kan* because of action for some other purpose.

The word *la* means a little like, but not exactly alike. To say *kan la* means that the thing spoken of is almost *kan*, or that it is a little like *kan*. Or it may mean that it is a little but not entirely *kan*.

The word *pi* means more than one or it may mean that which is done in a particular manner by many persons. *Kan pi* means the things that are *kan*. *Waci* means a dance and *waci pi* means dancing by a number of persons while *waci kan pi* means a dance that must be done by a number of persons and is *kan*. The young people say *wacipi wakan*, meaning a *waci* that is *kan*.

In the ceremonies of the Oglala the *wa wica kan*, or as the young people would say, the *wicasa wakan*, which means a holy man, use these words a great deal and this is what they mean when they speak them.

Kan is that which is established by custom and should not be changed, or it is something sacred that can not be comprehended.

A kan is that which is mysterious or supernatural. *Wa kan* when relative to the *a kan* is a God; when relative to mankind is a holy man or shaman; when relative to other things is sacred.

Wo kan is consecrated to the *wa kan* or for ceremonial purposes. *Ya kan* means to have supernatural potency. *Yu kan* means that a thing or person is sacred while being or doing something.

---

15. *Nagilapi.* George Sword. (CHS)

Nagilapi are the *niyapi* of animals and the smoke of inanimate things. *Nagila* is the same as the *ton* of anything other than *Tobtob Kin*. Each thing, animate or inanimate, other than *Tobtob Kin* has a *nagi* or a *nagila*. The *nagi* of an animate thing is its spirit and of an inanimate thing that grows from the ground is its smoke. This is the potency of anything.

---

16. *Nagipi* (Spirits). George Sword. (CHS)

There are many kinds of spirits *(nagipi)*. All the spirits of one kind are the same as one spirit. There are four classes of spirits, and four kinds of spirits in each class. The *Wakan Tanka* is a spirit but it is of four kinds. It is called *Wakan* because no man can understand it. The *Taku Wakan* is a spirit and it is four kinds and it is called *Taku Wakan* because it is akin to the *Wakan Tanka*. The *Wakan Tanka* and the *Taku Wakan* may be all called *Taku Wakan* because they are all akin to each other. When a prayer is made to *Wakan Tanka,* it is made to *Taku Wakan* also.

A *wakan* that is *Wakan Tanka* or *Taku Wakan* is *wakan* because it has power to do supernatural things and because mankind may gain its favor by pleasing it or incur its disfavor by displeasing it.

Wakan Tanka and *Taku Wakan* are spirits *(nagipi)* but many of them have material bodies. Some of them do not have a body of matter. These are all spirits that do good to mankind. There are other kinds of spirits that are *wakan* and these do evil to mankind.

The Evil Spirits are many kinds but they are not classed. There is one *Wakan Tanka* who is evil. The other Evil Spirits are not *Wakan Tanka* but they are *wakan*.

A Lakota has a spirit that goes to the spirit world and never dies. He has other spirit-like selves. His breath of life is like a spirit. His strength is like a spirit. His influence is like a spirit. These are all spirits but when his body dies, they go to where they came from and are no more.

The *Wakan Tanka* are the superior and the inferior and there are four of each kind. The *Taku Wakan* are of two classes and there are four of each class. These things are known by the holy men.

This much is known to the people: *Taku Wakan* (all kindred spirits) may affect the affairs of mankind, therefore the Lakota should secure their favor by ceremonies, by offerings and by prayer.

A Lakota may learn the will of *Taku Wakan* by seeking a vision *(hanblapi)*. A holy man should teach how to do this. All the people know that the spirit-like of things may be taken to the spirit world by the spirit of one of mankind. A holy man should teach how this may be done.

The *Wakan Tanka* that have material bodies are the Sun, the Earth, the Rock, the Moon. Those which have no material bodies are *Taku Skan Skan* (the Sky), *Tate* (the atmosphere or the wind), *Wakinyan* (the Winged), and *Wohpe* (the Meteor). The superior *Wakan Tanka* are the Sun, the Sky, the Earth, and the Rock. The inferior *Wakan Tanka* are the Moon, the Wind, the Winged and the Meteor.

The *Taku Wakan* have no material bodies. They may appear to sight as bodies but they are like shadows. They are the *Wakan* of love and of wisdom and of the weather and of games. This is one class. The other class is the spirits of mankind and the ghosts of mankind *(niyapi)* and the strength of mankind and the spirit-like of animals and things. There are four kinds in this class and many of each kind. But the many of each kind is the same as one. This is the knowledge of the holy men. The ceremonial bag or bundle is like a spirit and it must be regarded as such.

17. *Ni, Ini,* and *Initi.* George Sword (translated by Burt Means). (CHS)

The white people call it a sweat lodge. The Lakotas do not understand it so. The Lakota think of it as a lodge to make the body strong and pure. They call it *initi.* This means a tipi to do *ini* in. When a Lakota does the *ini,* he makes his *ni* strong and helps it to bring all out of the body that is hurtful to it. The *ni* of a Lakota is that which he breathes into his body and it goes all through it and keeps it alive. When the *ni* leaves the body of a Lakota, he is dead. When a Lakota says *inipi,* he means he does the *ini.* The *ni* goes all through the body all the time. Sometimes it is weak and then hurtful things get into the body. When this happens, a Lakota should *inipi* in an *initi.*

The spirit of the water is good for the *ni* and it will make it strong. Anything hot will make the spirit of water free and it goes upward. It is like the *ni* which can be seen with the breath on a cold day. An *initi* is made close so that it will hold the spirit of water. Then one in it can breathe it into the body. It will then make the *ni* strong, and they will cleanse all in the body. They wash it and it comes out on the skin like *te mini. Te mini* is sweat. It is water on the body. A Lakota does not *inipi* to make the water on the body. He does it to wash the inside of the body.

He may do this to cure himself when he is sick or he may do it to make himself feel strong. He should always do it when he is about to do some important ceremony so that he will be clean inside before the *Wakan* beings. When a Lakota says *ni,* or *ini* or *inipi,* or *initi,* he does not think about sweat. He thinks about making his *ni* strong so that it will purify him.

---

18. Foundations. Thomas Tyon, William Garnett, Thunder Bear, George Sword, and John Blunt Horn. (AMNH)

Iya is a giant who was the third person created after the sky and the earth. The sky was the first created. The earth was the second thing created. These were all created by *Taku Wakan.*

Iktomi was of the size of an ordinary man. His body was big and round like a bug. His legs and arms were slim like a bug's. His hands and feet were large and long and very powerful. He wore clothes made of buckskin and had a robe made of coonskins.

Heyoka was seen only in a vision. He was the one seen when one saw in a vision the Thunderbird or lightning, or a snow bird, or a swallow, or a horse, or a dog, or a night hawk, or a frog or a dragonfly. He was dressed in a shabby way, and did things that were strange.

When a man sought a vision and saw a white buffalo, he belonged to the White Decorated society.[18] This originated five generations ago. Then a man sought a vision and he saw a white buffalo. He was a Lower Brule. He painted his vision on a robe. Then he chose ten Indians and started the society or clan. The White Decorated carried bows and arrows at feasts and dances and when they were dancing they shot arrows into the sky and the earth. This was to defy *Wakinyan* and *Inyan*.

There was another society called the Silent Eaters or the Big Bellies. They were called this because they were old men and ate in silence, and they were usually fat men. They had a right to a seat in every council. If they wanted to speak, they had [a] right to do so at any time. They listened to all the talk of a camp. If anything was talked about that should not be, then they gathered together and considered the matter in silence, and after they had eaten then they counseled about it. Their decoration was a sash of white skin worn over the left shoulder and hanging down below the waist. They did not go on war parties unless there was a general war. They were warriors who had been on war parties but had grown old. They would fight if the camp was attacked. But they would go with the camp and defend the women and children. Their name in Lakota is *Ahinila wota,* which means those that have matured.[19]

Taku Wakan is all that is mysterious. It means all things mysterious taken together. To invoke *Taku Wakan* is to invoke all the spirits, but especially the mightier spirits. All beasts are *wakan.* These beasts are especially *wakan:* buffalo, horses, elks, wolves, weasels, bears, mountain lions, prairie dogs, ferrets, foxes, beavers, otters.

Some kinds of fish are mysterious. Spiders are mysterious. The dragonfly is mysterious. Some lakes are mysterious. Some cliffs and hills are mysterious. A cliff with round rocks in it is mysterious. Certain cliffs had hieroglyphics on them; they were mysterious. Certain birds, such as the swallows, spotted eagles, eagles, hawks (that is the gray grouse hawks), are mysterious.

Man has one spirit. It left his body when the man died. It went to the spirit world. Some said this was in the west, and some said it was in the south.

Wakan Tanka was the Great Spirit. He was above all spirits. He did nothing. He was chief of all things. Indians did not know much about him. They invoked only the spirits that were under him. They asked him to make the other spirits do as they wished. He stayed above as some Indians thought. He was the first of all things. The Sun was *wakan*. The Sioux worshipped the Sun. They asked him to protect them in battle, to shield them from harm, to help them in raids for horses and women. The Moon was *wakan*. They worshipped her in the place of the Sun at night.

Every person worshipped what he considered his patron. They sought a vision and what they saw in this vision they prayed to and had for their spirit. Persons who saw similar things, or things that belonged together, prayed to all these things, and they formed a sect of that kind. There was a chief to each sect or clan. He directed all the religious ceremonies. He promulgated the forms and customs and when present took the lead in all the ceremonies.

The Sun and the Moon were of the same kind, and they were related in this way. The Sun was a male and the Moon a female. The Earth was *wakan* like the Sun and Moon. The Sun they addressed as Grandfather (or venerable one). The Moon and the Earth they addressed as Grandmother (the same).

Inyan was the Spirit of the Rocks. He was a powerful spirit. The Indians invoked him more often than any other one. They made sacrifices to him frequently: when sick, when in want, when desiring anything, when going to a battle. The most acceptable sacrifice to *Inyan* was a piece of the skin of the person making the sacrifice. Anything could be given as a sacrifice to *Inyan*. The sacrifice was made on anything that represented *Inyan*. Usually this was a stone. A stone of a peculiar kind or shape was usually chosen. This stone was *wakan* until the sacrifice was made, and then it became a common stone. The sacrifice was *wakan* until after it was made and then it was like anything else of its kind. Anyone could take it, but the one who made the sacrifice never took it. Some stones were very *wakan* and no one took anything sacrificed on them. If one sacrificed a piece of their skin to *Inyan*, then they could offer buffalo chips as a sacrifice, and these chips represented whatever the one making the sacrifice wished them to do. The Indian never burned such chips except in ceremonial fires.

The Four Winds were *wakan.* The Indians invoked them. The West Wind was the first. All things that came from the west were *wakan.* There is where *Wakinyan* (the Thunderbird) lives. There is where the sun goes over the edge. All animals were created in the west. There is a high hill in the west, and on top of it is a great plain. There is where the West Wind has his home and the *Wakinyan* and all his family dwell there.

The eagles come from the west. They are the *akicita* of the West Wind. The West Wind is strong and mighty but he is good natured. He travels with the *Wakinyan.* He is invoked to protect from *Waziya,* the North Wind.

The North Wind is the second. He is strong and cruel. He is called *Waziya.* When an Indian is rich and stingy they say he is like *Waziya.* He delights in doing harmful things, and killing living things. He sometimes comes like a man. Then he is a large and strong man and is clothed with furs. The wolf skin is his favorite fur. For this reason many women will not handle the wolf skin. They fear that *Waziya* will kill their children. He has no pity on anything. The Sun and the South Wind are invoked against *Waziya,* and the West Wind also. *Waziya* is at war with *Inyan* and does all he can to harm him. He is at war with *Maka,* the Earth, and does all he can to harm her.

The East Wind is the third. He is not invoked, except when there is an invocation of the daylight or dawn. In the Sun Dance and in the Mystery Dance and in the Buffalo Ceremony, the East Wind is invoked just as the dawn is appearing. He is called on to help the dawn to appear for the dawn brings the day. The Sun begins his daily journey at the home of the East Wind. The East Wind is invoked to help the sun as he rises from his bed so that he may be strong and able to see everything over the whole world. His home is on an island which is rosy red.

Waziya has no *akicita,* except the man *Waziya.* This was his bastard son. His mother stole him away when he was born, for he would have killed him. But when he grew to be a man he went to help his father. The aurora are new born clouds, but *Waziya* kills them as fast as they are born.

The land of the ghosts is far away near the home of *Waziya*. Some Indians believe there are ghosts and say they have seen them. If they see a ghost, no harm will come of it. If they hear a ghost, bad luck will follow. If they hear a ghost mourning, then someone of the family will die soon.

Ghosts appear to war parties, and if they sing the song of victory the party will succeed, but if they mourn, then the party had better go home. When a war party is away, if a ghost is heard in the camp it foretells what is the success of the party. If it sings a song of victory, the party has succeeded, if a song of mourning then the party has met with disaster.

The Indians do not invoke the ghosts. They invoke the good spirits to keep the ghosts from them. When a camp or tipi is abandoned, the ghosts inhabit it. When a war party starts, they may kill an animal such as a deer, elk, or buffalo. This they dedicate to the Sun and Moon and the Earth or *Inyan*, or to the ghosts. They say, "We leave this for you that you may be pleased with us and help us." They may leave only a part of the animal which must be the best part. If they do not make such a sacrifice to the spirits they may help the enemy. This sacrifice is the most often made to *Maka*, the Earth.

A shaman is a wise man who has intercourse with the spirits. He is generally a medicine man. He knows about the medicines and what sickness they are good for. He is respected and feared by the Indians. He is usually the leader of a sect who have certain spirits they have intercourse with. He leads in all the ceremonies. He may promulgate ceremonies of a new kind. If he does this he must prepare himself by the sweat bath according to the customs and seek a vision. If his vision is right he will be told what to do. Then he may organize a new ceremony according to the directions he receives in the vision. Not many dare to attempt to do this. Only very old and very wise men would attempt to do this, for if one should do such a thing wrong the spirits would be displeased with it and punish such a one in some way.

The oldest and most revered ceremony is the *Inipi* (sweat bath). The next oldest is *Hanblepi* (seeking a vision). The sweat bath is to purify one. It drives away all evil things. This ceremony should be had before undertaking anything of importance. It should be done before all ceremonies. It should be done before undertaking to give medicines. It should be done before giving a feast. It should be done before doing anything out of the ordinary things done every day.

Hanbleyapi [the vision quest] is very old. It is very *wakan*. It should be undertaken before attempting to do anything of great importance. One should always perform the ceremony of the sweat bath before seeking a vision. To seek a vision is done in different ways. For most of the things one goes alone on a hill after doing certain things according to the customs, and there awaits the vision. If a vision is sought for things that are of great importance, he should seek the advice of a shaman who is wise on these matters, and do as he directs.

If one wishes for the best of visions, he must seek it of the Sun. He must gaze at the Sun until he sees the vision. The Sun Dance was like this.

If one sees *Wakinyan* or any of his lieutenants in a vision he becomes a follower of *Heyoka* and is a *heyoka*. He is different from all others except the *Heyoka,* and does things differently, and *Wakinyan* hates him. Each one believes in the spirits his sect believes in, and laughs at the spirits that another sect believes in. One seeks a vision to learn what sect he must belong to.

If one wants to become a medicine man he seeks a vision, and if he sees the right thing it will instruct him what he must do. It will also instruct him what medicine he must use. Then when he has related his vision to the wise men, they will tell him what he must do. When they have instructed him, he will belong to a cult in medicine.

The Bear medicine was the most sought because the Bear medicine men could treat all ordinary diseases, and only they were allowed to treat those wounded. The medicine sack was *wakan*. It could be prepared by a shaman only. Its colors were *wakan* and so were its decorations. But the medicines were what the person had been instructed how to use in his vision. One Bear medicine man could instruct another how to use his medicines.

The bird medicine men resorted to jugglery such as sucking through a bone and tricks of various kinds. All the medicine men invoked the aid of the spirits. There were bad spirits who always sought to do harm to mankind. They did not have names but there were many of them. Some of them had names like *Iktomi,* and *Hiya* [*Iya*], and *Can Otidan,* and *Anog Ite.*

Wanagi is the name of ghosts. They are like shadows. They cannot be felt but they can be seen and heard. *Waniya* is a spirit of a man or woman. It is that which makes him live and it leaves him when he dies. It begins when one is born but it continues after one is dead. They go somewhere after death of the body, but they may come back.

When one dies his spirit stays at the place where he dies for a short time, sometimes many days. But if the tipi in which he died is moved or taken down, then the spirit goes away. It may come back to another place. It sometimes comes back and foretells things which will occur. It is most likely to talk to a shaman. But it may talk to one of its kinspeople.

It is not known where it goes. Some think it goes to the place of the ghosts, and some to the home of the West Wind, and some to the home of the South Wind. It is someplace a long journey away and it should be provided with food for the journey. It should be given the things it enjoyed when the body was alive. The spirit cannot take these things with it, but the essence *(ton)* of the things it takes with it and uses them.

When things are given to the spirit, after it has taken the essence of them, then anyone may take the things and use them. But no one will do so unless he is in great want, for otherwise the things might be taken before the spirit has taken the mystery *(wakan)* from them.

The mysterious *(wakan)* of anything is the *tontonsni.* The *tontonsni* is that which causes it to act on other things or on mankind. It is that which causes medicines to act on people. It is that which spirits act on the people when they are not present. It is that from which the shamans and medicine men get their power. It is that which the spirits get from things which are offered them.

Iktomi was the first thing made in the west that matured. He invented language. He saw all animals when they were made, and watched them grow. So he gave them their names. He was very wise in many things, and very foolish in many other things. He delighted in playing jokes on everything. He would fool men and spirits to get something from them and would cheat and lie to them. He was like a man, but he was deformed.

Can Otidan were little beings who stayed in the woods. They would lure hunters away and lose them or they would frighten them so that they would lose their senses. They were like little men and women, but they were very ugly. The women could appear like beautiful young girls, and they would entice young hunters to follow them into the woods, where the males would chase them, and do horrid things to them.

The *Hohnogica* were little people with hair all over their bodies, and with horns and a tail. They were invisible until they wished to be seen. They stayed around the camps. They would stand by the tipi and listen to what the people were talking about. When a mother wished to frighten the children she would tell them that she would call the *Hohnogica*. They sometimes stole little children and carried them away. Sometimes the children would return and tell what the *Hohnogica* did to them.

When a child disappeared, *Maka* (the Earth) was invoked to help return them. The mysterious stones[20] were consulted to learn what had become of the child.

Anog Ite was like a woman with two faces. One face was very beautiful, and the other very ugly. She lived with the spirits of the woods. She was very cunning, and could hide anywhere. She delighted to frighten women who were with child. She would lure hunters away with her beautiful face, and when she had them in her embrace she would turn her horrid face to them and frighten them out of their senses. She had influence *(tontonsni)* over fruits of all kinds, and she would cause them to make sick one who would eat such fruits. Shamans and medicine men knew how to drive her influence away from the fruits or from persons who had eaten such fruits. She caused pregnant women to have pains. She would torture young babies and give them pains in the bowels. When she walks she makes queer noises with her feet, sometimes like bugs rattling, sometimes like bears shuffling, sometimes like stones knocking together, or like any noise. She has many ears and can hear everything for a long distance. It is hard to keep a secret from her. She tortures women during their menstrual periods.

The *tontonsni* of *Iktomi* is very powerful. He discovered colors and plumes and delights in them.

Taku Skanskan is *Wakan Tanka*. He was given power over everything. He especially supervises everything that moves. He presides over races, which he invented. He presides over the movements of camps and war parties and hunting parties. He presides over the flight of migratory birds, and the movements of herds of buffalo, antelope, elk, deer, and mountain sheep. He established the customs that govern in the movement of camps. The men who are entitled to sit in the Mystery Lodge[21] invoke his aid when there is about to be a movement of the camp or a party is about to go for any purpose. Each individual going on a war party is placed in his care. He presides over life and gives life to everything. When *Waziya* comes he is not pleased. He can cause the spirit to return to the body.

Unktehi are like animals. They stay in the waters and live in swampy places. They have four legs and horns which they can draw in or extend them to the skies. They have long hair on the neck and the head which is *wakan*. Their tails are strong and they can shoot or strike with them, and they use their tails as men use their hands. They are always at war with the *Wakinyan*. When they move they make the waves and they destroy all living things they can get hold of. They like dog meat and will give up anything to get it. When one is in the water they will shoot him with their tails and they will cramp and go down so that they may get them. The right thing to do in such cases is to give them a dog. They like a white dog the best. Their females live on the dry land, and their bones are often found in the badlands. Their teeth were like knives so they could cut anything. The females are called *Unhcegila*. Their power lies in their tails, and if they lose their tails they are weak and foolish and can do no harm.

Everything has a *tonwan* (spiritual essence). *Wakan Tanka* is the *tonwan* of all spirits. Red is the color that spirits like best. Blue they like also. And they like yellow, or brownish yellow. They like all colors but these they like best.

Red is the color that belongs to the Sun. He shows this color in the morning before he starts on his daily journey, and at evening when he goes over the steep. This color is invoked by shamans, and it represents the coming and the going of the Sun. When one wears red the Sun is pleased and will listen to such a one. The Indians are red, so they are the favorite people of the Sun. The Sun provides everything for them. White is the favorite color of *Waziya*. The white people are like *Waziya*. They have no mercy on the red people.

Wa is the white of *Waziya* (the snow). *Wasicun* is the *tontonsni* of the snow storms. White men are called *wasicun*.

---

19. *Wohpe* and the Gift of the Pipe.[22] Finger, March 25, 1914. (AMNH)

Question: You say that when *Wohpe* gave the pipe to the Lakotas she was in their camp for many days. Was it she that gave the first pipe to the Lakotas?

Answer: Yes.

Question: Can you tell me how she did this?

Answer: Yes, but it is a long story.

Question: Will you tell it?

Answer: (The legend of the giving of the pipe to the Lakotas)

In the long ago the Lakotas were in camp and two young men lay upon a hill watching for signs. They saw a long way in the distance a lone person coming, and they ran further toward it and lay on another hill hidden so that if it were an enemy they would be able to intercept it or signal to the camp. When the person came close, they saw that it was a woman and when she came nearer that she was without clothing of any kind except that her hair was very long and fell over her body like a robe. One young man said to the other that he would go and meet the woman and embrace her and if he found her good, he would hold her in his tipi. His companion cautioned him to be careful for this might be a buffalo woman who could enchant him and take him with her to her people and hold him there forever. But the young man would not be persuaded and met the woman on the hill next to where they had watched her. His companion saw him attempt to embrace her and there was a cloud closed about them so that he could not see what happened. In a short time the cloud disappeared and the woman was alone. She beckoned to the other young man and told him to come there and assured him that he would not be harmed. As she spoke in the Lakota language the young man thought she belonged to his people and went to where she stood.

When he got there, she showed him the bare bones of his companion and told him that the Crazy Buffalo had caused his companion to try to do her harm and that she had destroyed him and picked his bones bare. The young man was very much afraid and drew his bow and arrow to shoot the woman, but she told him that if he would do as she directed, no harm would come to him and he should get any girl he wished for his woman, for she was *wakan* and he could not hurt her with his arrows. But if he refused to do as she should direct, or attempt to shoot her, he would be destroyed as his companion had been. Then the young man promised to do as she should bid him.

She then directed him to return to the camp and call all the council together and tell them that in a short time they would see four puffs of smoke under the sun at midday. When they saw this sign they should prepare a feast, and all sit in the customary circle to have the feast served when she would enter the camp, but the men must all sit with their head bowed and look at the ground until she was in their midst. Then she would serve the feast to them and after they had feasted she would tell them what to do: that they must obey her in everything; that if they obeyed her in everything they would have their prayers to the *Wakan Tanka* answered and be prosperous and happy; but that if they disobeyed her or attempted to do her any harm, they would be neglected by *Wakan Tanka* and be punished as the young man who had attempted to embrace her had been.

Then she disappeared as a mist disappears so that the young man knew that she was *wakan*. He returned to the camp and told these things to the people and the council decided to do as she had instructed the young man. They made preparation for the feast and in a few days they saw four puffs of black smoke under the sun at midday, so they prepared for a feast and all dressed in their best clothing and sat in the circle ready to be served and every man bowed his head and looked toward the ground. Suddenly the women began uttering low exclamations of admiration, but all the men steadily kept their eyes toward the ground except one young man and he looked toward the entrance of the camp. He saw a puff of black smoke which blew into his eyes and a voice said, "You have disobeyed me and there will be smoke in your eyes as long as you live." From that time, that young man had very sore eyes and all the time they were as if biting smoke was in them.

Then the woman entered the circle and took the food and served it, first to the little children and then to the women and then she bade the men to look up. They did so and saw a very beautiful woman dressed in the softest deer skin which was ornamented with fringes and colors more beautiful than any woman of the Lakota had ever worked. Then she served the men with food, and when they had feasted she told them that she wished to serve them always; that they had first seen her as smoke and that they should always see her as smoke. Then she took from her pouch a pipe and willow bark and Lakota tobacco and filled the pipe with the bark and tobacco and lighted it with a coal of fire.

She smoked a few whiffs and handed the pipe to the chief and told him to smoke and hand it to another. Thus the pipe was passed until all had smoked. She then instructed the council how to gather the bark and the tobacco and prepare it, and gave the pipe into their keeping, telling them that as long as they preserved this pipe she would serve them. But she would serve them in this way. When the smoke came from the pipe she would be present and hear their prayers and take them to the *Wakan Tanka* and plead for them that their prayers should be answered.

After this she remained in this camp for many days and all the time she was there everyone was happy for she went from tipi to tipi with good words for all. When the time came for her to go, she called all the people together and bade the women to build a great fire of dried cottonwood, which they did. Then she directed all to sit in a circle about the fire and the shaman to have an abundance of sweetgrass. She stood in the midst of the circle and when the fire had burned to coals she directed the shaman to place on it the sweetgrass. This made a cloud of smoke and the woman entered the smoke and disappeared. Then the shamans knew that it was *Wohpe* who had given the pipe and they appointed a custodian for it with instructions that it was to be kept sacred and used only on the most solemn and important occasions. With due ceremony they made wrappers for the pipe so that it is *wakan*. The shamans instructed the people that they could make other pipes and use them and that *Wohpe* would be in the smoke of any such pipe if smoked with proper solemnity and form.

Thus it was that the Beautiful Woman brought the pipe to the Lakotas.

---

20. Consecrating a Pipe. Ringing Shield. (AMNH)

(This expression was used by Ringing Shield, an old shaman.) The Spirit Pipe *(Candahupa Wakan)* was consecrated *(wogluzepi)* by many shamans *(wicasa wakan ota)* by a binding dedication *(woiciconzipi)*. He said: the *Unktehi* are the greatest powers in the waters and no power can trouble them there. Their power lies in their horns and their tails. They can push these out or draw them in as they wish. They can push them up to the clouds. In old times, men have seen them do this. They wave with their tails and this makes the waves on the waters. They are friends to all animals and birds that live in or on the waters. The turtles talk with them.

Tunkan is the spirit which fell from the sky. It is a stone. It knows all things which are secret. It can tell where things are when they are lost or stolen. It is the friend *(kola)* of *Taku Skanskan* (the spirit or power which causes things to vanish like smoke or clouds that fade away).

(The North Wind) [. . .][23] *Wohpe* and a son was born who is *Woziya* [*Waziya*] (The Man from the North).

Iktehi [*Unktehi*] is *tuwa wakan* (that which is very mysterious). Plumes and down and red paint belong to him. The Shadow Lodge[24] is erected to him. He gives the *wakan* medicine bag. This must be made of the skin of an animal or bird, as it is shown in the vision. It must contain something of an animal and of a bird and of a reptile and of the vegetables.

---

21. Knowledge and Spirits. Ringing Shield. (CHS)

What a man knows is what has been done. What the spirits know is what has been done and what will be done in the future. The spirits can tell what is to be in the future. They can tell this to anyone. If one wishes to talk with the spirits he must purify his body. He must do nothing that the spirits do not want him to do. He must be a good man. He must purify his body by taking the vapor bath. When taking the bath, he must sing his song and use medicines that will please the spirits.

Sweetgrass and sage please the spirits. A shaman can tell him what other medicines he must use. He should ask a shaman how to do when he is taking the bath. He should seek a vision and if he sees the vision the spirits will talk to him. If he has pleased the spirits, they will tell him what he wants to know. If they do not want to tell him this, they will tell him something so that he will know that he should not be told the things he wants to know.

There are a great many spirits. They control everything; and they know everything. They can make a man do anything they wish. They can make animals and trees and grass do as they wish. They can talk with animals and they can make animals talk with men. The spirits go about in the world all the time and they make everything do as they please. Some spirits may want things done one way and others may want them done differently. Then the strongest spirits will overcome the weaker. Some spirits are very powerful and others are not so powerful. Any spirit is more powerful than a man.

A man may be hated by a spirit and then that spirit will do him harm. But he may employ a more powerful spirit and then defeat the spirit that wants to do him harm. Some spirits always try to do harm to someone or something. The good spirits watch them so that they must do harm secretly.

If a man is a good man he can please the good spirits so that they will guard him from the bad spirits. He can please them so that they will be his friends all the time and help him in everything that he asks them to.

Some spirits are very great and powerful. They do the mysterious things. The Great Spirits are all akin to each other and no other spirit can do anything that they do not wish. The Sun is a Great Spirit and knows everything and sees everything. The Spirit of the Air is a Great Spirit and he makes the grass and trees grow and the water flow. The Spirit of the Earth is a Great Spirit and he holds up everything.

Men should be careful and not offend the spirits. The spirits hate a coward or one who lies. They are friends to the brave man and the good hunter. They are pleased with the man who has many children and will listen to him and help him so that he may be successful in his hunting. They will help a brave man to get many women, and when he is in a war party. They will help him to get many horses. They love a man who bears the coup stick and has scalps in his tipi.

If a man is good and wise, he may become a shaman and be the friend of the spirits. He must learn the songs and the ceremony. Shamans will teach him these. If he is a wise shaman, the spirits will teach him how to do mysterious things. They will give him mysterious power over other men. The spirits love a generous man. They love an industrious woman and will help her in all her work. The shaman should know the word[s] of a shaman. He talks in the spirit language.

---

22. The Stars. Ringing Shield. May 1903. (CHS)

A wise man said this. The stars are *wakan*. They do not care for the earth or anything on it. They have nothing to do with mankind. Sometimes they come to the world and sometimes the Lakotas go to them. There are many stories told of these things. No medicine can be made to the stars. They have nothing to do with anything that moves and breathes. A holy man knows about them. This must not be told to the people. If the people knew these things, they would pull the stars from above. There is one star for the evening and one for the morning. One star never moves and it is *wakan*. Other stars move in a circle about it. They are dancing in the dance circle.

There are seven stars. This is why there are seven council fires among the Lakotas.[25] Sometimes there are many stars and sometimes there are not so many. When there are not so many, the others are asleep. The spirit way is among the stars. This moves about so that bad spirits can not find it. *Wakan Tanka* keeps the bad spirits away from the spirit way. The spirit way begins at the edge of the world. No man can find it. *Taku Skanskan* is there and he tells the good spirits where to go to find it. The winds will show a good spirit where to go to find the beginning of this trail. The bad spirits must wander always on the trail of the winds. The stars hide from the sun. They must fear him. So mankind should not try to learn about them. It is not good to talk about them. It is not good to fight by the light of the stars. They must be evil for they fear the sun.

---

23. Spirits. Short Feather, June 6, 1898. (AMNH)

The Sioux are more like the Great Spirits than any other of mankind. In the beginning the spirits talked with the Sioux. The Sioux and the Great Spirits were like friends. The spirits are still among the Sioux. The spirits are jealous of the Sioux but they are more friendly to the Sioux than to any other of mankind.

The region beyond the pines is beyond the pines that grow on the edge of the earth. There is where the spirits of good Sioux go when they die. The spirit of a bad Sioux can not find the trail to the region beyond the pines. It must forever wander in search of this trail.

Skan is the Great Spirit. He governs everything that moves. The color of *Skan* is blue. *Wakinyan* is not a Great Spirit. He is the friend of *Skan*. He is the enemy of the water monsters.

The water monsters make the floods. They spew them out of their mouths. They make springs. They inhabit swampy places. They are very large. Some men have seen them. They can reach the clouds with their horns and tails. When they take people or animals down to their places, they eat them. Or they may keep them. They took a girl down in the Missouri River and kept her for a long time. Her father threw a white dog in the river and the monsters took the dog and gave up the girl.

The Bear is the friend of the Great Spirit. He is very wise. He taught the shaman the secrets of the ceremonies. He teaches the medicine men about the medicines and the songs that they should sing.

He is a spirit that comes to the shaman when the shaman seeks a vision. When a man sees the Bear in a vision, that man must become a medicine man.

Iya is a Great Spirit. He is a bad spirit. He does harm to everything. He does not take part in the council of the Great Spirits. He is jealous of the Sioux and tries to do them harm all the time. A shaman who has *Iya* for his councilor is a bad shaman. The people all fear such a shaman. He can make people into animals. He can kill people by incantations. He can make bad medicines.

---

24. The Future. No Flesh, 1899. (CHS)

This is what the old men taught. This is what the Lakotas believed long ago. Some did not know about it but they all believed it. The wise men knew about it.

Men should ask the *Wakan* to help them and they should give gifts to the *Wakan*. The *Wakan* is everywhere and in everything. It can do things to men that no man can do. The Lakota should please the *Wakan* by songs and by ceremonies and by drums and by rattles. Everyone should have a song that will please his *Wakan*. Everyone should have the *Wakan* he chooses. No one should do anything without asking his *Wakan*.

The *Wakan* is like a spirit. The spirit lives forever. When a man dies, his friends should give gifts to his spirit. The spirit was not his life. His life was his ghost. His ghost is his breath. When a man dies, his spirit stays near for a time: the like-a-spirit of the gifts is pleasing to it. It takes them to the spirit land. The good spirit goes to the spirit world. The bad spirit does not go there.

No man knows where the spirit world is. It is at the other end of the spirit way. The ancient people said it was beyond the pines. The pines are at the edge of the world. It is beyond the path of the winds. There is no cold or hunger or work in the spirit world. The spirit stays in the spirit world. It can come to the world. It can talk to mankind. A *wakan* man can talk with a spirit. A spirit can talk with its friends. If a spirit talks to one, that one is in danger. One who hears a spirit should ask his *Wakan* to help him. He should make gifts to the *Wakan*. He should ask a *wakan* man to help him. He should do as the *wakan* man bids him.

---

25. The Medicine Bag. Red Cloud, Meat, and No Flesh. (CHS)

The medicine bag of the Lakota is called *wopiye*. It is *wakan*. The shaman makes it *wakan*. *Skanskan* taught the Lakotas about the *wopiye*. It is the place where good is. It should not be handled in a disrespectful way. If it is not kept as it should be, the *sicun* will bring disaster.

Wopiyepi should be given in the *Wacipi Wakan*. They should be made of something dreamed of. Medicine may be kept in them. *Wasicunpi* should remain in them.

A man can give his medicine bag to another. He can not give his medicines away. When the bag is given, the *sicunpi* go out of it. A medicine bag is not good for anyone except the one who has dreamed.

A medicine bag may be very large or it may be very small or it may be of any size to suit the one who has it. It must be like the dream.

Gnaska and *Gicila* fly from a medicine bag. Two-Faces flies from a medicine bag. *Can Oti* flies from a medicine bag.[26] A woman can have a medicine bag.

---

26. *Wakinyan.* Seven Rabbits. (CHS)

Wasicunpi may be seen in visions. They may be anything. They are the guardian spirits of the Lakotas.

Wakinyan is many in one. They are black and yellow and scarlet and blue. Their symbolic color is yellow. The black have four joints in their wings and six quills in each wing. They have long beaks. The yellow have no beaks; they have eight joints in each wing. The scarlet have strong beaks and eight joints in each wing. The blue are round like a ball and have no eyes or ears. The *Wakinyan* made the wild rice and the long and short awned grass.

27. Spirits. From Addresses by Shamans at a *Wacipi Wakan* (Holy Dance). (CHS and AMNH)

One shaman:

Everything has a spirit. A war club has a spirit. A bow has a spirit. A drum has a spirit. A prairie dog has a spirit. A prairie dog has two spirits: one the spirit like the tree and one the spirit like the breath of life. The breath of life is given by *Wakanskanskan. Wicasa Wakan* can talk with these spirits. The *wakan* plumes of birds have a spirit. The *wakan* plumes of the medicine bag are very powerful.

Unktehi gave the *Wacipi Wakan.*[27] His *akicita* are the lizards, serpents, owls, and eagles. There is war between the *Wakinyan* and the *Unktehi.* The *Wakinyan* gave the war ax and the spear.

Another shaman:

The Sun is *Wakan Tanka.* Indians should always address him in invoking the great powers. They should pray to him.

Another shaman:

Inyan is older than *Iktomi.* He is entitled to the red paint. He knows all things on earth. He can tell where stolen horses are. He can tell where the herds of buffalo are. They have gone back into the earth.[28]

28. Spirits. Thomas Tyon.[29] (AMNH)

In olden times, the Oglala Indians believed that there were spirits belonging to places, things, animals, birds, insects, and reptiles. Each of these spirits had possession of that which they belonged to and controlled it. The disembodied spirits of men were called shades or shadows. There was no well-recognized Great Spirit, though some Indians thought there was some great power like a chief over the spirits but they did not know what it was. Most of the Indians know nothing about this. There was no bad spirit or influence but nobody knew just what these were.[30] The spirits of the other things could use these evil influences or they could combat them and overcome them when they wished to do so.

When a shaman or a medicine man wanted to have the aid of the spirits, he called on them and made propitiatory offerings to them so as to please them and they came to his aid if they were pleased. The only time when these spirits were seen or talked to was when the person sought a vision. Then he did not know what spirit would come; but some spirits would come and talk to him. The spirits would come and aid one at times whether such a one called upon them or not, that is, when they were pleased with such a one. They would bring evil on one who did things which displeased them.

The evil influences would come on anyone if they could or some one might bring them onto another and hurt that other in this way. The good spirits could be called to aid one who was suffering from these evil influences. The spirits were pleased with invocation properly made, with doing good things, with feasts, with smoke of willow bark or of sweetgrass. These things drove away the evil influences and the smoke of the sage kept them away.

If one sought a vision and talked with a spirit, it would tell him what to do. If he did these things, the spirits were all pleased. But if he did not do them, then they abandoned him to the evil influences or brought them on him. These evil influences were the cause of most of the sickness of the older Indians. The way to cure the sickness was to get the aid of some spirit and drive them away.

These spirits were: *Wakinyan* (*wa,* snow, white in the air;

kinyan, to fly, flash; flashing white). The cause of thunder; a fabled bird, hidden in the clouds whose voice is the thunder and the glance of whose eye is the lightning. This spirit governs the weather, the clouds, and the rain and has little to do with the affairs of men. It may be invoked and pleased or displeased and will give good weather or bad as it sees fit.

Mahpiya (the heavens, the clouds, the sky). A presiding spirit over these, which hears invocations, is pleased or displeased, and shows this by giving or withholding pleasant weather, rains, storms, frosts, and dews or by hot winds sent as punishment.

Maka (the Earth). A presiding Spirit of the Earth which hears invocations and is pleased or displeased and shows this by giving good or bad seasons and by producing plenty or scanty vegetation. This spirit especially presides over the medicines that come from the earth and gives to them potencies for good or evil according to its pleasure and according to the familiarity of the shaman or medicine man with it and the methods of his invocations.

Waziya (*wa*, snow; *zi*, green; *ya*, doing with the mouth; *wazi*, green in snow, pines; *waziya*, mouthing of the pines; *ta*, at; *waziyata*, at the mouthing of the pines, the north). *Waziya*, a mythical giant at the north who causes the cold north wind by blowing from his mouth. He comes near during the winter and recedes during the summer and is in continual contest with the south winds. He presides over snow and ice and guards the entrance to the dance of the shadows of the north (the aurora borealis). The seven council fires burned (the seven nations of the Sioux confederacy lived) in a land where the trees were small and the leaves fell before the coming of each winter.

The seven fires were lighted in a circle (the nations were camped together) and *Waziya* appeared in the council. He was a large man and clothed in heavy furs. He said, "Why do you stay here where the trees are small and the leaves fall? Come with me and I will show you where the trees grow tall and the leaves are green all winter." So the shamans counseled together and agreed to send some of the people with him. They went on a journey of many days and found it was true that he had told them. Then the Dakotas went to that land. But all did not go. That is where the shadows of the dead dance.

(At present the Dakotas hold Christmas festivals and St. Nicholas is represented at the Christmas tree by someone dressed in heavy furs and the older Indians gave this character the name of *Waziya* and the younger children speak of this festival as "the time when *Waziya* will come.")

Wiyohiyanpa (*wi,* sun; *yo,* to do; *hi,* to arrive; *yanpa,* the place: the place where the sun arrives). The East, the Spirit of the East which presides over the day.

Okaga (to renew or make after the same kind). The South, the Spirit of the South which may be invoked; it presides over the south winds and warm weather and over the production of fruits and grains.

Wiyohipeyata (*wi,* sun; *yo,* to do; *hi,* to arrive; *hpeye,* to lie down, to retire; *ta,* the place: the place where the sun retires). The West, the Spirit of the West which presides over the evening and the coming darkness and is present at the death of man and animals.

Tatanka (*ta,* beast; *tanka,* great, large: great beast). The Buffalo Bull, the Spirit of the Buffalo Bull which presides over fecundity, virtue, industry, and the family. It also patronizes hunting. This spirit remains with the skull of the buffalo and is at continual conflict with the Spirit of the Coyote. It is the guardian of young women and women during their menstrual periods and during pregnancy.

(*Tatanka* appears to be partly mythical as a great beast that once inhabited the earth and was the mightiest of beasts and was seen by men in a vision. The large fossils of the mammoth and titanotherium were believed to have belonged to this mythical animal.)

Mato (the Bear). The Spirit of the Bear which presides over love and hate and bravery and wounds and many kinds of medicines. He was the patron of mischief and fun.

Mica[31] (the Coyote). The Spirit of the Coyote which presides over thieving and cowardice and all mischief of a malevolent kind. This spirit was continually trying to outwit *Tatanka.*

Sungmanitu (the Wolf). The Spirit of the Wolf which presided over the chase and war parties.

Sunka (the Dog). The Spirit of the Dog presided over friendship and cunning.

Hehaka (Male Elk). The Spirit of the Male Elk presided over sexual relationship.

Capa (the Beaver). The Spirit of the Beaver was the patron of work, provision, and of domestic faithfulness.

Wambli (the Eagle). The Spirit of the Eagle presided over councils, hunters, war parties, and battles.

Cetan (the Hawk). The spirit presided over swiftness and endurance.

Zuzeca (the Snake). The Spirit of the Snake presided over the ability to do things slyly, to go about unknown and unseen, and of lying.

Hnaska[32] (the Frog). The Spirit of the Frog was the patron of occult powers.

Hogan (the Fish). The Spirit of the Fish was the patron of ablution and presided over the powers of the waters.

Keya (the Turtle). The Spirit of the Turtle was the guardian of life and patron of surgery and controlled accidents.

Unktomi[33] (the Spider). Also a mythical being like a goblin. The presiding genius of pranks and practical jokes with powers to work magic over persons and things.

Unktehi. A mythical being like a goblin whose habitation was the waters and whose disposition was malicious. It presided over floods, drowning, and accidents in water. It also caused alkali and muddy or bad waters.

Unhcegila. A mythical monster of the land something like the dragon; it presided over mysterious disappearances or deaths.

These spirits were not separate from the things. They were the spirit of, but [also] the power of these things. Then there were other spirits that no one knew what they were or where they abode. These spirits could take the form of anything and so appear to anyone, or they could appear as a shade or a voice. There were spirits of places, as a hill, or a camping place or a battle ground or anywhere that was marked by some event. There were spirits of the forest and of the prairie.

The spirit of man was different. It was like this shadow. A man or woman might have two or more spirits. One spirit of a man might be good and the other bad. One might be brave and the other cowardly. One might be true and the other false.

When a man died, his shade left him and went to the land of the shades. First, after death it lingered for a time near where the man died. It then wanted the things it had during the man's life. It would try to communicate with anyone who was at the place where he died. After a little while it grew tired of waiting and started for the land of the shades. It might go a little way and then come back again. But it finally went on the journey. If it had the implements the man had used in life it could use them on this journey but if it had them not it could make the journey without them. But it was best pleased when it was supplied with all it had in life and then it would return and help the friends who supplied these to it. These were supplied by killing a horse and a dog and placing them together with the war and hunting and other implements with the body of the dead person. The spirit of all the things placed with a dead body went with the shade of that body.

If another, a friend or an enemy, died at or near the same time, the two shades made the journey to the land of the shades together. If it was a friend, they went together as friends and if it was an enemy, the stronger conquered the weaker and held it in bondage forever.

The land of shades is away in the northern skies and the shades dwell there in peace and plenty without sickness or sorrow of any kind and amuse themselves by games, singing, and dancing and with agreeable women and fine horses. They never know cold or heat or hunger or thirst. They visit and hunt at their pleasure. They may come to their people who are alive when they wish to do so and can hear the calls of their friends for their aid and can meddle with the affairs of the living. If one has been a coward or a very mean person when alive, the Spirit of the North meets him at a narrow place on the trail to the land of the shades and trips him up so that he falls into the waters, and *Unktehi,* the Spirit of the Waters, does with him as he will.

The spirits like to receive gifts and be praised and they will come and help anyone who knows how to please them. They can see and hear everything everywhere all the time. One spirit may want to do one way and another spirit may want to do another way. Then the strongest spirit prevails or the spirit that receives the most presents or is the best pleased will prevail. These spirits know what is past and what is now and what will be in the future and they can reveal these things to men.

The evil influences are in the air. They go about in the dark. They are under the direction of the other spirits and especially the Spirit of the Spider. They may abide in a person but can be driven out by the other spirits, by medicine, or by exorcism. Any new or strange thing is the work of the spirits. A shaman can, by his incantation, tell what spirit is accountable for anything. The

Indians did not worship the spirits. They only feared them and endeavored to propitiate them or obtain their help in what they desired to do.

---

29. The Spirit of the Buffalo. Bad Wound. (CHS)

The buffalo were given to the Lakotas by *Inyan*. They came from the earth. Their tipi is in the earth. They know all the ceremonies. They dance in their tipi. Where the round depressions are on the prairies is where the buffalo danced.

The Crazy Buffalo is very bad. Young buffalo cows may become like women. Their children will be like the children of men. If they run away, they become like cows, and their children become like calves.

The spirit of the buffalo stays with the skull until the horns drop off. If the horns are put on the skull, the spirit returns to it. The earth eats the horns and when they are eaten the spirit goes to the buffalo tipi in the earth. The way to the buffalo tipi is far in the west.

Tatanka is like a Buffalo Bull. He is like a spirit. He is *wakan*. He helps men who hunt. He helps women who work. If a woman is lazy or lewd, he will not help her. He is pleased to see a woman with child.

---

30. The Four Winds. Red Rabbit. (AMNH)

The Four Winds are *wakan*. They have their homes in the west and the north and the east and the south. In the west is a high mountain and on top of the mountain there is a flat place. This is where He of the West *(Wiyohpeyate Wicasa)* dwells. Sometimes he is called *Yata*.[34]

With him dwells The Winged Ones (*Wakinyan,* the Thunderbirds). They do not live in the same tipi with him. But they live on the same high mountain. They often travel together. When The Winged Ones fight anything, then *Yata* helps them.

Yata is a giant but he is invisible. In the long ago, men saw him and talked with him. Since then, men only have seen him in a vision *(ihanble).* Now he is never seen. His father was *Tate,* who had four other sons. He had no mother so he will never die. His father gathered stuff from the land of the spirits *(wasicunpi)* and from this he made his sons.

The land of the spirits is far beyond the place of the pines. When the *wasicunpi* dance and *Wohpe Wakan* dances with them, the light of *Wohpe Wakan's* hair flashes through the air and men can see the light as it dances far beyond the pines. When *Woziya* [*Waziya*] dances with them, his breath comes, cold and disagreeable.

The mountain where *Yata* dwells is surrounded with water. At night the sun lies there to rest, and when the moon is strong she takes his place and watches over the world. *Yata* is not wise and often does things foolishly. But he is not vicious, and when he does any harm he will try to remedy it. He is blind, or nearly so. He listens to the counsel of the other powers. His aides (*tonweyapi;* soldiers, marshals, or spies and counselors) are the hawks and bats. They are *wakan.* He is fond of ceremonies. He gives omens.

Woziya is the North Wind. He is a giant with a vicious disposition. What he touches grows cold and dies. When he breathes hard, it is cold weather. He causes the snow and frost and ice. He has a robe of fur and all his clothing is of fur. Sometimes he is jolly and full of fun. He is always at war with his brother *Okaga.*

Wohpe Wakan is *Okaga's* woman, and *Woziya* tried to steal her. That was before the world was. Since then these brothers have been at war. *Yata* tries to keep them from war. Sometimes he fights with them, sometimes helping one and sometimes the other. *Iktomi* stirs up strife among the Four Winds when he can so that he can have fun watching them fight.

Woziya has for his *tonweyapi* the white owl, the raven, and the wolf. His tipi is far away near the land of the *wasicunpi,* and he visits them and joins in their dances. His food is ice and his drink is snow water. He is invisible, but sometimes he visits the people, and then they can see him.He always comes to bring some tidings of things to come to pass or from people who have died and gone to the spirit land.

The manes *(wanagipi)* of the dead people pass by his tipi when they travel to the spirit world. He talks with them, and they tell him all they know. If they are worthy he permits them to pass on. If they are unworthy he pushes them off, and they must wander for all time in the world forever cold and hungry and naked. If a shadow has with it the shadow of an enemy, it may be substituted for itself and pushed off the trail instead of the first shadow.

The trail by the tipi of *Woziya* is high in the sky, and he keeps it covered with ice so that it is slippery and hard to travel. When one dies, his shadow must rest and prepare itself before undertaking the journey. It stays near the body, or where it left the body, for many days until it feels able to make the journey. So food and presents should be placed near the body for the manes until it has departed on the journey. Beyond the home of *Woziya* it is never cold and never hot. There is plenty of everything there. Birds and beasts fear *Woziya,* and when he comes, they fly to the home of *Okaga* and beg his help.

Wiyohiyanpa is the East Wind. In the mysterious language he is called *Yanpa.* Beyond the lands, in the waters is a flat island. This is the home of *Yanpa.* There he has a bed made of the down from water birds, and ornamented with the plumes from under the eagle's tail. Here he lies and sleeps the most of the time. The sands of this island are shining yellow. This is where the sun begins his daily journey to view the world. When the moon is eaten away by the mice and the gophers, or when *Heyoka* bites her, she gets her strength and grows again on this island.

The sun and the moon see everything and know everything on the earth, and they tell all this to *Yanpa.* His *tonweyapi* are the night hawks. The night comes up from the waters about this island. When *Yanpa* is not disturbed he is pleasant. When he is disturbed he is very unpleasant, but he does not destroy things. He sleeps the most of the time and goes abroad in the evening. If he is compelled to go about before evening he grumbles and quarrels with everything. So all ceremonial lodges have their doors towards the east, so that *Yanpa* may be pleased.

The sick people invoke *Yanpa,* that he may give them respite from pain, and give them rest, because he knows how good it is.

When *Yanpa* is seen in a vision he can tell all that has been. But he cannot tell what will be.

Itokaga is the South Wind. In the mysterious language he is called *Ito* and *Okaga*. His home is at that side of the earth where the sun stands when he has made half his journey over the world. His tipi is very large, and made of vines growing so closely that no rain or wind can pass through them. In this tipi it is always pleasant, though there is never a fire there. At the rear of the tipi, opposite the door is where *Okaga* rests. At the side of the tipi his woman, *Wohpe,* rests.

Okaga makes beautiful things. He first made the flowers and the seeds. When *Wohpe* first came to his father's tipi she fell from the stars and she had a beautiful dress. *Okaga* learned from this dress to make beautiful things. His younger brother, *Yamni* [*Yumni*], lives in his tipi. *Yamni* is small and weak, and he does no work. But he is the messenger for many of the supernatural people *(oyate wakan).*

Okaga is the giver of life. The water fowls and the meadow-larks are his *akicita.* The cranes are his criers. His breath is warm and brings good weather. He is ever kind, his heart is good towards all, so that it is not necessary to invoke him to get his help. His only contention is with his brother *Woziya,* who tried to steal his woman.

Tate always was. He is the younger brother of the sun. His tipi is far away towards the land of the *wasicunpi*[35] (the aurora borealis). He never appeared to mankind. He visits his sons in their tipis. He has nothing to do with the affairs of mankind or animals. Only very venerable shamans know anything of him *(wicasa wakan ksapapi,* rendered wise or venerable shamans). He presided at the institution of the *Wowaci Wakan* (the mysterious dance). He gave to all the mysterious people their *ton* (influence, or power, emission of power).

---

31. The Sacred Language. Lone Bear, August 1900. (ANMH)

Tobtob governs all things. This is the Great Spirit. *Tobtob* is all kinds of good spirits. It is Four-times-four. There are four of each kind of spirits. The bad spirits are not of the *Tobtob*. *Tobtob* is the language of the shamans.

Hunonp is of the language of the shamans. It is the Spirit Bear who is of the *Tobtob*. He taught the shamans all their secrets. No one can talk with *Hunonp* without understanding the language of the shamans. The Bear knows all things about *Tobtob*. He knows all things about medicines. He took pity on the Sioux when the spirits were angry with them. The spirits were angry with the Sioux because they left the middle of the world.[36]

32. *Iktomi*. Old Horse. (AMNH)

Iktomi[37] is of the oldest. He is full of tricks. He plays his pranks on the *Wakan* and on the Lakotas. When the Lakotas came from the middle of the world he would go into their lodges and then play tricks on them. He persuaded them to scatter about everywhere, and then they would be with their lodges alone, and when the enemy came upon them he would laugh at them.

Then the Wise One told them that *Iktomi* was trying to destroy them. So the Wise One told them to stay together. He told them to make a lodge for him, and he would meet them in the lodge and teach them.

So the Lakotas came together in one camp like they were in the middle of the world. Then they built a lodge for the Wise One. The Wise One met the shamans in this lodge and told them many things. He told them to make their camp in a circle so that each door of each lodge would be towards the door of every other lodge. Then if *Iktomi* came into a lodge, everyone would know it.

He told them to place the entrance of the lodge towards the east. Then every visitor who came to the camp must come in by the entrance. The entrance should be towards the east because the sun begins his journey there. Then he told them to always make a lodge for the camp, so that the wise men could meet in it. He told them to make a fire in this lodge when they met there to counsel.

Iktomi is a little one. His body is like a fat bug. His legs are like the spider's, but he has hands and feet like a man. He talks with men and beasts and with everything that lives and with trees and stones. He plays tricks on beasts and birds. He can make himself invisible. He is weak, and he must get things by his tricks. He is the friend of the great Evil Spirit, but he fools the Evil Spirit very often.

He can make himself appear like an old man. When an old man comes to a lodge, he should be watched. If he proposes a game, then it is *Iktomi*. Sometimes the women feed him, and then he will dung in the lodge, then they know that it is *Iktomi*. If a stranger meets one and proposes some game or trick, then it is *Iktomi*. The shamans can make a charm that will defeat *Iktomi*.

He is the friend of Two-Face. If a stranger proposes to lead a young man to a woman, then this is *Iktomi*. The woman is Two-Face.

Iktomi is *heyoka* for he talks with the Thunderbird. He will not play his tricks on the *heyoka*. *Iktomi* can ride on a dog, and then the dog's hair comes off and this makes sores on the dog. He rides wolves and coyotes. *Iktomi* is afraid of a sweat lodge. He cannot enter a lodge for the camp (*tiotipi*).

---

33. *Hanbleceya.* Thunder Bear. (AMNH)

A custom the Sioux Indians had for many years: if one wished to hold a Sun Dance and had not the time, they practiced this. If a child is sick and they wish it to recover, they promise to do this. If a child dies, they do this. If they are to have a fight with the enemy and want to conquer, they do this. If one wishes to marry a girl and fears that he may not get her, he does this. If they have a strong desire for anything, then they do this. To prepare for it they dress with a robe only and naked, take a pipe and take four flags, which they place to the points of the compass, and kinnikinic and tobacco mixed, which they tie in little bags on each flag.

This dreamer sees some animal who tells him about medicine. Then they go to the top of a hill and prepare a place by leveling it and putting up the flags about it and remain there until they have a vision, from one to five nights without eating or drinking. Before they go, they sweat and they do so after they come back. Before going up he calls medicine men to go in the sweat house and they advise him in regard to his undertaking and encourage him. After he comes back, he takes the same men into the sweat house with him. Some men are afraid to go in the sweat house with him. When he returns, then the head medicine man whom he has chosen advises him to tell the truth, etc., and then he tells what he has seen, if anything. This then becomes a matter of general knowledge.

This is a forewarning or foretells something. Among the Sioux Indians if a man wishes to become a medicine man he must *Hanbleceya* which means he must seek a vision in a peculiar manner. To *Hanbleceya* one must invite a number of medicine men to be with him and advise him in his preparation.

He then builds a sweat house by sticking slender poles into the ground in a circle about six feet across and then bending them and weaving them together so as to form a dome about four feet high and over this he places a covering of skins, robes, or other material, leaving a place just large enough to crawl in but which can be closed from the inside. When the invited men are assembled, they heat a number of stones and place them in the sweat house. Then they all strip and go into the sweat house. While in there, they pour water on the hot stones or they pour infusions of herbs on them. This fills the place with steam and causes those in it to sweat freely.

While in the sweat house, the medicine men exhort the one who wishes to seek a vision and advise him how to proceed and impress on him the importance of telling truly his experiences while seeking the vision. They tell him that if he is successful in his quest the Spirit of the Earth will come to him in some form and communicate with him and that this communication must be interpreted rightly and that he must govern his action according to this interpretation. They are expected to be present when he returns from his quest and to aid him in arriving at the true interpretation of the communication. After the exhortation and advice are ended, all come out of the sweat house, bathe, and clothe themselves and then the one who wishes to seek the vision gives a feast.

Soon after this, he prepares four small banners on four small wands, mixes kinnikinic, and fastens a small portion of this

Rocky Bear, 1900. Photograph by Heyn and Matzen, Omaha.
Smithsonian Institution National Anthropological Archives

Red Hawk, 1913. Photograph by Joseph Kossuth Dixon, taken
in New York. Wanamaker Collection, Indiana University
Museum

Thomas Tyon, ca. 1909. Graves Collection. Courtesy Mari San-
doz Society, Chadron, Nebraska

No Flesh. Undated. Photograph by N. W. Photo Company, Chadron, Nebraska. The Denver Public Library, Western History Department

Short Bull and Joseph Horn Cloud. Undated. Nebraska State
Historical Society

William Garnett, Charles Ash Bates (allotting surveyor), and American Horse, 1907. The Denver Public Library, Western History Department

Group from Pine Ridge attending Rodman Wanamaker's "Last Great Indian Council" at the Crow Agency, Montana, 1909. (See Joseph Kossuth Dixon, *The Vanishing Race*.) Photograph by Joseph Kossuth Dixon. Left to right: Bird Necklace, Little Wound, Good Lance, Jack Red Cloud, Iron Crow, Calico-Painted Buckskin, George Sword, Iron Bull, Afraid of Bear. Wanamaker Collection, Indiana University Museum

Blue Horse. Undated. Eddie Herman Collection, Smithsonian
Institution National Anthropological Archives

to each banner. He then strips himself naked and, throwing a robe about his body, takes a pipe, some kinnikinic, and the banners and goes to the top of a hill. There he clears a space of all vegetation, large enough to lie on, and, placing one banner each at the west, north, east, and south, he then implores the Spirit of the West, the North, the East, and the South to aid him. He then fills the pipe with kinnikinic and lights it and while smoking it makes an offering of the smoke to these spirits, facing first to the west, then to the north, then to the east, and then to the south, addressing each spirit in turn.

He then sits and meditates as long as he deems proper and then he rises and calls on the Spirit of the Winds and of the Clouds and of the Thunder to help him and makes an offering of smoke to these, addressing each in turn. He then sits and meditates for a longer period than before, after which he covers himself entirely with the robe and then calls on the Spirit of the Earth to come and speak to him, chanting a song in praise of the spirit.

After this he must at no time go from the space he has prepared for himself but may lie, sit, or stand, but must try to keep his mind on his quest. He must neither eat nor drink after this until the quest is over. The Spirit of the Earth may come to him either while he is awake or as a dream while he sleeps. It may come to him in the form of a man, an animal, or a bird or it may come as a voice only or only in his thoughts. When it comes, it will tell him something which will be a knowledge of some medicine or what to do in the future or a warning against some evil or to make another quest or to cease from seeking a vision. The communication is apt to be ambiguous and require an interpretation.

The spirit may not come at all and after maintaining his quest as long as he can endure the fasting, he returns and reports his failure. Or the spirit may come only after he has fasted for four or five days, when the communication is very apt to be ambiguous and very important and to require much time and consultation to be properly interpreted.

Soon after he returns from his quest, he calls together the medicine men who advised him in his preparation and they prepare and enter the sweat house as before and he then tells them while in the sweat house all he experienced, and if he failed to see the spirit they question him closely as to all he did and advise him how to proceed anew, which he may or may not do, as he chooses. If he saw a vision, he tells it to them and they question him closely regarding all the particulars relating to it. If the meaning of the communication is plain, then he is declared the proper custodian of the knowledge and the proper person to exercise it.

If the meaning of the communication is ambiguous, they come out of the sweat house, bathe, and clothe themselves and enter into council which continues until an interpretation is agreed upon, after which he is declared the custodian of the knowledge and the proper person to exercise it. If this knowledge pertains to the sick or to anything that may be used as a medicine, this knowledge constitutes him a medicine man so far as that particular medicine is concerned. But it gives him no other knowledge or power.

If the vision pertains to a particular kind or class of medicine, as, for instance, Bear medicine, he must become the pupil of some Bear medicine man and learn what the medicines are, how to prepare them, how to administer them, and the songs and ceremonies that pertain to them.

---

34. Instructing a Vision Quester. James R. Walker.[38] (AMNH)

After a pipe full of the *cansasa* has been consumed, the deputies address the candidate in substance as follows:

"You desire to seek a vision. This is a solemn matter. You should not undertake it from curiosity only. You must do this according to the forms which we will now teach you. You must find a high place where no one will interrupt you. You must take with you plenty of *cansasa* and a pipe. You must take with you good medicine which we will give you. You may take a robe with you. But everything else you must leave behind you, except a loin cloth and moccasins. When you have thus prepared yourself, go to the place you have chosen. When you come there, clear a place of every living thing. This place must be large enough for you to sit or lie upon. When you have cleared it of every living thing, then you must place the medicine wands, one at the east, one at the west, one at the north, and one at the south on the place you have prepared. When you have done this, you may enter upon it to seek a vision. After you have entered upon it to seek a vision, you must not step beyond its boundaries nor speak to any man, woman, or child until after you have seen a vision or until you know that you will not see one.

"When you have entered on this place, you should meditate only on seeing a vision. You may invoke the spirits in words or song and you must always address them in a reverential manner. First, you should make an offering of the smoke of the *cansasa*. Offer it first to the Spirit of the East, then offer it to the Spirit of the North. Then offer it to the Spirit of the South. When you offer the smoke to the Spirit of the East, ask it to send you a vision. Wait and meditate for a time and if this spirit does not send a vision, then call upon the Spirit of the West in the same manner. If it does not send a vision, then call upon the Spirit of the North and then upon the Spirit of the South.

"If these spirits do not send a vision to you, then offer smoke to the Spirit of the Earth and call upon it. If no vision is sent you by this spirit, then you may call upon the spirit of heaven, the Great Spirit. But do not offer smoke to the Great Spirit until after you are sure that the other spirits will not send a vision to you. When you offer smoke to the Great Spirit, you must stand and lift your face to the sky and when you have offered the smoke, you must bow your face to the ground. After this, you must not look upon anything until you have seen a vision or have given up the quest. If you are sleepy, go to sleep, for it may be the vision will come to you in a dream. The vision may come to you as man, a beast, a bird, or as some form that is not known. Or it may come to you as a voice only. It may speak to you so that you will understand its meaning or it may be that you will not understand. If you have done something which the spirits do not like, then you will see no vision. If you know that you have done something of this kind, you [had] better not attempt to seek a vision, for you will not see one.

"Do not be discouraged when you seek the vision, for the spirits may wait a long time before they bring a vision to you. When you have seen a vision, do not call upon the spirits any more but return to us and we will advise you about its meaning.

"You should be sincere in this matter and truthful to us and do not lie to us by telling us that you have seen a vision when you have not, for if you do, we may advise you to do those things which the spirits do not want you to do and so bring harm upon you."

After this advice is given, the candidate and his deputies come out of the sweat house and assume their clothing. Any one or more of the deputies then take four small wands about two feet long. These are generally made of sprouts of the plum tree because the wood of these sprouts hardens quickly. They fasten to the smaller end of each of these wands a little packet of medicine. There is no particular medicine used for this purpose, for the substance is immaterial as its efficacy is given it by the ceremony of preparing it. These wands with the medicine attached are given to the candidate and he is expected to set them up about the place where he is to make his quest for a vision.

The candidate, within a short time, not exceeding a few days, proceeds according to his instructions to seek the vision. He usually goes to the top of a mound-like hill and removes all vegetation from a spot about six feet square. One who seeks a vision in this manner usually asserts, and with evident sincerity, that he has seen a vision. This vision may be seen shortly after entering on the quest or only after prolonged fasting and invocation. It may be that the quest is so prolonged that the seeker becomes so exhausted that he barely has strength to come away and yet he may see no vision. The Indians look with suspicion on one who seeks a vision in this manner and fails to see one, for they believe that such a one is guilty of some wrong that places him in disfavor with the spirits.

If the candidate sees no vision he calls his deputies together and they advise him either to try again to have a vision or to abandon his desire for initiation as a *Hunka*. If he tries again, he may have the vision, but when it it known that he will have no vision, he is advised to abandon his efforts to become a *Hunka* and he usually does so. (This seeking a vision is usually the most difficult part for the white man who desires to become a *Hunka*.)

If he sees a vision, he calls them together and they hear what he has to tell them, and if the vision is plain and easily understood, they advise him as they see fit. But if the vision is vague, they go again into the sweat house and meditate upon the proper interpretation of it. If they soon agree upon this, they expound it to the candidate or it may be that they require some time to agree upon a proper interpretation, in which case they leave the sweat house and each goes to his home. They meet either with or without the candidate and discuss the matter at will until they come to an agreement, when they notify the candidate that they have agreed. They then meet with him and expound his vision and give him advice according to their interpretations of it.

The vision may be interpreted to relate to anything whatsoever and the advice is given according to the interpretation. If the interpretation pertains to the candidate's initiation in any way, he is advised as to this matter. It may be that the interpretation is that he should proceed no farther as a *Hunka Skita*[39] and if such is the case he must stop his candidacy, for no one will have anything to do with him as a candidate for initiation. But if the vision is interpreted as favorable to his candidacy, or for the government of his conduct as such, then he is advised according to the interpretation. If the interpretation is something entirely foreign to his candidacy, he is advised according to it and proceeds as a *Hunka Skita*.

---

35. Elk Dreamers.[40] Anonymous. (CHS)

Those who dream of the elk must wear sticks like elk horns with hide branches and rawhide ears. They must paint yellow. They must paint their hands and feet black and have black paint on their breast and back. They must have a circle made of eagle feathers on the right side. They must have a mask made of rawhide. They have poison in the circle. They can vomit poison in the hand. They can shoot poison. They can throw poison from a wooden ring.

---

36. Dreams and Obligations. Anonymous. (AMNH and CHS)

(Alluded to in a medicine man's talk while treating a sick man.) If one dreams of an elk, he will be very sick. If a young girl will give him

a pipe, this will cure him. Grasshoppers and the toenails (claws) of birds are poison to one who dreams of elks. Someone knows his dreams and gives these things to him.

One who dreams of a coyote must wear a coyote's skin until he gets the Spirit of the Buffalo. He must cover the skin with weeds, and paint it white on the inside. He must wear it like a coyote and crawl close to the buffalo. He must have a whistle made of the bone from an eagle's wing. He must blow carefully on this whistle and low like a bull. He must carry his bow in his right hand. When he shoots the buffalo, the Spirit of the Buffalo will be with him. He must leave the meat of the liver of the buffalo for the coyote. He must paint red around his mouth and on his hands when he is doing this. When he kills a buffalo, he may throw away the coyote skin. One who sees a white bear in a vision must not eat the heart or the liver of anything.

Song sung to the Spirit of the Buffalo:

> A man from the west
> A man from the west
> Four legs he speaks
>
> Singing says mysterious things
> Singing says mysterious things
> Four legs he speaks

37. "I Am a *Wicasa Wakan*." Red Hawk. (CHS)

I am a *wicasa wakan* and I know the *Wacipi Wakan*. I know the *Wakan Iya, Econpi,* and *Lowanpi* [*Wakan* speech, actions, and songs]. I am a warrior and can wear the split eagle feather. I am a medicine man and know the Bear medicine. *Hunonpa* came to me when I *hanblapi*. He came to me many times. He gave me wisdom. He told me of the Lakotas.

My *Hunka Ate* was a wise man. He knew all the stories of the Lakotas. All the people listened to him and he told many stories. He could talk with the *nagipi* from the regions beyond the pines. I have talked with them.

My medicine is good. It is very good in war. I have had a

revelation from *Wi*. Here are the scars. No man will dispute what I say. I am a Lakota. The Lakotas are superior to all others of mankind. All of mankind was made first and the Lakotas were made last. My *Hunka Ate* was my *kola*. He told me these things. They have been told from the beginning. When I die, I shall go to the land of the *nagipi*. My enemy's *nagi* waits to go with me. I have talked with it.

When I danced the *Wacipi Wakan*, they told me this. *Tunkasila* chose a good woman. He chose a good man. He placed them in the middle of the world. Their children were the Lakotas. When the Lakotas came among other people, the *Wakanla* were afraid of them. The *Tunkansi* told the people of the Lakotas how to talk with *Taku Wakan*. He taught them the ceremonies and the songs. He came among them like a wise old man. When he had taught them the *Wakan Wacipi*, then he went away and no man has seen him since. These are the songs I sing. I have talked with his *akicita*.

---

38. "I Was Born a Lakota." Red Cloud's Abdication Speech, July 4, 1903.[41] (AMNH and CHS)

My sun is set. My day is done. Darkness is stealing over me. Before I lie down to rise no more, I will speak to my people.

Hear me, my friends, for it is not the time for me to tell you a lie. The Great Spirit made us, the Indians, and gave us this land we live in. He gave us the buffalo, the antelope, and the deer for food and clothing. We moved on our hunting grounds from the Minnesota to the Platte and from the Mississippi to the great mountains. No one put bounds about us. We were free as the winds and like the eagle, heard no man's commands. We fought our enemies and feasted our friends. Our braves drove away all who would take our game. They captured women and horses from our foes. Our children were many and our herds were large. Our old men talked with spirits and made good medicine. Our young men herded the horses and made love to the girls. Where the tipi was, there we stayed and no house imprisoned us. No one said, "To this line is my land, to that is yours."

In this way our fathers lived and were happy. Then the white man came to our hunting grounds, a stranger. We gave him meat and presents and told him to go in peace. He looked on our women and stayed to live in our tipis. His fellows came to build their trails across our hunting grounds. With his trinkets and his beads he bought the girl I loved. He brought the *maza wakan*, the mysterious iron that shoots. He brought the *mini wakan*, the mysterious water that makes men foolish.

I said, "The white man is not a friend, let us kill him." Our chief, Bull Bear, made me ashamed before our people. For the white man he had a heart like a woman.

I was born a Lakota and I have lived a Lakota and I shall die a Lakota.[42] Before the white man came to our country, the Lakotas were a free people. They made their own laws and governed themselves as it seemed good to them. Then they were independent and happy. Then they could choose their own friends and fight their enemies. Then men were brave and to be trusted.

The white man came and took our lands from us. They put [us] in bounds and made laws for us. We were not asked what laws would suit us. But the white men made the laws to suit themselves and they compel us to obey them. This is not good for an Indian.

The white men try to make the Indians white men also. It would be as reasonable and just to try to make the Indians' skin white as to try to make him act and think like a white man. But the white man has taken our territory and destroyed our game so we must eat the white man's food or die.

The president promised us. The commissioners he sent to us promised to clothe and feed us if we would let the white people have our lands and they promised to feed us and clothe us until we could feed ourselves. We, the older Indians, told the commissioners that we would fight for our horses and for women and that we could hunt for our food and clothing but that we could not dig the earth to make food and clothing grow from it.

We told them that the supernatural powers, *Taku Wakan*, had given to the Lakotas the buffalo for food and clothing. We told them that where the buffalo ranged, that was our country. We told them that the country of the buffalo was the country of the Lakotas. We told them that the buffalo must have their country and the Lakotas must have the buffalo.

Now where the buffalo ranged there are wires on posts that mark the land where the white man labors and sweats to get food from the earth; and in the place of the buffalo there are cattle that must be cared for to keep them alive; and where the Lakota could ride as he wished from the rising to the setting of the sun for days and days on his own lands, now he must go on roads made by the white man; and when he crosses the bounds the white man has set about us, the white man says to us Indians, "You must not be on the lands that are not on the road."

They tell us that we are Indians and they are white men and that we must be treated different from the white man. This is true. But the white man should say how he should be treated and the Indian should say how he should be treated. It is not so. The white man says how the white man should be treated and the white man says how the Lakota shall be treated and the Lakota has nothing to say in this matter. The commissioners and the white people sent to us by the president tell us that the white people know what is best for us. How can this be? No white man was born an Indian, then how can he think as an Indian thinks?

The commissioners promised that our children would be educated so that they would be wise and think as the white people think. Many of our children have been in the schools but they were born of Indian parents and they think as their parents think.

Our children can not forget their own people, and when the older people tell them of the time when the Lakotas moved across the land as free as the winds and no one could say to them "go here or stay there"; of the times when men did not labor and sweat to stay in one place; of the times when to hunt the buffalo and keep the tipi was all the care there was; of the times when brave men could win respect and renown on the warpath—then they sing the Indian songs and would be as the Lakotas were and not as the white men are.

The priests and the ministers tell us that we lived wickedly when we lived before the white man came among us. Whose fault was this? We lived right as we were taught it was right. Shall we be punished for this?

I am not sure that what these people tell me is true. As a child I was taught the Supernatural Powers (*Taku Wakan*) were powerful and could do strange things; that I should placate them and win their favor; that they could help me or harm me; that they could be good friends or harmful enemies. I was taught that the Sun *(Wi)* was a Great Mystery *(Wakan Tanka)*, that he was the Supreme Mystery *(Iyotan Wakantu)*,[43] and that he was our [grand]father *(Tunkansila)*, and my people addressed him as Father *(Ate)*. This was taught me by the wise men *(wicasa ksapa)* and the shamans *(wicasa wakan)*. They taught me that I could gain their favor by being kind to my people and brave before my enemies; by telling the truth and living straight; by fighting for my people and their hunting grounds. They taught me that *Taku Skanskan* (the supernatural patron of moving things) was *Wakan Tanka*; that *Inyan* (the supernatural patron of immovable things) was *Wakan Tanka*; that *Wakinyan* was *Wakan Tanka*; that *Tatanka* was *wakan*; that *Anog Ite* was *wakan* for evil; that *Heyoka* was *wakan* for evil; that *Iktomi* was *wakan* for evil.

These things were taught before the Sun Dance. The Lakotas believed them and they lived so as to win the favor of the Supernatural Powers *(Taku Wakan)*. The shamans could heal the sick with the help of the Good Mysteries *(Wakan Waste)* and by driving away the Evil Mysteries *(Wakan Sica)*. Two Legs (the mythical Bear) taught the Lakotas what medicines were good.

When the Lakotas belived these things they lived happy and they died satisfied. What more than this can that which the white man offers us give?

Taku Skanskan is familiar with my spirit *(nagi)* and when I die I will go with him. Then I will be with my forefathers. If this is not in the heaven of the white man, I shall be satisfied. *Wi* is my father. The *Wakan Tanka* of the white man has overcome him. But I shall remain true to him.

Shadows are long and dark before me. I shall soon lie down to rise no more. While my spirit is with my body the smoke of my breath shall be towards the Sun for he knows all things and knows that I am still true to him.

39. Defying the *Wakinyan*.[44] From a speech by Red Cloud. (AMNH)

Anpeyoka, the first dawn, the power that awakens the people,
Anpaoluta, the red dawn which awakens the sun,
Itoka, The same as *Okaga*, the South Wind,
Woziya the friend of *Heyoka*.
Heyoka inflicts skin diseases and sore eyes.
Iya inflicts headaches and paralysis.
Wiyohpeyata wicasa, the Man from the West, the one whose voice is the distant rumbling thunder.

---

40. Sending Spirits to the Spirit World. Short Bull, February 11, 1898 (Thomas Tyon, interpreter). (AMNH)

(The U.S. Indian agent had sent U.S. Indian police to arrest a member of Short Bull's band for giving away his property when his son, a young man, had died.)[45]

. . . *Kola*, I have put the red stripe on your forehead and you are *Mihunka* (my brother by custom of the Lakotas). I put the black stripe on your cheek and this makes you *miakicita* (my messenger or envoy). Write what I say to you and tell it to the Agent. I went to the Indian Messiah in a far away country.[46] He taught me the Ghost Dance. I brought this ceremony to the Lakotas. I was the leader of the Ghost Dance among the Tetons. This was our religion. I taught peace for all mankind. I taught my people that the Messiah would make all things right and that they should not make war on anyone.

The white people made war against the Lakotas to keep them from practicing their religion. Now the white people wish to make us cause the spirits of our dead to be ashamed. They wish us to be a stingy people and send our spirits to the spirit world as if they had been conquered and robbed by the enemy. They wish us to send our spirits on the spirit trail with nothing so that when they come to the spirit world, they will be like beggars.

We blacken our faces and cause our blood to flow from wounds so that the *Wakan Tanka* will know that we sincerely mourn for our dead. We give to the departing spirits what they need on the trail and in the spirit world. If we enrich the spirits with our gifts, they will go into the spirit world with pride and honor and all we give will be there for us when our spirits come there. If we give nothing to the dead, then their spirits will come into the spirit world with only shame. Tell this to the agent and maybe he will not cause us to make our spirits ashamed.

---

41. "I Was Called by Jocko Wilson." Short Bull (interpreter unkown).[47] (CHS)

(*[Interpreter's comment]: wants to prove that he was not the cause of the trouble of 1890–91*). He saw a woman. It was told that a woman gave birth to a child and this was known in heaven. This was told to him and he wanted to see the child when they heard this. This man professed to be a great man, next to God; [he] told them that he wanted to be their intermediator and that they should dance and be together and he would be with them.

He had a look. He said as many nights and days as it would take to do that he knew all about it. He said Indians [are] like grass and flowers and they learn and they sing and pray. He said "Do nothing wrong." He said the people can't take away anything when they die. Whiskey is bad. Who drinks, they cause murders and suicides.

Across the ocean is a great church where he came from. "That church belongs to me. You may go as you please, but one church, one belief, one faith. When you listen to me when I pray or teach from my church all good people will come with me. The whole world will sing. The whole earth is now filthy and stinks. These murders and suicides are that which now stinks. You say, 'Father, oh Father, is that you? All that will say, say that the Father, God will look at you. Those that have done wrong, he will shake the earth. This part of the earth will get it."

First heard of this man at Rosebud in the year When Red Shirt's Sister Committed Suicide.[48] I did not see the child. I do not know where it was born. I was called by Jocko Wilson to go and I went to see him. I went to the Rabbit Blanket [Paiute] Indians. I went in March. I was a long time in going. I first went to the Arapahoe Agency. I do not know how long I was there. I was six days at Pocatello. I went to the Bannocks and was there nine days. Then I got on the train. I was on the train two days and the third day in the evening, I came to the Fish Eaters[49] and I was there eight days. There were many whites and Indians there. I left there.

I left there on [a] train and on the hills above Pocatello, there was an accident. Big river washed out [the] bridge and [the] train upset. [I] came to Arapahoe Agency [Wind River Reservation], came from Arapahoe Agency on horseback. To my home it took fourteen days.

Red Star went. At Rosebud heard that this man had sent representative[s] to Rosebud and Pine Ridge and told them to have Short Bull come over there. He wanted a man who would be straight and would not lie. Rosebud Indians called a council and tried to pick out a man to go and they chose me. There was a paper at Rosebud that called for such a man made by the Oglala chiefs.

I first heard that this was a holy man. Said that God's daughter gave birth to a child and we should go and see it. I do not know where. I did not see this woman. All I saw was the man and his wife. Dance for five days; first pray and address. The other four all dance.

---

42. Ghost Dance. Short Bull. (CHS)

First: purification by sweat bath. Clasp hands and circle to left. Hold hands and sing until a trance is induced, looking up all the time. Brought to pitch of excitement by singing songs prescribed by the Messiah. Dressed as prescribed. Froth at mouth when in trance. They must keep step with the cadence of the song. The[y] go into trance in from ten minutes to three quarters of an hour. Each one described his vision. Each vision is different from others. Men, women, children have visions.

The ghost shirt is *wakan*. It is impervious to missiles.

---

43. The Buffalo. Short Bull. (CHS)

The buffalo were given by the Spirit of the Earth to the Indians. The Spirit of the Earth and of the Buffalo are the same. *Iktomi* named all the animals. He [gave] food for all animals. But he did not give food for Indians.

The Oglalas should venerate the Spirit of the Buffalo. An Indian went to a hole in the ground and found the buffalo. They were given to him for his food. He drove some of them up on the earth. From these came all the buffalo.

Part III

Narratives by
Thomas Tyon

The content of documents in this section pertains directly to Lakota beliefs, yet these texts have two important differences from the preceding ones. In the first place, they all have the same guiding theme, the *wakan* quality in various life forms. In the second place, they were all written in Lakota by Walker's friend Thomas Tyon. Most, if not all, are records of interviews with holy men that Tyon held for Walker. Unfortunately, he never mentioned the names of his informants. The documents remained untranslated until we prepared English versions for this volume.

Most of the texts describe the ritualistic knowledge of the holy men. They are an important addition to our knowledge about how the Lakotas viewed the interrelationships among different life forms, and they show how those interrelationships formed the basis for Lakota beliefs about disease and its prevention and cure. Each document is an exciting record of thought processes. Each shows how holy men articulated their understanding of *wakan* qualities intrinsic to various animals and objects. Because what is *wakan* constitutes the very ground of being, it is the basis for important interrelationships among life forms. All applications of knowledge are based on perceived relationships, and effective action is bound up in an intimate, causal way with the very structure and energies of a universe understood as *wakan*. Therefore, as the holy men comment on how they perceive what is *wakan*, they also show how they apply their perceptions, especially for the purposes of healing.

The English term *sacred* has too many limiting connotations to serve as an adequate equivalent for *wakan*, so we have kept the Lakota term. The single exception is the expression *wicasa wakan*, which we have translated "holy man." These texts, as well as many of the preceding documents, are in themselves the best commentary on the meaning of the Lakota term. Many of Tyon's texts include in their title the word *yuwakan*. The prefix *yu-* indicates causation. According to George Sword, the use of this prefix with the word *wakan* indicates that the *wakan* quality is indirectly caused through action taken for some other purpose (see document 14). The only way to translate this concept would have been "is made *wakan*." Such a translation has the advantage of consistency but the disadvantage of suggesting non-Indian concepts of causation, not to mention the clumsiness of the English expression. Therefore we have retained the Lakota sense of a participatory world view and translate *yuwakan* as simply "is *wakan*" while adding the Lakota titles to the documents so that readers can follow the occurrence of the concept.

---

44. The Pipe Is *Wakan (Cannonpa Yuwakanpi)*. Thomas Tyon (translated by the editors). (CHS)

The pipe is very *wakan*. It is used for doing all things. *(Taku woecon kin iyuha el woilagyape lo.)* It is used in all *wakan* actions. First I will tell something. When men gather together to smoke, it is a rule that nobody goes in front of them. If someone goes in front of them, they empty and clean out the pipe.

And another thing is as follows: when they first light the pipe, they raise it up. They raise the pipe to the above and they say this, "Behold, *Wakan Tanka,* I give this to you." They say, "I will live long and I will have horses; also, I will kill an enemy." Or, "I will steal a woman," they say. They present the pipe to the four winds and they make these speeches.

And I will relate another different thing. If a man's child is sick, he takes a pipe filled with tobacco to a [medicine] man. Then the medicine man takes the pipe and smokes it, it is said. Now, he sets it aside *(wana yaguna)*. "Listen. Go home. I will arrive in a little while." That is what he says.

In all *wakan* acts, they use the pipe. When going to war or in the Sun Dance, the leaders carry *(yuhaxkan)* the pipe. So they think that the pipe is very *wakan*. Ever since the standing people have been over all the earth, the pipe has been *wakan*. *(Ehantan najin oyate maka sitomniyan cannonpa kin he uywakanpelo.)*[1] Even to this day the pipe is very *wakan*.

Long ago a people were camping and two young men from the camp were going on ahead, it is said. They were going along a ridge. Then suddenly a very beautiful woman appeared climbing the hill. She was coming, carrying something. So they stood watching her, it is said. Then one of the young men said, "Well, my friend, I will do it with her *(kicimu kin ktelo)*."[2]

"Look, my friend, see clearly! She is not a woman, probably

something *wakan,*" the other said. But the young man was not afraid. Then the woman heard him. She said, "Come here! We will lie down." So he went there but no further, for from the sky a very big cloud fell on them, it is said. And when it cleared away, the young man was nothing but bones lying there, it is said.

The woman-who-was-not-a woman *(winyan sni)* was coming in a *wakan* manner. But the poor young man did not know it. Thus he was entirely devoured by snakes, it is said.

So the other young man stood there trembling, it is said. Then the woman said this: "Young man, do not fear me! Because that one was foolish, I did this *(witkotkoka ca heca muwe),*" she said, it is said. "Listen boy *(hokxila),* I am bringing home news. I am bringing something so the people will live; it is the Buffalo Calf Pipe. They will live in a *wakan* manner *(taku wan awau kin le ptehincala cannonpa ca oyate unipi kta ca wicawaka u we).* I will assist all of the people by showing them good ways *(oran waxte).* I will go there." She left saying, "Now after a while, I will arrive bringing news."

So the young man hurried home with the news, it is said. And then the crier took it and since the camp circle was large, the crier walked all around proclaiming the news, it is said. "*Howo!* Something is coming but it is coming in a *wakan* manner so no one think anything evil. Follow good ways. In a very *wakan* manner it comes," the crier proclaimed, it is said. And so all the people prepared themselves *(Cankelaka oyate qon ataya iyarwayela unpi),* it is said.

Now the woman came among the tipis, it is said. And she told them she had something, it is said. "The Buffalo Calf Pipe arrives here," she said, it is said. Anyone who does bad deeds and uses this pipe will be rubbed out *(Tuwa wicoran xica econ can na cannonpa kin le un yapakintapi kte),*" she said, it is said. The woman was a very beautiful woman, it is said. She was completely naked, it is said. Her hair was very long, it is said.

So it is that the pipe is very *wakan.* If a people quarrel, then they make peace *(wolakota kagapelo)* using the pipe. She instructed them *(wicaxipelo)* in the girls' menstrual ceremony *(Ixnati Awicalowanpelo,* singing over those living alone)[3] and in the *Hunka* ceremony. And the man who was the leader was always to have the pipe. The pipe is their heart; all hold firmly to it. Thus it is believed to be *wakan.* The Indians *(Ikcewicaxa kin)* in everything they undertake, they do it with the pipe. Well, this is what I know about the *wakan* pipe. So it is.

---

45. The Vision Quest Is *Wakan (Hanpleceyapi Yuwakanpi kin).*[4] Thomas Tyon (translated by the editors). (CHS)

When a man cries for a vision, it is nearly like the Sun Dance. When a man's wife or child is sick, he has faith *(wacinyecanontka),* but finally, in any case, he makes a vow. He says as follows, "*Wakan Tanka,* pity me. If my wife lives, I will cry for a vision," he says. Then perhaps the fortunate man's wife is cured.

When he understands that his wife is really well, he takes a pipe filled with tobacco to the lodge of a holy man. The pipestem is rubbed with red paint. Then the holy man takes the pipe and smokes it, it is said. And when he is completely finished *(tanyerci yaguna),* he says, "All right, boy, you want something; why did you bring me a pipe?" it is said. That is what the holy man says. Then the man says, "All right, my friend, my wife almost died on me but I vowed to cry for a vision and then she lived for me. But I do not know how to do it; therefore, I want you to teach me and so I gave you this pipe," it is said. This is what the man who will cry for a vision says.

And then the holy man says, "Now listen! From this time on take good care of your own." He is speaking in a *wakan* manner. Then he says, "Well, when a man cries for a vision, from that time on he can think nothing bad. Try to live well! My friend, later, in this way, I will prepare you," he says. In this way they talk together, it is said. Perhaps now, at this time, the holy man says this to the man who made the vow, it is said. "Now listen, seek out a red blanket and four pieces of cloth and from them make tied tobacco *(canli waparta).* And you must also have ready a buffalo hide with the hair on it. Also seek out a pipe."

As soon as the man seeking the vision has these things, he sends word, it is said. When he has everything, he tells the holy man, it is said. Therefore he follows the commands of the holy man. Then he [the vision seeker's helper] goes to a distant hill and the holy man commands him to make a place *(owanka)* there, it is said. Therefore, the helper *(wowaxi)* goes now, they say. Then he goes to a very high hill, it is said. Now he carefully makes a place, it is said. The place is ten feet square and the earth is very well prepared, it is said. And then he returns home, it is said.

Then the holy man tells him the following, they say. At that time *(hehanl)* he orders them to make a sweat lodge, it is said. So now he says, "Bring some willows!" The helper goes and now he builds a sweat lodge. Now the man who will cry for a vision goes there, it is said. Also men from all around go there, they say. Therefore many men take part in the sweat bath, they say. Inside the sweat lodge everything is well covered with a blanket of sage, it is said. Now the vision quester goes into the lodge, it is said; also all of the other men. Now they bring into the lodge all of the hot rocks they say, it is said. And they cover the door; then they pray very earnestly *(lila ceyapi)*, it is said. All those men sitting in the lodge advise the man who will cry for a vision with the *wakan* knowledge that they have and so the holy man instructs the vision quester, they say. "My friend, perhaps something frightening comes to you and you want to run away; stand with a strong heart! In this way you will become *wakan*." Saying this, he instructs him, it is said. "Pray to inquire wisely and well into everything! You will be a coward if you learn nothing," he says, it is said. The holy man leaves and then they come out of the sweat lodge.

So now the vision quester, wearing only a furred robe around his shoulders and with a pipe and kinnikinic *(canli canxaxa)*, carrying a filled pipe and wearing the robe, he stands ready, they say. The bowl of the pipe that he carries is sealed with tallow, it is said. Thus the tobacco will not be scattered. So it is. And now they go to the young man [the helper] who has been sitting there a long while, it is said. Therefore the vision quester is frightened *(lila cante xica*, a very bad heart), it is said. Possibly some bad-tempered *(ocin xica)* animals might come there. That is why they are very afraid of the night, they say.

Now the vision quester wraps his robe around himself with the fur side out, and until the sun rises, he stands looking east, pointing with the pipe that he holds, praying as hard as he can. All night long he stands in this way, it is said. At last the dawn seems to be visible and so he stands, rejoicing greatly, it is said. And then possibly, he becomes very drowsy, so very slowly he lies down flat, they say. And with his arms very properly uplifted in prayer, now as he lies there, he hears something stamp the ground behind him, coming towards him, creeping up stealthily, little by little. He is very excited *(lila cantiyapa)*. So perhaps, all of a sudden, he thinks to raise up his head as it goes by, they say. And he looks at the thing that comes stamping the earth. And then it is very little even though he heard the sound of its breath *(taninyan honaran)*, it is said. It was only a grasshopper walking although it came stamping the ground, they say.

Therefore, it is said, the man at once thinks, "Alas I have done harm to myself. When I came, they commanded me not to be afraid of anything," he thought at once. And again he lay down, they say. "Well, being impatient, I heard the sound of something but I will not anticipate it again," he thought. Now again he was impatient and he fell fast asleep, it is said. Then he dreamed, it is said. Perhaps in the dream a man came there, it is said. Again he thought he was afraid, but he was asleep. Therefore, in no way could he flee.

The man looked at him as he lay, it is said. Then the man who came spoke to the vision quester, they say. "Boy, look towards the south," he said. And he stood pointing towards the south. Then he looked there. And it was a very large camp of people, it is said. It was very clear as he stood. And then in a tipi he saw a man, a skeleton *(hunhun)* lying down, they say. Then the man said, "Look towards this place!" So the vision quester looked there and the man showed him some snakeroot *(waptaye)*, it is said. "Recognize these roots well! They will be thanked for giving life *(niciyin kte)*," he said, they say. The man told about those medicines, it is said. "If you learn these well, then the sick man who lies there will stand because of you," he said. And he went away home. And then the man stood and he said this. At last the man was like a buffalo bull and he spoke, it is said. Well now, the vision quester finally woke up. And then absolutely nobody was there, it is said. So it is.

Now it was time for the vision quester [to return]. Therefore, the helper again made a sweat lodge but the fire for the rocks was not yet built in place before the vision quester was brought back, they say. And now at last he lighted a fire at that place, it is said. When the vision quester returned, all the men living around said, "Well, now I will go participate." And from all around they came to the sweat lodge, it is said. And then they all went inside the lodge. The door was covered and again they prayed earnestly, it is said. Then the door was opened and they smoked tobacco there, and the holy man asked questions of him who had cried for a vision, they say.

"Listen, without jesting, tell about your vision! In a *wakan* manner you arrived home," he said, it is said.

"Yes," the vision quester said, "in this manner, I dreamed something," he said, and all of what he dreamed, he told about, it is said. Then all those sitting in the lodge said in chorus, "Haye," it is said.

From the time the man dreamed, he knew how to doctor people, it is said. He knew about the medicines and all other things used for doctoring. The man was a buffalo dreamer. That man also served regularly for the girl's menstrual ceremony. That man also did the *Hunka* ceremony. Those ceremonies he did for the people. Therefore the buffalo dreamer was very famous. He was not under any other medicine men. He was very *wakan,* they believe. Well, those medicine men dream of animals. And then they doctor people. Well, those buffalo dreamers had many rules but I do not remember them all. So this is the end.

---

46. The Rock Is Believed *Wakan (Inyan Wakan Wicalapi kin).* Thomas Tyon (translated by the editors). (CHS)

A man dreams of Rock and therefore he begins to follow certain customs. Whenever someone loses something, he makes a feast for the Rock dreamer: this is called the *Yuwipi*[5] feast. Now all of the holy men come there to the feast. The leader of the holy men, he himself, is completely tied up, hand and foot. Then the fire is entirely extinguished and they beat the drum and shake the rattle while they sing loudly. And now perhaps the man who is tightly tied up, he is the one who says, "Poke up the fire!" so they make the fire blaze. Now whatever the man had lost appears (ahipi), it is said. The holy man who was tightly tied up is completely untied, it is said. It is the Rock that does this, they say. The man sitting there has that which was lost, they say. Well for that reason, the Rock dreamers are very wakan, they think.

So it is that if someone loses a horse, they quickly make a feast for the Rock dreamer and they have him look for it. So the rocks tell about whoever stole the horse, even the name and the place; they come to report everything, they say. Therefore they are considered very powerful (wowitunpekelo). These Rock dreamers are called the Yuwipi society. Still, even today, they are believed to be wakan.

And again there is a different kind of wakanla rock; they are the sweat lodge stones (tonkan yatapika), as they say. These act differently. When a man is sick, they make a sweat lodge for him. They do it in this way. Ten or twelve saplings (cowanjica) are completely bent over and they use a tent or even a robe to cover it completely, leaving no holes. And in the very center, the earth is dug out in an exact circle. Next, they fill the fireplace with rocks that are glowing bright red all over. Then the sick man is commanded to go inside. And afterwards the holy man also goes inside. Men very frequently make the sweat lodge. Inside the sweat lodge the entire floor is well covered with a blanket of sage. Everything is done with reverence. So it is. Now the robe is thrown down [to cover the door], and then the holy men speak (woklakapelo). They speak in the spirit language (he hanploklakapi eciyapelo). These are the things they say.

"Sweat lodge stones (tonkan yatapika), pity me! Sun, pity me! Moon, pity me! Darkness of night (hanokpaza kin), pity me! Water, standing in a wakan manner (mni wakanta najin kin),[6] pity me! Grass, standing in the morning (pejihinyanpa najin kin), pity me! Whatever pitiful one is scarcely able to crawl into the tipi and lie down for the night (takuxika teriya tiyoslohanhan hinyunke), see him and pity him. Unhappiness causes coldness within the body so that even the place of eating and the place for lying down and the place for seeing become as nothing (cuwita tanmahel taku iyokipi xni na owate na oyunka na owakita kin lena ekayex koye ecetu xni kin). This way the sweat lodge stones frantically persuade the Spirit of the Sky (heun tonkan yatapika Ite Peto knaxkinya ciyelo).[7] The holy man makes this kind of speech. He tells these things from his vision. Well, they say very many things but only that which is clear I write. So it is.

Now a water bucket is passed inside and also a bowl. So now the holy man takes the bowl and the water and pours it on the rocks. Then it becomes very hot and steaming. The men sitting inside all sing loudly and some cry out. They do not cry out because of the heat. A sick man is sitting inside; they want him to be cured and for that reason, humbling themselves *(unxi icicar)* they cry out. And also some love a woman but are rejected, so for that reason they pray. And some want to kill an enemy and so they pray for an enemy. The men cover the rocks well with water because they want everything they pray for to come to pass. The breath of the rocks is very *wakan*, they think.

Also, long ago, if a man dreamed of Rock, then the people believed in this manner, it is said. The man who was the Rock dreamer could not be shot even by a bullet, they thought, it is said. And this they believed, it is said. So the men who could not be shot made war medicine *(wotawe)*, it is said. Well, this much of the *wakan* rocks is told. There is also much more but only so much did the leader tell. I have related all.

---

47. The *Wakinyan* Are *Wakan* (*Wakinyan Yuwakanpi kin*). Thomas Tyon (translated by the editors). (CHS)

The man who dreams of *Wakinyan* is called *heyoka*.[8] In all their speech, the *heyoka* talk in opposites *(unzinhe-kta kinya eca-iyapi kin unwelo)*. The *heyoka* dreamer is very frightened whenever there is thunder and lightning. He thinks he hears human voices from the clouds; therefore he escapes by running into a tipi. He gets inside the tipi and immediately burns cedar *(rante zilyapelo)*. They think that the *Wakinyan* are afraid of cedar. This tree is very *wakan*. Whenever they burn cedar, they think the *Wakinyan* can do nothing to them *(Wakinyan kin tokelran okihipi xni)*. They do not think the *Wakinyan* hate the cedar; rather they think they are friends. Therefore they do this out of respect.

The *Wakinyan* often command the man who dreams of them to do certain things *(wakinconzapi)*, it is said. But some *heyoka* do not follow their commands closely and the *Wakinyan* will surely kill them. The *Wakinyan* dreamer is made to do these things, it is said. They command him to commit murder *(tiwicakte xipi)*, it is said. And if he does not do it, they will make him kill, it is said.

Then the *Wakinyan* command the *heyoka* to do the *Heyoka* ceremony *(Heyoka Woze, "heyoka* ladle out [of a pot]")* it is said. This is the way to do the *Heyoka* ceremony. They put up an old, smoke-darkened tipi in the middle of the camp circle and then two *heyoka* helpers *(heyoka wowaxi)* wear robes with the hair side out over their shoulders. They both wear a single leather strap around their waist. And they strangle a dog. Then they singe it in the center of the camp circle and cut it up entirely. And they cook it in a kettle until it is boiling hard. Then all of the *heyoka* move quickly *(lila xkanpelo)* around the kettle. Then they rub medicine on their hands.[9] The kettle and the soup are very hot but the *heyoka* thrust their hands in the kettle and dip out the pieces of dog meat. But none of them scald their hands. Therefore they are believed to be very *wakan*.

Well, these *Wakinyan* dreamers have many songs. The round skin tent that is erected for them as the *heyoka* tipi is an old smoke-darkened tipi. It is an old buffalo hide tipi, I mean. The *Wakinyan* dreamers purposely make people laugh. Everything they say is very good to hear *(onaron waxtexte)*. There is only one bad thing they are directed to do. They are commanded to murder someone. Well, the man who dreams of the *Wakinyan* kills an enemy and so completes what he has been commanded to do. From that time on, he does not fear the *Wakinyan*. And if he does not do something that they direct him to do, then every day he is agitated *(cantiyapa)*. At last he murders someone. This is how it is but these *heyoka* men are believed to be very *wakan*.

When the *Wakinyan* come, a *heyoka* stands looking at them and sings loudly. He stands with his hand raised up and the clouds are pushed aside, it is said. Therefore, the people have a strong belief in the *heyoka*. Also, they doctor people. And again, their medicine is very good. They have a medicine; the water is very hot but they rub it all over their hands so the water does not scald them. Therefore, they are believed to be very *wakan*. The *heyoka* are directed to do *heyoka* things *(heyoka wawicakicanzapi)*. And this is so. They are commanded to kill a child *(cinca wanji kikte-wicaxipi xkelo)*, it is said. If they do not do it, then the *Wakinyan* will kill them, it is said. Thus they are very frightened.

Men and women have *heyoka* dreams of the *Wakinyan* but they do not understand them so a holy man teaches them, it is said. A mirror is placed above the dreamer in which to see, then the holy man somehow sees the entire dream in the mirror, it is said.[10] Therefore, an ordinary man is afraid to look, so a *heyoka* leader looks in the mirror. Then the dreamer must also join the *heyoka*; it is said. Probably you know that. The *heyoka* are very badly dressed. They have burlap sack cloth shirts and leggings. And some of them rub mud all over their bodies. Everything they do, they do backwards, which is very funny. Well, these are the customs of the *heyoka*.

---

48. Bears Are *Wakan (Mato Wicayuwakanpi kin)*. Thomas Tyon (translated by the editors). (CHS).

A man dreams of the bear, and so he is very *wakan*. Also he belongs to the Bear society.[11] The man who dreams of the bear is leader of the whole society. These are the rules of the Bear society. First there was only one Bear Dreamer. Little by little, the society grew larger. This is the way it grew. Many men are wounded by bullets or the like; the Bear doctors make all of them well. So those who have been wounded and made well by the Bear doctors are taken into the Bear group. From that time on, men who were wounded participate in the ceremonies of the Bear society *(Mato Okolakiciye qel taku kuwapi kin)* and learn everything about them. Because many wounded men are taken in, the Bear society includes many men. The Bear Dreamer society is the only one the people find very astonishing *(wowinihanyan)*. The members cure men who are very badly wounded, so to this day, Bear medicine is still considered *wakan*. This is the way it is administered *(lecel econpelo)*.

When a man is wounded, a big tipi is set up in the middle of camp and the wounded man moves into the tipi. Inside the tipi the entire floor is completely covered with sage. And all those who consider themselves Bears, these and only these, move into the tipi with the wounded men. And when the Bears doctor, they all have round drums. They sing many very good songs. And so the Bear leader moves about *(xkanyelo)*. All those who have been wounded stand and move about. Those who have different types of medicine *(pejuta)* move about. They are all thought to be very *wakan*. There is a very white medicine and it smells very good. All men find it very pleasing. When they smell it, then the wounds do not fester. They are cured. So it is that for four nights the ones who were wounded will participate in ceremonies *(wakiciyaotaninpelo)*.

Then all those who had been wounded will come out. So an old man goes about proclaiming this aloud. Perhaps some of the women are menstruating, so none of them come near. The old man goes along. Around the camp, on the inside of the camp circle, the crier goes along. So then the people stir about *(Wana oyate kin lila wicoxkinciyelo)* and men crowd all around the Bear tipi. Then, as the Bears sing, all of the people stand looking intently at the entrance to the Bear tipi. Suddenly the Bear leader begins to move quickly towards the tipi entrance. Growling ferociously, he comes out of the tipi. His body is painted entirely red and his hands white; he carries a knife. All of the onlookers flee. Then one of the wounded comes out after him, carrying a short staff painted entirely red. Slowly he comes out. The staff is forked at the end. And then the Bear singers come out, singing as loudly as they can. Therefore, the Bear leader and the one who was wounded bend down and move about furiously *(ihunkulkul iyaya ohitiyela xkan yelo)*.

Perhaps the spectators standing there have a dog. If the knife bearer sees it, he chases it and if it is unwell, he overtakes it and immediately tears it to pieces, and even though it is raw, he, the Bear leader, that is, eats it.

Well now the wounded begin to walk and they stand facing the south. Then they turn and stand facing the west. Again they turn and stand facing the north. Again they turn and they stand facing the east. They all stand with their arms raised in prayer. Throughout, they sing the songs. Therefore, the Bear leader moves about. And now when they have completed the four directions they go back to the tipi from which they came. Again they go inside. The doctors place the wounded at the *catku* [place of honor at the rear of the lodge]. At last they apply the healing root. Throughout they command that no woman come near.

When the Bear society is moving *(iklakapi)*, the wounded ones walk ahead of the others. When they move, they walk and nobody goes before them. The wounded never go against the wind. They carefully see to this.

When the wounded one is completely cured, he takes part in the Bear society. From that time on, he knows about the Bear medicine. So not just anyone takes part in the Bear society. It is because a Bear doctor has caused him to live that a man takes part in the society. There are many doctors but this is the way the Bear doctors increase in number. Therefore, the Bear doctor songs are very good.

Here is another thing. If a menstruating woman tans a bear skin, then she becomes a bear *(ehantan mato ayaxkelo)* and the woman is black all over, it is said. And her face is hairy all over, it is said. Therefore women are very much afraid of bear skins. So it is that the bear skin is also believed to be *wakan*.

Sometimes the leader of the bear dreamers sleeps in his tipi during the day. And then suddenly they wake him up; they frighten him and he becomes wild *(knaxkinyan)*, it is said. Finally his canine teeth grow very long and become visible, it is said. Then, lying down, he paws at the earth and a wild turnip slips out from it, it is said. And again, he comes outside and he goes around a wild plum tree, growling like a bear. He grasps the plum tree in his hand and shakes it. And then some plums stick to it, it is said. So it is, the Bear dreamers are believed *wakan*.

Well, there is another thing. Bear dreamers imitate the bear *(mato kaga)*, it is said. The bear skin completely covers his head and on the right side of the back, an eagle tail feather is fastened, it is said. Then from the center of the camp he goes around the inside of the camp circle, it is said. He has a knife in one hand and even though someone shoots him with a gun, he does not die, it is said. He himself often says he is going hunting. He thrusts his knife into something and he heals the wound, it is said. I have not seen the knife wounds with my own eyes. I have heard them say these things. So it is. Because of these bear customs, they believe bears to be *wakan*.

49. Wolves Are *Wakan (Xungmanitu Yuwakanpi kin)*. Thomas Tyon (translated by the editors). (CHS)

Because of these customs, wolves are *wakan*.[12] In the beginning a man who dreamed of wolves always went towards the enemies' tipis like a wolf, it is said. He was, therefore, very inconspicuous, hence nobody was able to see him. This is right, so far. A man was wandering, lost in the wilderness, when a wolf came there and they went together towards the camp, it is said. Therefore, they believe the wolf to be very *wakan*. And so far, it is also right, it is said. The men who dreamed of wolves had certain customs, it is said. Some they told about, it is said. Those they told the people about, it is said.

When there were many buffalo somewhere, a wolf came to tell the wolf dreamer, it is said. Therefore the man as well as the wolf is believed to be very *wakan*. Also when a man shoots a wolf with a gun, the gun will be no good the next time it is used, it is said.

This too is right. When a horse is used to chase a wolf, that horse will not be good again, it is said. From that time, the horse is always lame, it is said. So it is that in the past the people considered wolves very *wakan*. And to this very day, when they hear a wolf howl, they say, "It will be very bare *(lila waxmi kte lo)*"; or perhaps they say, "Something will be wrong *(Taku toketu kte lo)*." Also, the man who dreamed of the wolf was not very much on guard *(awaniciklake xni),* but would haughtily close his eyes, it is said; yet the man was very much on his guard.

Long ago a woman lived with wolves, it is said. Then the wolves took great pity on her. The wolves went scattering away and when it was evening, they came home to the woman with meat, it is said. Therefore they believe the wolf to be *wakan*. Well, so it is. Even now they consider the wolf *wakan*.

50. Toads Are *Wakan (Witapir'a Yuwakanpi kin).* Thomas Tyon (translated by the editors). (CHS)

If a man dreams of toads, he is a doctor *(wapiya),* it is said. Whatever these toads suck, they suck hard. So it is that a man who dreams of a toad is very *wakan,* they believe. From the time of his dream, he doctors people using his mouth. He takes all the bad blood out of the body, it is said. Those men who become doctors, Indian doctors, do not do it intentionally. The dreams they have of animals are what cause them to believe they are doctors. Those who dream of the toad believe that it is their leader.

Also men who dream of bears are doctors: also those who dream of fish are doctors, it is said. Also anyone who dreams of the belted kingfisher *(hoyazela),* or birds; so they mean them. [They function as bird doctors.] Thus those men who are doctors dream of animals. That is why they are doctors. The people believe in them. There is much more but this is all I remember well.

---

51. The Medicine Men Called Bone Keepers[13] *(Wapiye Wicaxpi Qeya Hunhunyuha Ewicakiyapi).* Thomas Tyon (translated by the editors). (CHS)

Many medicine men secretly make a society for themselves. No other will be able to join them. Those who own medicine bundles *(wopiyeyuhapi)* call each other to meet together again and again. No one at all knows what they do. Only the medicine men practice certain things. What they do is very bad *(Taku kuwapi kin hena lila xicelo).* For that reason, they do not want others to know about it, it is said. They sometimes kill men by using medicine, they say. Therefore the people believe the Bone Keeper society to be very *wakan.*

The Bone Keepers often make love potions for a young man, it is said. The young man for whom the love potion is made will now go there to court the woman. When the woman does not want to be courted and she does not hold the young man dear to her heart, then the young man again appeals to the medicine men, it is said. He says, "I want to marry *(opluspin kta)* a woman, but she dislikes me." He says bad things about her to the medicine men, it is said. Then the medicine men become very angry and they instruct the young man, it is said. Again they tell him, "Go to the woman!" And, again, "Quickly come back with a hair pulled from the head of the woman you desire!" Therefore, the man now goes again to the woman. But again she treats him as before; she strongly dislikes the young man. Therefore, he immediately pulls out a hair from the woman's head, takes it, and quickly brings it back, it is said. The medicine men take the hair and secretly make a sweat lodge, and they resolve to cause the woman hardship, it is said. They say, "The woman will have violent nosebleeds," it is said. And so such women are very sick. Therefore, the woman's father hurries to make a feast for the Bone Keeper society, it is said. He says, "My heart is destitute *(lila cante unxiya)*, my friends. These medicines you have are good medicines. If you cure my daughter, she will marry that young man." And he pleads with the medicine men *(wopiye qon hena cekiya)*, it is said. Then they take pity on him and hear him, it is said. Therefore his daughter is cured. And so she will now marry the young man, they say. Therefore on account of this, they strongly believe the Bone Keeper society to be very *wakan*. When the man with the love potion goes to the woman, she says nothing. Suddenly she goes home with him. They are afraid that if she refuses to marry him, her violent nosebleed will begin again.

The Bone Keepers, the name Bone Keepers, does not refer to bones. It refers to medicine. When the Bone Keeper society has a feast, they make a rule that no matter how much food they have, all must be eaten up, and nobody may laugh while eating. None of it is spilled out on the ground. It is very *wakan*. Nobody disregards this and laughs at them. And so the customs are *wakan*, it is said.

And they make people sick, it is said. In case of sickness again, it is the Bone Keepers who cure them, it is said. Therefore, they are very much afraid of the Bone Keeper medicine men. They believe them to be *wakan,* not men. Therefore, if someone is sick, it seems that the Bone Keepers did it; they blame them. And at once, they make a feast for them. This they order them to do. If someone finally dies, the Bone Keepers defend themselves strongly. Therefore the Bone Keepers are very much hated *(lila warte wicalapi xniyelo).* But the people are very much afraid of them. They are believed to be very *wakan.* Therefore, the Bone Keepers make love potions for young men. So women are frequently seduced. The men are no good but they are feared, that is why the women marry them. But I know well that the Bone Keeper society dreams of all the things that move on the earth *(taku wamakaxkan).* Among the people, certain men have medicine bundles *(wopiye yuhapi).* These bundles contain medicines. However, only those men who consider themselves *wakan* have them. Therefore, the people fear them. If during a feast, one of the medicine men spills from the kettle, they all say together, "Wo-ho-ho!" No food at all may be tossed away *(yupsicapi).* The Bone Keepers have only a round drum. They shake rattles and they sing. Well, this is the way the Bone Keepers act *(xkanpelo).*

---

52. Mourners Are *Wakan (Waxikla Wicayuwakanpi kin).* Thomas Tyon (translated by the editors). (CHS)

Mourners become *wakan* in this way. If a man or a woman or a child dies, they make a sweat lodge for them. Inside the sweat lodge, they counsel the mourners. These are the things they say.

"Well, recently your heart was grieved but they want you to mourn properly. Therefore medicine men will give you advice. So now listen well as you sit here," they say. "Your heart is grieved, but think of your relatives who are living. Pity yourself, cry! And take up your gun and go cry away from camp *(mani-takiya).* And try to shoot a deer. And when you shoot one, come back home with a good heart. And when you return home, call those who live around you and eat with them with a good heart. And then think of nothing bad. And when the dawn comes, go outside, look at it, raise your arms in prayer and from that time always live in goodness. In that way you will please others. Get in the habit of being poor. Be thankful! And when something displeasing happens to you, defend yourself well. Live in goodness and do not listen to evil. Don't have just any thoughts you please. When you itch, use a chokecherry branch to scratch with. If you use your hand, you will be infested with lice. And when you eat and still want more, stop at that point. And live thinking about those who suffer. If you help all of these, they will be grateful to you."

So it is. When men mourn, they are regarded as *wakan* for one month *(hehanyan wiwakta)*. When someone does it exactly so, then he is thankful, it is said. They become very *wakan*. Therefore, still, to this day, people follow these customs. When someone does not do this, he is completely destroyed. So it is. When someone mourns, they hurry to make a sweat lodge and the mourners cleanse themselves. From then on, they are glad. Well, this is all.

---

53. Ghosts Are *Wakan*[14] *(Wanagi Yuwakanpi kin)*. Thomas Tyon (translated by the editors). (CHS)

Dead people exist among the tipis, the people believe; and on that account everyone is always afraid of the night. That is why the members of each household really believe these things and when they eat they always give food to the ghosts. They do it in this way. They take a little bit of food and spill it out near the fire. They say this as they do it. "Ghosts, say for me 'I will live long,'" they say. The ghosts accept it, they think. If they don't do this, the ghosts take offense, they say.

And yet a second thing, at a meal a child may spill out soup or hot coffee for the same reason, it is said. It is this way, it is said. Perhaps someone who does not observe the custom might dream of ghosts and then they are "ghost killed," they say. When they say the ghosts killed someone, this is what they mean.

Ghosts cause the mouth to become crooked, they say. For that reason people are very much afraid of ghosts.

In a household on a still night, everybody there may suddenly hear a pleasing sound like someone whistling. Suddenly they hear it, so the man in the tipi says, "Alas," it is said. "Something may happen, someone is whistling behind the tipi," he says, it is said. Ghosts bring messages, they believe.

And too, it is as follows. If a man walks about at night, far from camp, and suddenly hears a human voice, he faints from fright. When he regains consciousness, his mouth and eyes are twisted, it is said. That is why, to this day, people are very frightened of ghosts.

And it is also as follows. When they bury someone and they are wailing, then the wind comes up, it is said. The *wakan* ones do this *(wakanpi xka heconpi kin)*; that is why it happens. Also, even to the present time, when an owl hoots at night, the people believe that its call is very *wakan*. Hence it is so. The people prepare ghost feasts for them, they say. And also, when they deeply love someone, they keep the spirit *(nagi yuhapelo)*. In this there are very many rules. But I have now told everything that is clear. The people believe that ghosts are *wakan*. So it is.

---

54. Double Woman Dreamers[15] *(Winyan Nonpapika Ihanblapi)*. Thomas Tyon (translated by the editors). (CHS)

When a woman dreams of the Double Woman, from that time on, in everything she makes, no one excels her. But then the woman is very much like a crazy woman *(lila witkowin)*. She laughs uncontrollably and so time and time again she acts deceptively *(knayan xkinyelo)*. So the people are very afraid of her. She causes all men who stand near her to become possessed *(wicayuknaxkin)*. For that reason these women are called Double Women. They are very promiscuous *(lila hinknatunpi s'a,* repeatedly have many husbands). But then in the things they make nobody excels them. They do much quillwork. From then on, they are very skillful. They also do work like a man.

The Double Woman is frequently at rocky cliffs. First, people hear their voices, it is said. After that, the first thing that happens is that they dream of the Double Woman, they say. Whoever dreams, she herself, sometimes imitates her in the camp circle *(hocokagapelo)*. When the camp is in a circle, she goes around the inside of the circle. Two women [Double Woman dreamers] go all the way around the circle from their home bound together by a single rope. And in the middle of the rope, they tie up an imitation of a baby. And bearing it, they go along laughing uncontrollably. Therefore, they cause all the men who stand near them to become possessed *(iyuhawica yuknaxkinyanpi)*. This is the song they sing as they walk along. "Someone is meeting me here," they say. And then, "He is the one!" they say. And then they laugh uncontrollably. So they cause all the young men to become possessed, it is said. I myself, personally, have never seen it. I have heard them tell about it. Even now, they believe these things are *wakan*.

Then too, some Double Women are doctors. Whoever walks about at night is very afraid of these Double Woman dreamers. They do not wish to hear their voices. They are very afraid of the night. Nobody sees them but they do not want to hear their voices. When they hear the voices, only women dream about the Double Woman; men never dream of her. Whoever dreams in this way seems to be crazy *(witkotkoke selececa)* but then everything she makes is very beautiful. Well, so it is. They believe them to be *wakan*. This is the end.

---

55. The White-tailed Deer Is *Wakan*[16] (*Can Tarca Yuwakanpi kin*). Thomas Tyon (translated by the editors). (CHS)

A man loves a woman and he is always thinking of her. Perhaps when he has gone to shoot deer, the very woman he loves is sitting in the forest, laughing and looking at him, they say. So the man goes to the woman and suddenly he touches her *(iputaka)*, they say. And finally they lie together, they say. Then when he finishes, the man stands up and the woman too begins to stand, they say. So the man looks at the woman. And then the woman says as follows, "I am a White-tailed Deer Woman (*can tarca winyela*, female woods deer), but I make myself look like a woman and the man is deceived," they say.

From that time, the man loves her *(teriyaku)*, they say. The man who lay down with the deer returns home. The holy man tries hard to cure him, they say. He is very deranged *(knaxkinyan)*, they say. If the man is very strong *(wakix'ake)* he will be able to live, they say. Some are not able to live and so they die, it is said. Therefore, the white-tailed deer are very much feared.

---

56. The Black-tailed Deer Is *Wakan (Sinte Sapela Yuwakanpi)*. Thomas Tyon (translated by the editors). (CHS)

The deer called black-tailed are very *wakan*, they believe. A man goes to shoot deer and he sees a black-tailed deer *(sinte sapela heyuga)*, so he shoots at it but his shots are bad, they say. He uses up all the bullets he has, they say; and he is not able to kill the deer. When he returns home, he is very deranged, they say. The holy men doctor him a great deal *(lila piyapi)* but one by one they find they can not help him, they say. Only those men who are strong are able to live, it is said. So it is. The Lakota believe the black-tailed deer to be very *wakan*. The men who doctor the victims give them charcoal *(carli)* to eat and so they live, it is said. So it is.

---

57. Horses Are *Wakan (Xunkawakan Yuwakanpi kin)*. Thomas Tyon (translated by the editors). (CHS)

A man values a horse very highly. Perhaps the horse is sick. Then the man says this. "My horse, if you get well, you will be painted red. I want recovery!" Thus they speak to the horse, and they deceive him. After a while, the horse is injured, or the man is injured, it is said.

Also this is right. When a horse is lean, the man who owns it speaks to it as follows, "My horse, for one month, no one will ride you," he says, they say. And it is not yet one month before they ride the horse. And so the horse falls and breaks its neck, it is said. So it is, the horse is very *wakan*.

They have a rule that a woman may not ride a swift horse. If a woman rides such a horse, then from that time, the horse is slow, they say. Therefore, they made a rule that if a horse is swift, a woman may not ride it. And this is right. If it was a good horse, then they judge that the household will die. If people do not hold to these customs, after a while the household becomes very poor, they say. Therefore, they are very frightened and they try to follow the customs. So it is until today, they still believe these things. They believe that horses are *wakan*. This much I know.

---

58. The Weasel Is *Wakan (Itunkasan Yuwakanpi kin)*. Thomas Tyon (translated by the editors). (CHS)

If a man wears a weasel skin shirt and continues to lie with a woman—even though the weasel is very *wakan*, he does this—then for that reason, the man becomes a weasel, it is said. And for that reason, his legs and his hands too hurt all over and so he dies, it is said.

And also if a woman comes in contact with a weasel skin while she is menstruating, she becomes very sick, it is said. Medicine men treat her but still she is very sick, it is said. Some die, it is said. If one lives, her leg is dislocated, it is said. Therefore, the weasel is very *wakan*. Right until today it is so. The otter is like this too; also the otter skin, but still they are *wakan*. So it is.

---

59. The Mountain Lion Is *Wakan (Ikmu Tanka Yuwakanpi in)*. Thomas Tyon (translated by the editors). (CHS)

Whoever mutilates *(wicayupxun)* a mountain lion or a wild cat or even a house cat will have terrible things happen to him, it is said. That man's hand or leg or foot becomes completely dislocated *(ataya napxunpsun)*, it is said. Therefore, nobody eats cats, they believe. They are very afraid of them, all cats. This is the end of information on cats. So it is.

60. Gophers Are *Wakan (Wahinheya Yuwakanpi)*. Thomas Tyon (translated by the editors). (CHS)

Men, women, boys, girls, and babies all get scrofula, which they believe is caused by gophers.[17] For you know, where those gophers are, the earth is entirely pulverized. This is why people think about gophers as they do and why they so believe. Holy men doctor them and extract gophers' whiskers from them. Then they cure people. Some are not treated quickly so these develop scrofula of the throat, it is said. Hence no one goes near to where the gophers burrow in the earth. They fear that perhaps the gophers will shoot them. Those who go to where gophers live hide their throats. They still believe in this custom to this day.

Whoever has been shot by a gopher does not eat potatoes. They think that the potato is gophers' food. They think the same way about everything that comes from the ground. So it is that the holy men form their opinion *(iyukcanpi)*. In this way they form their opinion.

Also some animals are able to kill gophers, so they rub their fat on those who have been shot by a gopher. Thus they say that they rub badger fat on anyone who has been shot by a gopher, it is said. Therefore they also believe that the badger is *wakan*. Badgers are able to kill gophers. These are the customs that the holy men dream about. That is how they know them. Thus they believe the badger to be *wakan* too, in this way. Whoever kills a badger takes out everything from the body cavity *(cuwi mahel)*, leaving only the blood. And when the blood reflects well, like a mirror, then someone can see himself in it. If the man sees himself in the blood and his entire head is white, then he will become an old man, they believe. And if another looks long inside, and sees himself sick, he will die, they say. If someone sees a red head, then he will kill an enemy. And so it is this way, it is said. This is the way it is.

61. The Spider Is *Wakan*[18] *(Iktomi Yuwakanpi kin)*. Thomas Tyon (translated by the editors). (CHS)

If a man is going to kill a spider, it is proper to say this first and then kill it. "Grandfather, *Wakinyan* are killing you!" he says and then he kills the spider. Then that man is never bitten by spiders, it is said. When someone does not say that before killing a spider, then the spider is offended and spiders bite the man, it is said. So it is. Spiders are very *wakan*, the people believe. This is the end. This belongs to the Spider *(Iktomi tawayelo)*.

62. Springs Are *Wakan (Wiwila Yuwakanpi kin)*. Thomas Tyon (translated by the editors). (CHS)

When a man drinks from a spring during the night, this is what he says before he drinks, it is said. If he does not say this and drinks the water, then the spring shoots him *(opi)*, it is said. Therefore, the people are very much afraid of springs and no one drinks water from a spring at night.

When a man has been shot by a spring, he returns home and the medicine men doctor him assiduously *(wapiyapi kin lila kuwapelo).* Whoever is strong *(wakix'ake)* can be made to live, it is said. But some they can not cure, it is said. The medicine men draw out the scum from those shot by the springs and then they live, it is said. These medicine men draw out the scum by sucking, it is said. To this very day, the Lakotas have this belief. This is the way it is.

IV

Ritual

The documents in this part pertain to three major ceremonies: the sun dance, the *Hunka* and the *Tatanka Lowanpi* (Buffalo ceremony). These are the ceremonies that Walker described in detail in *The Sun Dance,* but the documents presented here all include additional information and add important dimensions to the published accounts. Short Bull's two paintings of the sun dance and the commentaries on the details of the paintings are here published for the first time. The various documents attributed to the holy men are the primary sources upon which Walker based his synthetic descriptions of the ceremonies. All of these primary documents emphasize the particular character of an individual's understanding of a ceremony.

Thomas Tyon's text on the sun dance (document 63) adds to our knowledge of the ceremony in ways that are possible only through the unity of a single individual's viewpoint. While most of the facts that Tyon mentions can be found in Walker's own account of the ceremony, Tyon's text has specific emphases and stylistic traits that enable the reader to relate to the ceremony as an event in which one's attention is drawn from one significant point to the next. Tyon's account has a highly visual quality. We have decided to maintain the constant repetition of the English word *now* in the published translation because its presence in Lakota indicates a specific kind of transition from one idea to another; it is a stylistic feature that emphasizes the visual aspects of the text.

The accounts of the *Hunka* ceremony by the various holy men (documents 71–82) record the rich traditions surrounding the ceremony. They also add to our knowledge of the personal attitudes of some of the holy men and help us to understand why they chose to share as much information with Walker as they did. Walker wrote several long drafts of an essay describing the *Hunka* ceremony. He originally intended to use the ceremony as the focus for describing as many features of Lakota life and religion as possible. We have selected the last of these drafts for publication (document 83). This long account not only describes the many features of the ceremony as known to Walker but is also a superb example of Walker's method of synthesizing data. The account of *Hunka* printed in *The Sun Dance* (pp. 141–51) is stripped of the symbolism and detail included in this earlier draft.

Similarly, the description of the Buffalo ceremony printed here (document 85) is a draft earlier than the account published in *The Sun Dance* and incorporates many more details.

---

63. Thomas Tyon Tells about the Beginning of the Sun Dance,[1] 1910–11 (translated by the editors). (CHS and AMNH)

If a man's child is very sick, or his wife, or if enemies shoot at him in a fight and he fears very much, yet he survives and is not killed, in such case he may vow the Sun Dance. Hence on account of such vows, they seek a good man, one without offense who knows the complete ceremony. The man who is to dance the Sun Dance bears a pipe and at sunrise he goes and extends the pipe and prays for that which he desires. When he is finished, the man, from then on, proceeds very carefully. In the days to come, the one who is to dance the Sun Dance should always try to do what is proper. When he decides a thing is not proper, he is afraid of it, it is said. Something the Sun Dancers know is that in the Moon When the Sage Is Long,[2] then it is time to go, it is said. Therefore the leader of the Sun Dancers, along with the people living about, fills a pipe and carries it in procession on foot. And they select a place for the camp circle so that all may come together properly in camp and do all things properly.

Now the leader of the Sun Dancers erects a tipi in the middle of the camp circle for them and inside the tipi he covers the floor well with sage. The man who will dance the Sun Dance now makes a sweat bath for himself in a formal way and cleanses himself *(sapa sni igluhan)*. Whoever is an attendant must do the same as the leader does. Now they do things in this manner. They strip themselves completely and over their shoulders they wear furred robes with the hair out. And now they will live in the tipi. Before the Sun Dance there are strict rules made for them. No one swims. They can only take the sweat bath.

Well now, the people all camp in a big formal camp circle, and then the Sun Dancers will properly observe the rules made for them. No one laughes in the tipi and they regard everything within as *wakan*. Also, outside, around the tipi, they spread a blanket of tree leaves. They make a good place inside. They place a buffalo bull head inside. They place a pipe there also. The pipe belongs to the leader. Well, these men dress themselves as follows: They fold blue blankets around themselves and they also use scarlet blankets for skirts. Then the men repeatedly paint themselves red. They wear twisted sage around their head; they have buffalo hair tied on both wrists and on both ankles. They also have the same made of rabbit skin. Also they make a hoop covered with otter skin and they wear an otter skin cape.

Well, having finished these things properly, now during the nights, they feast. An old man cries out for those men who are skillful singers to assemble there; women also go. They sit in the tipi and they make no fire and sing the first song (first song on the phonograph records).[3] There are many songs but they sing the first. When the men who will dance the Sun Dance are singing, then all the Sun Dancers wail. Well now, they feast each night for four nights and [in this way] four days pass and then those who are to seek the *wakan* tree get busy with their work.

Now the men who are leaders decide how to divide up the work agreeably. And now the beloved children[4] are gathered together; they assemble them, and they command them to go to seek the *wakan* tree. Only the children who are relatives go. Well now, before they finish the search themselves, a good man selects the *wakan* tree and marks it, it is said. Well, when the seekers go, they all intermingle. They sing this song. They sing the second song. All who go are on horseback. They go here and there, round and round. All the people stand looking toward them and when the seeker returns they will again completely intermingle. Again they sing this song (song number three).

Now they finally arrive home so all the people bustle about (*skinciyapi*). They will now go and bring the *wakan* tree. But they do not go yet to bring the *wakan* tree. A good man goes on foot to where the *wakan* tree will be erected. They select a man who has done nothing bad and have him dig a hole in the ground, it is said. And while the hole is being dug they begin to erect leafy tree branches the height of a man. Now the entire people go to bring the *wakan* tree. Now they go there together. When they arrive at the *wakan* tree, a holy man again stands there and talks. Then he sings. They sing this song (song number four). During this time all the people stand very quietly. Then the men who are leaders gather the beloved children together again. Again the holy man talks there, and again he sings (song number five). And then he stands and looks toward the four winds and now he stands by the *wakan* tree holding an ax and in that place he talks again, and he pretends to strike the *wakan* tree three times and the fourth time he strikes it. Then he stops striking with the ax. Therefore the leaders now meditate. This is the song of their meditation (the sixth song).

They dance the White Owners dance *(Ska yuha wacipi)*.[5] At this time, those who choose to give to them make many presents to the children one by one in a line, and when they have finished there, then they choose a good woman and she alone cuts down the *wakan* tree and completely separates the branches from it. And when they have completely finished this, they pick some very good men who have never done anything bad. And those will bear the *wakan* tree as they go, returning to camp.

Well those on horseback are there and again they are prepared to hurry about *(skanpi)*. Those who bear the sacred pole return on foot and they will make three pauses and each time they will howl. The fourth time, the last, they howl like dogs.[6] Now those on horseback will race vigorously to the place in the camp circle where the *wakan* tree is to be erected. They make their goal an enemy and he who first strikes that will really kill an enemy in the future. They wish for this and race vigorously.

Well now, all the people returning arrive on foot at the camp circle, and where the *wakan* tree will stand they bring yellow clay and the *wakan* tree. Then all the various societies sit in a circle and sing: White Owners and Kit Foxes and White Marked and Bare Lances and Pawnee[7] and Omaha. Then they sit around while they cook food in kettles and sing while cooking. These societies set up their tipis.

Well now the place where the sacred pole is has been made *wakan*; no one goes near that place. Now again the holy man goes there and commands them to bring the offerings. The *wakan* tree is forked. The top of the tree is towards where the sun goes down. First are the stems of chokecherry bushes that have no leaves and then the fat of a ruminant's heart and then red clay and then the fat of a buffalo loin, and a wooden rod, the stem of a chokecherry bush completely peeled, thrust into the buffalo loin. They mix the red clay in one of a pair of parfleches.

They paint red the entire green bark of the forks. They mix Pawnee and common tobacco and put it on, and a feather decorated with red-dyed porcupine quills down the middle. Then they wrap the chokecherry stems in a bundle. And now they put them in the forks of the *wakan* tree.

Now all the people stand respectfully and quietly. They make an image of a man of rawhide and paint it entirely red. They place a plume on the head completely reddened. And they also make an image of a buffalo and paint it entirely black. They tie on the pole two small thongs so they will hang down from it. Now they carefully push upright the *wakan* tree, the forked tree. Now they place it erect and the people all shout together excitedly. Then all the women sing. At the top of the tree they tie a red blanket and then they paint the *wakan* tree on the sides of the four winds. Then the women raise the tremolo *(ongna kical)*.

Well now, the entire people move about very excitedly and they set up the Sun Dance lodge. When they finish the lodge, a man again proclaims in a loud voice. Now all the young men paint themselves red. Now they will have the ground-smoothing dance. So now all the young men come according to their band *(tiyospaye)* to the middle of the camp circle. Each band has thirty-five or forty. In this way they come.

Well now, when they come to the place of the Sun Dance they run excitedly around the lodge. And now they go within the lodge. Within the lodge they dance around firing guns. They shoot both the image of the man and the image of the buffalo. This is the song for the dance (song eight). Then this song is for the *wasicunpi* (song nine). Now they come outside altogether, moving quietly. Now those who will dance the Sun Dance separate and the Sun Dancers go together into the tipi.

Now they have finished the lodge for the Sun Dance so they come around the lodge praying. Now they stand at the entrance of the lodge. They go to the *catku*. The leader of the Sun Dance goes first, formally bearing the buffalo head. Bearing it to the *catku*, he stands there. He feigns four times to lay it down and then lays it down. And again they feign laying their hands on it three times and the fourth time they really lay their hands on it formally and then take them away. They all sit at the *catku*. These men will sing but they will not use a drum. A dried buffalo hide is used for the singers. They use quite a long wooden rod with a ruminant's tail tied on the end to beat the dried buffalo hide. And again they sing the first song (the first and second songs). And then they dance all around the lodge. They sing a song. This is song number ten. Well, from now on they dance throughout the night. And thus the day passes.

So now the leader of all the Sun Dancers prepares the ground. At first he stands facing the west. He talks. Then the people stand looking toward him and say, "We wish you life." And with an ax he feigns three times to strike the ground and the fourth time he strikes it. And then in the same manner he strikes towards the east. And then he strikes the middle of the ground. Well now, he digs the ground and pulverizes it. Now he replaces all the earth and makes a star at the center of it. And there he sprinkles Pawnee tobacco and red clay. And then he erects on this pulverized earth a pipe and a rod of chokecherry stem completely painted blue. This pipe is formally filled with tobacco. And then he places the pipe on a dried buffalo chip.

Well now, the sun is at the meridian, so they will now mark the Sun Dancers. So they first take two braided thongs and approach the *wakan* tree and then tie them to the *wakan* tree so that they will hang suspended from it. And now when the sun is at the meridian the holy man again sings. He sings song number eleven, and also song number twelve. Men, for the sake of the people, give names to the children. As long as they are Sun Dancing, they run to give away presents.

The men drink no water while they dance and they do not eat. They will compose and sing songs on this day. While dancing in the circle they will use these songs. They use songs number thirteen through twenty-three. Songs number twenty-four and twenty-five are scalp songs or victory songs.

Well now, the ceremony is completed and the people disperse widely. All go to whatever place they wish. All the Sun Dancers sound a large whistle while dancing and look at the sun as it moves *(hinapa)*. And the words of the songs for the dance are such as are appropriate. If they wish for many buffalo, they will sing of them; if victory, sing of it; and if they wish to bring good weather, they will sing of it.

64. The Holy Men Tell of the Sun Dance. Little Wound, American Horse, and Lone Star, September 14, 1896 (Antoine Herman, interpreter). (AMNH)

The Sun Dance is the greatest ceremony that the Oglalas do. It is a sacred ceremony in which all the people have a part. It must be done in a ceremonial camp. It must be conducted by a shaman who knows all the customs of the people. He must know all the secret things of the shamans. He is the chief and *wakiconza* of the ceremonial camp. Other shamans should help him as his council. He appoints the *akicita* of the ceremonial camp.

The Sun Dance must be done in a dance lodge made for that purpose. This lodge must not be used for any other purpose. . . . The Sun Dance must be done around a sacred pole. This pole must be at the center of the dance lodge. . . .

One who wishes to dance the Sun Dance should make this known some time before the time for doing this dance. This is because all the people have a part in this ceremony. All should have time to prepare for the Sun Dance. . . . One who wishes to dance the Sun Dance must give feasts and many presents. He must give away all that he possesses. His people must give feasts and presents. . . . He must choose someone to instruct him for the dance. The one he chooses becomes his grandfather. He must think and act just as his grandfather tells him. He must submit to his grandfather in everything until he dances. He must obey the rules for one who is about to dance this dance. . . .

The ceremony of the Sun Dance is in four parts. One part for the dancer and the people to prepare for the dance; one part to gather at the place for the dance; one part for the camp and the ceremonies before the dance; the last part for the Sun Dance. . . .

Anyone may dance the Sun Dance if he will do as the Oglalas do. A man or a woman or a child may dance. But for women and children the dance is done differently. They are not attached to the stakes or the pole as men are. Women nearly always dance in the name of some absent one. . . .

If one wishes to become a shaman of the highest order, he should dance the Sun Dance suspended from the pole so that his feet will not touch the ground. . . . If one has scars on his breast or his back that show that he has danced the Sun Dance, no Oglala will doubt his word. He is eligible for leadership of a war party or for chieftainship. . . . The ceremony of the Sun Dance may embrace all the ceremonies of any kind that are relative to the Gods. . . .

---

65. Instructing the Sun Dance Candidate. George Sword, June 17, 1909 (Thomas Wells, interpreter). (AMNH)

The one who instructs a candidate to dance the Sun Dance is the *tunkansila*. This means more than a grandfather. The candidate then becomes like a babe. His instructor governs him in everything. He must do nothing but as he is told by his instructor. The instructor thinks for him and speaks for him and tells him how to think and how to speak. The instructor gives rules and the candidate must obey them exactly. The instructor becomes the candidate's other self. He is like the candidate's spirit. . . .

The candidate is a sacred person until he dances. . . . The *tunkansila* is like a sacred person until when the candidate is to dance. . . . When the candidate begins to dance, the instructor has nothing more to do with him. . . . One who has danced the Sun Dance should always respect the one who gave him his instruction. He should treat him as if he were his *Hunka*. You have chosen me to give you the instruction and I am your grandfather according to the Lakota customs.

---

66. Sun Dance Symbols. George Sword. (CHS)

A hoop covered with otter skin ceremoniously is a symbol of the sun and of years. The years are a circle. An armlet of rabbit skin is an emblem of fleetness and of endurance on long journeys and during marches. A cape of otter skin is an emblem of power over land and water. A skirt of red worn by a man is an emblem of holiness. A blue skirt is an emblem of *Taku Skanskan*, that is, of the heavens, and indicates that the wearer is engaged in a sacred undertaking. Armlets and anklets are emblems of strength and of love and cunning in the chase.

---

67. The Sun Dance Pole. Bad Heart Bull. (CHS)

The sacred Sun Dance pole must be cottonwood because the ghost-like [*nagila*][8] of the cottonwood is not dense when it is dry.

When the tree is cut down it must be trimmed, all but the forks at the top. These must not be trimmed because this is the head of the tree and its spirit-like is there. The leaves must not be taken from the top, for these leaves are like the scalp of mankind and they control the spirit-like of the tree. The tree is captured and if its scalp is left on it, it will serve those who capture it. The bark and limbs must be taken from the body of the tree because its ghost-like is in these, and if they are left on the tree, the ghost may haunt the dancers.

---

68. Notes on the Paintings of the Sun Dance. Short Bull, 1912.[9] (CHS)

Painting 1 (Plate 1). The Third Day of the Sun Dance.

Lower left hand corner, coming to dance.
Man at bottom, dried buffalo head, must go round the circle.
Figure of man and buffalo hung to pole.
Black space [represents a] bundle of chokecherry bushes.

Inside [the] bundle a bag and in the bag, buffalo hair and sweetgrass.

Thongs for suspending dancers.

At right corner one with [buffalo] head and pipe, to be suspended.

At foot of pole red flannel wrapped around fat from heart and
loins of buffalo; flag of red flannel.

Man below carries flags for drummers.

At left of door, dried buffalo hide and drum.

Drumsticks ordinary and for dancers.

Painting 2 (Plate 2). The Fourth Day of the Sun Dance.

Crowds belong in tipis.

Tipis painted as in former times.

Designs on tipis represent dreams in usual sleep.

Dream of bears.

Black tipi represents night; should have light.

Moon and stars, the light of night.

Antelope is brother-in-law.

Red stripe is roads.

Calf-hide door.

Speckled tipi of bear.

Rainbow and sky, a clear day.

Blue, a clear day.

Speckled top, small clouds.

At left, young man courting.

Lower right, the same.

Black blotches, tipi of dreams.

Scarlet tipi of fire.

Buckskin skirts with porcupine [quillwork].

The sacred pole.

Dancers cut fingers and carried buffalo hides.

Hoops of other hides all carry.

Two feathers as horns of antelopes.

Sage wreaths.

Horns like a buffalo's made of feathers.

Whistles made of eagle bones.

Gaze at the sun.

Big hoop, elks.[10]

Move a brush of feathers over dancers when they weary.

Red staff.
Banners for dancers.
Musicians.
Only two suspended.
Should be only two dancers.
When one breaks loose, the other dances.
Beds for dancers.
Gifts for dancers.
Two days and one night; dancers fast and pray.
After first night, young man with water tempts them.
They sing a song to resist temptation.
Legend of origin of Sun Dance.[11]

69. Short Bull's Painting of the Third Day of the Sun Dance. J. R. Walker.[12] (CHS)

The painting [plate 1] representing the area of the formal camp circle for the Sun Dance shows only such tipis and lodges as are permitted on this area and only such persons as take an active part in the ceremony of the Sun Dance. The time is the morning of the third day of the ceremony, and the first day of the dance, when the dancers are formed in line to march to the dance lodge. Except that one figure represents a candidate dancing the buffalo head form of the dance which occurs on the second day of the dance. This is given here because in this form, the farther the buffalo heads are dragged, the greater the merits of the dance and the dancer is permitted to leave the dance lodge and drag the heads about the area until he falls from exhaustion.[13]

Only circular tipis or lodges are permitted in the camp circle or on the area. These may be decorated with designs or colors but each decoration should indicate something of note relative to the occupant.

The entrance of all tipis should be toward the center of the area. The entrances of the lodges should be toward the dance lodge and the entrance to the dance lodge should open toward the sun at midday.

Beginning at the right of the painting the explanation of it in detail is as follows: the first tipi is that of the shaman who conducts the ceremony, indicated by the red banners at the top of his tipi poles. It is colored yellow as an indication that he has communicated in a vision with the great God *Inyan*, the Rock, and that his *wasicun* or ceremonial bag has the potency of that God; the inside of the tipi is colored black as an indication that he has supernatural powers through his *wasicun*.[14]

The next tipi above is that of an associate shaman in the conduct of the ceremony whose tipi is decorated as that of the first, except that there are no red banners on the poles.

The next two tipis are the sacred lodges, or preparation lodges, where the candidates must remain from the beginning of the ceremony until its close, passing through the entrance only to march to the dance lodge or on returning from it. These lodges are colored red to indicate that the occupants are sacred persons, and no one is permitted to come near them except those who do so as a part of the ceremonial rites, or their attendants chosen by themselves or appointed by the council of the ordinary camp. These lodges are colored blue inside, emblematic of *Wanagi Tanka*, or the Great Spirit, *Taku Skanskan*, the Sky. This is to propitiate him because he gives life and strength and his aid will be needed by the candidates in their fast in the lodge and their dance during the ceremony.

A consecrated buffalo calf skin is hung as a flap over the entrance to the sacred lodge as a [propitiatory] act toward the Buffalo God who prevails in the formal camp for the Sun Dance. This skin is taken and hung upon the sacred pole during the dance.

The scarlet tipi above the sacred lodges is that of a very old and powerful shaman who, because of his repute, may place his tipi where he desires. The scarlet color of his tipi indicates that in a vision he has seen a fire, the *akicita* of the Sun, which is evidence that he has the favor of all the Gods and especially that of the Sun, and that his *wasicun* is of the most potent. Therefore, he may take precedence in any ceremony or alter or stop any ceremony. The circular emblems on his tipi indicate the supernatural powers he communicates with and whose potency his *wasicun* may exercise, except that of the Sun.

The one [emblem] above the entrance indicates that he has had communication with the Sun, through the fire, but the potency of the Sun is imparted to no other thing than the fire. The emblem on the right indicates that he communicates with *Wanagi Tanka*, the Great Spirit, the Sky, and with *Unci*, Grandmother, the Earth, and *Wakinyan*, the Winged One. Because he has communicated with the Winged One, commonly translated the Thunderbird, he is *heyoka* and must [stay] apart alone in all ceremonies. Therefore he is pictured sitting alone in his tipi watching the ceremony. His face is black, which ordinarily indicates either mourning or enmity, but he, being a *heyoka*, must do contrary to the ordinary actions of mankind and his black face indicates rejoicing and approval.

The emblem at the left indicates that he may communicate with *Inyan*, the great God, the Rock, and with *Eya*,[15] the great God of evil. *Inyan* is the God of destruction and *Eya* is the God of all manner of magic for evil. Therefore, the *wasicun* of the shaman is to be feared as well as respected.

The lower figure of a man with banners over his shoulder represents the shaman who conducts the ceremony. The red sash about his waist is the badge of his office. The red designs on his face are his personal emblem. His red hands indicate that he is entitled to touch and handle holy things. He bears his fetish in his right hand, its color, red, indicates that it is potent in holy things. In his left hand are banners emblematic of various supernatural powers he has communicated with in vision[s]. He is beside the candidates and will so march with them whenever they go outside the preparation or dance lodge.

The group of figures next above the shaman represents the candidates to dance the Sun Dance. They are in line, single file, except the two leaders of the dance, who are side by side. They march in this order when outside the preparation or dance lodge. They are all prepared alike, each with his body painted red, except his hands, and naked except for a skirt of deer skin from his waist down. He has four eagle plumes attached upright to his scalp as an emblem of his good repute and a badge showing that he has a part in the ceremony of the Sun Dance.

About his head is a chaplet of sage, because sage is the favored herb of the Sun and is offensive to all evil beings. Around his neck is a necklace to which is attached a disk of rawhide colored in an emblematic manner. The disk is a symbol of the world and of time, and therefore, of all things. Tied to the center of the disk is the central quill from an eagle's tail so that it will hang in front of the wearer. This is a symbol of bravery and fortitude.

About his wrists and ankles are bands made of the shed hair of the buffalo, in which abides the potency of the God Buffalo, who is the patron of the chase and of the tipi.

The leader on the right bears in his two hands a filled pipe because the potency of the Mediator of the Gods abides in the smoke of the pipe. The leader on the left bears in his two hands a buffalo head ornamented with colors and having wisps of sage stuffed in its nostrils which is borne with the muzzle pointing forward [because] the God the Buffalo prevails in the camp and the sage in the nostrils banishes all evil from about their march.

The next group above the candidates represents the attendants chosen by the candidates or appointed by the council to wait upon the candidates and accompany them in the ceremony. Each of these is prepared and adorned like the candidates, except that their bodies, including their hands, are painted red, indicating that they can touch and handle sacred things, and the chaplet is of green grass and the anklets of sage. Each bears in his left hand a whistle made of the wing bone of an eagle, which he will deliver to the candidate he attends when dancing. In his right hand he bears a bunch of sage to be used to wipe the face and body of the candidates when they rest during the dance.

The shaman, the candidates and the attendants are the only persons permitted to come near the sacred lodge after the candidates first enter it.

The dance lodge is represented at the center of the picture as a circular bower sided and covered with green leaves and with its entrance toward the sun at midday. The frame of the lodge is made by forked posts set in the ground in two circles, one within the other. Poles are laid on these posts so as to make a supporting frame that will hold the branches having green leaves on them so as to form protecting sides and cover, except at the entrance, which is left vacant. Banners of the symbolic colors of the Gods are fastened to the tops of the inner circle of posts.

The area of the lodge is divided into two parts, the dancing and resting space. The resting space is the outer portion between the two circles of posts and under the covering. It is divided into two parts, the dedicated and the common part. The dedicated part is on the side opposite the entrance, colored red in the painting. At its middle, exactly opposite the door, next the wall of the lodge, is the *catku,* or honor place. Those who are entitled to rest on the dedicated part are the shaman conducting the ceremony and the two leaders of the dance at the honor place; next to these on the right and left are the candidates for the dance; next to these, the members of the societies taking part in the ceremony; next to these the four women who felled the sacred tree and the four men who struck it first with the ax; next to these, the mothers whose babes are to have their ears pierced and the men who are to pierce them.

Whoever wishes to do so may sit on the common part, but seats in the lodge are ceremonial and whosoever sits there must observe due decorum as is indicated by the red dashes in the painting.

The dancing space is all within the resting space and is occupied only by those taking an active part in the ceremony. On this space, next to and at the left of the entrance is placed the dry hide of a ruminant, preferably that of a buffalo, and a dance drum, and beside the hide are placed long wands with the dried tail of a buffalo tied to the smaller end of each. These are to be used by the drummers to drum on the dry hide when singing the ceremonial songs. Beside the drum are placed common drum sticks and two drum sticks that have been ornamented by a maiden chosen because of her good repute. The common drum sticks are to be used in making music that is not ceremonial and the two ornamented sticks are to be used in the selection of renowned warriors to dance the preliminary dance for the instruction of the candidates. The space about these implements is reserved for the musicians.

About this space the sacred posts are set as shown, colored red in the picture. Those who dance the form called "standing tied" are tied to these posts by thongs which pass through the flesh of the breasts and back.

The sacred pole is erected at the center of this space as shown in the picture. It is colored red to indicate its sacred character, and is forked near the top. The image of a man and of a buffalo made of the dry hide of a ruminant are suspended from the fork of the sacred pole. These are made with ceremony and colored black, which gives to them the receptivity of an enemy and of the Demon Buffalo [*Tatanka Gnaskinyan*] so that whatsoever is done to these images occurs to the enemy and to the demon. In the fork is tied a sacred bundle composed of a number of trunks of the chokecherry bush around a parfleche and digger. The parfleche contains such articles as are acceptable as offerings to the Gods and the bundle is consecrated by appropriate ceremony before it is tied in place. Near the top of the pole a red banner is placed, the sacred color of the sun, showing the disposition of the people to give allegiance to his will. At the top of the pole is a bunch of leaves left there when the tree was prepared as a pole so that the spirit of the tree might be appeased and lend itself to the purpose of the pole.

The figure of the man below the entrance to the lodge represents him dancing the buffalo head form of the Sun Dance. The number of buffalo heads he may choose are fastened to him by thongs passing through the flesh of his back so that the blood will flow. These he drags while dancing and the greater distance he drags them the more meritorious is his dance, so he is permitted to leave the dance lodge and drag the heads about the camp area and he should dance dragging them until he falls from exhaustion. In this form the body is naked except for the breech clout, though the dancer is permitted to carry two staffs, provided they have been made red with ceremony.

The group to the right above the dance lodge represents the maiden assistants chosen because of their good repute after having passed the ordeal of biting the snake to establish their chastity.[16]

The one in the center is canny *(wakan)*, because her eyes are crossed and she has supernatural powers as shown by this. Such are chosen to ornament the drum sticks for the Sun Dance because they are by nature *wakan* or canny. Each of these maidens has the four eagle plumes erect at the scalp lock, the sage chaplet and necklace with the dry hide disk. But she has not the eagle quill attached to the disk, though she may carry an eagle quill at her belt, provided she will give it to a man during the ceremony. She has wristlets of the shed hair of a buffalo, but no anklets. These maidens are entitled to sit with the musicians and take part in all the songs of the ceremony but they are not permitted to sit on the dedicated space. The tipi behind and above them is the lodge where they assemble for the ceremony.

The group next to the left of them represents the four women who felled the sacred tree standing together and a mother who is to have her babe's ears pierced standing near to the left of them. They are adorned as are the maidens, except that they are not permitted to carry the eagle quill and they have anklets of shed buffalo hair. Any number of mothers may choose to have their babe's ears pierced and all such belong with this group. This group is entitled to sit on the dedicated space and to take such part in the ceremony as they may be requested to do, usually, to minister to the comfort of the dancers as much as the customs will permit.

A mother who wishes to have her babe's ears pierced should make a bed of sage on the dedicated space on which the babe will lie while a man pierces its ears.

The next group beyond and below the women represents the members of the societies who take part in the ceremony. They are adorned as are the candidates except that their anklets are of sage. Their hands are painted red and in the right hand they bear whistles made of the wing bones of eagles, which indicate that they will dance, and in their left hands are bunches of sage with which they will refresh themselves during the dance. Their lodges are above and behind them.

The next group below these represents the Brave Heart or Silent Society[17] composed of the elders of the camp among whom are the four men who first struck the sacred tree with the axe and those who bore the sacred pole from where it was prepared to its proper place. These are all adorned as are the other members of the societies except that their eagle plumes are wrapped with scarlet and their anklets are of rabbit skin. They bear the whistles and bunches of sage indicating that they intend to dance. They are entitled to sit on the dedicated space and take such part in the ceremony as may be required of them. Their lodge is behind them, with a scarlet flap over the entrance to indicate the character of the occupants.

This is as a Brulé Sioux would read the picture.[18]

---

70. Piercing the Ears. Rocky Bear, February 1, 1905.[19] (CHS)

Piercing the ears is a custom that the Oglalas and Lakotas have practiced from ancient times. This is done to show that they are

Lakota. Anyone may have his ears pierced, a man, a woman, or a child. This is a sign that the one having his ears pierced will live according to the Lakota customs and obey their laws. It obligated such a one to side with the Lakotas against all others of mankind. Usually the parents had their children's ears pierced when the children were small. It was so in former times.

Then when the Sun Dance was danced, all the children whose ears were not pierced and who had been born since the last Sun Dance, had their ears pierced while the dancers were dancing. But it was not necessary to have the ears pierced at a Sun Dance. Anyone might have the ears pierced at any time. Usually someone was chosen to do this. A shaman or holy man was usually chosen to perform the operation. The ears were pierced with anything sharp enough to do so. Formerly this was done with a pointed stone or an awl. The shaman performed a ceremony and sang his song to his ceremonial bag. Then he pierced the ears and exhorted the one whose ears were pierced, or the parents of such a one, to live as Lakota and to observe all the customs of the Lakotas.

If the one had a name he might keep it, or the one who pierced the ears might give a new name when the operation was done. If a new name was given, the one who gave it became godfather to the one who received it. Then presents were given, both to the one who gave the name and to the one who received it, and also to the shaman. If this was done when there was no Sun Dance, a feast was given after the operation.

* * * One who had a child's ears pierced thereby became responsible for the instruction of that child relative to the customs of the Lakotas. * * * One whose ears are to be pierced is laid on a bed of sage. Then the one who is to pierce the ears harangues, telling of his feats and why he is qualified for piercing ears. He should then kneel at the head of the person whose ears he is to pierce and place a block of wood under the ear and with a knife or awl pierce the ear, one or more times as has been agreed upon. Then he should pierce the other ear in a like manner. The hole made by piercing may be large or small as agreed upon and it may be at any part of the ear desired. A bit of sinew or of tanned skin is placed in the hole to keep it from closing by healing. This is moved often to keep the hole open. One who pierces an ear is obligated to know that the one whose ear is pierced is taught the customs of the Lakotas. A holy man or the

council may proclaim that anyone is entitled to have the ears pierced. One who wins the right to wear a quill from the eagle's tail is entitled to have his ears pierced. One whose ears are pierced is entitled to the respect of the people, except he has disgraced himself.

---

71. Legend of the First *Hunka*. No Flesh. (CHS)

Before the Seven Council Fires the Sioux Indians all made their winter camp together. Before then, in ancient times, there was a head chief of all the Sioux who had four sons. These sons were cunning hunters and brave warriors, so they were Foxes, and two of them were the stake holders for the camp. (*A stake holder among the Sioux is a member of the association of Foxes who is chosen because of his bravery and daring for the place. There are two of them, and their duty is, when the camp is attacked by an enemy, to care for the helpless, to guard the rear when a camp is retreating, and to rescue women and children from danger or when taken prisoners.*)[20]

During the summer hunt the camp was attacked by the enemy, and one of the stake holders was killed while trying to rescue an old woman, and the other was killed while trying to keep the enemy from the retreating camp. The other two sons were chosen stake holders, and went on a war party to win the right to carry the banner of the Foxes, when they were both killed. The chief mourned for his sons, and gave away everything he possessed, even his tipi and his clothing and his women's clothing. Then he sought a vision, going naked to the top of a high hill. The people camped about the hill, and all stayed in their tipis while the chief was on the hill.

The chief invoked *Tate* (The spirit of the Wind), and he sent his youngest son, *Yomni* (The spirit of the Whirlwind), which talked with the chief. It said to him, "Travel towards the pines until you find a lone tipi. Go into the tipi, and what you find in it bring back with you."

The chief came and told the people what he had seen and heard on the hill, and they gave him clothing and food and he traveled towards the pines [north]. On the fourth day he came to a lone tipi. He went into it and found a baby boy and a baby girl. He took them and brought them back to his camp and proclaimed to all the people that he took this boy and this girl for his son and his daughter.

Then the people made a great feast, and sang and danced, and played games and gave presents to the chief, and to his women, and to his son and daughter, so that he had more than he had before he gave away everything when mourning for his sons. He then called together the councilors and the keeper of the mysterious pipe and the shamans and when they had feasted and smoked, he told them that they were called to choose a name for the boy and the girl.

They made a smoke with sage, and then with sweetgrass, and then they smoked willow bark in the pipe, and while they were smoking, a shaman said to the chief, "What was the last word *Yomn* said to you?"

The chief said, "The last word *Yomn* said was '*Hunka.*' "

Then the shaman said, "This boy and this girl are *Hunka*, and you are *Ate*. So they will be forever. When they are a man and a woman, then we will know what to name them."

The boy became a hunter when he was a man, and a leader in the buffalo driving; and he became a brave, and a great warrior, and he took many scalps of the enemy, so that in the chief's tipi there were many scalps for each one of his sons that the enemy had killed. The girl was industrious and generous. She had food always ready so that no one went hungry from the chief's tipi. The fire always burned in the tipi, and she gathered herbs and sweetgrass. She could tan skins so they were soft and white, and paint dreams on robes so that *Iktomi* was afraid of them. She could make moccasins and leggings, and ornament them with designs that the spirits would respect. So the people named the boy Bull Bear, because he was a leader of the people, and because he was brave and cunning. They named the girl Good Heart, because she was industrious and generous.

Bull Bear was chosen as a Fox, and taught the mysteries of the mysterious pipe. He was chosen a councilor, and made a Silent Eater. He was made the head marshal *(akicita)*, but the old chief would not consent that he should be made a stake holder, for he feared that he would lose him as he had lost his other sons. Bull Bear led many war parties, and his sister often went

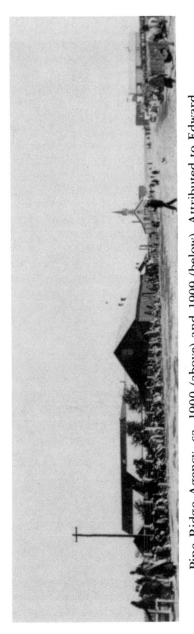

Pine Ridge Agency, ca. 1900 (above) and 1909 (below). Attributed to Edward Truman. Walker Collection, Colorado Historical Society

Dancing at Pine Ridge, July 3, 1891. The Denver Public Library, Western History Department

Painting a hide. Sioux homes in background. Pine Ridge or Rosebud Reservation, ca. 1898. Photograph by Jesse Hastings Bratley. Crane Collection, Denver Museum of Natural History, negative number BR 61-187

Lakota homes on Lower Medicine Root Creek. Undated. Walker Collection, Colorado Historical Society

Above: Before entering the sweat lodge. Negative number BR 61-278

Three views of the purification lodge, or sweat bath. Probably taken on the Rosebud Reservation, 1898. Photographs by Jesse Hastings Bratley. Crane Collection, Denver Museum of Natural History

Opposite, above: Sweat lodge with cover raised. Negative number BR 61-168

Opposite, below: Just out of the sweat lodge. Negative number BR 61-264

Sun dance lodge at Pine Ridge, 1882. Fred B. Hackett Collection, Colorado Historical Society

Council or ceremonial lodge at Pine Ridge. Undated. Walker Collection, Colorado Historical Society

A *Hunka* ceremony at Pine Ridge, 1907. Photographs by Edward
S. Curtis, from Edward S. Curtis, *The American Indian,* vol. 3.
Smithsonian Institution National Anthropological Archives.
Above: Bringing the buffalo skull for the altar
Below: The altar completed

Omaha dancers inside a log dance house. Undated. Walker Collection, Colorado Historical Society

with him on the warpath, so the people all expected that he would be the head chief when the old chief died.

Then a shaman said to the chief: "Now you are an old man. You will soon travel to the ghost land. Before you go you should do this for your people. Make a great feast for your people. Proclaim this to the people. *Yomn* taught you this thing. When one's heart is good towards another, let them be as one family. Let them proclaim this to the people. Let them do so with feasting and presents."

Then the chief made a great feast for all the people, and he counseled with the councilors, and with the chiefs and with the shamans, and it was agreed that this thing should be for a law forever. Then the chief had the head marshal *(akicita)* proclaim to the people that as long as they were a people, when anyone wished to do a great favor to another he should choose him as a *Hunka,* or as an *Ate.* The people agreed to this, and ever since that time this has been the law among the Sioux, until the missionaries taught them that this is wrong.

When they performed the ceremony over them with horses' tails, then the shamans became the head men of the *Hunkayapi,* and they taught them what they should do.

This is what the missionaries said was wrong.

---

72. Origin of the *Hunka* Ceremony. Little Wound. (CHS)

I am now old. My day is nearly ended. I see the shadows of night coming. I will tell you of my people and of their old customs. I am a chief, and my father was the head chief of the Oglalas. He was murdered by Red Cloud in a cowardly way. My father was a *Mihunka* to all the people. He told me stories *(hunkankanpi)* of the old times. He told me of the year when They Made the Ceremony over Each Other with the Horses' Tails[21] (established the ritual of the *Hunka Lowanpi*). His name was Bull Bear. This year was before he was born. His father's name was Stone Knife. He was shaman and the head chief of the Oglalas. He helped to make the ceremony of the horses' tails.

It was this ceremony that was performed when an Oglala

chose a *Hunka* or an *Ate*. They used to perform this ceremony, but now the people have forgotten it. Only the old men remember it. I know the ceremony and I can perform it. I am a *Hunka* and an *Ate* many times. I can wear so many red stripes that they would hide my face. I do not wear them any more, because the young people have forgotten what they mean, and they do not show proper respect *(hunkayasni)* for them.

In old times everything had its shadow (ghost or spirit). The shaman could invoke the spirit of the *Tatanka,* or of the *Inyan,* or any other good and powerful influence *(ton)*, and it would come and do his bidding. Now the shamans have lost their power. The spirits no longer come to help men. In ancient times, before my grandfather helped to make the ceremony of the horses' tails, anyone could choose another for a *Hunka.* If such were a person with a good heart, he would give a feast and make presents. The chiefs and the councilors and the shamans counseled about this and they proclaimed that it was not good.

A shaman sought a vision. His vision was a ghost like a cloud. He followed this ghost and it led him into a great hole in the earth. When they came into this hole it was like a great council tipi, and there were many people there. All were feasting and singing and giving presents. *Tate* and *Okaga* were there. They taught the shaman the songs and the ceremony. Then *Tate* carried him through the air back to his people, and told him that when one chose a *Hunka* or an *Ate,* then this ceremony and these songs should be done and performed.

So he taught the ceremony and the songs to the chiefs and the councilors and the shamans. This he did by waving horses' tails over all the people. When he did this, a mysterious whirlwind *(tate homni wakan)* came and proved to the people that this pleased the spirits.

Since that time when a person is made a *Hunka* it is done with this ceremony. The secrets of the ceremony were mysterious *(wakan)*. They are not good now. No one cares for them now. They will be lost when the *Hunkayapi* are all dead. I will tell them to you. You may write them, for the spirits of the ancient times no longer visit the people. They will do me no harm. If they do, I am an old man and ready to die.

My friend I make you my *Hunka* when I tell you these things. You must look on me as your *Ate (miye Hunkakeya)*. If you will do this, I will tell you the secrets of the *Hunkayapi*.[22]

That which I tell you you must remember at all times, then the spirits will help you. If you forget it, then the spirits will do you harm.

Inyan dwells in the stone. *Tate* dwells in the air. *Okaga* dwells in the south. *Tatanka* governs the love and the hate of all men and all animals. I am a shaman. I am familiar with these spirits. I am familiar with all spirits and the ghosts of dead men. They will do my bidding. When I make a medicine that is good, and when I make an incantation that pleases them, then they will care for one whom I ask them to care for. This ceremony belongs in the tipi of *Inyan*. *Tate* and *Okaga* have taught it to the shamans. *Tatanka* watches all and if any who have had this ceremony performed over them act in a bad way, he makes all men and all animals hate such a one.

Inyan wants one with a straight tongue. *Tate* wants one who is brave and cunning. *Okaga* wants one who has a good heart and is generous. *Tatanka* watches all *Hunkayapi,* and if they do wrong he informs all spirits of this and they punish such a one.

Okaga comes in the moon when the grass begins to grow. To the sweetgrass he gives his spirit. His spirit is in the smoke of the sweetgrass. *Waza* [*Waziya*] is the chief of the bad spirits. He brings cold and death. He hates *Okaga,* but he runs from the spirit of *Okaga.* The smoke of sweetgrass and a good song will drive the spirit of *Waza* away.

Tate gives his spirit to the sage. The smoke of the sage is strong, and all evil spirits fear it. They will fly from it.

Red is the most beautiful color. The spirits are pleased with red. *Inyan* is the Spirit of the Earth that dwells in the stone. It pleases *Inyan* to have red placed on a stone. When you would please the spirits put red paint on a stone.

That all may know that you are *Hunka* you may wear a stripe of red paint on your forehead and cheek. When you wear this red paint you must act so as to please the spirits and live as your *Ate* teaches you.

By this red streak, the spirits will know you. They will respect *(hunkaya)* you, and treat you as their child.

If you wear this red streak without being entitled to do so, or if you act contrary to what your monitors *(Mihunka)* have taught you, then *Tatanka* will inform all men and all women and all animals that you are a sham, and the spirits in medicine will go from them. Disease and hardships will come upon you.

These are the secrets of *Hunkayapi*. You must not talk of them with anyone except a *Hunka* or *Ate*. My friend I have told you the secrets of the *Hunkayapi*. I fear that I have done wrong. But the spirits of old times do not come to me any more. Another spirit has come, the Great Spirit of the white man. I do not know him. I do not know how to call him to help me. I have done him no harm, and he should do me no harm. The old life is gone, and I cannot be a young man again.

73. The *Hunka*. George Sword. (AMNH)

The Oglala Sioux for the ceremony is *Hunka Lowanpi*. The accent is on the second syllable of *Hunka,* and the first syllable of *Lowanpi*.[23] *Hunka* appears to be a borrowed word from some other Indian language. *Lowan* means a song or singing. *Lowanpi* means singing with ceremonies or performances.

This ceremony has been practiced among the Oglalas for many years. There is a year named for the time when it was given the present form. It was practiced before that time. The name of this year is When They Waved Horses' Tails over Each Other [1805].

Before the Oglalas came onto a reservation they practiced this ceremony a great deal. Now they practice it very little. Hardly anyone knows just how to perform the ceremony now. Only old men know how to do so. It costs a great deal to have the ceremony performed rightly. The ceremony could be performed now, if one would make the right preparations and provide the right things and give the right feast. The older Indians would rejoice to have the ceremony performed in the old way.

The ceremony was performed to make the Indians akin to each other. It would make two Indians brothers. Or it would make them brother and sister. Or it would make them sisters. Or it would make them father and child. Or it would make them mother and child. When Indians became of kin in this way, it was like kin by birth. When they were kin in this way they could not marry.

In old times when there were many wars, a *Hunka* was

bound to help his *Hunka* kin in every way: in going on a war party, in a fight; and if he was a prisoner his *Hunka* must not rest till he was released. If he took horses, he must help him. If he had horses taken, he must help him to get them back. If he took women he must help him to keep them, and if his women were taken he must help him to recover them. If he took children he must help him to care for them, or if his children were taken he must help him to recover them. If he gave a feast he must help him to provide for it. If he was sick he must help him to get the medicine men and to pay them. If he wished to steal a wife he must help him to do so and must be ready to fight for the wife. If he wanted to give love medicine he must help him to do so. If he played in games he must not play against him. If he was poor and hungry he must feed him and give him whatever he needed.

The ceremony could be performed by anyone who was acquainted with it. To perform the ceremony properly, a shaman or a medicine man should conduct it. The one who had the ceremony performed chose the one who should conduct it. A *Hunka* is anyone who has had the ceremony performed for him or her. A *Hunka* may be an Oglala, or any other Indian, or a white man, or anyone. A *Hunka* must choose to adopt one before that one can have the ceremony performed for his or her benefit. A *Hunka* may choose to adopt anyone as his or her child, or brother, or sister, or parent. When a *Hunka* chooses to adopt anyone, she or he gets the consent of the one to be so adopted. Or if it is an infant, then he gets the consent of the parent of the child. When a *Hunka* has the consent of one to be adopted, he then makes the preparation for the ceremony.

The preparation for the ceremony is to choose the one to conduct it, to invite the friends, to provide the feast, to provide the presents. He may ask his friends to help him in this. It was the greatest honor to provide all these things without help.

If one was poor, the ceremony did not amount to much. If one was unpopular, the ceremony did not amount to much. If one had much, the ceremony was largely attended and lasted many days. A brave warrior was sure to have a popular ceremony. A big chief was sure to have a popular ceremony. A wise shaman was sure to have a popular ceremony. A medicine man who could do many mysterious things was sure to have a popular ceremony. Anyone who had many horses, or dogs, or robes, or other things that could be given as presents was sure to have a popular ceremony. An infant whose parents had much, or if the father was a brave, or a wise shaman, or a renowned medicine man, was sure to have a popular ceremony.

The friends to be invited were the kinspeople, by blood and by *Hunka;* also braves, shamans, medicine men, and chiefs. Oglalas and other Sioux and other Indians could be invited. White men were not invited unless they were to be made *Hunka.* A few white men have been made *Hunka.*

The invitation to the ceremony was by sending word or by personally inviting them. Honored guests, such as shamans, medicine men, braves, and chiefs were invited by sending or giving them invitation wands. Invited guests received the invitation some time before the ceremony was to be performed. Invited guests were expected to bring food and presents to the gathering. All invited guests were looked after by the one who gave the ceremony. Every invited guest was expected to help to make the occasion enjoyable.

In former times there were very many *Hunka.* There are not many *Hunka* now. In former times when the Indians dressed and painted themselves for any occasion a *Hunka* painted himself so that his *Hunka* could tell that he was a *Hunka.* A *Hunka* painted his face in a particular way. If it was a woman, she painted the parting of her hair red and her face was painted like the men who were *Hunka.* A *Hunka* painted the face by making marks on it that showed him to be so. Sometimes, at present, a *Hunka* paints his face so that he is known.

The *Hunka* ceremony is hardly ever performed now. The young people do not care for it now. In former times it was good, because it helped *Hunka* very much. It is no help to be a *Hunka* now. The *Hunka* ceremony taught the *Hunka* to be what the Indians thought was good. The Indians' way of being good is not the same as the white man's way. The white man's way of being good is now accepted by the Indians.

---

74. *Hunka* and the White Man. Afraid of Bear. (AMNH)

The *Hunka* ceremony was performed by our fathers, by our grandfathers, and by their fathers. It came with our people when they came from the Land of the Pines. The Spirits of the North perform it in the Moon When the Ducks Come Back (April), and in the Moon When the Wind Shakes Off the Leaves (October). The Man from the Land of Pines came to the shamans in my grandfather's time and taught them how to perform this ceremony right. He told them the secrets of it.

That year was When They Waved Horses' Tails over Themselves (1805). I was born the year When They Brought In the Captives (1843). My father told me these things. He was born the year When the Good White Man Came (1802). He was two years old when the Man from the Land of the Pines came *(the mystical man who has much to do in the mythology of the Oglalas)*.[24] He was three years old when this man came. His father told him all about it.

Before this time anyone could perform the ceremony. This man said this was not right. He came from the spirits to tell the right way to do this. He told the shamans how to perform the ceremony right. My grandfather was a shaman, and he told him. My grandfather told my father. My father told me.

I know how to perform the ceremony right. I know the secrets of the ceremony. Some Indians pretend to perform the ceremony but they do not know how. Before the Man from the Land of the Pines came, anyone could perform the ceremony. Other Indians could perform it. But it was not right. The spirits saw that it was not right, so they sent the Man from the Land of the Pines to teach the Oglalas how to perform the ceremony right. When the ceremony is performed right, the spirits are pleased.

I can perform the ceremony for anyone who is chosen in the right way. I can do it for a white man. One must be chosen by a good *Hunka*. Guests must be invited. A feast must be given. Presents must be made to me and to the guests. I must have time to prepare for the ceremony. I must first seek a vision to learn if I can do this for a white man. A white man would be like an Indian if he becomes *Hunka*. I do not know whether the spirits would aid me if I were to undertake to perform the ceremony for a white man or not. I could find this out by seeking a vision. I would have to have presents before I would seek a vision.

A white man would be my brother if he became a *Hunka*. The *Hunka* are not what they were in olden times. They do not look on each other as they did before the Indians came onto a reservation. The spirits do not come and help us now. The white men have driven them away. I can bring the spirits sometimes now. But they will not come quickly as they did in former times. I can not tell the secrets of the *Hunka* to a white man, but if he becomes a *Hunka* I will tell them to him.

A *Hunka* is the brother of all other *Hunka.* He will help a *Hunka* in anything he undertakes. If he thinks a *Hunka* is about to undertake anything bad, he will advise him not to undertake this. These things will have to be provided for the ceremony: two *Hunka* wands; two *Hunka* rattles; a mysterious ear of corn; a meat scaffold; dried meat, both fat and lean; dried willow bark; tobacco; a pipe; sweetgrass; an eagle feather; an eagle plume; mysterious paints, red, black, and white; invitation wands; a mysterious fire stick; a mysterious counting stick; a buffalo skull; presents for the shaman; presents for the *Ate*; presents for the guests; a dog for the feast; plenty of food for the feast; two tipis; a drum.

The following persons will be necessary to perform the ceremony: *walowan* (the master of ceremonies), *pte pawa* (the marker, assistant to the master), *wowasi* (helper, assistant to the marker), *wahuwapi yuha kin he* (bearer of the mysterious corn), two *Hunka koza kin* (two bearers of the wands).

A white man would have to get a *Hunka* to propose him for the ceremony. The *Hunka* would consider whether they would accept him as a *Hunka* or not. They might refuse to accept him. He could be initiated as a *Hunka* anyway. But if he was rejected by the *Hunka,* they would not recognize him as a *Hunka.*

---

75. The Secret That the Spirits Told. John Blunt Horn. (AMNH)

I am a *Hunka.* I know about it when it was done as it is now. I also know how it was done before They Made Medicine by Waving Horses' Tails over Them. My grandfather was a *Hunka.* His father told him all about this thing. He told me about it. The *Hunkas* were among the Sioux from the beginning. When they lived in the Land of the Pines, then one was made a *Hunka.* This is the way it was done then.

The Moon When the Ducks Come Back (April), the Lakotas went to hunt. They traveled far away and hunted until The Moon When the Leaves Are Brown (October); they hunted towards the winter camp. They all came together for the winter like one family. Some had plenty of meat and robes and skins. Some had but little of these things. If a man had plenty and his friend's child pleased him, he would say, "I will take this child as my own." And then he would give a feast and give away his meat and his robes and his skins.

If a man did this, he was considered a generous man and everybody gave him something. If a man's heart was good towards an old man, he would say to that old man, "I will take you for my father." And he would give a feast and while everybody was happy, he would say to them, "I take this man for my father." And he would give away all he had. He would keep this old man as his father and everyone would say that he was a good man and they would give him things to eat and to wear and they would give to this old man also.

If such a man had much to give away, he had a big feast and everybody came and ate and sang and danced and played games. This was in the winter time. Anybody could choose anybody in this way.

The year When Many Pregnant Women Died (1799), the old men and the wise man and the medicine men counseled together and they said so many women died who were pregnant because their children were given away in a manner that was not pleasing to the *Tatanka* (the mythical Great Beast or the Bull Buffalo).

So for five years there was no one made *Hunka*. In the fifth year, in the Moon When the Chokecherries Are Ripe (July), many Lakotas came together at the River of Muddy Water (Missouri) and they had plenty of buffalo meat and plenty of fresh robes and plenty of chokecherries and plenty of wild turnips. There was there an old man and an old woman. They had nothing and no children. Then a man said, "I would make this man and this woman my *Hunka* but I am afraid the pregnant women will die if I do this thing."

The people all talked about this. Then the old men and the wise men and the medicine men said they would counsel and make medicine and talk with the spirits and find out about this thing. So they gave a great feast and went into the sweat lodges and then they all sought a vision. Every man sought a vision by himself.

Then they went into the council lodge and stayed there two days and two nights. The council lodge was in the center of the camp. No one would go near it. And many persons saw ghosts the first night. The second night the ghosts danced so that it was light like the moon (the Aurora Borealis). While the ghosts were dancing, the old men and the wise men and the medicine men came out of the council lodge and danced in a circle around it. Many saw ghosts dancing with them. So all were afraid and went into their tipis. In the morning one of the old men called aloud to the people to come out of the tipis and look on the sun when it was rising. And all the people came out and stood looking at the sun, and while it was rising, the old man cried in a loud voice that the spirits were pleased, that they had told them how to perform the ceremony of the *Hunka* in the right way.

Then that day the man said to the old man and the old woman, "I will take you for *Mihunka*." So they made a great feast and the councilors showed him how to do this thing right. And when they performed the ceremony, they told the secret which the spirits had told them. And they made mysterious medicine with each other in the council lodge. And they fastened horses' tails to wands and waved them over each other. And they waved these horses' tails over all that were in the lodge. Since that time, no one is permitted to perform the ceremony but one who knows the secret which the spirits told.

---

76. The Obligations of the *Hunka*. John Blunt Horn. (AMNH)

The *Hunka Lowanpi* was very good for the Oglalas before they lived on a reservation. It was like the church among the white people. Any good Oglala could be a *Hunka*. Any other Indian than an Oglala could be a *Hunka*. If any other Indian was a *Hunka*, the Oglala would treat him like a brother. They would not take his horses. They would not take his women or children. They would not take him a prisoner. If some other Indian took him prisoner or took his horses or his women or children, then a

Hunka would get them and give them back to him. If a *Hunka* were hungry or naked and another *Hunka* knew this, he would give the hungry one something to eat, even if he had to take it out of his mouth to give it. He would give him something to wear, even if he had to take it off himself to give it. The braves were all *Hunka*. The shamans were all *Hunka*. The wise medicine men were nearly all *Hunka*.

Little children that were *Hunka* were like the children of everyone that was *Hunka*. Old people that were *Hunka* were like parents to the children that were *Hunka*. Sometimes the *Hunka* had meetings to which no others were allowed to go. There were some secret things that were told to a *Hunka*, and to no one else. These secrets must not be told, except to a *Hunka*.

The Indians do not pay much attention to a *Hunka* now. To be a *Hunka* would not be of much benefit to an Oglala now. A *Hunka* was taught to do things that he would not be allowed to do now. The Oglalas did not think these things were wrong, but the white people do. A *Hunka* was taught to steal horses from other Indians than the Oglalas, to steal women from other Indians than the Lakotas. He was taught to take a woman wherever he could get one to go with him. He was taught to fight his enemies and the enemies of his friends and of his *Hunka*. He was taught that he must not do these things to a *Hunka* even if the *Hunka* was any other Indian than an Oglala. He was taught that he must protect a *Hunka's* horses, his wife, and his children the same as if they were his own. He was taught that he must help a *Hunka* on a war party or on a raiding party. That he must help a *Hunka* in love. He was taught to have all the wives and children he could get. He was taught to give his wife to another *Hunka* if he wanted her and he was a good friend. He was taught that he might sell his wife to any other but must give her to a *Hunka*. He was taught to give his children to an *Ate Hunka*. He was taught to believe a shaman who was a *Hunka*. He was taught to believe in the medicines of a medicine man who was a *Hunka*.

A *Hunka* was taught that it was stingy to have much—horses, or dogs, or robes, or food—when other *Hunka* near him had little. He was taught that it is right to ask everyone to eat when he had plenty of food, and to give away his robes or anything he had plenty of. He was taught that he must not permit his *Ate* to be naked or hungry or in trouble, that he must steal or fight if necessary to provide for his *Ate Hunka,* that he must not have carnal intercourse with the woman belonging to another *Hunka* without the consent of the one to whom she belonged.

---

77. The Spirits Taught the Oglalas. Ringing Shield.[25] (AMNH)

My grandfather told these things to my father and my father told them to me. I have talked with the old men of the Oglalas and they say they are so. A long time ago the Indians talked with the spirits. When they wanted to do something of importance they asked the spirits about it. If the spirits said it was good then it was done. If they said it was bad then it was not done. They sought a vision and the spirits came and talked with them. Now the spirits will not come. This is because the white men have offended the spirits.

The spirits taught the Oglalas how to perform the *Hunka* ceremony right. When the Lakotas came from the Land of the Pines, they did not know how to do this right. Then when a Lakota had a good heart towards another he made him his brother. If a Lakota's heart was good towards another he could show this by making the other's child his child also. In this way a Lakota could adopt a brother, or a sister, or a parent, or a child. Before the spirits showed the Oglalas how to perform this ceremony, if a Lakota wanted to adopt one, he did so without asking anyone about it. Only if it was a child he asked the parents, or if it was an adult he asked the person first.

The Lakotas all lived together a long time ago. They had many chiefs. They scattered over much country when they hunted. They tried to come together sometimes. When they came together, they rejoiced greatly. Then they had games and singing and dancing. Then if a man had much to give away he would adopt someone and give a great feast and give away all he had. That was before there were any Oglalas. All were Lakotas. There were some bands, but I do not know which.

There were *Hunkas* among other Indians. Probably the spirits had shown them how to perform the ceremony. I do not know this, but think they did not know how. The spirits showed the shamans and the medicine men how to perform the ceremony before there were white men among the Lakotas. Before this time there was no ceremony. Sometimes there was a great feast, and the shamans talked of the spirits.

When the Good White Man Came (1803), the shamans were ashamed. The next year they could do nothing, and the braves laughed at them. The next year They Made the Hair on the Horses Curly.[26] The next year ten shamans sought a vision together. The Spirit of the Great Beast, and of the Horse, and of the Dog talked with them, and taught them how to perform the *Hunka* ceremony. Since that time the *Hunka* ceremony has been performed this way. This ceremony is mysterious.

---

78. The Spirits No Longer Come. Blue Horse. (AMNH)

The *Hunka* ceremony was mysterious for the Indians. It was good when the Indians did not know the ways of the white man. It made the Indians like one family. Bad Indians could not become *Hunka*. It was not the white man's way of teaching.

Sometimes many Indians camped together to perform this ceremony. Then there were good times. This was usually in the summer time. It might be in the winter time. The winter was not a good time for this ceremony, because food was not plenty during the winter. When many Indians gathered together for this ceremony, the old men counseled and the young men played games. The women provided plenty to eat. The children were happy and were never hungry. The young people made love. Many sought a vision, and talked with the spirits. The good spirits attended such gatherings. The bad spirits also came.

The Lakotas have practiced this ceremony for many years. It was not always the same. The shamans first learned how to perform it right. These shamans became Oglalas. The other Lakotas learned how to perform it from the Oglalas. Other Indians are *Hunkas,* but they are not full *Hunka* like the Oglalas.

The young people do not become *Hunka* now. It is of no use

to them. The old people do not pay much attention to a *Hunka* now. The *Hunka* are not what they were in old times. Some old Indians could perform the ceremony right. No young Indian knows how to perform it right. An old Indian who wears the gee string and leggings could perform it. He might be afraid to talk like the Indians did before they lived on a reservation. It would not be right to teach the young Indians what was taught to the *Hunka* in old times.

There are some secret things taught to a *Hunka*. These secrets are not good now. They are about the spirits. The spirits will not come now. These are the spirits of the Skies, of the Earth, of the Clouds, of the Thunder, of the Land of the Pines, of the Coming-light, of the Sunset, of the South, of the Winds, of the Waters, of the Flying Things, of the Beasts, of the Insects, of the Growing Things, of the Great Beast, and of the Spider. There are bad spirits also. There are ghosts and the Man from the Land of the Pines. One spirit is stronger than another. One spirit is chief, and can influence all other spirits. These spirits come no more to the Indians.

---

79. Counseling the *Hunka*. Bad Wound. (AMNH)

Anyone may desire to become a *Hunka*. If an old man is a *Hunka*, he may choose someone younger to be his *Hunka*. He may choose a young man to be his son. He may choose a young woman to be his daughter. He may choose a little child, even a baby. If he chooses a young child or a baby to be his *Hunka*, then he should counsel with the child's parents in the matter. A woman who chooses someone to be her *Hunka* must do the same as a man. A young man may choose an older man to be his *Hunka* father or an older woman to be his mother or one near his own age to be his brother or sister or he may choose a child for his adopted child. A woman must do as a man does when she is a young woman. If a man chooses to become a *Hunka* and chooses a father, then he must counsel with him as follows.

He must choose three friends to counsel for him. It is best if these three friends are *Hunkayapi*. He should ask these three friends to advise him. If they think he should not try to become *Hunka*, they should tell him so. If they are willing to act as his friends, then he should give them a feast. When he has given them a feast he should say to them:

"My friends I have chosen you as my *kola wicaya* (deputies) because you are *waste* (of good repute) among the *Hunkayapi* and I am sure that your heart is good (friendly towards me). I know that your tongues are not forked (you will not lie), and that you are *kolaya* (friendly to me) and that I can depend on you. I *Hunka Skita*[27] (seek to become a *Hunka*) and I have chosen [someone] to be my *Ate* (*Hunka* father).

"*Kola*, go to his tipi. Take with you the pipe (handing them a pipe) and this *cansasa* (dried willow bark) (handing it to one of the friends) and this *wacanga* (sweetgrass) (handing it to another) and tell him I have chosen him to be my *Ate*. Tell him this because I honor him and that I wish him to teach me so that I may become such a man as he is. Tell him that if he will become my *Ate* I will give him suitable presents and will honor and obey him in all things and will be a true *Hunka Towa*[28] (*Hunka* child) to him."

The friends do what is asked of them. If the one chosen consents not, then the one who has chosen him must stop or he may choose another. If he accepts, then he and the friends smoke the willow bark and burn the sweetgrass and smell it and their hearts are made good. When they smoke the pipe, they smoke it in the Indian way: one whiff at a time, then pass it to another. The *Ate* smokes first. When all have smoked once, then the *Ate* smokes again. When the *Ate* has smoked the second time, he says to the friends, "I am *Kaniga Ate*[29] (chosen for an *Ate*). Tell who has chosen me to prepare presents and the feast. When he has done so, let me know that I may appoint the day." Then they counsel about these things.

If an old man or woman chooses a young person for a *Hunka*, then he says to that person, "I have chosen you to be *Hunka Towa*. Let us counsel about the matter. Bring your friends and we will talk about it." Then the young person asks his parents or relatives or friends about it and takes counsel with them and two or three of them go with him to the tipi of the older person and they receive the pipe and the sweetgrass from him and hold council.

And the older person says, "I wish to make this one my *Hunka.* I wish to do this because my heart is good towards him (gives the reason, which may be because the one has been sick and gotten well or because of friendship to the person or his parent or because a medicine man has told him to do so or as a reward for some reason).

"If he is my *Hunka Towa,* I will be a father to him and will teach him to be a good and true man." They then smoke the pipe and talk of the matter. If it is a little child that is chosen, then the parents must answer for it and the same things are done. Then when this thing is agreed upon, the friends and the two principals have a meeting, generally in the evening. The one who proposes the relationship must provide the place of meeting and build the fire and furnish the willow bark and the sweetgrass. When the fire is burned to coals, the *Ate* sits at the west, opposite the door, the *Skita* near the door and the friends at the east, north and south side of the tipi.

The *Skita* must fill the pipe and light it and hand it to the *Ate,* who smokes first and then hands it to the friends. The *Kaniga Ate* sprinkles the sweetgrass on the fire. When they smoke the second time, the *Kaniga Ate* waves the pipe over the coals in the smoke of the sweetgrass and should say, "Spirits, hear these my friends." He then smokes and hands it to the one in the east, who does so and says, "Oh Spirits of the East we offer this smoke. Give us a bright day for the ceremony."

He then hands it to the one in the north. He then smokes and does the same and says, "Oh Spirits of the Land of the Pines (north), give us a warm, pleasant day for the ceremony." He then smokes and hands it to the one who is in the south, who says, "Oh Spirit of the South, we offer you this smoke. Give us a generous day for the ceremony." He then smokes and hands it to the *Kaniga Ate,* who waves it in a circle five times in the smoke of the sweetgrass and the first time he should say, "Oh Spirit of the East, we have invoked you." The second, "Oh Spirit of the North we have invoked you." The third time, "Oh Spirit of the South we have invoked you." The fourth time he should say, "Oh Spirit of the West we have invoked you," and the fifth time, "Oh Spirit of the Earth give us much on that day." He then smokes and lifts the pipe above his head and says, "Oh Spirit of the Skies, we offer this smoke to you, cause the spirits we have invoked to listen to us."

The *Kaniga Ate* then proposes the *alowanpi* (master of cere-monies),[30] *ptepaowa* (skull painter), *wowasi* (helper), *wahuwapi yuha kin he* (custodian of ear of corn). They agree upon these. They discuss who are to be invited and what presents should be given.

---

80. Changes among *Hunka*. Thunder Bear. (AMNH)

If a man's heart is good towards a child because he likes the child, or because he likes the father, or the mother, then that man may adopt that child as his own. In old times this was done by initiating the child as a *Hunka*. The man then became like her father. The man must be like her father at all times. If her own father leaves her mother, she would live with her mother, and after a while her own father would have nothing to do with her. But her *Hunka* father would always be like a father to her. Sometimes she would live with her mother, and sometimes she would live with her *Hunka* father. Even if her *Hunka* father changed wives she would still go to his tipi and stay sometimes. But she was only like a friend to this man's children. She could marry one of his sons if she wanted to. She played with his children, and they acted like brothers and sister. If it was a boy, it was the same.

If an old man adopted a young man or a young woman, then the one adopted was like a son or a daughter to him. If a woman adopted anyone, it was the same as if a man did so. If two men or two women adopted each other, then they became like brothers and sisters. They would not marry one whom they had adopted as a *Hunka*. Sometimes one would go with the *Hunka*, and leave the blood relations.

A *Hunka* was supposed to live a good life. We now call good men, like the catechists of the church, *Hunka*. In old times the *Hunka* were taught what the Indians believed to be good. This would not all be good now. They were taught to be industrious, generous, brave, and to tell the truth. They were also taught to have many wives, to steal horses from an enemy, to kill the enemy, to steal women and children from the enemy, to kill anyone who was the enemy of himself or a *Hunka*. They were taught to take the scalp, to torture prisoners, to kill little children, to believe in the powers of the medicine men and in the spirits of animals.

A man that was a good *Hunka* would be a good man now. A man that was a good *Hunka* wanted to do right. He would try to do right now. He would spit on the bad things that were taught him in the old times.

The young people laugh at the old *Hunka* when they tell of the spirits. Probably some of the old Indians could perform the ceremony in the old way. I think they would not tell the secrets to a white man. These secrets are foolishness. I was told them, but I have put them out of my mind. I do not believe them, though I once did. I cannot tell them now.

---

81. Implements Used in the *Hunka* Ceremony. Takes the Gun. (AMNH)

My *Ate* told me the meaning of the implements used in the ceremony of the *Hunka*.[31] I will tell them as he told me. The wands are mysterious.[32] A *Hunka* should make them. A shaman should give them power by his magic. They should be made of wood. They should be painted by the shaman. They should be adorned by the feathers from the tail of a young eagle. They should have attached to them two horses' tails, or tufts of hair from a horse's tail. They should have other ornaments. The feathers and horses' tails are necessary.

The Indians had only dogs. Then they moved camp slowly. The brave Indians got horses. They could move swiftly and could ride on them. To show that his heart was very good an Indian could give a horse to a friend. When an Indian became a *Hunka,* there were not horses to give to all. So a horse's tail was waved over him. This showed that the heart of all who had the horse's tail waved over them was as good as if they gave a horse.

The eagle is the bravest of birds. His tail feathers are his best mark. The spirit of the eagle goes with his tail feathers. The eagle feathers above the head make a brave man. To wave eagle feathers over one is to say that he is a brave man, or it is to wish him to be a brave man, or it is to promise to help him in time of need, or it is to wish one to be an industrious woman, or it is to wish happiness to a woman.

To wave eagle feathers over anyone at any time means these things. To wave an eagle wing over anyone means to wish them peace and happiness. The horses' tails and the eagle feathers on the wands are to wave over one who is to be made *Hunka,* to wish that one prosperity, peace, happiness and to promise help to that one. And it is waved over all those present to show that they all join in this.

The rattles may be made of anything that will rattle. They should be made of the dried skin of the scrotum of a buffalo, or of the dried skin of any animal shaped over something round, like a stone, when it is green, and sewn together and dried in this shape. Or it may be made of a pumpkin skin (a gourd). The rattles should be painted and ornamented. The best ornament is hair from a horse's tail and an eagle plume. The best color is red. There should be blue stripes on them, one stripe on each rattle, but there may be more. The red color represents the day. The blue represents the sky. The hair from the horse's tail represents a horse running. The eagle plume represents an eagle flying. The rattle represents a power over the spirits. The rattle pleases the good spirits and frightens the bad spirits. When the *Hunka* songs are sung and the rattles are rattled, the good spirits come near, and the bad spirits go away.

The ear of corn is *wakan* (mysterious). It should be chosen by a wise man (a shaman). The spirits will tell him which ear [is] to be chosen. He must be alone when he chooses the ear. Everyone must permit him to examine their corn. No one knows whether they have the *wakan* corn or not. Only the shaman can tell. The spirits will show him. He must make medicine first and call on the spirits to help him. No one may watch him when he examines the corn. He must not tell when he finds the *wakan* ear. He may take many ears. He will know the *wakan* ear. He will take the *wakan* ear to his lodge secretly. He will make medicine over it. It will then belong to the spirits.

He will paint the rows of grains on the ear. Some of them he will paint red. Some of them blue. Some of them he will not paint. He may paint the rows only part of the way from the small end. He must begin to paint at the small end.

This ear of corn represents the Spirit of the Earth. It represents plenty of food that comes from the earth. It is carried before one and kept near one who is to be made *Hunka* to show that if such a one pleases the Spirit of the Earth, this Spirit will always give him plenty. The red paint on the ear represents day. The blue paint represents sky, and it represents night also. The spirits of the day and of the night are pleased by these colors.

Talo, the meat, is made *wakan* by making medicine over it. This pleases the Spirit of *Tatanka* (the Great Beast, Buffalo Bull). It represents food that is from animals. It represents plenty of meat and of robes and of skins.

The sage makes the bad spirits sick. They go away from it when it is burned. It does not make the good spirits sick. They will not leave when it is smoked. Sweetgrass is pleasant to all the spirits. Good spirits like it. Bad spirits like it. All like it. The smoke of sweetgrass is pleasant to the good spirits. They come to the smoke. They are pleased with one who makes this smoke. They will listen to what such a one asks. But the bad spirits come also to enjoy the smoke. So sage must be burned to make them sick.

When one wishes to ask something of the spirits, he must burn sweetgrass to please them. If it is good, he must burn sage to drive away the bad spirits. If one wishes to do something bad he must burn sweetgrass and make bad medicine. Then the bad spirits will help him. Each one makes his own medicine. He knows which medicine is good and which is bad. Some medicine men made very bad medicine.

The Spirit of the Buffalo comes to its skull. The Spirit of *Tatanka* is pleased to see the skull of a buffalo. The spirit of *Tatanka* cares for the family. It cares for the young man or the young woman who should live together. It cares for the woman who lives with a man. It cares for little children. It cares for the hunters. It cares for the growing things (vegetation). It cares for everything that has young.

The buffalo skull is at the ceremony of *Hunka* because the Spirit of *Tatanka* is to be pleased. The meaning of the songs, that is a secret. The meaning of the paint, that is a secret. It is told to one who is made a *Hunka*.

82. Preparing the *Hunka* Implements. Feather on Head. (AMNH)

I am a great medicine man. I have mysterious powers. I learned them from the spirits and from visions I have sought. The spirits talk to me as a familiar. I can give magic power to things. I can make the mysterious things. I have power over the Indians to do mysterious things to them. I can cure the sick and I can make the well sick. If they come to me and listen to me, I can do mysterious things for them. I know the roots of the earth. I know the deadly things. I know the medicines that are good. The Spirit of the Earth is a friend to me. The white man's way leads away from the Indian's way. The young Indians no longer listen to the wise medicine men.

I am a shaman. The secret things I will not tell. I know the secrets of the implements of the *Hunka*. These I will tell you for pay. *(He is paid.)* The wands are a horse's tail and the eagle's feathers. The horse's tail is to go far and fast, to go without fatigue. The eagle feathers are to be brave and chief of the air. The wand is to be strong. The ornaments are to have plenty.

By the power of my medicines I can give these properties to these wands. A wand that has not had good medicine made over it is bad. A *Hunka* made with such a wand will not be good. The secret of my medicine I must not tell anyone. The Spirit gave it to me. The wand should be painted red. The paint should be put on with ceremony. They should be red because this is the day and summer time. It is the time to be prosperous and happy.

The *cowahe* (scaffold) should be *wakan* (mysterious). It should be made with ceremony. Good medicine should be made over it. It should be painted blue. This is the earth and the sky. The earth gives meat and the sky dries it for winter. Meat from a scaffold that is not mysterious will not give a *Hunka* a good spirit. It will not make him strong. It will not make him generous.

The *wagamuha* (rattles) should be made mysterious by the spirits. Good medicine should be made over them. If mysterious they frighten the evil spirits. If they are not mysterious, the evil spirits do not fear them. They are the rain that rattles on the dry earth. If they are not mysterious they are the hail that destroys everything.

The *cansakalan peta* (fire wand) is mysterious. If it is not, it is evil. It should be painted red. This is the fire and the light. The mysterious fire should not be touched only with the mysterious fire wand. If it is, the *Hunka* will be cold and weary. The rattles should be painted red with blue stripes. This is the earth and the sky. Rain comes from the sky to the earth.

There is a spirit pipe. It is *wakan*. No one may see this pipe but those who should see it. It must not be handled by everyone. It is kept by one man. His father kept it. His grandfather kept it. His son should keep it. It is very old. Many brave men and wise men and great medicine men have smoked this pipe. It was made by wise men and the spirits showed them how to make it and what ceremonies to hold over it and what medicines to make over it. This is the pipe of great councils. The pipe for the *Hunka* ceremony should be like this pipe. It should be made mysterious by a medicine man. This will please the spirits. If the *alowanpi* [master of ceremonies] makes this pipe, he will have power with the spirits. If he smokes some other pipe the spirits will ask, "Where is the pipe?"

The Spirit of the *Tatanka* dwells in the skull of a buffalo. It is with it in the lodge of the *Hunka*. It is pleased with the ceremony when it is rightly performed. It is the mighty beast that rules all other beasts. Its voice frightens away the spirits of evil beasts. The *alowanpi* should have nothing to do with implements that are not *wakan*. *Wakan* implements that have been used many times have great power with the spirits. The old men, our fathers' fathers knew these things best.

---

83. The *Hunka* Ceremony.[33] James R. Walker, 1912. (AMNH)

According to traditions of the Oglala Lakota Indians, the *Hunka* ceremony was performed among them in ancient times without definite forms or rites, and during the year when They Waved Horse Tails over Each Other, the shamans took charge of it and gave it forms and rites such as it has had ever since then. (The Lakotas gave each year the name of some notable thing that occurred during it, and as the *Hunka* ceremony is sometimes called "Waving Horse Tails over Each Other," it is probable that it was first performed as hereafter described during the year so named, which corresponds to A.D. 1805.)

The ceremony is performed for the purpose of giving a particular relationship to two persons and giving them a relation to others that have had it performed for them. It is more or less elaborate according to the will of the one who conducts it and the means of the one for whom it is conducted but it has certain essential features which are: a shaman must conduct it; it must be performed for two persons at each time; the horse tails must be waved; the *Hunka* corn must be exhibited; the *Hunka* meat must be given; generosity must be inculcated; and presents and a feast must be given. (According to information given by an old shaman named Running Shield, for many years actual horse tails were waved during the ceremony but later tufts of long hair from horse tails were attached to wands of much older origin and the wands thus decorated were called horse tails or *Hunka* wands. These wands are two round tapering rods of wood about twelve hand breadths in length and as thick as a man's thumb at their larger ends. They are painted red and must be decorated with not less than four quills from the tail of the golden eagle, attached by their quill ends about one fourth the distance from the larger end and so that the other ends are held in such a manner that when they fall away from the rods, they will hang expanded in a fan-like manner. This is all that is essential to the wands in their original form but other decorations may be added, provided each decoration has some symbolic meaning. This wand has mystic powers and pertains to the Gods and Sun and the Buffalo.

(The *Hunka* corn is an ear that a shaman secretly selects from corn recently gathered. He subdues its *wakanla* or potency by his mystic powers and with the aid of his fetish compels it to do his will. It is a symbol of the Great God, the Earth, and he paints stripes of red on it as a symbol of the Sun and blue as a symbol of the Sky, so that it is a symbol of these three great Gods, the Sun, the Sky, and the Earth. It is then attached near the smaller end of a tapering rod of plum wood about six hand breadths in length and as large at its smaller end as the largest quill from an eagle's wing so that this end will project beyond it about a hand breadth. An eagle plume with the skin from the head of a mallard drake wrapped about its quill is attached to this projecting part. The eagle plume is a symbol of constancy and virtue and the skin from the mallard drake's head of the God *Okaga* (the South Wind) and of comfort. The *Hunka* meat is meat that is to be partaken of to teach generosity and charity.)

The relationships that are established by the *Hunka* ceremony are similar to those of parent and child, or brothers, or sisters. Anyone of mankind of either sex or any age may become *Hunka* if another will assume this relation with such a one; but in the case of small children the parent, usually the father, must take its place in the ceremony and become sponsor for it. If the relationship is that of parent and child, the one who is as parent is called *Ate Hunka*. (*Ate Hunka* means "father *Hunka*," but this title is assumed by a woman who assumed the relation of a parent to a child by the ceremony of Hunka.)

One who assumes the relation of a child is *Hunka* to his *Ate* and those who assume the relation of brothers or sisters are *Hunka* to the other. When an Oglala speaks of a *Hunka*, he always means the one he has assumed the relation of brother with and when he speaks of another for whom the ceremony has been performed he calls him *Hunkaya* or if of more than one such he calls them *Hunkayapi*. Elderly *Hunkayapi* of good repute are called by all *Mihunka*. (*Mihunka* is a term of reverence and respect which is sometimes applied to the Gods, especially to the Sun.)

The *Hunkayapi* have no formal organization as a society but they are a kind of brotherhood that should give preference to each other. A parent may have his child become *Hunka* to one to do honor either to the child or to the one chosen as *Ate,* or that the child may be benefited. Or one may seek to become *Ate Hunka* either from affection for the child or to get material benefits from its parents. Two may become *Hunka* to each other from affection or for the benefits of the brotherhood or anyone may seek to become *Hunka* to comply with a vow or a vision. If one becomes *Hunka* he can not withdraw from this relation without the consent of his fellow *Hunka*.

The fullest form of the ceremony is when two men become *Hunka* and the following description is of this form. (This description is based partly on notes taken while observing the ceremony and partly on information gotten from Indians who had conducted it. The quotations are interpretations of utterances heard during the ceremony.)

When one wishes to become *Hunka,* he should consider well whether he can provide suitably for the feasts or not, for the standing of a *Hunkaya* among the *Hunkayapi* is in proportion to the lavishness of the gifts and feast at the ceremony that establishes his relation with them. He should give all his possessions for the occasion and should ask his kinspeople and friends to give for him. If this does not enable him to provide suitably, he should proceed no farther in the matter. If it does, then he should proceed as follows. He should invite two friends to a feast and then tell them of his intentions, asking their advice. If they advise him not to undertake to become a *Hunka,* he should do as they advise. But if they encourage his intentions, then he should give them a pipe and smoking material and a present and ask them to carry them to the one he has chosen for his *Hunka* and get his formal consent. (It is probable that these two have already agreed upon the matter and this is only a required formality.)

They go with the pipe and present and, entering the tipi, they fill the pipe and offer it unlighted to the one whose consent they seek. (To enter a tipi and formally fill a pipe and offer it unlighted signifies that the one offering the pipe wishes to make a request of the one the pipe is offered to. To take a pipe so offered signifies that the request will be heard, to light the pipe after the request is made signifies that it will be considered, and to smoke the pipe in communion signifies that the request will be granted. To smoke a pipe in communion is to light it and smoke a few whiffs, usually four, and then pass it to another, who does likewise, and so on until each who is interested has smoked and then repeat until the pipeful is smoked. This is similar to the ordinary passing the pipe in social smoking but is done with more formality.)

If he takes the pipe, they tell him their errand and if he lights and offers it in communion, then they give him the present and discuss the matter with him. Then they should return and report to him who sent them and he should set a day for another feast and invite to it the same two friends and the one who is to be his *Hunka.* At this feast, after they have eaten, they should all four smoke in communion so that the Mediator may harmonize their spirits and predispose the Gods in their favor. By this smoke, the one who asked the other to be his *Hunka* becomes the candidate and the one who consented becomes his fellow candidate.

Then the provision for the ceremony is discussed and a shaman who is *Hunkaya* is chosen to conduct it when the two friends are delegated to go with pipe and present and get his consent. This they do, and if he refuses the pipe, the candidates should proceed no farther in the matter, for the will of the shaman is the will of the Gods in all such matters and to oppose this would anger the shaman and the Gods and they would bring some misfortune on one who did so. But if the shaman lights and offers the pipe in communal smoke, then they give him the present and he thereby becomes the *walowan* of the ceremony and all preparations for it. (A literal translation of *walowan* is "one who sings," but the concept expressed by the word used in this connection is the one who conducts the ceremony and sings the formal songs. So the word *walowan* will be used in this paper to designate this person.)

When the friends report this to the candidates, they should set a day for a feast and invite the two friends and the *walowan* to it, and when it is partaken of and the Mediator has been propitiated by a communal smoke, the spirits of all will be harmonized and the *walowan* will probably advise the candidates to seek a vision so that the will of the Gods may be known in regard to their important undertaking, or if he knows what this will is, he may then reveal it to them. In any event they should not proceed without an assurance that it is not against the will of any God. Then they will discuss the ceremony and preparation for it in a general way and the *walowan* will appoint a time for meeting the candidates for the first formality of the ceremony proper. This should be an evening and they should meet with none other present and sit in a tipi about a fire of coals without smoke, for the *ton* of the Great God, the Sun, abides in such a fire, so that what is done in its presence is solemn and binding. The *walowan* should fill his ceremonial pipe and, holding it over the fire so that the *ton* of the Sun may be upon it, he should move the mouthpiece in a circle as the Four Winds goes upon his trail around the edge of the world and thus secure the authority of the greater God, the Sun, over the lesser God, the Four Winds. He should move the pipe so as to complete this circle four times because of the four kinds of Gods and while moving it, he should pray to *Wohpe,* the Mediator, saying, "Ho, potency of the pipe, we will smoke this pipe to you. Let your *ton* be in it so that the smoke may go to the Gods." (The *ton* that is the imparted potency of the Goddess *Wohpe,* the Mediator, abides in the smoke of the pipe and of sweetgrass and can be imparted to no other thing. She is sometimes addressed as the potency of the pipe, sometimes translated "the spirit of the pipe.")

He should then light the pipe and hand it to the candidate, who will elevate the mouthpiece towards the west and say, "*Yanpa,* the *ton* of this smoke goes up to you. Give us a clear day for the *Hunka* ceremony." He will then smoke four whiffs and hand the pipe to his fellow candidate, who will elevate the mouthpiece towards the south and say, "*Okaga,* the *ton* of this smoke goes up to you. Give us a pleasant day for the *Hunka* ceremony." He will then smoke four whiffs and hand the pipe to the *walowan,* who will elevate the mouthpiece and move it in a circle as before and say, "*Tate,* we have offered smoke to your sons. Command them to give us a good day for the *Hunka* ceremony." (*Tate,* the Wind, is one of the Great Gods, the father of the God, the Four Winds, who is four in one, subject to the commands of his father. When he is the West Wind, his ceremonial name is *Yata,* and he controls storms.[34] When he is the South Wind, his name is *Okaga* and he controls pleasant weather.)

When they have thus propitiated the Gods, the *walowan* should interpret any vision either of the candidates may have had in compliance with his instructions and all should be in strict accord with his interpretation. Then they should discuss [whom] they wish to take an active part in the ceremony and the *walowan* will appoint a marker, a helper, two bearers of the horse tails (or *Hunka* wands), a bearer of the *Hunka* corn, two rattlers and two singers and drummers. Then they will agree upon the day for the ceremony.

Those appointed at this meeting should be notified soon after so that they may prepare for the occasion, as it is expected that they will contribute liberally for the presents and the feast.

Soon after this meeting the candidates should send invitation wands to those they especially desire to be present at the ceremony. (Invitation wands are made of the sprouts of the plum tree because it is an emblem of hospitality. They should be about as long as the longest quill from an eagle's wing and ornamented with paints or colored quills of the porcupine or in some manner that will indicate that they are invitations. The sticks of the guessing game may be sent as invitations but this is not good form. If an invitation wand is received, this indicates that the invitation is accepted, but if it is rejected, this indicates not only that the invitation is not accepted but hostility also.)

They should send wands to every prominent person in the camp and adjacent camps of friendly people and they must send wands to seven *Hunkayapi,* preferably *Mihunka.* Invited guests are given precedence at the ceremony and feast but all who may come are welcome.

Guests may come to the place for the ceremony at any time before the day appointed for it, but they should bring their tipis and goods so that they may not be a burden on the candidates or those who are to supply the feast and presents. They may occupy themselves in any manner they see fit and they usually devote themselves to pleasure. If there are a large number of tipis, a formal camp may be established and it may remain for an indefinite time after the ceremony.

On the eve of the ceremony, the *ton* of the Gods the Mediator, the Buffalo, and the Whirlwind will predominate the camp and there will be feasting, singing, gaming and merriment far into the night. (The Goddess the Mediator is the patron of happiness. The God the Buffalo is the patron of hospitality. The God the Whirlwind is the patron of sports and gaming.)

As it grows dark, a wise old woman will go to the top of a nearby hill and wail a potent song to warn the wolf and coyote from the camp, so that none may be in trouble or have sorrow on the morrow. (The wolf is the *akicita* or servant of *Eya* [*Iya*], the principal God of evil and misfortune, and the coyote of the Demon and Two Face, the Gods of evil that incite to cruelty and lust.) She will also charge [*Waziya*] and *Iktomi* to stay away from the camp. (*Waziya* is a superhuman man of uncertain moods who may do harm or good according to his humor. He is often called the Old Man. *Iktomi* is the supernatural son of the Great God, the Rock, who is denied a place as a God and whose chief delight is to play tricks on others that will make them uncomfortable or ridiculous.)

If the day appointed for the ceremony is unfit for it, the *walowan* should appoint another, usually the next, and he should propitiate the Gods, especially the West Wind and the South Wind; ceremonies which as a shaman he will know. If the dawn promises a fair day, the people should bestir themselves in preparation for the ceremony. They should have their morning meal and be dressed before the Sun appears in sight. Those entitled to insignia of dress, feathers, emblems or paint should display them.

(At one ceremony observed, in addition to those who wore eagle quills or bore banners indicative of some position or deed, the *Hunkayapi* all put red stripes on their faces and the seven *Mihunka* painted their bodies red. Three *akicita*, or marshals, painted three black stripes perpendicular on their right cheeks as badges of their authority. The women who had had the Buffalo ceremony performed for their benefit painted the parting of the hair red and some of them the right half of the forehead. Two women who were *Hunkaya* put the red stripes on their cheeks. At this ceremony, the *walowan* painted his body red as an emblem of his sacred office and put a number of fine red stripes on his cheeks, said to have been one for each time he had taken part in the *Hunka* ceremony. He painted red zigzag lines down each arm from his shoulders to his hands as a symbol of his mysterious powers and he painted his hands red to indicate that he was about to do solemn things of which the Gods would take notice. His regalia was a headdress of skin with the hair on, having a buffalo horn at each side attached so that they stood as if grown there, and the headdress was adorned with hawk feathers and weasel skins. Since then the author has been informed that only those who have accomplished much are entitled to wear the buffalo horns; only those who have much power to do mysterious things are entitled to wear hawk's feathers and only those who are very cunning are entitled to wear the weasel skins. Anyone may wear either of these, but to do so without the right is contemptible.)

The *walowan* with his regalia on should go to the top of a nearby hill to await the appearance of the Sun. The regalia of the *walowan* is any peculiar article of dress or adornment that he had adopted to wear when he is formally acting as a shaman. He should face the Sun and sing a song in his praise as he first appears in sight; and as he leaves the edge of the world, the *walowan* should invoke his favor for the people and for the ceremony and then pray the God the Four Winds to give a fair day. When the people see that he has done this, they should shout "*nunwe*." (*Nunwe* is an exclamation of approval used at ceremonies with a meaning like that of "amen" in English.)

Then the women should quickly erect a large tipi with its door towards the east to be used as the ceremonial lodge and about forty paces south of it a small tipi with its door towards the south to be used as the preparation lodge. In the meantime, the *walowan* will return to his tipi and when the lodges are erected he will come forth with his ceremonial pipe and fetish[35] in his hands. (A shaman's fetish is a material that has a supernatural potency imparted to it and the bag or wrappings about it. By proper invocation, the potency of the fetish may be exercised as the shaman wills. The fetish has been called a medicine bag, which is a misnomer as it has nothing to do with medicines.)

He [the *walowan*] should chant of his accomplishments and powers and then harangue the people relative to what should be done on that day. Then he should command the marker and helper to prepare the ceremonial lodge, which they will do by leveling the place of honor and covering it with sage and making an altar between it and the fireplace. Then they will place a stone on one side of the altar and the skull of a buffalo with the horns on it on the other. (The place of honor in a lodge or tipi is the inside rear opposite the door. The fireplace is the center of the lodge or tipi. An altar is a square of earth four, or some multiple of four hand breadths in length with a horn-shaped process at each corner.[36] This is dug, pulverized, and leveled. The stone is an emblem of the Grandfather of all things, the Great God, the Rock. The potency of the Buffalo abides in its skull while the horns remain on it and this potency is a medium between mankind and the God the Buffalo.)

Then they will place the meat scaffold on the south side of the altar. (The *Hunka* meat scaffold consists of three round rods of wood about half as thick as a man's little finger. Two of them are about six hand breadths in length, forked at one end and pointed at the other. The other is about eight hand breadths long. The scaffold is placed by sticking the two forked rods in the ground so that the other can be laid in the forks and then laying it there.) They then place the *Hunka* meat on the scaffold and the drum inside next [to] the door, on the south side. (The *Hunka* meat should be supplied by the candidates or their friends and should be of the choicest flesh of the buffalo, both fat and lean in equal quantities, enough so that a small bit can be given to each invited guest.)

They will then inform the *walowan* that the lodge is prepared and he will go to his tipi and fetch the counting stick, the fire stick, the horses' tails, the *Hunka* corn, and the rattles. (The counting stick is a square rod of red cedar wood about as thick as a man's great toe and about twelve hand breadths long. It is used to make a record by notching it. Its use in this ceremony other than [as] an emblem of the office of marker is unknown to the author. The fire stick is a round rod of ash wood about as thick as a man's thumb and about eight hand breadths long. One end is made flat for about a hand breadth, and split and held apart by a wedge. It is painted red to signify that it is to be used to carry coals of fire in which abides the *ton* of the Great God the Sun.)

He [the *walowan*] will then present the counting stick to the marker, the fire stick to the helper, the *Hunka* wands to the bearers, the *Hunka* corn to the bearer, and the rattles to those appointed to rattle them. He will then begin to chant a song to the Four Winds and the people will form behind him for a procession, first the bearers of the implements and then others, and they will march in a circle by the tipis going in the direction that the Four Winds travels in his trail around the edge of the world. (The Four Winds travels on his trail going always in one direction from west to north and thence to east and then to south and thence back to the west.)

They should march around this circle four times, the *walowan* singing during the entire march and such others joining the song as wish to do so. When the procession arrives at the west the fourth time, the *walowan* should address the people, saying, "My friends, we have marched around the world with The Four. The West Wind has closed the door so that the Winged One can not come this day. *Iktomi* has gone to the place of *Eya*. The Buffalo is in the lodge. (The God the Four Winds is sometimes simply called The Four. The God the Winged One, sometimes called the Thunderbird, dwells in a tipi on the mountain that the Sun goes down over at the end of his daily journey. The West Wind can close the door of his tipi and prevent the Winged One from flying abroad so that the glance of his eye will not cause lightning. When the God the Buffalo is in the lodge, peace and plenty are there. The lodge here referred to is this ceremonial lodge.)

When this procession starts to march, the candidates should go into the preparation lodge and strip off their clothing except the breechclout, leggings, and moccasins and the fellow candidate should come out and tie the door flap.

When the *walowan* has declared that the Buffalo is in the ceremonial lodge, he should go and examine the preparation lodge on the outside and then say to the people, "There is an enemy in this tipi. Who will help me to take him?" He should then cry in a loud voice, "*Hunka* must die for each other." He will then say to the fellow candidate, "We will capture this enemy." He should then rush to the door of the preparation lodge and cut the strings and go in as if attacking an enemy. In a short time, he should lead the candidate outside, singing the song of victory that returning warriors sing, and lead him towards the ceremonial lodge. The people should follow and as many wish may join the song of victory. When they arrive at the ceremonial lodge, the *walowan* should say, "We should kill this enemy, but if anyone will take him for *Hunka* we will not kill him."

Then the fellow candidate should say that he will take him for *Hunka* and the *walowan* should say, "If you want him for your *Hunka*, I will make him *Hunka*. You take him into the lodge." Then the fellow candidate will lead the candidate into the ceremonial lodge and seat him between the altar and the fireplace and then others should enter and seat themselves as follows: the helper at the left of the place of honor and the marker at the right; the bearer of the *Hunka* corn at the right of the marker and the bearers of the *Hunka* wands at his right; the seven *Mihunka* at the left of the helper and the two drummers at the drum on the south side of the door; then the kinspeople or friends of the candidates, as many as can get seats, the men on the north side and the women on the south. Those who can not find seats in the lodge should sit in a circle before the door, the men on the north and the women on the south side. (It is not seemly for men and women to sit together at a ceremonial of any kind.)

While the people are seating themselves, the *walowan* should sing this song:

> The meadowlark, my cousin.
> A voice in the air.

(The meadowlark is an *akicita* or servant of *Okaga*, the South Wind. The meaning of the song is that the messenger of the South Wind promises the *walowan* a fair day and pleasant time.)

After all others are seated, the *walowan* enters the lodge in a formal manner and takes his seat on the place of honor, facing the altar and the candidate. He should then direct the fellow

The Third Day of the Sun Dance. By Short Bull, 1912. American Museum of Natural History

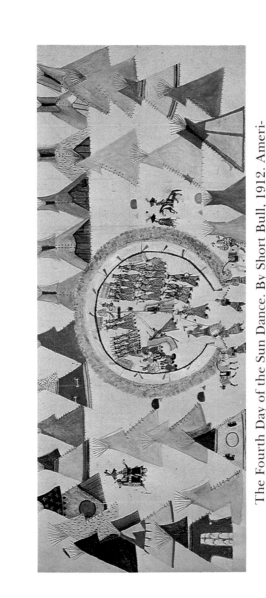

The Fourth Day of the Sun Dance. By Short Bull, 1912. American Museum of Natural History

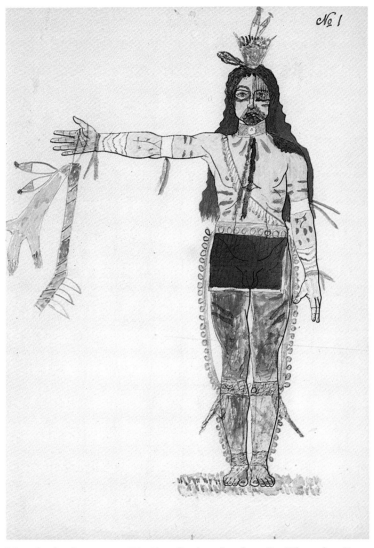

War Insignia, no. 1. Kit Fox Society leader. By Thunder Bear, 1912. Walker Collection, Colorado Historical Society

War Insignia, no. 2. Holy Bow Carrier, a Cheyenne. By Thunder Bear, 1912. Walker Collection, Colorado Historical Society

Ehanaui easa kinle
Blo to hunka to kapte sa
ta hin on Blo to hunka eyapi kin he
le cetu zanya yekten i yu k can nahin
Zan yu wo hi na he on i ta con
tu we ni to kaki i ta con okihi iwin
i sin la i ta con nahin on makin
i yo ti la ta yu i ta con pi

War Insignia, no. 3. War Party Leader. By Thunder Bear, 1912.
Walker Collection, Colorado Historical Society

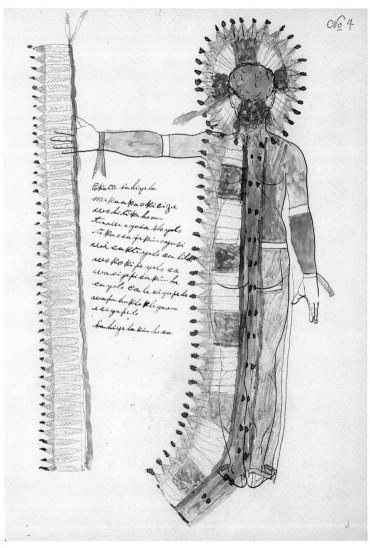

War Insignia, no. 4. Striped Warbonnet, a Cheyenne. By Thunder Bear, 1912. Walker Collection, Colorado Historical Society

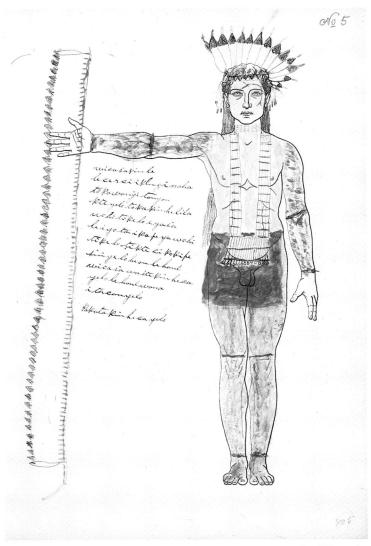

War Insignia, no. 5. A Man Who Killed an Enemy. By Thunder Bear, 1912. Walker Collection, Colorado Historical Society

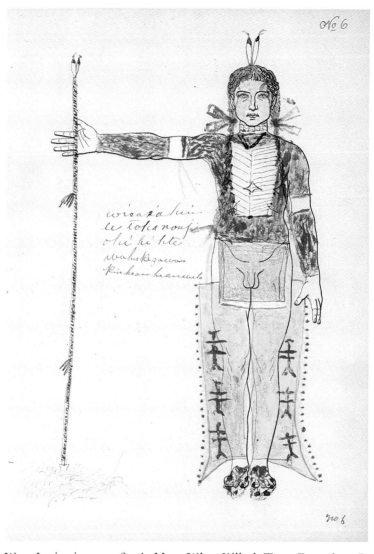

War Insignia, no. 6. A Man Who Killed Two Enemies. By Thunder Bear, 1912. Walker Collection, Colorado Historical Society

War Insignia, no. 7. Leader of the Beaver Society. By Thunder
Bear, 1912. Walker Collection, Colorado Historical Society

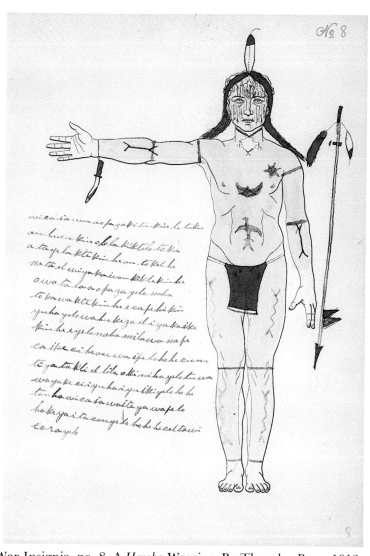

No. 8

wicaⁱⁱᵃ woma⁻ᵃᵖᵃgᵃᵖᵉ⁻ⁱᵘ⁻Ki⁻ⁱᵉ⁻ᵗᵘˢᵉ
aⁿ⁻ˡᵘᵉⁿ⁻Kⁱⁿ⁻ᵉᵏᵃ⁻Kⁱᵏᵗᵉˡᵒ⁻ᵗᵒᵏⁱᵃ
aⁱᵗᵘ⁻yᵉ⁻ˡᵃⁱᵏᵗᵉⁱᵏⁱⁿ⁻ʰᵉⁱᵃⁿ⁻ᵗᵒᵏⁱⁱ⁻ˡᵘ
ⁿᵒⁱᵗᵃⁱ⁻ˢᵉˡᵘⁱyᵃⁱKᵘⁱⁱwᵃⁿ⁻ᵏⁱˢᵏˡᵉˡⁱᵏⁱⁿ⁻ˡᵘᵉ
ᵒⁱwᵒⁱᵗᵃⁱˡᵃⁱᵃˢⁱᵖᵃⁱ⁻ᵍᵃⁱyᵉˡᵒⁱⁿᵃˡᵘᵃ
ᵗᵒⁱᵏᵃⁱwᵃⁱⁱKᵗᵉⁱKⁱⁿ⁻ˡᵘᵉⁱᵉⁱᶜᵃⁱᵖᵉⁱˡⁱⁱᵏⁱⁿ
yᵘⁱˡᵃⁱyᵉˡᵒⁱwᵃⁱˡᵘⁱᵏᵉⁱᵍᵃⁱᵉˡⁱⁱyᵃⁱˡᵘᵃⁱⁱᵏᵃ
Kⁱⁿ⁻ˡᵘᵉⁱᵉⁱyᵉⁱˡᵒⁱⁿᵃˡᵘᵃⁱᵐⁱˡᵘⁱwᵃⁱⁱⁿᵃⁱᵖᵉ
ᶜᵃⁱⁱᵏᵘⁱ⁻ᵉⁱⁱˡᵘᵒᵘⁱwᵃⁱⁱˢⁱᵖᵉⁱˡᵒⁱˡᵘᵒⁱˡᵘᵉⁱᵉⁱⁿⁿᵃ
ᵗᵉⁱyᵃⁱᵗᵃⁱᵏˡⁱⁱˢˡⁱⁱˡⁱˡᵃⁱᵒᵏⁱⁱⁿⁱˡᵘᵃⁱyᵉˡᵒⁱᵗⁱⁱⁱwᵃ
wᵃⁱyᵃⁱᵏᵉⁱᵉⁱⁱⁱyᵘⁱˡᵘᵃⁱⁱⁱyᵘⁱⁱᵏⁱⁱyᵉˡᵒⁱˡᵒⁱˡᵘᵉ
ᵗᵒⁿⁱˡᵘᵃⁱwⁱᶜᵃⁱⁱᵃⁱwᵃⁱˡᵘᵗᵃⁱyᵘⁱwᵃⁱᵖᵉⁱˡᵒ
ˡᵘᵃⁱᵏᵉⁱyᵃⁱⁱⁱᵗᵃⁱᶜᵘⁿⁱᵍᵉⁱᵗᵒⁱˡᵒⁱˡᵘᵉⁱˡᵘᵉⁱˡⁱᶜᵃˡⁱᵗᵒᵘⁱⁱ
ᶜᵒⁱⁱᵃⁱyᵉˡᵒ

War Insignia, no. 8. A *Heyoka* Warrior. By Thunder Bear, 1912.
Walker Collection, Colorado Historical Society

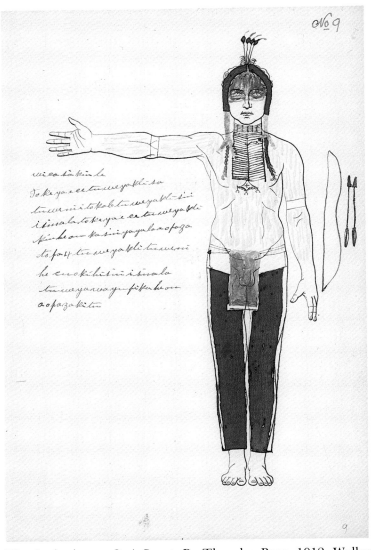

War Insignia, no. 9. A Scout. By Thunder Bear, 1912. Walker
Collection, Colorado Historical Society

War Insignia, no. 10. Lance Bearer of the *Sotka* Society. By Thunder Bear, 1912. Walker Collection, Colorado Historical Society

War Insignia, no. 11. Lance Bearer of the Otter Society. By
Thunder Bear, 1912, Walker Collection, Colorado Historical
Society

War Insignia, no. 12. A *Heyoka* Warrior. By Thunder Bear, 1912. Walker Collection, Colorado Historical Society

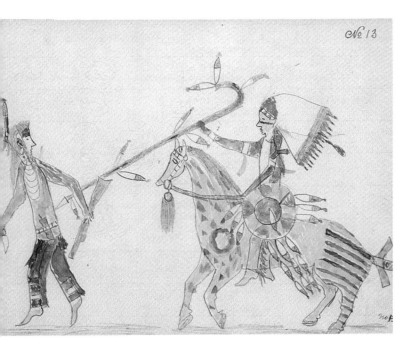

War Insignia, no. 13. Lance Bearer of the Brave Society. By
Thunder Bear, 1912. Walker Collection, Colorado Historical
Society

War Insignia, no. 14. Leader of the *Sotka* Society. By Thunder
Bear, 1912. Walker Collection, Colorado Historical Society

candidate to take his seat beside the candidate and when this is done, he should fill and light a pipe and hand it to the helper, who will hand it to the candidate. The candidate will smoke a few whiffs and hand it to his fellow candidate, who will do likewise and hand the pipe to the helper, and then the pipe will be passed and all in the lodge smoke in communion, the last smoking being the *walowan,* who should then say, "The Grandfather, the Father and the Sons are with us. The Bear and the Buffalo are in this lodge. We have smoked in communion and the Mediator has gone up to the White God. I will now make sacred smoke to drive away the evil powers."

(The God the Bear is the patron of wisdom and his presence at a ceremony insures that it will be correctly performed. The Rock is the Grandfather, the Wind the father, the Four Winds the sons, and the Winged One the White God whose presence in the summer clouds makes them white. The meaning of this speech is that the supernatural powers named have been propitiated by the communal smoke and will look with favor on the ceremony. Any ceremony that has to do with an altar always includes the God the Earth.)

The helper should arrange the buffalo skull on the altar so that it will face the *walowan* and place the stone so as to support it in this position. The *walowan* will then fill his ceremonial pipe with a mixture of the bark of the red willow and Indian tobacco which has been made potent by proper ceremony. While he is doing this, the helper will bring on the fire stick burning coals and place them beside the altar. (To carry burning coals on a ceremonial fire stick and place them together makes a spirit fire that attracts disembodied spirits of former friends and they will give good counsel.)

When he has thus made a spirit fire, he should take a burning coal on the fire stick and hand it to the *walowan,* who will light his ceremonial pipe with it. (The smoke from the contents of a ceremonial pipe lighted with a spirit fire are very potent for invoking the good and exorcising the evil powers.)

Then he will address the altar and say, "Grandmother, you have taken the horns from this skull. The *wakanla* of this buffalo still watches for the dawn. These horns we will honor."

(Grandmother is the ceremonial appellation for the God the Earth, who removes the horns from the skull of a buffalo after the beast has been dead for some time and then its *wakanla,* that is, its immaterial self, leaves the skull. When the skull is honored by replacing the horns on it, its *wakanla* returns to it and will serve the one who so honors it. To watch for the dawn indicates that one is strong and vigorous.)

He [the *walowan*] will then smoke his ceremonial pipe and while he is doing so the helper should place the horns on the skull and arrange the meat on the scaffold, carefully separating the fat from the lean. Then the *walowan* will address the skull, saying, "*Hunka* of the Buffalo, this meat was yours but you gave it to us. If there is a portion of it that you want, tell us and we will give it to you." (The animal buffalo is the *Hunka* of the God Buffalo, and this address alludes to the legend that the God gave the animal to the Lakotas for meat and that when he did so, [commanded] that a portion of each animal should not be eaten by the one who killed [it], each man's taboo to be revealed to him in a vision.)

He should then sprinkle over the meat some material that he has made potent by proper ceremony and while doing so he should say, "My preparations are good and they make this meat sacred." He will then hand a wisp of sweetgrass to the helper, who will sprinkle it on the spirit fire and this will incense the lodge with pleasant odors which will please the Gods and insure the intercession of the Mediator.

While the incense of the sweetgrass is in the lodge, the *walowan* should address the Gods and say, "White God, favor us this day. West Wind, keep the Winged One in your camp this day. Sun, we beg you to keep *Iktomi* and *Anog Ite* from this camp this day."

He will then address the people, extolling himself and the ceremony and admonishing them to observe the precepts taught by it. (In one performance of this ceremony observed, during this address the *walowan* said, "I know how to wave the horse tails as our ancestors did. I will do it that way now. The young people forget how to do this. The shamans will soon be cold and hungry." This alludes to the passing away of the old customs of the Lakotas and the disregard and neglect of the shamans who were their custodians.)

He [the *walowan*] will then say, "This young man desires to be a *Hunka*. I will make him a *Hunka* as our ancestors were made *Hunkayapi*. The Sun looks on us and the Wind is pleased. The Wolf has gone to the hills. The Earth and the Rock and the

Buffalo are in this lodge. They will help me to make this young man a *Hunka*."

He will then formally empty his ceremonial pipe on the chopping board and hand it to the helper, who will empty this refuse on the spirit fire. (The chopping board is a part of the paraphernalia that belongs with a ceremonial pipe. It is a square board about three hand breadths long on each side and as thick as a man's finger. It is used to cut and mix the smoking material on. The refuse from the pipe is emptied on the spirit fire because it would be sacrilegious to throw it on the ground where it might be trampled on like common matter.)

He will then fill and light the ceremonial pipe in a formal way and go to the door of the lodge and elevate the mouthpiece towards the Sun and say, "*Mihunka*, we will bring you a grandson today." He will then return to his seat and give the helper sweetgrass and he will incense the lodge with it and when the smoke rises, the *walowan* will say to the candidate, "I will now make you a *Hunka*. I will teach you how to live as a *Hunka*. These men whose bodies are painted red are *Mihunka*. They will tell you of the *Hunkayapi*. When they speak, let your ears be open."

Then each of the seven *Mihunka* should address the candidate relative to the obligations of a *Hunka* and the benefits derived from being a *Hunkaya*. These will probably occupy some time and when they have finished their addresses there should be an intermission of the ceremony for a short time. During this intermission, the women should begin the preparations for the feast.

At the will of the *walowan,* he will return to the ceremonial lodge and sing this song:

> Kinspeople mysterious come,
> They come this way.
>
> Kinspeople mysterious come,
> They come from the west.

(The kinspeople alluded to here are the buffalo people, who are a supernatural people in the forms of buffalo. They are the people who live under the world and in whose midst the Sun remains during the night. In the beginning they were relatives of the Lakota.)

While he is singing, the people will enter the lodge and seat themselves as during the previous part of the ceremony. When the people are seated, the *walowan* will fill and light his ceremonial pipe and the helper sprinkles sweetgrass on the spirit fire and while he incenses the lodge the *walowan* will say, "The *ton* of the pipe goes to the mysterious brothers and they will carry it to the Buffalo God, who will be pleased with the *ton* of the sweetgrass." (The *ton* of the pipe and the *ton* of the sweetgrass are the same and it is the *ton* of the Mediator. The mysterious brothers are the buffalo people.)

After formally smoking and emptying his ceremonial pipe, he will direct the bearers of the *Hunka* wands to stand and wave them and as they do so, he will say, "These horse tails are sacred. Our grandfathers made them, and the *tonwan* of the Sun is in the eagle feathers and the *ton* of the Sky is in the hair. When one is made a *Hunka* these horse tails are waved over him. The *tonwan* in them will do good for him. It will cause him to remember his comrades. It will shield him from the sight of the Winged One so that he shall not be *heyoka*. *Okaga* gave the horses and he is pleased this day. I will wave these horse tails over you."

(The *tonwan* of a supernatural being differs from the *ton* in that the *ton* can be imparted only from the being, whereas the *tonwan* may be imparted by an *akicita* or chosen messenger of the being. The *ton* of the Sun can not be imparted to anything and abides in the fire, but the eagle is an *akicita* of the Sun and the *tonwan* of the Sun abides in its tail quills.)

Then the *walowan* will formally fill and light his ceremonial pipe and stand between the altar and the fireplace and extend it with the mouthpiece towards the trail of the Four Winds around the world, pausing at the north, east, south, and west and at the latter place bowing low and then lifting the pipe on high. (This is a ceremonial recognition of the Four Winds and of the mysterious brothers, the buffalo people who come from the West.)

He should then stand in the door of the lodge and hold the mouthpiece of the pipe extended towards the sun, elevated in both hands, and say, "*Mihunka,* we have offered smoke to your messengers and to the West Wind, whose tipi is where you are going. They will tell you that we will bring you a younger son this day."

He will then return to the place of honor and take both wands, one in each hand, and wave them from side to side over the two candidates and while doing so he will sing a *Hunka* song, the substance of which should be that the *ton* of the eagle and the horse are in the wands and these will be imparted to the candidates. When he begins to sing, the drummers begin drumming in time and the people join in the singing. This song should be repeated several times and then the *walowan* will address the candidate relative to the duties and obligations of the *Hunkayapi*.

(At one ceremony observed, the substance of this address was as follows: "My grandson, these *Mihunka* are painted red to please the powerful one, the Sun. They have told you how the *Hunkayapi* should live. If you will do as they have done, then the women will sing your praise. The *Hunkayapi* will be as brothers to you and your robe will be good and your moccasins will be new. You will know what gifts to make to the Rock when you see red stripes on a stone. The Great God will give you the eagle feathers. The Buffalo will make your women industrious and they will bear you many children. The Sun will protect you in war and will keep your women and children from the enemy. If you will listen to the Buffalo, he will help you in the chase, and you shall have plenty of meat and robes so that the Wolf shall be afraid of you. I sought a vision and the Bear spoke to me. This is what he said, 'A blue horse and eagle feathers. Women singing in a circle.' The council lodge and a large robe with a buffalo cow painted on it. This is what he showed me. I am a shaman and I know the language of the shamans. If you are in trouble, if you know not what you should do, if a bad *tonwan* is on you, then you should ask the shamans. They will tell you. They speak with the Relative Gods.[37] This is what the Bear said to me: 'The young man should have the sacred horse tails waved over him with the eagle feathers. He will provide for his women and his children. He will be brave and truthful so that the people will listen to him. He will have plenty and he will give freely. His women will be industrious and bear him many children and he will never cut their noses.' My grandson, I have made a charm. I will give it to you. If you will listen to its *ton,* it will be this way with you. This is the Bear's charm. He told me how to make it. Then I asked Two Legs what he would tell me. Standing like a man he said, '*Iya* and *Iktomi* they are traveling.' This I will explain to you. If you are lazy or a coward, then you will sleep with the coyote. Then you should not cut your women's noses. No woman will cut her flesh for you. The Buffalo will laugh at you. If you lie, *Iktomi* will play tricks on you. *Anog Ite* will show both her faces to you. Your women will suffer and your babies will have pains in their bowels. If you listen to the shamans, *Okaga* will stay with you. If you laugh at the shamans, *Waziya* will stay with you. I will now wave the horse tails over you."

(An explanation of this address was given as follows: Red is a sacred color, the symbol of sacredness and especially symbolic of the Sun, and men painted their bodies red to indicate that they had performed some sacred ceremony or were engaged in something that called for the favor of the Gods and for this reason the *Mihunka* referred to had their bodies painted red.

(Women only sang the praise of those of good repute. To say that one's robe is good and his moccasins are new signifies that he is considered prosperous. The God the Rock was propitiated by those who were on a hunting or a war party, either to secure power to destroy or to avert such destruction from themselves. Stones where such propitiation could be properly made were marked with red stripes indicating what offerings should be made at that place. The God the Buffalo presides over the family affairs and the chase and if he is pleased, he will give prosperity and happiness. The shamans usually sought visions of the God the Bear, who is often referred to as Two Legs, and here this shaman tells his vision in the incoherent manner that they mostly told them. "A blue horse and eagle feathers" seen in a vision is interpreted that the one for whom the vision was sought would be a successful warrior, as the horse and the eagle are both *akicita,* or messengers of the Sun, who is the God of war; or, a blue horse is a war horse and eagle feathers are only worn by those entitled to do so by some valorous deed. "Women singing in a circle" indicates that one will take a scalp and, as is the custom, the women will sing in a circle about it. "The council lodge and a large robe with a buffalo cow painted on it" signifies that one will be sufficiently esteemed to have an honorable place in the council of the camp and have a large relationship and following.

(The reference to cutting women's noses alludes to the custom of cutting off a woman's nose as a punishment for infidelity. This was done by the husband and if the man was able to establish the woman's guilt, none dared to resent it. To say that one slept with the coyotes indicated that he was considered disreputable and unworthy of association with the people. To say that no woman would cut her flesh for a man indicated that if he were to die no one would regret it. To say that the buffalo laughs at one indicates that such a one is unsuccessful in the chase. The relation of *Iktomi* and *Anog Ite* to mankind have been explained. To say that *Okaga*, the South Wind, remains with one means that such a one has a pleasant life, but to say that the superhuman being *Waziya* remains with one means that such a one has a hard life with many misfortunes.)

He then should wave the wands over the candidates and over every *Hunkaya* in the lodge, chanting a *Hunka* tune while doing so, the drummers drumming in time with it. He should then take the two rattles, one in each hand, and say, "These rattles are sacred. The color of the Sun is on them. The color of the Earth is on them. The *ton* of the Relative Gods is in them. Their sound calls the attention of the Gods. The plumes on them give them potency." Then he should sing a *Hunka* tune without words and sound the rattles vigorously in time with the song, the drummers drumming in time with the sound of the rattles. He should sound the rattles over the heads of the candidates and then over the heads of each of the *Hunkayapi* in the lodge, after which he should return to his seat on the place of honor and then say, "The *wakanla* of the Buffalo is *Hunka* to all who have the *Hunka* ceremony performed over them. It should be pleased."

He should then formally fill his ceremonial pipe and light it with fire from the spirit fire and on his hands and knees blow smoke from it into the nostril cavities of the buffalo skull and then hand the pipe to the candidate, and while he smokes, the *walowan* should say, "You smoke with the *wakanla* of the Buffalo and you are his brother. He will help you that you may have plenty of meat and buffalo hides."

He should then remove the skull from the altar and say, "We will smoke to the Rock," and then blow smoke on the stone on the altar and hand the pipe to the candidate, who should also blow smoke on this stone. He should then say, "We have smoked to the Rock, and he will be your friend and make you strong and healthy so that you will not grow tired easily." Then he should say, "We will smoke with our grandmother," and then blow smoke on the altar and hand the pipe to the candidate, who will do the same. Then the *walowan* should say, "We have smoked with the Earth, and she will provide all things for us."

He should then take the *Hunka* corn and thrust the stem it is bound to in the altar and say, "Our grandmother gave us this corn. She sent it by the buffalo women because she was pleased with the Lakotas. *Okaga* came with her. She gave it in the summer. This ear of corn is sacred. If we give it to her, she will give us much more for it. She teaches the *Hunkayapi* to give to the hungry. The drake's feathers are *Okaga*. The plumes are the Buffalo. These embrace the Earth, and her children are many. These things a shaman can tell you."

("Our grandmother gave us this corn" refers to a Lakota legend that in the long ago, a Lakota men took for himself a fair-haired buffalo woman and because of jealousy she fled from him and her children and hid by burying herself in the ground. Standing near her, he bewailed his loss when she repented and besought the Earth to restore her to him. The Earth would not do this but in pity for her children caused her to grow as a plant with a fair head and changed her breasts to an ear of corn that is at first milk and then grain for the food of mankind.[38]

("The drake's feathers are *Okaga*" has already been explained. "The plumes are the Buffalo" alludes to the plume of the eagle as a symbol of valor and virtue and to the God the Buffalo, the patron of the virtues. "These embrace the earth and her children are many" is a metaphor meaning that if the products of the ground are cultivated, there will be plenty, and if the virtues are cultivated there will be happiness. "These things a shaman will tell you" means that the shamans are the proper persons to explain difficult and obscure matters in the mythology or ceremonial of the Lakotas.)

Then accompanied by the drum and rattles and waving of the horse tails in time with the song, he sould sing this song:

> *Hunka, Hunka, Hunka* in the west.
> *Hunka's* voice, hear it.

(This song is the declaration of the *walowan* as a shaman that the God the Buffalo is pleased with the ceremony as it has so far been conducted and that he will continue it.)

He should then remove the ear of corn from the altar and give it to the bearer and replace the buffalo skull as it was supported by the stone on the altar and then seat himself on the place of honor and display paint pouch and paints and say, "These paints are consecrated, for I have prepared them with proper ceremony and their *ton* is good."

He should then hand the paints to the marker and direct

him to paint the insignia of a *Hunka* upon the buffalo skull, and the marker should paint a red stripe from the right eye cavity down across the cheek to the nasal cavity and behind this a black stripe. (The red stripe is the insignia of a *Hunka*. The black stripe is the insignia of an *akicita* or marshal of either a camp, a ceremony, or expedition, and in this instance it indicates that the Buffalo is not only a *Hunka* but has authority among the *Hunkayapi* that must not be disputed.)

The marker should then paint the upper part of the stone red. (The symbolic color of God the Rock is yellow, but red is put on a stone in veneration of the Rock, for red is sacred and the Rock is pleased with this mark of reverence and may bestow perseverance and endurance on one showing it.)

Then the helper should sprinkle sweetgrass on the spirit fire, and when it has incensed the lodge the *walowan* should take lean meat from the scaffold and give it to the candidate and bid him give of it to all within the lodge, giving him a knife to cut it with. The candidate should cut the meat and give a morsel to each person in the lodge, reserving a bit for himself.

Then the *walowan* should take the fat meat from the scaffold and cut it into bits and give a portion to each one present but reserve none for himself, giving to the candidate last. Each should eat the meat as it is given to them, and as the candidate places the fat in his mouth, the *walowan* should say that he is hungry and has no fat meat to eat and ask the candidate for some. If the candidate should say he has no meat, then the *walowan* should say to him that he has some in his mouth and advise him that as a *Hunka* he should be ready to take the meat from his own mouth and give it to a hungry *Hunkaya*.

Then the *walowan* should say, "My moccasins are old and my feet are sore," and after waiting a short time he should say to the candidate, "You should take the moccasins from your own feet and give them to a *Hunkaya* who has none." Then he will take the moccasins of the candidate and say to him, "I am cold and have nothing to cover my body," and then say to the candidate, "As a *Hunka* you should take the covering from your body and give it to a *Hunkaya* who has none." Then he should take the candidate's shirt. Then he should say, "My leggings are old and ragged," and then say to the candidate, "As a *Hunka*, you should strip yourself naked and give all you have to a *Hunkaya* in need," and then he receives the leggings of the candidate. He should then address the people, saying that the candidate has proven himself worthy to be made a *Hunka,* for he has taken fat meat from his mouth to give to a hungry *Hunka* and has stripped himself of all his clothing to give to a *Hunkaya* who was in need so that he is now naked and without food. "I will put the red stripe on his face for he is a *Hunka.* I will put this stripe on his face so that when the people see it, they will know that he has given away all that he had and then they will give to him. I put the red stripe on his face and on the face of his *Hunka* so that they may remember this day and when they see a *Hunkaya* in want they will give to such a one."

He should then direct the candidate and his fellow candidate to sit closely side by side and the marker and helper to hold robes so suspended that they would hide the candidates from the sight of the people. He should then take his fetish in his hands and incant the invocation of its potency and continue this incantation while he should take from the wrappings of the fetish a talisman or familiar which he has prepared with proper ceremony, usually tied in a small package and painted red. With these held reverentially he should move slowly and solemnly into the folds of the suspended robes and give the talisman to the candidate, instructing him as to its potency and the proper use of it. And then he should name to the candidates what thing is taboo to them until they have freed themselves from the taboo by some deed approved by the people.

(The taboo established during this ceremony was usually a portion of some animal that must not be eaten during the taboo. An act or deed was generally prescribed to be done which would lift the taboo, such as to kill an enemy or take a scalp or capture horses or women from an enemy. But it might be any deed.)

During the time the *walowan* is hidden under the robes, the drummers should sound the drum and then drum and sing a *Hunka* song, the people joining in the singing. When it is seen that he has risen as if about to come from the screen, the drummers should begin another *Hunka* song and during this the marker and helper remove the screen of robes and the *walowan* returns to his seat on the place of honor, exposing the candidates bound together, arm tied to arm, leg tied to leg. The candidates should each have a red stripe painted on his right cheek from his forehead to his chin. (One is entitled to have a red stripe painted on his cheek for each time the *Hunka* ceremony is performed for him, either as a candidate or fellow candidate, and thus one may have several such stripes when exposed at this part of the ceremony.)

Then the *walowan* should address the candidate in substance as follows, "You are bound to your *Hunka* as if he were yourself. When you put the red stripe of the *Hunkaya* on your face, remember this. What you possess should be as if it were his. What he possesses he will give to you if you desire it. You should help him if he is in trouble. If anyone does harm to him you should take revenge for it as if the harm was done to yourself. If you have horses or women or meat, they are his as if they belonged to him. If he has these things, they are yours as if they belonged to you. His children will be yours and your children will be his. If he is killed in war, you should not rest until you have provided a companion for his spirit. If he takes a ceremonial bath or seeks a vision, you should help him to prepare his potencies and aid him in making gifts to the shamans and medicine men. If he is sick, you should make presents to the shamans and the medicine men. As you do these things for him, so he will do them for you. The *Hunkayapi* are as your kinspeople. If you are a true *Hunkaya,* they will not permit you to want. You should choose a mentor and listen to his teachings. You should be as a son to him."

(The reference made in this address to the giving of women is in accordance to an ancient custom among the Lakotas by which if a man had more than one woman, when he had a guest or friend to whom he wished to show especial courtesy, he did so by giving the guest or friend one of his women to use as long as he remained in the tipi with the giver. The exhortation to provide a companion for the spirit alludes to the custom of killing an enemy in the name of one who has been killed in war, when the spirit of the enemy killed must accompany the spirit of the one in whose name he was killed and serve it on the spirit trail and forever be as a captive to it. The potencies used in ceremonial baths and seeking a vision are material things to which supernatural powers have been imparted by proper ceremonies, usually done by shamans or medicine men who must be recompensed with gifts. "You should choose an *Ate,*" literally translated, would be, "You should choose a father," but the concept is mentor rather than father.)[39]

When he has closed this address, the *walowan* should stand

and declare the candidate a *Hunka,* which will end the ceremony. Then the new *Hunka* and his *Hunka* will rise and leave the ceremonial lodge still bound together and go to the preparation lodge, where they will unbind and clothe themselves and join the people. When the new *Hunka* has left the ceremonial lodge, the people rise and silently go, leaving the *walowan* alone in it. He will then invoke the Gods and wrap the implements of the ceremony in their appropriate coverings and carefully preserve them for future use because the more often such implements are used the more potent they are. Before leaving the lodge, he should level the altar, because the God the Earth would be annoyed were this thing made of her substance to be left uncared for, and he should turn the buffalo skull with the horns down so as to free its *wakanla* that it may depart when it desires to do so. After this, no one should enter the ceremonial lodge and it should be taken down in a short time.

When the two *Hunka* join the people, presents are made by those who wish to give them. It is expected that the *Hunka* and their kinsfolks will give liberally and that those who receive presents from them will give something in return, except the *walowan* who should receive much but is not expected to give anything.

(At one *Hunka* ceremony observed, when the *Hunka* joined the people his father harangued the assembly, praising the *walowan* and his son, and announced his intention to give away all that he possessed. This he apparently did, beginning by giving a horse to the *walowan.* While he was giving, he sang a song of the White Horse Society[40] and others were incited to harangue and give so that there were several singing or haranguing and all giving at the same time. The presents were first displayed either by spreading them on the ground or draping a horse with them. Some who wished to give employed elderly men to harangue for them and announce who was giving and to whom it was to be given. Soon there was shouting, singing, and hilarity among all present. The *Hunka* and his father gave much but they received about as much in return, so that they were little the poorer for making the presents.

(When the giving ceased, the *Hunka* took all that he had received and laid it at the feet of an old man, thus signifying that he had chosen him for his mentor. The old man gave presents to the *Hunka,* which signified that he agreed to be his mentor.

Then the father shouted the praises of the mentor and his son and invited all to the feast of dog flesh. At this feast, all sat in a circle on the ground except the women who were serving it. The shamans sat together and next to them the *Mihunka* and elderly men; next to these the new *Hunka* and his fellow *Hunka;* next to these were the men and boys and then the women and girls and children. The feast continued far into the night.)

If the candidate is a woman, the ceremony would be nearly the same, except that she would not be stripped of her clothing in teaching her generosity and she would be lectured to be hospitable, industrious, and submissive to her man.

If the candidate is a young child, one of its parents would take its place in the ceremony and it would be placed in the arms of its *Hunka* instead of being bound to him. If one becomes a *Hunkaya,* he cannot voluntarily withdraw from this relationship, but if he is stingy or guilty of cowardice, the *Hunkayapi* may refuse to recognize him as one of their number.

84. Explanation of a Diagram of the Ceremonial Lodge of the *Hunka Lowanpi*. Antoine Herman. (AMNH)

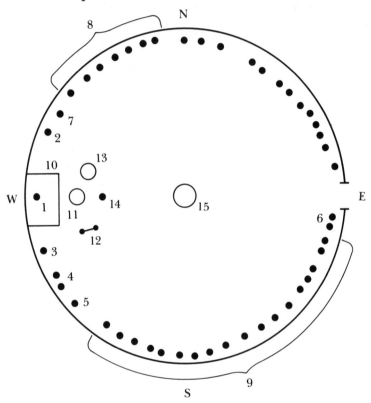

N – north; E – east; S – south; W – west.
The circle represents the walls of the lodge; the dots within the circle represent the people.

1. the *walowan* (conductor of the ceremony)
2. the *ptepaowa* (marker)
3. the *wowasi* (helper)
4. the two bearers of the wands and rattles
5. the bearer of the ear of corn
6. the drummers

7. the *Hunka*
8. the *Hunkayapi,* the first seven men [to the right of no. 7 on the diagram] with bodies painted red
9. women, some *Hunka* and some buffalo women
10. *catku* (honor place)
11. altar of earth
12. *wakan* meat scaffold
13. spirit fire
14. candidate
15. fireplace

---

85. *Tatanka Lowanpi,* The Buffalo Ceremony.[41] James R. Walker. (AMNH)

The *Tatanka Lowanpi* or the Bull Buffalo Ceremony has been practiced among the Oglala Lakotas from very ancient times. One of the Buffalo Women, a woman belonging to *Tatanka,* taught this ceremony to the Lakotas. *Anog Ite* was luring her (Buffalo Woman's) daughters to the home of *Iya* and *Iktomi* and was persuading them to do foolish and disgraceful things. With the aid of the messengers of *Wi,* the Sun, and of *Okaga,* the South Wind, she drove *Anog Ite* and *Iktomi* away from the tipi of the buffalo and purified her daughters and made good women of them so that they were industrious and hospitable and were true to their men.

When the Lakotas were on the plains for the buffalo, she [the Buffalo Woman] saw *Anog Ite* lurking near their camp, so she taught them the Ceremony of the Bull Buffalo, so that they could purify their daughters at their first menstruation and thus drive from them evil *tonwan* or influences and incline them to become industrious and hospitable and to live such lives that the men who owned them should never have to cut their noses for infidelity.

This ceremony, like the *Hunka Lowanpi,* to which it is closely related, is based on the beliefs and practices of the shamans and is performed to impress on the minds of young women their duties to themselves and to the men who shall own them and to *Taku Wakan* and the shamans.

When a girl is young, she is like a boy, but when she has her first menstrual flow, a *tonwan*[42] possesses her which gives her the possibility of motherhood and makes her *wakan* and this *tonwan* is in the products of her first flow, making it very powerful for either good or evil as it may be used.

At this time, *Anog Ite* and *Iktomi* lurk near her and if a man approaches her, they may plague him with eruptions and palsy or it may be with madness, and if she permits this, she may sleep with the coyotes and her children will be a shame to her. She should live alone during this period in a tipi put up for this purpose, called the lonely tipi,[43] and ever afterwards when she has her menstrual flow this is called her lonely time, when she should not take part in any feast or ceremony nor talk with men, so that the *wakan tonwan* of her flow may harm no one and so that all may know that she is not with child.

The tipi where she stays during her flow is *wakan* and the evil powers lurk about it to do harm to any man who may enter it. The *Can Otila,* the imps of mischief, hide near the door to hear secret things, which they are sure to tell.

Parents should teach their girls to carefully preserve the products of their first flow and wrap them in bundles so that it may be known what they are, and to place these bundles in some out of the way place where the coyotes cannot get them. They should be placed in a living tree so that its spirit may guard them, and it is best to place them in a plum tree, for it is fruitful and its *tonwan* may influence the girl to bear many children. If a man meddles with such a bundle, he is apt to be plagued with pimples and boils until a shaman or medicine man exorcises the evil *tonwan* from him.

Iktomi persuades his friend, the coyote, to seek for such bundles, and if he gets one he devours it and thus gets a power over the girl by which he can compel her to do ridiculous or disgraceful things. But if he does not know which girl made the bundle, its *tonwan* operates against him and makes him lean and mangy.

Some shamans can make philters of the first flow of a girl by mixing it with medicines known only to themselves and by incantation and magic. If such a philter is mixed with the food or drink of a young person, he or she will desire the one who mixes it and will go to the one so desired. If one wants a philter of this kind, he must secretly get the first flow of a girl and as secretly take it to a shaman who will make medicine to ward off the evil consequences and then make the philter.

The spirits which take possession of the body of a girl when she becomes a woman squeeze the blood from her body and cause the flow. Each moon they return and do this unless she becomes with child, when they are pleased and let her alone, except *Anog Ite,* who may still plague her with pains.

The parents should have the Buffalo Ceremony performed for their daughter as soon as practicable after she has her first flow. If this is at a time when they have plenty, it should be performed as soon after the flow ceases as the friends can be gathered together for this purpose. But if it is at a time when there is not plenty, then they should announce that their girl has become a woman and that they will have the ceremony performed as soon as they can make the proper provisions for it so that she may become a buffalo woman.

If a girl has no father, then her friends may have the ceremony performed for her. But it is no disgrace to a woman if the ceremony has never been performed for her benefit, for such a one may, by her skill and industry, make herself as desirable as if she had been made a buffalo woman.

This ceremony may be performed in a simple way with few present and little or no feasting or giving, or the occasion may be made an elaborate festival. The social prestige of the woman is in proportion to the number of guests, the amount of the feast and the prodigality of the giving at this ceremony which is her debut as a woman. There is no fixed ritual governing the ceremony, but each performance should be like the others in the rites and songs and their sequence.

When a girl's first flow comes upon her, she should be placed alone in a tipi and her mother or female friends should teach her how to care for and dispose of the products and how to purify her body after the flow ceases by bathing or, better still, by the *ini* or the sweat bath. And they should instruct her as to the part she is to take in the ceremony.

The provisions for the ceremony which her parents are required to make are: a tipi for the lodge, preferably a new one; a dress for the girl, preferably one that has not been worn; a breechclout for the girl, preferably one that is ornamented; a wooden bowl, preferably a new one; chokecherries, either fresh or dried; an eagle plume with the quill wrapped with the skin from the head of the mallard drake; sage brush; dried wood, either box elder or cottonwood; a drum; a pipe; dried willow bark to smoke in the pipe; sweetgrass; food for the feast and presents for the guests.

Anyone who knows the songs may conduct the ceremony, but it is preferable to have a man do so. The father may conduct it, but it is preferable that another man and a shaman do so. If another than the father is chosen, he is thereby given a kind of fostering relation to the girl which continues until some man takes her for his woman, and his advice should be sought and followed in all matters pertaining to the ceremony or to the welfare and disposition of the woman.

The one who is to conduct the ceremony should seek a vision relative to it and be controlled by the communication he receives from *Taku Wakan*. This vision he should relate during the performance. He should provide a buffalo skull with the horns on it and a staff made of cherrywood and a *wakan* fire stick and the ceremonial pipe. The father, mother and the girl may invite the guests and invitation wands are sent to show especial honor to those receiving them. Anyone should be welcome to the feast whether invited or not, except one to whom a dried bone has been sent, which indicates that the presence of such a one is not desired. Guests should bring their tipis and provisions so that they may not be a burden on the host, and they may come before and stay after the day appointed for the ceremony, prolonging the festival over several days. The day appointed should be devoted to the ceremony, from dawn to sunset, and guests should not occupy themselves with anything not connected with it. The following is a description of the ceremony as conducted by Ringing Shield, an old shaman.

In the morning, when the dawn was well defined, the shaman stood at the door of his tipi and sang this song.

> A voice, *Anpao,* hear it.
> Speaking low, hear it.

This was an invocation to *Anpao,* the dawn, to awaken the sun gently that he might begin his daily journey in a good humor and command the Four Winds to give pleasant weather during the day. Immediately the people busied themselves getting their morning meal and preparing for the ceremony. Before sun-up, the mother of the girl, with the help of other women, put up the tipi that was to be used as a lodge with its door towards the east so that the rising sun might shine on the *catku,* or place of honor, in the tipi. The father leveled the *catku* for a space of about three feet square with each corner projecting so as to symbolize the four legs of *Tatanka* and the Four Winds. Between the *catku* and the fireplace at the center of the tipi, he built a small mound of earth as the tipi of the Spirit of *Maka,* the Earth. On this he placed the buffalo skull so that the Spirit of the Buffalo might overlook all in the lodge. He then brought an armful of sage and laid it beside the *catku* and laid a bundle of sage by the door.

In the meantime, the mother and other women were building a fire at the north side of the lodge with the dried cottonwood, of which an abundance had been provided. While doing so, the mother was chanting this song:

> The spirit of the dry wood.
> Those coming are pleased.
> The spirit of the dry wood
> *Waziya* is going away.

The meaning of this song is that a spirit fire built of the dry wood will please the supernatural powers that may come to the ceremony and their beneficent *tonwan* secured and the malevolent *tonwan* of *Waziya* will be driven away. This fire was kept replenished so that there were plenty of coals from it during the ceremony.

As the sky grew red before the rising sun, the shaman stood facing it and said, "*Anpao,* I am your friend. I have prepared the red paint which you like best. I have mixed it with good marrow fat. Tell this to *Wi* that he may be pleased. Give your *tonwan* to this paint." He then waited until the sun was rising, when he said, "Grandfather, look with pleasure on us. Command the *Taku Wakan* to do as we ask them. We will do nothing to displease you this day. Tell *Yata*[44] that I am his friend, so that he may keep *Wakinyan* from the skies." The father then placed the pipe, willow bark, sweetgrass, wooden bowl, chokecherries, and eagle plume in the lodge near the *catku* and told the shaman that all was ready for the ceremony.

The girl had been alone in her tipi from the evening before and when the shaman was chanting his song to the dawn, she came out with the bundle containing the products of her flow and carried it over a hill and placed it in a plum tree and she returned to the creek, where she washed her hands to cleanse them from any evil *tonwan* that may have gotten on them from the bundle. Then she went into her tipi to prepare herself for the part she would take in the ceremony, by putting on the breechclout and an extra dress and letting her hair down about her shoulders as those who mourn wear their hair, to indicate that she mourned for her departed childhood.

The shaman then went into his tipi and put on his regalia, which was a skin cap with buffalo horns at the side and a skin pendant to hang down the back. It was adorned with hawks' feathers on the cap and weasels' skins on the pendant, and the tail of a buffalo was attached to the lower end of the pendant. He stripped his body, wearing only his leggings and moccasins, and painted his face and body red and put three stripes of black across his face, from his right eye to his jaw, the red to indicate his *wakan* power and the black stripes to indicate his authority to perform the ceremony. When he appeared, he held his pipe in his right hand and his *wakan* medicine bag and the staff of cherry wood in his left, with his arms crossed over his chest so as to bring these articles against his shoulders, thus imparting to them the *tonwan* of his familiar spirit. He then sang this song:

> The sun is going.
> The sun is going.
> Traveling they go.
>
> My kinsman is going.
> My kinsman is going.
> I do this thing.

This song means that the sun on his journey is driving away the evil beings and that the shaman has painted himself red to symbolize the good powers of the sun and he held the pipe and medicine bag and staff against his body so as to impart to them some of the powers of the supernatural beings.

While he was chanting, the people stood about him giving respectful attention, and when he stopped singing, he addressed them, lauding the girl and her father and reciting his own proficiency in performing the ceremony and exhorting all to have a proper spirit for the occasion. He then announced that the ceremony was about to be performed and the people went into the lodge and seated themselves as follows: the father seated himself at the north side of the *catku* and the men seated themselves around the north side of the tipi to the door; the mother seated herself at the south side of the door and the women seated themselves around the south side of the lodge to the *catku*. The drummers sat between the mother and the fireplace. Many could not get into the lodge and seated themselves in a circle east of the door, the women on one side and the men on the other, in compliance with the customs that women should not sit with a man in public.

After the people were seated, the shaman walked with slow and long strides to the fire at the north side of the lodge and sprinkled some sweetgrass on it to subdue the spirit of the dry wood and induce it to do his bidding. He then entered the lodge, and passing around the south side to the *catku*, he deliberately scanned each woman, so that none who were having their menstrual flow might take part in the ceremony, for this would throw an evil spell over the ceremony and prevent its efficacy. He then returned to the door by the way he had gone, so as not to pass between the *catku* and the mound and thus desecrate them and deprive them of their *wakan* attributes. Then he scanned each man so that no objectionable one could take part in the ceremony.

He then took his seat on the *catku* and gave the *wakan* fire stick to the father, who brought coals from the fire outside and laid them together between the mound and the *catku*, making a spirit fire. While he was doing this the shaman spread sage over the *catku* and the space between it and the mound and around the spirit fire so that the *tonwan* of the sage would keep all evil *tonwan* away.

He then lighted the pipe with the spirit fire and blew some of the smoke from it into the nostrils and eye sockets of the buffalo skull and then handed it to the father, who took a whiff and handed it to the one next to him and so on around the lodge. While the people were smoking, the shaman painted the right side of the forehead of the skull, down to the eye socket, red to show that this ceremony belonged to the Buffalo and that the girl for whom it was to be performed would thereby become a buffalo woman. He then stuck two wands in the mound so that they stood within the curves of the horns of the skull, each wand having fastened near its top end a small package of medicine tied in red buckskin to please the Spirit of the Buffalo and let it know that its *tonwan* in the medicines on the wands was respected.

He then sprinkled sweetgrass on the fire to get the attention of the supernatural powers and lighted the ceremonial pipe and, rising, held it with the mouthpiece pointing towards the north, the east, the south, and the west, to please the Four Winds, the messengers of *Wakanska*,[45] who presides over all moving things.

He then said, "My friends, we have smoked with the Spirit of the Buffalo and the *tonwan* of *Tatanka* will be in this lodge." He then sang this song.

> Buffalo bull in the west, lowing.
> Buffalo bull in the west, lowing.
> Lowing he speaks.

Then he laid a bit of red cloth on the skull as a sacrifice, saying, "My older sister, I give this robe to you." He then directed that the girl should be brought, and her mother led her into the lodge and seated her at the north side of the mound, she sitting crosslegged as boys and men sit. The shaman then sprinkled a bit of sage on the fire and said, "*Iya,* go away from this place that this girl may not be a lazy woman." Sprinkling another bit on the fire, he said, "*Iktomi,* go away from this place that this girl may not do foolish things." Again sprinkling on the fire, he said, "*Anog Ite,* go away from this place that this girl may not do shameful things when she is a woman." He sprinkled the sage on the fire the fourth time and said, "*Hochnogia* [*Hohnogica*] go away from this place that this girl may not have trouble when she is a woman."

When the sage ceased smoking, he sprinkled sweetgrass on the fire and said, "*Tatanka,* I have painted your woman's forehead red and have given her a red robe. Her medicine is within her horns. Command her to give her *tonwan* to this girl so that she may be a good buffalo woman and bear many children."

He then said to the girl, "You have lived alone for the first time. The *tonwan* of the *Taku Wakan* had possession of you. You are now a woman and should be ashamed to sit like a child. You should sit like a woman."

Her mother came and drew her feet together so that she sat with her limbs together at one side, after the manner of the Lakota women. The shaman then said to her, "You should always sit as you are now sitting. If you should sit as a man sits, then your mother would be ashamed and the young men would say that the coyotes had eaten your bundle."

He then arose and walked around the girl four times, scanning her closely to see that she was properly prepared for the ceremony. Seating himself, he said to her, "I sought a vision and saw the messenger of the White Buffalo Cow. I sang this song:

> The messenger of the buffalo in the West
> The messenger of the buffalo in the West
> The messenger of the buffalo in the West
> I will give you a robe.

"Then the messenger said, 'A spider, a turtle, the voice of the lark, a brave man, children, a smoking tipi.' I have spoken with the *Taku Wakan* and I will tell you what this means. The spider is industrious and builds a tipi for its children. It provides them with plenty of food. The turtle is wise and hears many things and does not tell anything. Its skin is like a shield so that arrows cannot wound it. The lark is cheerful and brings the warm weather. It does not scold its people. It is always happy. If a brave man takes you for his woman you may sing his scalp song and you may dance his scalp dance. He will kill plenty of game so that you will have skins and robes. You will bear him many children and he will make you happy. There will always be a fire in your tipi and you will have food for your people. If you are industrious like the spider, and wise like the turtle, and cheerful like the lark, then you will be chosen by a brave man and have plenty and never be ashamed.

"Then these are things I saw in the vision. A coyote and worn-out moccasins and I heard a voice in mourning. The Buffalo sends this message to you. If you listen to *Iktomi* or to *Iya* or to *Anog Ite,* then you will be lazy and poor and miserable. A brave man or a good hunter will not give a dog for you. Your robes will be old and ragged and your moccasins will be worn and without color on them. The buffalo horns are on my head and I speak *Tatanka.*[46] The buffalo tail is behind me and this makes me *wakan.* I am the buffalo bull and you are a young buffalo cow. I will show you what the bad *tonwan* would have you do. I will show you what the good *tonwan* would have you do."

He then lighted the ceremonial pipe from the spirit fire and while he smoked the drummers drummed and sang a song without words, some of the women joining in the singing. The drummers stopped and the shaman sang this song:

A man from the north gave me a cane
I told this girl so.

She will live to be old
Her tribe will live.

He then went to the south side of the lodge and the drummers began drumming and singing a song without words and the shaman danced towards the girl, keeping time with the drums. As he danced, he uttered a gutteral cry something like "un-hu-hu-hu-ah." He continued to dance backwards and forwards about the girl in faster and faster time until his motions and cries appeared frantic.

He then got on his hands and knees near the door and bellowed like a bull, pawing the earth and throwing it up as bulls do. Then he sniffed as if trying to scent something and then came on his hands and knees slowly towards the girl, lowing as the bull does when mating. He approached the girl on the right side and sidled up against her when her mother came and placed a bunch of sage under her right arm so that it would cover her right breast.

The shaman then approached in the same way on the left side, when the mother placed sage under the girl's left arm so that it would cover her left breast. The shaman then approached the girl in the same manner from behind when her mother placed a bundle of sage in her lap.

The shaman then went to his seat and said to the girl, "The bull tries to be intimate with the young cow but she drives him away until she belongs to him. Your mother has shown you how the good will keep away the evil and you should not allow a man to be intimate with you unless you belong to him. If you do, then you will be ashamed of your children and no man will pay a price for you."

He then took the wooden bowl and, putting water in it, mixed chokecherries with the water, singing a song without words while doing so. He then said to the girl, "We are buffalos on the plains. Here is a water hole. It is red to show that it is *wakan*, and belongs to the buffalo woman. Drink from it." He placed the bowl in front of the girl and she stooped and drank from it.

The shaman then got on his hands and knees and so went to the bowl and drank from it, and rising with the bowl in his hands, he said, "My friends, this girl gives you this red water that you may drink from it and be her friends. Let all who are her friends drink of it."

He then handed the bowl to the father, who drank from it and passed it to the one next to him, who drank from it, and so it was passed on around until all in the lodge and out of it had drunk from the bowl, which the shaman replenished as needed with water mixed with the chokecherries.

He then directed the girl to stand up and take off her dress and she did so, taking off the outer dress and handing it to him. He spread it over the buffalo skull and said, "This girl gives her dress to the buffalo woman. Anyone who wants it may take it."

A woman from without the lodge came in and took the dress, and the shaman gave the girl a bit of sage and told her to eat it, and while she chewed it, he said to her, "Sage is bitter. Your mother has shown you that it will keep away bad things." He then gave her a bit of sweetgrass and told her to eat, and while she was chewing it, he said to her, "Sweetgrass is good. It pleases *Taku Wakan* and you should remember these things."

He then took the wands from between the horns of the skull and, handing them to her, said, "This is your buffalo medicine. You should always keep it for it will keep bad *tonwan* away from you. It has the *tonwan* of *Tatanka* and of the Spirit of the Buffalo. It will keep *Anog Ite* away from you. It will bring you many children."

He then directed the mother to arrange the girl's hair as a woman, which she did by parting it carefully across the top of the head and braiding each half.

The shaman then painted red the right half of her forehead and a streak across her head at the parting of her hair, saying while doing so, "You see your oldest sister on the altar.[47] Her forehead is painted red. This is to show that she is *wakan*. Red is a *wakan* color. Your first flow was red. Then you were *wakan*. You have taken red water this day. This is to show that you are akin to *Tatanka* and his woman. *Tatanka* is pleased with an industrious woman. He is pleased with a woman who gives food to those who are hungry. He will make brave men desire her so that they will pay a large price for her. She may choose the man she desires. If he has other wives, she will sit next the *catku*. They will carry wood while she makes moccasins. You are now a buffalo woman. You may paint your face this way."

He then tied the eagle plume to the hair at the top of her

head, saying while doing so, "The spirit of the eagle and the duck will be with you. They will give the *tonwan* of *Wi* and *Okaga*. They will give you many children."

He then handed to her the staff of cherry wood and said, "This staff is of the *wakan* cherry wood. It will help you to find the plums and chokecherries so that you may make plenty of pemmican."

He then directed the mother to remove the girl's breech-clout, which she did without exposing her person and handed it to the shaman, who handed it to the father and said, "You are now a woman. The buffalo woman is your oldest sister. Go out of this lodge."

He then began to chant a song without words and the girl arose and looked confusedly about and then went from the lodge. After she had gone out all the others went out excepting the shaman, who remained singing as an expression of his gratitude to the supernatural powers and spirits who had aided at the ceremony. When he stopped singing, he leveled the mound of earth so that it might not be desecrated, and defaced the *catku* and turned the buffalo skull with its horns to the ground, so that its spirit might find rest as the buffalo rest on the ground at night, and then he came from the lodge to his own tipi, where he divested himself of his regalia.

When the father came from the lodge, he brought the breechclout of the girl with him and threw it outside the camp and then addressed the people in praise of the shaman and of the ceremony and said that his daughter was now a woman and a buffalo woman and that if a brave man or a good provider should choose her, he could have her if he paid the price of a woman.

The tying of the eagle plume to the girl's hair was to indicate that she had matured as a woman and the throwing away of the breechclout was done to show that the parents would give her their consent to her being taken by the right kind of a man as his woman.

If at any time during the feast that followed this ceremony, any man offered the father three or more wands of an equal size, this is considered as offering as many horses as there are wands offered or their equivalent in value for the girl. If the father refuses the offer, then the one making it may steal the girl, provided he can get her consent, except when the father and the one making the offer are both *Hunkayapi,* that is, bear an adopted relationship to each other, in which case neither can take the women of the other without the other's consent. If the father accepts the offer, then the one making it may at any time take the buffalo woman upon paying the price he has offered.

Such offers are made only at this ceremony and the woman is not taken until some years afterwards so that she may learn industry from her mother and become skillful in the work of a woman before she leaves her parents. In the meantime, some other man may take the woman, in which case the father must pay the one who made the offer an equivalent of his offer. But if the one making the offer does not take her by the time she has gotten her full growth, then his claim upon her ceases. A woman who has had the Buffalo Ceremony performed for her benefit is entitled to paint her face as the shaman painted it at that time, at any time she wishes to do so, and she should do so whenever she paints her face formally for any occasion.

After the father had addressed the people, he gave a horse to the shaman and then many of the guests gave him and the young buffalo woman and her mother many presents and they gave many presents in return. During the giving, men were calling out the names of the givers, the persons given to and the things given with speeches in praise of all concerned and other remarks calculated to please the people and make them merry.

After the giving, there was a feast provided by the parents of the young buffalo woman to which the guests contribute largely. The principal viand at this, as it is at nearly all the formal feasts of the Lakotas, was boiled dog meat. This closed the formal ceremony.

The buffalo women form a class distinct from other women, but they do not form an association or society and the duties and obligations impressed upon them are those to the men who may take them as their women.

86. Explanation of a Diagram of the Ceremonial Lodge of the *Tatanka Lowanpi.* Antoine Herman and James R. Walker. (CHS)

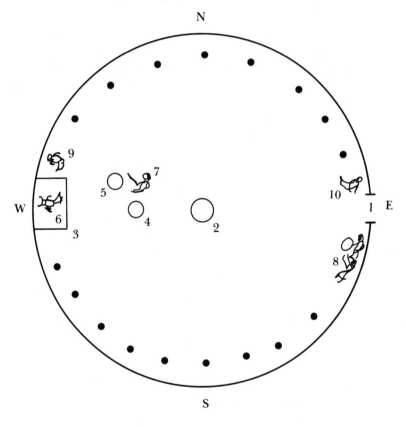

This was made at the time of taking notes on the ceremony.
N – north; E – east; S – south; W – west.

The circle represents the walls of the lodge; the dots within the circle represent the people.

1. door of lodge
2. *oceti,* fireplace in center of lodge; fire kept burning during the ceremony.
3. *catku,* rear of lodge; place of honor opposite the door

4. mound with buffalo skull
5. spirit fire
6. shaman
7. girl for whom ceremony is performed
8. drum and drummers
9. father
10. mother

V

Warfare

Walker collected data on men's societies and on warfare as part of his collaboration with Clark Wissler. Some of this material was incorporated in Wissler's 1912 monograph *Societies and Ceremonial Associations in the Oglala Division of the Teton-Dakota*. Although Walker's investigations of these subjects were neither systematic nor extensive, he recorded valuable information on the identity and ritual of the societies and on their symbolic relation to the realm of the sacred. Thomas Tyon contributed two texts (documents 89 and 90) on the insignia and ritual of the societies and provided an origin story for the societies, evidently borrowed from the Cheyennes.

In addition, Thunder Bear drew a series of depictions of war insignia. Most of these drawings were done on printed forms showing an outline of a nude male body. These forms were used by Wissler to collect information on body painting and insignia, evidently with the intention of having them redrawn by museum illustrators prior to publication. Within the limitations imposed by the form, Thunder Bear did a creditable job of depicting a wide range of war insignia. To most he added brief captions in Lakota.

It is unknown whether Walker's discussions of these drawings were based on interviews with Thunder Bear or whether there were other sources. Many of the interpretations seem to be idiosyncratic; it should not be assumed that all Lakotas would have interpreted these symbols in the same way. The system of insignia for war honors was undoubtedly not as systematically defined as Walker implies. It is also possible that Walker himself contributed the symbolic data from Lakota myth and religion used to explain the insignia. There are inconsistencies and some details that the editors cannot identify, but as a whole, this material represents the most extensive available record of Lakota war insignia. The collection is a real contribution to our knowledge of Lakota life and, as such, it deserves further study.

87. Associations among the Oglala Sioux.[1] Thomas Tyon and John Blunt Horn. (CHS)

In former times, before the white people interfered with the organization of the Indians, the Oglala Sioux had the following associations, which were first established in this way. A man in whom the people had confidence sought a vision and in the vision was instructed in the forms and ceremonies for establishing an association, and what the duties of such an association were. He would instruct others in these matters and associate them for the purposes of the organization in compliance with his vision.

These associations were: *Tokala,* Foxes; *Ihoka,* Badgers; *Cante Tinza,* Brave Hearts; *Wicin Ska,* White Badges [White Marked]; *Kangi Yuha,* Crow Carriers [Crow Owners]; *Ainila Wotapi,* Silent Eaters; and *Sotka Yuha,* Wand Carriers [Bare Lance Owners].

The Foxes were composed of men chosen for their distinction in bravery or some other trait that met the approval of the Foxes. No one was supposed to seek admission to the society. When the Foxes desired anyone to become a member of the society, they sent two members to such a one to inform him that he had been chosen and to explain to him the duties and obligations of the association. If such a one did not wish to assume these obligations, he declined and this ended the matter. Some would not care to assume the obligations, they were so strict and exacting.

If the one chosen agreed to become a Fox, he was told to be present at a meeting of the Foxes when he would be installed as a member. This was usually at some public gathering of the people. On such occasions, when the candidate appeared, the Foxes took charge of the meeting and gave it a formal character by organizing it as follows.

There were fourteen officials at a meeting of this kind: one *wakiconza,* custodian of the pipe; one *cancega yuha,* custodian of the drum; four *wahukeza yuha,* bearers of the wands; two *glahapa,* bearers of the whips; two *wakapamini,* distributors of food; and four *hoka,* singers. There is in addition a committee of four headmen of the association, one of whom must be the custodian of the pipe, who are councilors in all matters of the association. In a formal meeting, the custodian of the pipe presides and has charge of all ceremonies, subject to the advice of the council. He sits opposite the opening into the tipi or lodge where the meeting is held and the custodian of the drum and the singers sit at the right of this opening. The bearers of the wands and of the whips sit on the left of the fireplace, which is in the center of the tipi or lodge, and the distributors of food on the right.

Anyone who wishes to do so may be present at such meetings, but the Foxes have the place of honor, which is farthest from the opening or door.

There were songs that belonged to the association of the Foxes and were sung at their formal meetings. These could be sung by anyone at any time, but at the meetings all joined in singing them, whether Foxes or not, and no other songs were sung. After the Foxes had taken charge of a meeting and placed the proper officers about the lodge, they sang a Fox song and danced the Fox dance, in which only Foxes might participate.

Then the two who had informed the candidate that he had been chosen to be made a Fox led that one before the custodian of the pipe and told the custodian that the Foxes had chosen this one to be made a member of the association and that they had informed him of this and he had consented to assume the duties and obligations of a Fox. The custodian of the pipe then explained to him the various officers at the meeting and what their duties were, *i.e.,* that his own duties were to preside at that meeting, subject to the advice of the four councilors, and to hold and care for the mysterious pipe *(canduhupa wakan)* of the Foxes. That the custodian of the drum held and cared for the mysterious drum *(cancega wakan)* of the Foxes. That the four wand bearers carried the wands that belonged to the association which were peculiar and distinguished the association like banners. That the four bearers of the whips had whips of a peculiar kind with which they would scourge anyone who was derelict to his vows and obligations as a Fox. That the four distributors of food were to teach generosity and the singers were those who chose the songs and led in the singing.

When these explanations were ended, the custodian of the drum began drumming and the singers began a song of the Foxes, in which all joined, and all the Foxes present, except the custodian of the drum and the singers, joined [in the dance] and if a Fox present did not dance, the bearers of the whips lashed him until he joined in the dancing.

After this, the custodian of the pipe invoked *Yata* and *Iya*[2] for their aid in the ceremonies and their propitiation in regard to the candidate. These two invoked are supernatural beings, the sons of *Tate,* and are referred to as *Taku Skanskan,* or the Spirit which presides over moving, hunting, and war, [and] *Inyan,* the Stone Spirit, or the Spirit that presides over bravery, generosity, and endurance. Originally it appears that they were the offspring of *Tate,* the Wind, and were the North Wind and the East Wind.

After this invocation, the candidate is called before the custodian and remains standing during the time when the lectures are given him. These lectures are given by the custodian of the pipe and the councilors, or by any distinguished Fox. They inculcated bravery, generosity, chivalry, morality, and fraternity for fellow Foxes, from the point of view of the Indians.

They taught that one should be brave before friends and foes alike and undergo hardship and punishment with fortitude. That one should give to the needy, whoever it might be, excepting an enemy, of everything one possessed. That one should search for the poor, weak, or friendless and give such all the aid one could. They inculcated that a Fox should not steal, except from the enemy, should not lie, except to the enemy, and should set an example by complying with the recognized rules of the hunt and camp. That if a fellow Fox were in trouble of any kind he should help him to the best of his ability and if a Fox died or was killed and left a widow, he should keep that widow from want. That he should not take the wife of a brother Fox without his consent. That he should treat all his women the same, showing no more favor to one than to another. That if he captured women, he should treat them the same as his own women, and his children by such a woman should be treated the same as children by women of his own people. That if he put a woman away he should see that she was not in want until some other man took her. That if a fellow Fox had no wife, he should give him one of his women if he had more than two.

If the candidate agreed to be governed by these lectures, he was then declared a Fox and he was presented with a wand of the kind belonging to the Foxes, but smaller than those the wand carriers bore, and was instructed to preserve it as a reminder of his duties and obligations.

The singers then began a Fox song and all Foxes joined in a dance and while the custodian of the drum drummed vigorously, the new member was first lashed by the bearers of the whips until he danced vigorously, and the bearers of the wands waved them over him while he danced. After this dance the distributors of the food served all present with food which had been prepared, serving the Foxes last and the new member after all others had been served. Then another Fox song was sung and Fox dance danced, after which the meeting was continued, usually with Fox songs and dances, but not formally, as long as desired by the attendance.

The Brave Hearts is a very ancient association. Their headdress was of a peculiar kind, made with horns that rest on the sides of the head in imitation of the buffalo and of eagle feathers placed close together so that they lie down. They carried a lash or whip of a peculiar kind. Their especial obligation was to care for the helpless in time of danger and if the old or women or children are in danger in time of war, their obligation binds them to go to their rescue.

The White Badges are distinguished by a white stripe across their shields and on their bodies. The emblem carriers carry a wand something like the Mystery Bow,[3] the wand being decorated with beaver fur and sweetgrass and crow's feathers.

The Silent Eaters is composed of only chiefs and headmen. They are who consider the politics of the camp, and after a session, they eat in silence. A modern name for them is "The Big Bellies," which is given because of their manner of eating and because the association embraces most of the corpulent men of the camp.[4]

88. The White Badge Society and the Silent Eaters. Thomas Tyon and John Blunt Horn. (CHS)

The White Badges originated five generations ago among the Lower Brules. A man sought a vision and saw a white buffalo. He painted his vision on a robe. He chose ten men and originated the White Badges. They danced wtih bows and arrows and would shoot the arrows while they danced. Their badge was a white sash over the left shoulder. This sash was made of white skin. They had a white stripe on their bodies and arms. They had a white stripe across their shields.

The *Ahinila Iota* (Silent Eaters) were only braves accepted by the people. They did not dance and only gave feasts at their initiation.

---

89. Oglala Men's Societies. Thomas Tyon, 1911–12 (translated by the editors).[5] (CHS)

Because of a dream a man created it, they say. The man considered himself *wakan,* so they say. They were named after their *wotawe* (war charm). So it is; on account of that they made societies, it is said. The first man to understand (*iyukcan,* create) it was a holy man, it is said. You know, in the beginning when the people were growing up, they lived with their enemies. Therefore, on account of a man's dream, they put their trust in something (*wacinyepica*).

He took four men and with them he made a society, it is said. It was the Kit Fox society. And then they made some regalia (*canwounye*),[6] it is said. When they say regalia they mean spears and also they mean whips and also they mean swords. Well, only those who had been scouts in war had a right to all the regalia. Also, that which they trusted in, that was the *wotawe,* he said. That which is called the *wotawe* and whatever is the *waxicun* (war bundle) are really the same.[7]

Wherever there is a house they customarily nail a horseshoe above the door. That is similar to a slight degree. That *wotawe* was something *wakan* that the Kit Fox society had with which to act *(taku wan wakan yuha xkanpi).*[8] Therefore they acted with brave hearts. And on account of it they were enabled to accomplish many deeds in war.

When a Kit Fox member was wounded, the people thought, "The young man has secretly done something unmanly, it seems." "The Kit Fox society member failed to carry out a vow," they thought, it is said.

By *wotawe* they mean the regalia. Spears and *wapaha*—by *wapaha* I do not mean a warbonnet but that is what they call the [feathered] spears.[9] That word signifies they will strike something *(apapi)* by raising the hand. Therefore they say *"wapaha."* Well, they also say "spears" *(wahunkeza).*

Well, the Kit Fox society has very many customs. I do not remember them well but as far as I am able I will here write them all.

Well, there are many different societies, Bare Lance Owners *(Sotka yuha),* White Marked *(Wicin ska),* Badgers, Crow Owners, Mandans *(Miwatani),* Brave Hearts, White Owners, and Omaha. Well, these are the societies; all have similar regalia with which to act. All the regalia are used in war; because of them, they try to perform deeds. Well, in this way they act. And if one society has bad luck, then the other societies will strongly ridicule them. Therefore they are very much on their guard. Well, [now] all these are at peace and yet they want to be praised when they tell about the deeds they have done, and so it is.

Thus if a young man carries one of the pieces of regalia and does a great deed, his name will be well known. Perhaps in time he will be a leader among the people. So, on that account, still to this day those who have them accomplish deeds *(wicoran kin hena yuha xkanpelo).* Well, when someone takes one of the pieces of regalia, no one knows how he will do. And then in this manner the regalia will help him to kill. Well, [now] there is no fighting, so he thinks, "I will care nothing for this regalia." You see, those who have regalia only accomplish things in fighting. But now there is no fighting. Therefore, whoever has a piece of the regalia makes the people live and repeatedly he gives much away. In the past a Kit Fox regalia holder was very brave because of it, they thought. He did not cling to his property so he believed himself to be brave.[10]

Well, therefore in the past years they had many customs. Now those are poorly remembered, for no one still follows them. Now only the Omaha society has all the regulations. These are very little different, they say, and of all of them I will write here. The Omaha [society], too, has regalia. And about these I know a little well. The Kit Fox society had the kit fox skin as its *wotawe*, while the Omaha have the crow skin. Well, so it is.

Now the Omaha have four men as leaders. And they have a drum, two crow skins, two whistles also, two whips, and six drumsticks. Of the drumstick owners, two are leaders. And they have a single serving stick and a single spoon. In the beginning there was only one dance. So it is. Now when they want dances the Omaha leaders create them. And in that way, they say, they dance. And when they dance, the whistle owners play for them a great deal. Then they come and there they act with everything *(taku kin iyuha el xkanpelo)*. Then when a good crowd of people gathers, they sing the song of the first one to dance. Then when he dances everyone helps him and from that time the dance runs.

Then all those who have performed deeds complete telling about them. Then, before they eat, both whistle owners stand and put the kettle at the *catku* [place of honor at the back of the tipi]. And with pleasant smelling sweetgrass they incense it; also the crow skins are incensed. Then both crow skins are laid in place at the *catku*. And these men [the crow skin owners] sit near the singers. And then when they sing they move about as if they were frantic *(knaxkinyes'e xkanpelo)*. And suddenly standing, they pass by and go around the fire dancing. And they come dancing towards the *catku*. And the dancers finally put on the crow skins and with them they go dancing towards the doorway. They dance four times around the fire. Then the two whistle owners also dance, following them. And when the song ends, they sit down.

Then the whistle owners again stand and again the kettle is placed at the *catku* and again they incense it. And now they are finished. Then the serving stick owner comes dancing and they thrust the serving stick into the kettle. Then he sits in his place. Then the spoon owner stands and comes along and the leaders who were sitting come dancing towards there. He picks up the spoon and he puts it in the mouths of the Omaha leaders. And after this they eat. And they continue to eat until they are finished.

Well, thus the Omahas have many rules, very many, but now they carry out very few. Therefore I will tell about some of the Omaha rules. Whoever is an Omaha member is commanded to think nothing bad. And when they hear anything bad about people, they pay no attention to it. They are commanded not to fight with anyone. They are commanded not to lie. And whatever they give, they are commanded not to take back. Each day they are commanded to think good thoughts.

Well, if a man's wife or child has died, they quickly have an Omaha feast and the mourners are painted red. They are called "Red painted ones." When they take things given to them, the mourners' hearts are gladdened. And also, this is how it is. If a man does something bad, the Omahas quickly oppose him. And they invite that man. And then they advise him. When the man understands the bad deed, he has been made well *(akisniyapelo)*. This is the Omaha rule.

Well, in this way, too, the Kit Fox rules are all similar. All the Kit Fox society customs by which they act are *wakan*. And they are filled with dreams and bravery and honor; in such ways they act. It is as before. In this way they have very much regalia with which to act: spears and *wabaha* [feathered staffs] and swords and rattles and whips and a drum and drum beaters. Besides, I forgot, some drum stakes.[11] All of this regalia is the same. All are commanded to use it in killing enemies. Therefore they accept them. So if anyone who bears a piece of the regalia is a coward, then no one speaks of that youth as a man. Therefore many of the society regalia bearers killed people in battle. All of this regalia was alike, but each society was different from the others. So it is.

Also another thing I will tell about, those called the Silent Eaters. *(Ainila wota)* Those young men were extremely brave. They join of their own accord; they are not invited. They learn about it from others and only so do they join the Silent Eaters society. That society alone does not have regalia or spears. They only have ideas with which to act, it is said *(Wiyukcanpi ecela yuha xkanpi xkelo)*. They sing nothing. The meetings are held secretly.

Kit Fox or Bare Lance or Badger or White Mark Owners, Crow Owners or Mandans or Brave Hearts or White Owners or the Omahas, each society has different regalia in their lodges and they make it for war. The regalia that they make are made to be *wakan*. Therefore nobody is allowed to laugh. It is considered very *wakan*. It is the same as what they call *wotawe*. White men soldiers have things to act with. These *wotawe* or regalia are similar.

Now I notice that we do not well remember the order in which the societies came. I asked which society was created first and I asked which regalia were created first. But I remember all the regalia that the Kit Fox society acted with, so here I wrote about it all.

Well, so far I understand it. Well, some Lakota old men are still alive, but their minds are dead.

Also, maybe all these societies belong to the Crow Indians, it is said.

Whatever I forgot, I will write of again.

---

90. Origin of the Kit Fox Society. Thomas Tyon, 1911–12 (translated by the editors).[12] (CHS)

From the beginning, this is what they told. A people were camping. Then a boy shot a buffalo calf and carefully skinned it. When he was finished, a man came from someplace. He asked for the meat, they say, but he would not agree to it, it is said. The boy was the one [who would not agree]. Then the man persisted and took the calf on his own accord, it is said. Then the boy became angry and clubbed the man to death, it is said. Having done this, he went on home, it is said.

Then the people knew and they came upon him from all around, it is said. Then the boy said, "Grandmother, I have done a terrible thing, so they will kill me," it is said. And he stood ready, it is said. That boy lived with his grandmother, they say. Now the people came and stood around. Then a kettle of soup was sitting there, boiling hard. Then they said that the boy had gone inside the kettle. Then the kettle went high in the air and burst, it is said. The boy went veiled in steam and hot water, it is said. Therefore all the people fainted from fear, it is said.

A big hill was close by. And they stood looking towards it. Then suddenly a wolf was returning home, so they stood watching it. And then beyond, the boy came and stood, peeking over, it is said. Therefore all the people together chased him. Then the boy threw something. Then this was kit fox bones, he said, and a kit fox song he came singing. Again he went back inside the hill, it is said. He did this four times, it is said.

All the society regalia, those are what he threw, it is said. The very last thing he threw was a kit fox skin. And from then they did not see him a second time, it is said.

And so the boy lived unknown to the people, it is said. Then, perhaps, many winters passed. They forgot the boy. And then in some place the boy became a youth. And suddenly he returned home, it is said. And then he made the Kit Fox society, it is said. Bare Lance Owners and White Marked and Badger Owners and Crow Owners.

That boy was Cheyenne, it is said.

---

91. The Kit Fox Society among the Oglala Sioux.[13] Anonymous. (CHS)

They are so named because they were supposed to be like the kit fox in activity and cunning. It was originated by chiefs and headmen for the purpose of aiding the poor and helpless. Brave young men of good repute were chosen as members. It was gotten up when the Cheyennes, Arapahoes, and Sioux were associated together and all other Indians were considered enemies. This society was originated for the purpose of holding these Indians together and keeping them friendly to each other.

They have a sacred pipe. They have especial prayers. They invoked the four directions. They invoked *Inyan,* whom they called *Tunkasila* [Grandfather], the revered or reverend one. Their prayer was:

> Help me in what I undertake.
> Be with me in my undertakings.

> Have pity on me.
> Help me to defeat others.

They initiated with a ceremony and after the ceremony they presented the banner to the initiate. The young man then prepared himself as if for death. The women mourned for him as if he were already dead. He was then ready to do anything, even if it cost him his life. The older Foxes could tell of their deeds. The young Foxes could not tell of their deeds until they had done some notable thing. When the older Foxes would tell of their deeds, the younger Foxes would wail their death songs.

In time of war it was the duty of the Foxes to defend the old, weak and helpless.

A Fox song is:

> I am a Fox.
> I am supposed to die.
> If there is anything difficult,
> If there is anything dangerous,
> That is mine to do.

---

92. War Insignia.[14] Thunder Bear, 1912. (CHS)

One who kills a renowned enemy is entitled to wear a feather suspended from the pierced ear. Or he may wear an ornament of some kind suspended from his ear, provided the ornament is such as to signify his deed.

If during a battle the enemy charges on the Lakota and the Lakota meet the charge and drive it back, a Lakota who strikes one of the enemy with a club or stick is entitled to wear an eagle quill fastened upright to his scalp lock. If he was wounded, he is entitled to color the quill red, but if he was not wounded then the quill must not be colored. A Lakota who has been wounded by gunshot is entitled to wear a lead bullet suspended about his neck.

A Lakota who when scouting finds signs which lead to the discovery of the enemy is entitled to wear a small quill from the eagle's wing, such as are white, tipped with black. He is entitled to wear one such quill for each time he so discovers signs. He should wear such quills suspended from his scalp lock.

A Lakota who has fought with an enemy is entitled to wear a quill from the eagle's tail, such as are white with a black tip. He may wear it suspended from his scalp lock, or about his person, or suspended from a staff or any implement of war that he carries. If a Lakota kills an enemy, he is entitled to wear a quill from the tail of the eagle, such as are white, tipped with black. He should wear it fastened to his scalp lock so that it will stand upright. If he was wounded he may color the quill red. If during a fight he strikes coup on the body of an enemy, he is entitled to wear the quill in the same manner as if he had killed the enemy.[15]

A Lakota who has had a personal encounter with an enemy during a fight and has escaped is entitled to wear the quill from an eagle's tail colored yellow. He should wear it attached to his scalp lock so that it will stand upright. He is entitled to wear this kind of a quill and in this manner if he has had his horse shot from under him during a fight with the enemy. If he was wounded in the body he should put stripes of blue across the yellow quill, or if he was wounded in his limbs he should put stripes of red across it. (The blue is emblematical of the protection the *Wakan Tanka* gave him and prevented his spirit from leaving him. The red is emblematical of *Wakan Tanka,* who preserved his life and gave him strength to escape even with his limbs wounded. *Wakan Tanka* as represented by the blue is *Taku Skanskan* and when represented by red is *Wi.*)

A Lakota who is *blotanhunka,*[16] or in command of a war party, and who returns from a foray bringing scalps, women, or horses, is entitled to wear a quill from the tail of the eagle colored blue. He should wear this quill fastened to his scalp lock so that it will be upright. The blue is emblematical of the care that *Wakan Tanka* has given to the movement of his party. *(Wakan Tanka* in this case is *Skanskan.)*

A Lakota who takes horses from the enemy is entitled to wear the quill from the tail of the eagle with the color green on it. He should wear it suspended from his scalp lock. (The color green is emblematical of *Wakan Tanka,* who gave him success in his taking the horses, and *Wakan Tanka* in this case is the Earth.)

A Lakota who has done deeds of desperate daring in the

presence of an enemy is entitled to wear a quill from the tail of the eagle notched at its sides. This should be worn dangling from the forelock or the pierced ear, or it may be worn attached to a necklace, or it may be hung to the upper end of the red staff.

A Lakota who has taken a scalp is entitled to carry the red staff. This is made from a chokecherry bush, about two short paces long, and forked at the smaller end. It should be as large as a man's great toe at its larger end, and painted red. He may attach the scalp to the forked end and may also attach such other insignia to it as he is entitled to have. A *blotahunka* should have such a staff.

A Lakota who has struck coup on the body of an enemy is entitled to wear a miniature red bow attached to his scalp lock. A Lakota who has been wounded with a lance is entitled to wear a miniature red lance attached to his scalp lock. A Lakota who has been wounded by an arrow shot by an enemy is entitled to wear a miniature red arrow with a fringe attached, fastened to his scalp lock.

A Lakota who, after he is wounded, strikes coup on the body of the enemy is entitled to wear a quill from the tail of an eagle colored red and split halfway down from its tip.

Insignia No. 1 (Plate 3). Kit Fox Society Leader.

The yellow color of the body, face and arms indicates a membership in the society of the Foxes.[17] The red color on the hands indicates a compliance with Oglala ceremonies that entitles [one] to handle sacred things and lead a war party. The red color on the thighs, legs, and feet indicates having danced the Sun Dance.

The yellow fox skin suspended from the right hand is the badge of a member of the Fox society. The eagle quills attached to it indicate a leadership in the Fox society and the red bird plumes attached to the tips of the quills indicate a leadership in war, one such quill for each war [party].

The war club suspended from the right hand indicates a warrior ready to do battle when called upon. The wristlets of otter skin with the fur on indicate compliance with the sacred ceremonies of the Oglala. The irregular colored stripes around the forearm indicate having been [made] a captive by the enemy and having made an escape from his captors.

The armlets indicate compliance with the customs of the

Oglala. The wisp of sweetgrass dangling from the armlet on the right arm indicates a willingness to comply with the customs of the Oglala. The red eagle plume dangling from the armlet on the right arm [indicates] an observance with the great virtue of bravery. The red dangle of tanned skin on the armlet of the left arm indicates having been wounded in the arm by an enemy. The blue or green dangle from the armlet on the left arm indicates reliability or trustworthiness.

The red marks on the right upper forearm indicate wounds by cutting. The red dots on the left upper forearm indicate wounds by arrows or spears. These marks or dots may be placed on any part of the body. The horizontal red lines on the arms and body indicate having been in battle, as do also the red lines radiating from the neck. One such line can be placed on each arm, the body, and from the neck, for each battle.

The eagle quills worn at the scalp lock, if worn upright, indicate having killed an enemy. One quill may be worn for each enemy killed. If the enemy was killed in battle, a red bird plume should be attached to the tip of the eagle quill. If the quill has no such plume, the enemy killed as indicated was not killed in battle. Eagle plumes and quills may be worn as indications of many things, but the indication is shown by the position of the quill, the color painted on it, and the manner of cutting it.

The red roach worn at the parting of the hair in front of the scalp lock indicates having attacked the enemy when the enemy was protected in some manner. The eagle plume at the scalp lock (colored black in the illustration, but should be white as it is taken from the eagle), indicates a good repute.

The hair unbraided when on the warpath indicates a willingness to do desperate ventures. The dark ring around the eyes indicates membership in the society of the Owls,[18] and willingness to undertake or having done warlike things at night, or having surprised and defeated an enemy. A black horizontal line across the cheek indicates having killed an enemy who was not a Lakota. Black around the mouth and on the chin indicates having returned from a war party bearing the scalp of an enemy killed in battle.

A collar with streamers indicates a warrior who has fought against the enemy. Each streamer indicates a battle he has fought in. If the streamer is red, it indicates that the wearer was wounded in the battle; if it is any other color, it indicates he was not wounded in the battle. One streamer may be worn for each battle the wearer has fought in.

The diagonal black stripes on the thighs indicate having been in battle on foot, the black crosses that he was in battle on horseback. The sash over the right shoulder and across the chest is of antelope hoofs, a charm prepared by a shaman to protect against wounds. The belt with disks upon it is a charm prepared by a shaman to secure sustenance when on the war path. The string of tinkling bangles from waist to ankles indicates that the war dance has been done. None but the warrior who has fought the enemy may dance in this dance and wear the badge of having done so. The leg ornaments, if of otter skin with the fur on, indicate having scouted against the enemy.

Insignia No. 2 (Plate 4). Holy Bow Carrier, a Cheyenne.

Lakota inscription: "This man, a Cheyenne Indian, in furious battle can never be shot by the enemy. He is very skillful."[19]

The indicative insignia are: the eagle quill worn at the scalp lock, the red stripes on head and face, the armlets, and the red stripes on the moccasins.

The quill and armlets have already been explained in Insignia No. 1. The red stripe on the head indicates that the man was a Cheyenne.[20] The perpendicular red stripes on the face indicate that the enemy was killed in a hand-to-hand contest. The red stripes on the moccasins indicate that the enemy was killed while on foot.

The holy bow at the left, but not in hand, indicates that the warrior who wears the insignia shown in the illustration is entitled to carry the holy bow.

Insignia No. 3 (Plate 5). War Party Leader.

Lakota inscription: "In the past, this man, a *blotohuka*, repeatedly killed enemies. The reason why they say *blotohuka* is this. He thinks to go on the warpath and also go to war bravely, therefore he is the chief. Nobody is able to go before the leader. He alone is chief. And then he leads the others beneath him."

The distinctive insignia are the eagle quills at the scalp lock, the red forehead with black perpendicular stripes on it, the yellow arms and lower limbs, the diagonal red stripes on the thighs, the black rabbit tracks on the lower limbs, the war pipe in hand, and the scalp shirt.

The red forehead with black perpendicular stripes on it and the diagonal red stripes on the thighs indicate intention to war against an enemy. The yellow coloring of the body is the symbolic color of the God the Rock, the patron of revenge, destruction, and violence. Rabbit tracks on the sides of the lower limbs indicate rapidity of action and that the war will be made on foot.

The war pipe should have a black stem ornamented with either an actual or an imitation human scalp attached to it. When carried or smoked, it indicates warlike intentions.

A scalp shirt is an ordinary skin wamus ornamented in any manner, but it must have at the seams of the sides and arms fringes made of human hair representing human scalps. To don it indicates intention to do an act of bravery. To habitually wear it indicates a brave who has done a notable act of bravery. To wear it temporarily indicates a position of responsibility that may be dangerous. One who organizes a war party and leads it may don it temporarily, and if the party is victorious in battle he may wear it habitually.

Insignia No. 4 (Plate 6). Striped Warbonnet, a Cheyenne.

Lakota inscription: "A Cheyenne Indian fought furiously on foot. Therefore who he was, his name, was known to all the enemy. He killed them. So they were very afraid of him. So he was depended upon. Thus they thought. They called him Striped Warbonnet. He was Cheyenne."

The significant insignia illustrated are the red body, the armlets and wristlets, the warbonnet, and the banner.

The red body indicates compliance with Lakota customs. The armlets and wristlets have been explained.

A warbonnet is made of a headpiece to fit like a cap to which is attached at the rim a circle of quills from the tail of a young golden eagle that are white, tipped with black, so arranged that they project upward. A warbonnet may be ornamented in any manner to suit the fancy of the owner and a significance may be given to the ornamentation which will be recognized by the people. One ornamentation is a long pendant behind to which is attached a row of quills like those on the bonnet. Another conventional ornament is an eagle plume attached to the center of the headpiece so that it will project above the quills.

Only braves of renown were permitted to wear the warbonnet, the pendant indicating greater renown and the plume a greater repute than a warbonnet without these ornaments. The coloring in the illustration, the blue of the headpiece and plume and the bird feather plumes at the tips of the quills, indicate protection by the Great Spirit. The red pendant and squares on the bonnet and pendant indicate having fought furiously and the dark spots of the pendant indicate having fought on horseback.

The banner is a coupstick to which are attached tertiary quills from the wing of a young golden eagle that are white with black tips. A coupstick is a long rod so designed that it indicates that the bearer has touched the body of an enemy while at war. If the body was dead and killed by another, the coupstick should be plain and without dangles of any kind. If the body was dead and killed by the one who touched it, the coupstick should have a dangle made of an eagle quill. If a scalp was taken, the coupstick should have as a dangle from its upper end a scalp, either real or imitation. If one touched a number of bodies of enemies, his coupstick should have eagle quills attached so as to form a banner similar to that shown in the illustration. The quills may be attached to all or only a part of the coupstick.

Insignia No. 5 (Plate 7). A Man Who Killed an Enemy.

Lakota inscription: "This man dresses in this way and then kills an enemy honorably. The enemy was very dangerous but this man was the more to be feared as dangerous. He was not afraid of being killed. So now he is a good man. Now he is a leader. He is Lakota."

The distinctive insignia in the illustration are the yellow color on the face and body and the red color on the limbs and feet; the armlets, wristlets, and anklets; the warbonnet and banner; and the irregular red line about the left eye. All these have been explained except the red line. This is an irregular line forked at both ends and is the symbol of *Wakinyan*, the Winged God. It indicates having been irresistible in war.

Insignia No. 6 (Plate 8). A Man Who Killed Two Enemies.

Lakota inscription: "This man was able to kill two enemies. Therefore he has a coupstick."

The distinctive insignia in the illustration are two eagle feathers upright at the scalp lock, the yellow color on the face and red color on the body, the red line around each temple, the armlet with yellow dangles, and the coupstick. The eagle quills and colors have been explained. The red lines about the temples and the yellow dangles on the armlet indicate that he was able to kill two enemies. The eagle quills upright indicate that they were killed in war and the coupstick that he touched their bodies.

Insignia No. 7 (Plate 9). *Leader of the Beaver Society.*[21]

Lakota inscription: "This man wears a warbonnet because he has killed enemies. Therefore he is a good man. And men make him a leader because of his many deeds in battle. He has killed many men from all tribes of Indians and white men, too. Therefore he won leadership. So it is."

The distinctive insignia in the illustration not already explained are the unbraided but bound hair, the otter skin sash, and the war club. The unbraided but bound hair indicates having done desperate deeds and readiness to do them again. The otter skin sash is the badge of chieftainship of the Beaver band [society] of the Oglala Teton Lakotas. Habitual carrying of a war club indicates a warrior ready to go on the warpath at any time.

Insignia No. 8 (Plate 10). *A* Heyoka *Warrior.*

Lakota inscription: "I will tell what a man does when he wears a feather in this way. He kills an enemy directly. That is why he places a quill there on his head. It is placed upright in his hair. When he kills an enemy that way, he has his scalp. It is tied to the coupstick. A knife is tied to his hand because he has scalped. So it is. And he returns home and there he is very much honored. They all rejoice, praising him. From this he is counted a good man. At last he is a leader. This is his custom."

The significant insignia on his person not already explained are the symbols of the Sun, the Moon, and the Winged God. The star, crescent, and bird are these symbols. They indicate having received a vision from each of these. Such symbols may be painted on the person and his implements or the tipi. It is unusual to paint them on the person but common to paint them on the tipi and the shield. The forked lines on the limbs indicate a communication from the Winged God. Such lines may be straight, but usually they are zigzag. It is usual to paint them on the person and implements, but not on the tipi.

The knife suspended from the wrist indicates a warrior who fights with the knife, an unusual method, done by *heyoka*, or one who has seen the Winged God in a vision.

Insignia No. 9 (Plate 11). A Scout.

Lakota inscription: "This man is always the first scout to return. No scout returns home before him. He alone is the first scout to return. Therefore he wears the four stripped feathers of a returned scout. Nobody else may do this, only an expert scout. Therefore he wears the feathers."

The insignia signifying a successful scout are four eagle quills with their webs from the black tips down trimmed from the shafts and hanging, adorned with red bird plumes attached to the tips and worn erect at the scalp lock. A bow and two arrows carried in the hand indicate readiness to act. The red color from the top of the forehead to below the eyes indicates compliance with Lakota customs. The yellow color on the body indicates readiness to do destructive things, or go to war.

Insignia No. 10 (Plate 12). Lance Bearer of the Sotka Society.[22]

This may be painted on the tipi or shield. On horseback, indicating a horse was ridden in some notable event, usually in battle. The red deerskin dangle from the bit indicates the horse was ridden in battle. The tail bound with red indicates a war horse. The spear ornamented in the manner shown indicates the *Sotka* [Bare Lance] society, in which there were two spear bearers who were obligated to do some notable deeds. To each of these was given a warbonnet, one with red dangle and the other plain.

The eagle quills attached to the shaft of the spear indicate the number of enemies killed by the spear bearer and the red dangle at the butt of the spear indicates that the present bearer was wounded in battle. The black dangle indicates that he killed an enemy. The stripped quills upright at the butt indicate the number of forays the bearer has been on. The red belt with small eagle quills dangling (this may be arranged around the horse's neck) indicates a desire to touch the body of an enemy so as to bear a coupstick banner. The hair worn unbound indicates willingness to do desperate deeds. The spear bearers of the *Sotka* society must do some notable deed within two years from the time of their appointment. If not, others are appointed. If either of them does so, they hold the position indefinitely, but may be deposed for sufficient reasons.

Insignia No. 11 (Plate 13). Lance Bearer of the Otter Society.[23]

Insignia may be painted on tipi or shield. On horseback, indicating some notable deed done on horseback. Tail bound indicates a war horse. Scalp dangling from bit indicates a scalp taken when fighting on horseback. Warbonnet with unornamented headband and dangle indicates a lance bearer of the *Ptan* (Otter) society, and in war as such. Gun in hand indicates a gun was used in war. War horses are usually painted, each according to the fancy of the owner, often with designs indicating some notable deed done on horseback.

Insignia No. 12 (Plate 14). A Heyoka Warrior.

May be painted on the tipi. A *heyoka*. On horseback, indicating some notable deed done on horseback. The horse's tail bound, but down, indicates the war horse of a *heyoka*. The red banner at the bit indicates a *heyoka* who has been in war. The headdress is the buffalo bonnet, made from a strip of buffalo skin from the shaggy forehead to the tail, the tail included, forming the lower part of the trailer while the shaggy part is the headpiece. Small buffalo horns are attached, the larger at front and smaller behind. This is the warbonnet of the *heyoka*.

The zigzag stripe across the forehead and temples is the sign of a *heyoka* and indicates having received a communication from *Wakinyan*, the Winged God, and therefore is a *heyoka*. The zigzag stripes on shoulders and arms are the same emblems of a *heyoka*. The wooden sword in the right hand indicates he was in battle with few offensive implements and a willingness to do so again. The shield is ornamented in compliance with the communication given by the swallow, the messenger of *Wakinyan*. The crescent on his chest indicates that he received his vision during the crescent moon. This emblem also appears on the upper part of the shield. A bull buffalo is the central figure on the shield and below it is the emblem of *Wakinyan*. The shield is red with the figures on this red background. Two eagle quills are attached at each side of the crescent, and the apron of the shield is ornamented with four rows of eagle quills with four quills in each row. The entire shield is a sacred implement which may be used in ceremonies pertaining to *Wakinyan*. The blue stripes on the horse indicate the God *Taku Skanskan* and invoke him to give strength and rapidity to the horse.

Insignia No. 13 (Plate 15). Lance Bearer of the Brave Society.[24]

On horseback, indicating some deed done on horseback that made him eligible to the society of Braves [Brave Hearts]. The lance or wand of the Braves is long and crooked at one end, wrapped with otter skin with the fur on, and ornamented with four clusters of eagle quills, two quills in each cluster, two clusters on the shaft of the wand and two on the crook. Two lance bearers are chosen annually by the Brave society who must lead the society in case of war and show deeds of valor. In the illustration the lance bearer is shown touching a Crow Indian in war, thus entitling him to carry a coupstick. His war horse is dotted with paint on his neck and forequarters to protect it against wounds, and its hindquarters are striped, each stripe indicating some notable deed done. The warbonnet is individual property. The hair worn unbraided indicates readiness to do desperate deeds. The shield is figured according to a vision, the four colored projections indicating the Four Winds and the center the Wind.

The eagle quills are attached according to the vision, both to the shield and the apron. The circle on the horse indicates that the spots were made with due ceremony to make them effective.

Insignia No. 14 (Plate 16). Leader of the Sotka Society.

Head man of the *Sotka* [Bare Lance] society. May be painted on the tipi. Lance borne is wrapped with otter skin with the fur on, curved with a crook at one end and a lance point at the other. Decorated with twelve clusters of eagle quills, two quills in each cluster, one cluster at the end of the crook. A cord of sinew across from the tip of the crook to the shaft of the lance indicates the leadership of the bearer. Warbonnet, scalp shirt, hair unbound, and shield are as before explained. Tomahawk in hand is the same as war club in hand (Insignia No. 7). Eagle quills on shoulders indicate leadership.

Insignia No. 15 (missing).

Insignia No. 16 (not illustrated). **Akicita.**

Insignia of an *akicita* or marshal of the camp. A black stripe painted on the right cheek from the outer corner of the eye to the lower edge at the angle of the jaw is the insignia of an *akicita*, or the marshal of a camp. It is first painted there by a shaman or one who has been appointed by the council. Afterwards it may be renewed by the one wearing it as often as necessary. A red parallel stripe indicates a marshal of a ceremonial camp. The marshal of a civil moving party should have such a stripe on each cheek. The marshal of a war party should have two black stripes on the right cheek. A black stripe on the cheek and one across the forehead is the insignia of the herald of the camp. If there are parallel red stripes, they indicate a herald of a ceremonial camp.

Insignia No. 17 (not illustrated). **Buffalo Dreamer.**

A red circle at the middle of the chest indicates that the one who wears it had a vision and a communication from the Buffalo God. This indicates that he will be a successful hunter and a good provider. This insignia usually is shown by young men.[25]

Appendix I: The Authorities

The following list gives the names of Walker's informants and interpreters at Pine Ridge. Lakota names, reservation district, and approximate birth dates are taken from the Pine Ridge censuses of 1896–1904 (National Archives and Records Service, Record Group 75, Microcopy M595, rolls 362–69). Only those persons who contributed to the documents reproduced in this volume are listed, and no attempt has been made to go beyond the census records to locate those who cannot be so identified. The purpose of this listing is to validate the existence of Walker's authorities and to indicate the range in their ages and places of residence. In some cases the existence of several people with the same name makes exact identification impossible.

Afraid of Bear (Matokokipapi). Wakpamni district; b. ca. 1842. Older brother of George Sword.

American Horse (Wasicun Tasunke). Medicine Root district; b. ca. 1840.

Bad Heart Bull (Tatanka Cante Sica). White Clay district; b. ca. 1840.

Bad Wound (Oosica Hoksila, "Young Man Bad Wound," or Taopi sica, "His Bad Wound"). Pass Creek district; b. ca. 1833.

Blue Horse (Sunka Hinto). Wakpamni district; b. ca. 1821.

John Blunt Horn (He Wotoka). Wounded Knee district; b. ca. 1857.

Feather on Head (Wiyaka Peyohankle). Wounded Knee district; b. ca. 1832. Porcupine district; b. ca. 1845.

Finger (Nape, "Hand," or "Finger"). Pass Creek district; b. ca. 1839.

William Garnett. Interpreter; son of Colonel Richard Garnett, U.S. Army, and a Lakota woman. Medicine Root district; b. ca. 1855.

Good Seat (Toyanke Waste Win, "Her Good Seat Woman").
White Clay district; b. ca. 1827.

Antoine Herman. Interpreter. Medicine Root district; b. ca.
1861.

Antoine Janis. Interpreter. Wakpamni district; b. ca. 1859.

Little Wound (Ta Opi Ciqala). Medicine Root district; b. ca.
1829.

Lone Bear (Mato Wanjila). Porcupine district; b. ca. 1829. Pass
Creek district; b. ca. 1849. Medicine Root district; b. ca. 1854.

Lone Star (Wicarpi Wanjila). Wakpamni district; b. ca. 1871.

Meat (Talo). Pass Creek district; b. ca. 1855.

Bruce Means. Intepreter. Not on the census rolls.

Bert Means. Interpreter. Wakpamni district; b. ca. 1886.

John Monroe. Interpreter. Medicine Root district; b. ca. 1869.

Charles Nines. Interpreter. Not on the census rolls.

Richard Nines. Interpreter. Not on the census rolls. The Nines
brothers were the sons of a quarter-blood Mohawk Indian
from New York and a white woman. They were fluent in
Lakota and for years were licensed Indian traders at Pine
Ridge.

No Flesh (Conica Wanica). Porcupine district; b. ca. 1845.

Old Horse (Sunkwicarca, "Old Man Horse"). District unknown;
b. ca. 1860.

Red Cloud (Marpiya Luta). Wakpamni district; b. ca. 1823.

Elmore Red Eyes (Ista Sa). Interpreter. Medicine Root district;
b. ca. 1877.

Red Hawk (Cetan Luta). White Clay district; b. ca. 1829.

Red Rabbit (Mastincala Sa). Medicine Root district; b. ca. 1851.
Wounded Knee district; b. ca. 1855.

Rocky Bear (Inyan Mato). Wounded Knee district; b. ca. 1836.

Ringing Shield (Wahacanka Hotun). This man, described by
Walker as "an old shaman," does not appear on the census
rolls. However, a man who is probably his son does appear,
Porcupine district, b. ca. 1872.

Seven Rabbits (Mastincala Sakowin). Medicine Root district; b.
ca. 1833.

Short Bull (Tatanka Ptecela). Known as Short Bull no. 2. White
Clay district; b. ca. 1852.

Short Feather. Unidentified from the census rolls.

George Sword (Miwakan). Wakpamni district; b. ca. 1847.

Takes the Gun (Maza Wakan Icu). Sex listed as female. Wak-pamni district; b. c. 1820.

Clarence Three Stars (Wicarpi Yamni). Interpreter. Pass Creek district; b. ca. 1864.

John Thunder Bear (Mato Wakinyan). Wounded Knee district; b. ca. 1847.

Thomas Tyon. White Clay district; b. ca. 1855.

Thomas H. Wells. Interpreter. Son of Phillip F. Wells and a Lakota woman. Pass Creek district; b. ca. 1886.

Appendix II: Phonetic Key

Walker rarely used diacritical marks to indicate the phonetic system of Lakota, relying on the reader's knowledge for pronunciation. In this volume we have retained Walker's usage. However, in our footnotes, we use a simplified version of the standard literary form of Lakota (see Buechel, *Lakota-English Dictionary;* for a more sophisticated introduction to the problem of Lakota phonetics, see Allan R. Taylor, "The Colorado University System for Writing the Lakhóta Language," *American Indian Culture and Research* 1 [1975]:3–12).

The phonetic symbols we use which have special significance are the following:

c is pronounced *ch*

ġ is pronounced as German Ma*ch*en

ḣ is pronounced as German a*ch*

n, following a vowel, is not pronounced separately, but indicates that the preceeding vowel is nasalized (frequently written ŋ)

š is pronounced *sh*

We have not indicated aspiration, glottalization, phonetic values of vowels, or stress. The symbols above are given only because they are sounded significantly differently than they are in English.

The phonetic system used by Thomas Tyon is a standard one, used to write Lakota by Samuel and Gideon Pond, missionaries to the Santees. The special values of his symbols, where they differ from ours, are as follows:

h is sometimes used for ḣ

kl is used for gl

q is used for a glottalized k
r is used for ħ
x is used for š
ʼ is sometimes used to indicate strong glottalization

Notes

Part I. James R. Walker: His Life and Work

1. Part I is based in part on materials compiled by Maurice Frink and on Frink's biographical sketch of Walker in his manuscript "Pine Ridge Medicine Man," CHS.

2. "Declaration for Invalid Pension," Bureau of Pensions, CHS Documents folder 14, no. 1, p. 9; interview, Emeline Wensley Hughes with Maurice Frink, Denver, Colorado, 1971.

3. "Declaration for Invalid Pension," p. 1; "To all whom it may Concern" (army discharge), CHS Documents folder 1, no. 1.

4. "Declaration for Invalid Pension," p. 5; "Oldest Member of Red Cross is Denver Visitor," undated newspaper clipping, CHS Printed Material folder 24, no. 8.

5. Frink interview with Mrs. E. W. Hughes, 1971.

6. Untitled biographical sketch of Walker by his daughter, Maude B. Wensley, courtesy of Mrs. E. W. Hughes.

7. *Annual Report of the Commissioner of Indian Affairs, 1893*, serial no. 3210, pp. 165–67.

8. "Report of the epidemic of small-pox among the Winnebegosh-ish Chippewa Indians during the months of January and February 1883," CHS Documents folder 2, no. 2; "White Priest of Indian Tribe Writes Record of Religious Beliefs," unidentified newspaper clipping, CHS Printed Materials folder 24, no. 2.

9. Walker, White Earth Agency, Minnesota, to Commissioner of Indian Affairs, June 16, 1893, copy in CHS Documents folder 6, no. 2.

10. Ibid.

11. *Annual Report of the Commissioner of Indian Affairs, 1893*, p. 167.

12. Frink, "Pine Ridge Medicine Man," chap. 3.

13. *Annual Report of the Commissioner of Indian Affairs, 1891*, serial no. 2934, p. 65.

14. Charles Alexander Eastman, *The Indian To-day: The Past and Future of the First American* (Garden City, N.Y.: Doubleday, Page & Co., 1915), pp. 140–41.

15. *Annual Report of the Commissioner of Indian Affairs, 1893,* pp. 292–93; *1894,* serial no. 3306, pp. 291–92.

16. "White Priest."

17. *Annual Report of the Commissioner of Indian Affairs, 1899,* serial no. 3915, pp. 336–37.

18. Ibid., *1900,* serial no. 4101, p. 379.

19. Walker, Pine Ridge, to Wissler, January 7, 1907. All correspondence between Walker and Wissler, unless otherwise noted, is in the correspondence files of the Department of Anthropology, American Museum of Natural History.

20. Walker, Pine Ridge, to Paul Kennaday, Secretary, Tuberculosis Committee, Charity Organization Society, New York, enclosure in Walker to Commissioner of Indian Affairs, February 5, 1906, Letters Received by the Commissioner of Indian Affairs, 1906–13371, Record Group 75, National Archives and Records Service, Washington, D.C. The letter was written in response to Kennaday's request for information on steps taken for the prevention of tuberculosis at Pine Ridge.

21. "Tuberculosis among the Oglala Sioux Indians," *American Journal of Medical Science,* n.s. 132 (1906): 600–605; reprinted in *Southern Workman* 35 (1906): 378–84.

22. Letters Received by the Commissioner of Indian Affairs, 1906–16389, Record Group 75, National Archives and Records Service.

23. Copies in CHS Documents folders 9–11.

24. Copy in Brennan's personal letterbook, Brennan Papers, South Dakota Historical Society, Pierre.

25. Alfred L. Kroeber, *The Arapaho,* Bulletin of the American Museum of Natural History, vol. 13 (1902–1907), pp. 1–229, 279–454; Clark Wissler, General Introduction, American Museum of Natural History, *Anthropological Papers* 16 (1921): viii.

26. For a discussion of the method, see Edward Sapir, "Time Perspectives in Aboriginal American Culture: A Study in Method" (1916), reprinted in *Selected Writings of Edward Sapir in Language, Culture and Personality,* ed. David G. Mandelbaum (Berkeley: University of California Press, 1949), pp. 389–462.

27. See George W. Stocking, Jr., "The Basic Assumptions of Boasian Anthropology," in Stocking, ed., *The Shaping of American Anthropology, 1883–1911: A Franz Boas Reader* (New York: Basic Books, 1974), pp. 1–20; Margaret Mead and Ruth L. Bunzel, eds., *The Golden Age of American Anthropology* (New York: George Braziller, 1960), pp. 340–43.

28. Clark Wissler, "Societies and Ceremonial Associations in the Oglala Division of the Teton-Dakota," American Museum of Natural History, *Anthropological Papers* 11 (1912): 3.

29. CHS Letters folder 2, no. 2.

30. Ibid., no. 4

31. Alice C. Fletcher, *The Hako: A Pawnee Ceremony*, Smithsonian Institution, Bureau of American Ethnology, Annual Report 22, 2 (1904).

32. James R. Walker, "Sioux Games," *Journal of American Folk-Lore* 18 (1905): 277–90, 19 (1906): 29–36.

33. CHS Letters folder 3, no. 2; Clark Wissler, "Measurements of Dakota Indian Children," *Annals of the New York Academy of Sciences* 20 (1911): 355–64.

34. Clark Wissler, "Some Dakota Myths," *Journal of American Folk-Lore* 20 (1907): 121–31, 195–206.

35. Brennan to John Brown, Superintendent, Fort Shaw, Montana, December 26, 1908, Personal Letterbook, Brennan Collection, South Dakota State Historical Society, Pierre.

36. See Walker, *Sun Dance*, pp. 56–57.

37. The classic statements of Boas's theoretical position are his *The Mind of Primitive Man* (New York: Macmillan, 1911) and Introduction to *Handbook of American Indian Languages*, Smithsonian Institution, Bureau of American Ethnology, Bulletin 40, 1 (1911), pp. 1–83.

38. Walker, "Sioux Games," p. 277.

39. Interestingly, most of the criticism of Walker is passed through anthropological oral tradition. For an example of published criticism, see Paul Radin, *Primitive Man as Philosopher*, (1927; rpt. New York: Dover Publications, 1957): p. xxxviii.

40. See Walker to Wissler, November 13, 1911; February 7, 1912; and March 20, 1912, all in AMNH correspondence file. The Kit Fox society text is printed in Wissler, "Societies and Ceremonial Associations," pp. 21–23.

41. Walker's recordings were transferred from AMNH to the Archives of Traditional Music, Indiana University, where twenty-three songs have been preserved on tape. Recordings of sun dance songs are in CHS; see below, note 3, Part IV).

42. George A. Dorsey, *The Arapahoe Sun Dance*, Field Museum Anthropological Series 4 (1903); idem, *The Cheyenne II: The Sun Dance*, Field Museum Anthropological Series 9, no. 2 (1905).

43. CHS Letters folder 4, no. 3.

44. Ibid., no. 4.

45. Tyon's texts are printed in this volume as documents 44–63 and 89–90; Walker's typed copies of the sun dance text are in AMNH and CHS MS folder 64.

46. George A. Dorsey, "Legend of the Teton Sioux Medicine Pipe," *Journal of American Folk-Lore* 19 (1906): 326–29. Ironically, the second part of Walker's "Sioux Games" appeared earlier in the same volume, yet Walker was obviously unaware of Dorsey's article. In retrospect, the puzzling question is why Wissler did not draw Walker's attention to the current literature.

47. James R. Walker, "Oglala Kinship Terms," *American Anthropologist* 16 (1914): 96–109. A retranslation of the Tyon text will appear in *Lakota Society,* forthcoming.

48. CHS Documents folder 12, no. 4, and Letters Received by the Commissioner of Indian Affairs, Central Files, 52038-1913 (Pine Ridge 734), Record Group 75, National Archives and Records Service.

49. J. C. Bratton, Acting Chief, Civilian Reference Branch, National Personnel Records Center, to Frink, October 23, 1968, CHS.

50. The interview with Finger is printed in part in Walker's *Sun Dance,* pp. 154–56, and in part in document 19 in this volume.

51. Walker seems to be unique in identifying *Anog Ite* with the Double Woman. Perhaps this is an error, although it is repeated in *Sun Dance,* pp. 82, 162.

52. Walker, *Sun Dance,* p. 55.

53. In one of the introductions to his "Oglala Mythology" Walker wrote, "This mythology is much like that of ancient Egypt, Greece, and Rome in that the phenomena of nature were personified and given superhuman attributes" ("Introduction to Oglala Legends," MS 30 (15), Boas Collection, American Philosophical Society Library, Philadelphia).

54. Walker to Wissler, March 19, 1918, and November 8, 1919.

55. CHS MS folders 15–29.

56. Interview, Mrs. E. W. Hughes with Elaine Jahner, Denver, Colorado, 1978; the Oglala mythology will appear in *Lakota Myth,* forthcoming.

57. For a good discussion of nineteenth-century concepts of primitive man in the context of the development of anthropology, see George W. Stocking, Jr., "The Dark-Skinned Savage: The Image of Primitive Man in Evolutionary Perspective" in his *Race, Culture, and Evolution: Essays in the History of Anthropology* (New York: Free Press, 1968), pp. 110–32. For the concept of the noble savage as applied to American Indians, see Roy Harvey Pearce, *Savagism and Civilization: A Study of the Indian and the American Mind* (Baltimore: The Johns Hopkins Press, 1965).

58. See Ella Deloria, Rosebud, South Dakota, to Boas, June 28, 1938, and Deloria, Fort Defiance, Arizona, to Boas, May 12, 1939, Deloria correspondence with Boas, MS 31, Boas Collection, American Philosophical Society Library, Philadelphia; Deloria, Dakota Commentary on Walker's Texts, MS 30 (X8a.5), Boas Collection, American Philosophical Society Library. In 1937 Edgar Fire Thunder told Deloria that "the medicine men did not tell their secrets to one another" and that therefore "they were not corporately keeping anything secret from the rest of the people" (pp. 27–28).

59. Walker's stay at Pine Ridge was actually eighteen years. This document has been pieced together from three partial drafts of what Walker intended to be an introduction to his Oglala Mythology. See

"Introduction to Oglala Legends," MS 30 (15), Boas Collection, American Philosophical Society Library, Philadelphia; CHS MS folder 28, nos. 1 and 2, and folder 67, no. 1. *Long Knife* and *Gray Goose* in this document are evidently pseudonyms for George Sword and Thomas Tyon.

60. Evidently this is McLaughlin's report to the commissioner of Indian affairs, June 14, 1898, Inspections file, 1898–28158, Office of Indian Affairs, Record Group 75, National Archives and Records Service. In this report McLaughlin praises Walker as "an excellent man for the position," adding that "his successful practice has gained for him the confidence of the Indians to a wonderful extent."

61. From an untitled lecture, CHS MS folder 57, no. 1.

62. Edmund C. Bray and Martha Colemen Bray, eds., *Joseph N. Nicollet on the Plains and Prairies* (St. Paul: Minnesota Historical Society Press, 1976). The most significant of the earlier travelers' accounts are William H. Keating, *Narrative of an Expedition to the Source of St. Peter's River* (1824; rpt. Minneapolis: Ross & Haines, 1959), 1: 407 ff., and George Catlin, *North American Indians*, 2 vols. (1841; rpt. Edinburgh: John Grant, 1926), 1: 261 ff.

63. Donald Dean Parker, ed., *The Recollections of Philander Prescott, Frontiersman of the Old Northwest, 1819–1862* (Lincoln: University of Nebraska Press, 1966).

64. These manuscripts are in the Pond Papers, MS P437, Minnesota Historical Society, St. Paul. An English translation prepared by Ella C. Deloria in 1941 is in MS 30(X8a.17), Boas Collection, American Philosophical Society Library, Philadelphia.

65. James Owen Dorsey, *A Study of Siouan Cults,* Smithsonian Institution, Bureau of American Ethnology, Annual Report 11 (1894), pp. 351–544. The Bushotter texts are in MS 4800, National Anthropological Archives, Smithsonian Institution. An English translation prepared by Ella C. Deloria about 1937 is in MS 30(X8c.3), Boas Collection, American Philosophical Society, Philadelphia. A listing of the Bushotter texts is given in Raymond J. DeMallie, "A Partial Bibliography of Archival Material Relating to the Dakota Indians," in *The Modern Sioux: Social Systems and Reservation Culture,* ed. Ethel Nurge (Lincoln: University of Nebraska Press, 1970), pp. 316–24. For a biographical sketch of Bushotter, see DeMallie, "George Bushotter: Teton Sioux, 1864–1892," in *American Indian Intellectuals,* ed. Margot Liberty (St. Paul: West Publishing Co., 1978), pp. 91–102.

66. James Mooney, *The Ghost-Dance Religion and the Sioux Outbreak of 1890,* Smithsonian Institution, Bureau of American Ethnology, Annual Report 14, pt. 2 (1896), pp. 816–927.

67. The Beede manuscripts are in the Chester Fritz Library, University of North Dakota, Grand Forks, and the North Dakota State Historical Society, Bismarck.

68. For a biographical sketch of Eastman, see David Reed Miller,

"Charles Alexander Eastman, Santee Sioux, 1858–1939," in *American Indian Intellectuals,* ed. Liberty, pp. 61–73.

69. These manuscripts are part of the Neihardt Papers in the Western Historical Manuscripts Collection, University of Missouri, Columbia.

70. Many of Deloria's manuscripts are deposited in the Boas Collection, American Philosophical Society, Philadelphia, and the Institute of Indian Studies, University of South Dakota, Vermillion. A summary of Lakota life based on Deloria's manuscripts was written by Jeanette Mirsky and published in *Cooperation and Competition among Primitive Peoples,* ed. Margaret Mead (1937; new ed., Boston: Beacon Press, 1966), pp. 382–427.

Part II. Belief.

1. Little Wound's father was Bull Bear, the Oglala head chief who was killed by Red Cloud in 1841. See documents 38 and 72; cf. James C. Olson, *Red Cloud and the Sioux Problem* (Lincoln: University of Nebraska Press, 1965), p. 20.

2. *Tatanka gnaškinyan.* See documents 13 and 29; Walker, *Sun Dance,* pp. 88–89; Bushotter text in Dorsey, *Siouan Cults,* p. 477.

3. See document 14; Walker, *Sun Dance,* p. 152.

4. *Iya,* the Giant, the God of Evil. See Walker, *Sun Dance,* p. 88; Ella C. Deloria, *Dakota Texts,* Publications of the American Ethnological Society, vol. 14 (New York: G. E. Stechert & C., 1932), pp. 1–7.

5. Little Wound is apparently referring to the distinction between the superior *Wakan* and the *Wakan* relatives; see document 5. In this instance we have retained the capital *T* in *The* to mark the distinction. The superior *Wakan* are the Sun, Sky, Earth, and Rock (*Sky* is often used as the English translation of *Taku Škanškan*). See Walker to Wissler, January 13, 1915, p. 35 in this volume; Walker, *Sun Dance,* pp. 81, 154–56; Alice C. Fletcher, "Indian Ceremonies," *Report of the Peabody Museum of American Archaeology and Ethnology,* vol. 3 (Salem, Mass.: Salem Press, 1884), pp. 289–95; Dorsey, *Siouan Cults,* pp. 445–47; Frances Densmore, *Teton Sioux Music,* Smithsonian Institution, Bureau of American Ethnology, Bulletin 61 (1918), pp. 205–6.

6. This is an etymological translation: *ta,* "a ruminant," and *tanka,* "great, large." Cf. document 28.

7. *Iya* is intended here to designate the West Wind, not the Evil God. In his synthesis (*Sun Dance,* p. 84), Walker gives *Eya* as the name of the West Wind in the shamans' language. However, in his manuscripts Walker frequently wrote *e* for the sound usually written *i* in Lakota. He evidently intended, toward the end of his studies, to differentiate between *Eya,* the West Wind, and *Iya,* the Evil God. We have reproduced the names of these gods as Walker wrote them in each document, and have pointed out apparent inconsistencies.

NOTES (pp. 72–101) / 295

8. Walker varies in writing the name *Yata* and *Yate;* he frequently used *a* for the sound written *e* in Lakota.

9. Cf. Walker, *Sun Dance,* pp. 57, 152–53.

10. The Buffalo Calf Pipe, believed to be the first pipe brought to the Lakotas by *Woȟpe* and kept by the Sans Arc tribe. See documents 8 and 44; Edward S. Curtis, *The North American Indian,* vol. 3 (1908; rpt. New York: Johnson Reprint Corporation, 1970), pp. 55–60; John L. Smith, "A Short History of the Sacred Calf Pipe of the Teton Dakota," South Dakota University *Museum News* 28 (1967): 1–37.

11. The terms *woteȟila* and *teȟila* are equivalent. The prefix *wo-* (contraction of *wao-*) "is used to form generalized nouns, particularly abstract nouns" (Franz Boas and Ella Deloria, *Dakota Grammar,* Memoirs of the National Academy of Sciences, vol. 23, no. 2 [1941], p. 125). Thus *teȟila* is a verbal concept while *woteȟila* is an abstract noun. Stephen R. Riggs, *A Dakota-English Dictionary,* ed. J. Owen Dorsey, Contributions to North American Ethnology, vol. 7 (1890), gives *teȟila,* "to forbid"; John P. Williamson, *An English-Dakota Dictionary* (Yankton, S.Dak.: Pioneer Press, 1902), gives *teȟinda* (the Santee and Yankton form), "taboo."

12. Cf. the edited version of this document printed in Walker, *Sun Dance,* p. 156. This provides an opportunity to check the kind of editing done by the AMNH staff to Walker's original interview notes.

13. *Canšaša,* "red, red wood," probably from *canhaša,* "red bark." This is the dried willow or dogwood bark that the Lakotas mix with tobacco to smoke ceremonially; it is referred to in English as kinnikinic.

14. For further information on Lakota medicines, see Melvin Randolph Gilmore, "Some Native Nebraska Plants with Their Uses by the Dakota," *Collections* of the Nebraska State Historical Society 17 (1913): 358–70; idem, *Uses of Plants by the Indians of the Missouri River Region,* Smithsonian Institution, Bureau of American Ethnology, Annual Report 33 (1919), p. 43–154; "Medicines," in Eugene Buechel, S.J., *A Dictionary of the Teton Dakota Sioux Language: Lakota-English, English-Lakota,* ed. Paul Manhart, S.J. (Pine Ridge, S.Dak.: Red Cloud Indian School, 1970), pp. 729–30; Bray and Bray, *Joseph N. Nicollet on the Plains and Prairies,* esp. pp. 280–81; Densmore, *Teton Sioux Music,* pp. 244–71. See also "The Causes of Diseases (Told by No-flesh)," in Walker, *Sun Dance,* pp. 161–64.

15. Cf. Walker, *Sun Dance,* pp. 78–92.

16. *Iyo* appears frequently in Walker's manuscripts as a variant of *Iya.*

17. In Walker, *Sun Dance,* p. 153, *tan ton* has been changed to *ton ton;* evidently Walker decided that the latter form was correct. However, Riggs, *Dakota-English Dictionary,* gives *tanton,* "to have a body, be in the body; to be substantial," and notes the Teton use of the term to mean "to be ripe."

18. The White Marked society. See documents 39, 87, and 88, and Wissler, "Societies and Ceremonial Associations," pp. 34–36.

19. We are unable to reconstruct this etymology. The *Ahinila wota* is

the Silent Eaters society. See Wissler, "Societies and Ceremonial Associations," p. 75, and documents 87–89.

20. *Tunkan:* see documents 20 and 46; Dorsey, *Siouan Cults,* pp. 447–48; Densmore, *Teton Sioux Music,* pp. 204–38.

21. Evidently a reference to the council lodge.

22. This document is a continuation of the interview with Finger printed in Walker, *Sun Dance,* pp. 154–56. The decision to omit this section from the publication was evidently made by Wissler. Cf. document 44.

23. A blank in the manuscript, evidently intended for "raped"; see document 18, which identifies *Waziya* as the bastard son of the North Wind, and document 30, which reports the North Wind's attempt to steal *Wohpe Wakan,* the wife of the South Wind.

24. See Alice C. Fletcher, "Shadow or Ghost Lodge," in "Indian Ceremonies," pp. 296–307; Dorsey, *Siouan Cults,* pp. 487–89; Curtis, *North American Indian,* pp. 99–110; Densmore, *Teton Sioux Music,* pp. 77–84; Joseph Epes Brown, ed., *The Sacred Pipe: Black Elk's Account of the Seven Rites of the Oglala Sioux* (Norman: University of Oklahoma Press, 1953), pp. 10–30.

25. For the Seven Council Fires, see Walker, *Sun Dance,* p. 72. *Seven Stars* is a Lakota name for the Big Dipper.

26. *Gnaška,* evidently a form of *Gnaškinyan,* the Crazy Buffalo; *Gicila,* Dwarfs; *Can Oti,* Tree Dwellers. See document 13; Walker, *Sun Dance,* p. 89; James H. Howard, "The Tree Dweller Cults of the Dakota," *Journal of American Folklore* 68 (1955): 169–74.

27. For the connection between the *Unktehi* and the *Wacipi Wakan,* see Dorsey, *Siouan Cults,* p. 440.

28. See documents 29 and 43; Walker, *Sun Dance,* p. 84.

29. Most of this document was incorporated in Walker, *Sun Dance,* pp. 78 ff.

30. Tyon seems to be speaking here from the perspective of a Christian. He evidently means that just as there was no well-recognized Lakota concept of "Great Spirit" or God, so there was no concept comparable to the Devil, and therefore the Lakotas did not understand the true source of evil.

31. Riggs, *Dakota-English Dictionary,* gives *mica, micaksica,* "a small wolf"; Buechel, *Lakota-English Dictionary,* gives only the second form; Williamson, *English-Dakota Dictionary,* gives *mica,* "coyote".

32. Riggs, *Dakota-English Dictionary,* and Williamson, *English-Dakota Dictionary,* both give this form; Buechel, *Lakota-English Dictionary,* gives *gnaška.*

33. *Unktomi* is the Santee and Yankton form for *Iktomi.*

34. Here *Yata* is used for the West Wind; Walker's synthesis places him as the North Wind; cf. Walker, *Sun Dance,* p. 84.

35. I.e., the land of the spirits, not the land of the white men. See Walker, *Sun Dance,* pp. 87–88.

36. See "How the Lakota Came upon the World," Walker, *Sun Dance,* pp. 181–82.

37. The trickster. See Walker, *Sun Dance,* p. 90; Dorsey, *Siouan Cults,* pp. 471–73; Deloria, *Dakota Texts,* pp. 1–46.

38. This account of the vision quest was apparently part of an earlier draft of Walker's study of the *Hunka.* A brief summary appears in Walker, *Sun Dance,* p. 68. Compare the similar but fuller account by Thunder Bear in document 33 and that written by Tyon from an unspecified informant in document 45.

39. *Skita,* evidently from *yuskita,* "to bind or tie," a reference to the tying together of the two participants during the ceremony.

40. See Fletcher, "The Elk Mystery," in "Indian Ceremonies," pp. 274–88; Wissler, "Societies and Ceremonial Associations," pp. 85–88; idem, "The Whirlwind and the Elk in the Mythology of the Dakota," *Journal of American Folk-Lore* 18 (1905): 257–68; Densmore, *Teton Sioux Music,* pp. 176–79.

41. On this occasion Red Cloud abdicated his position as head chief in favor of his son, Jack Red Cloud. Eli Ricker, interviewing Walker in 1906, noted that the doctor had recorded the speech (Ricker Manuscript Collection, tablet 25, p. 69, Nebraska State Historical Society). Walker entitled this document "Part of Red Cloud's abdication speech."

42. Here begins a second document, to which Walker gave the title "Red Cloud's Confession of Faith"; it is not certain that this is a continuation of the same speech, although it appears to follow logically.

43. *Iyotan,* as an adjective, indicates "great" (used comparatively); as an adverb it indicates "most, very" (Buechel, *Lakota-English Dictionary*). *Wakantu* is clearly *Wankatu* "up above." Thus *Iyotan Wankatu* may be translated "Great Above." Cf. document 5 for the designation *Wakan Wankantu,* "Superior *Wakan.*"

44. The title of this document was given by Walker. See document 18, which refers to the ceremonial defying of *Wakinyan* by members of the White Decorated society.

45. With the establishment of courts of Indian offenses in 1883, the giveaway became a punishable offense. See Francis Paul Prucha, ed. *Documents of United States Indian Policy* (Lincoln: University of Nebraska Press, 1975), pp. 160–62. The court of Indian offenses was not established at Pine Ridge until 1892. See *Annual Report of the Commissioner of Indian Affairs, 1892,* serial no. 3088, p. 454.

46. Short Bull was one of the delegates sent by the Lakotas in 1889 or 1890 to visit Wovoka and learn about the Ghost Dance. See Mooney, *Ghost-Dance Religion,* pp. 819–20.

47. About the same time Short Bull dictated another account of his

visit to Wovoka (also known as Jack Wilson), printed in Natalie Curtis, ed., *The Indian's Book* (1907; rpt. New York: Harper and Brothers, 1935), pp. 45–47.

48. Given as 1889 in the No Ears winter count, to be printed in Walker, *Lakota Society,* forthcoming. Note that since the Lakota "winter" covered parts of two calendar years (from snowfall to snowfall), the assignment of a single calendar year date is arbitrary and might better be expressed as 1889/1890. However, we follow Walker's assignment of dates.

49. Perhaps the designation given by the Lakotas to the Paiute community at which they met Wovoka. The Pyramid Lake band of Paiutes call themselves *Kuyuidika,* "Eaters of the Cui-ui fish." See Omer C. Stewart, "Tribal Distributions and Boundaries in the Great Basin," in *The Current Status of Anthropological Research in the Great Basin,* ed. Warren d'Azevedo et al., Desert Research Institute Publications in the Sciences and Humanities, vol. 1 (Reno, Nev., 1966), p. 218.

Part III. Narratives by Thomas Tyon

1. This sentence is unclear. The reference might be to upright beings (humans); or it might be to "standing peoples," which Black Elk used to refer to trees (see Brown, *Sacred Pipe,* p. 69).

2. *Kicimu* is the reciprocal form of *ecamun,* "I do," a euphemism for sexual intercourse. Deloria called it a man's word; see "Commentary on the Bushotter Texts," MS. 30 (X8c.3), Boas Collection, American Philosophical Society Library, Philadelphia, text 7.

3. Also called *Tatanka Lowanpi,* "Buffalo Bull Sing." See document 85.

4. See Part II, note 38.

5. See Densmore, *Teton Sioux Music,* pp. 204–41, for references to sacred stones; for a description of the modern ceremony, see William K. Powers, *Oglala Religion* (Lincoln: University of Nebraska Press, 1977), pp. 143–54.

6. According to a present-day Lakota holy man, *tunkan yatapika* designates the sweat lodge stones. Another person suggested that *mni wakanta najin kin* refers to the steam rising. When it steams, water "stands."

7. *Ite Peto* is part of the spirit language. According to a present-day Lakota holy man, it refers to the Great Spirit. It may be etymologized as *Ite* (face) + *pe* (top of) + *to* (blue), most likely a reference to *Taku Skanskan.*

8. For *Wakinyan,* see Walker, *Sun Dance,* p. 83, and document 26. For *heyoka,* see Walker, *Sun Dance,* p. 68; Dorsey, *Siouan Cults,* pp. 468–71; Densmore, *Teton Sioux Music,* pp. 157–72; Ella C. Deloria, *Speaking of Indians* (New York: Friendship Press, 1944), pp. 53–55.

9. Gilmore, "Native Nebraska Plants," p. 362, identifies the medicine as *Malvastrum coccineum* (Pursh.) A. Gray. Densmore, *Teton Sioux Music*, p. 168, makes the same identification. Buechel, *Lakota-English Dictionary*, p. 174, concurs, giving the colloquial names "red false mallow or prairie mallow, a gray moss root".

10. Densmore, *Teton Sioux Music*, p. 249, records a medicine man's use of a mirror to see disease reflected in it. Fletcher, "Indian Ceremonies," p. 284, mentions the use of a mirror on the altar of an elk dreamer to symbolize light.

11. See Wissler, "Societies and Ceremonial Associations," pp. 88–90; Densmore, *Teton Sioux Music*, pp. 195–97.

12. See Dorsey, *Siouan Cults*, pp. 478–79; Densmore, *Teton Sioux Music*, pp. 179–84.

13. Deloria, investigating Walker's material in the field in 1937, recorded from Edgar Fire Thunder that medicine men were known as Bone Keepers *(Hohu Yuha)* (Deloria, Dakota Commentary on Walker's Texts, pp. 2, 27). This seems to be the only reference in the literature to the use of this term to indicate medicine men.

14. See Dorsey, *Siouan Cults*, pp. 484–93.

15. See ibid, p. 480.

16. See ibid, pp. 480–81.

17. This Lakota word is variously translated as gopher (Dorsey, *Siouan Cults*, p. 496), pocket gopher (Buechel, *Lakota-English Dictionary*, p. 517), and mole (Walker, *Sun Dance*, p. 162). The animal referred to is actually a pocket gopher (family Geomyidae), not a mole. See Ralph S. Palmer, *The Mammal Guide* (New York: Doubleday & Co., 1954), pp. 198–203.

18. See Dorsey, *Siouan Cults*, p. 479.

Part IV. Ritual.

1. This is the title of the text in Lakota. Walker had the text rewritten by Tyon's daughter so that the spelling conformed to Riggs, *Dakota-English Dictionary*. He then had a copy and an interlinear translation prepared by John Monroe (CHS MS folder 63; for the identification of Monroe as the translator, see Walker to Wissler, August 14, 1911, AMNH correspondence files and CHS Letters folder 7, no. 5). Finally, Walker prepared the text for bilingual publication with interlinear and free translations of his own. (Copies are in CHS MS folder 64 and AMNH.) The translation by the editors printed here is based on Walker's work but corresponds stylistically to the other Tyon translations in this volume.

2. This is not a usual Lakota designation for a month. According to Alice Fletcher, "The Sun Dance of the Ogalalla Sioux," *Proceedings of the American Association for the Advancement of Science, 1882*, vol. 31 (1883), p.

580, the sun dance took place in late June or early July: "The time is fixed by the budding of the *Artemsia Indoviciana*." Bushotter wrote that the sun dance was held late in June (Dorsey, *Siouan Cults*, p. 452). According to Curtis, *North American Indian*, p. 89, the sun dance took place at the summer solstice. Walker, *Sun Dance*, p. 215, indicates that the ceremony occurred "when the chokecherries are ripe."

3. These songs were recorded on a graphophone. The original wax cyclinders are in the CHS. Each cylinder container has a label pasted on it with the number and name of the song in Lakota in George Sword's handwriting. Taped copies of these songs are available from the CHS. For music and lyrics of Lakota sun dance songs, see Densmore, *Teton Sioux Music*, pp. 98–151; Densmore's original recordings are preserved in the Archive of American Folk Song, Library of Congress, Washington, D.C.

4. The text has *tawicaȟilapi (tewicaȟilapi)*, "they love them," a reference to the "child beloveds" who have been honored by the *Hunka* ceremony. Cf. Deloria, *Speaking of Indians*, p. 63.

5. The dance of the White Owners society. This was a chiefs' society among the Oglalas. The name is said to refer to the ownership of white horses. See Wissler, "Societies and Ceremonial Associations," p. 41.

6. Tyon wrote *šunka*, "dog," possibly for *šungmanitu*, "wolf."

7. This reference to a Pawnee society among the Lakotas seems to be unique. We are unable to identify it.

8. See document 15.

9. The paintings by Short Bull were done in 1912. Short Bull chose the colors of water paint he wished to use and Wissler sent them from New York. The paintings are executed on ducking canvas, 29¼" wide; that of the third day is 68½" long, and that of the fourth day is 66¾" long. Short Bull was paid twenty-five dollars for his work (see Walker to Wissler, May 13, 1912). Walker sent the paintings to the American Museum in 1918. This document is Walker's translation of "descriptive notes of the paintings dictated by Short Bull, and written by his son in Lakota. The script and orthography of the son are peculiar to himself and therefore almost impossible to translate" (Walker to Wissler, March 19, 1918). The original Lakota document has not been preserved among Walker's papers. Walker was especially interested in visual representation, since he himself never saw a sun dance, although it is commonly believed that he had actually witnessed the ceremony. See Mead and Bunzel, *The Golden Age of American Anthropology*, p. 342.

10. See documents 35 and 36.

11. See Walker, *Sun Dance*, pp. 212–15.

12. Walker prepared this extensive description of the first of Short Bull's paintings; if he prepared a similar description of the second painting, it has not been found among his papers.

13. For a discussion of the four forms of the sun dance, see Walker, *Sun Dance*, pp. 61–62.

14. Medicine bundle; see document 13 and Walker, *Sun Dance*, pp. 87–88.

15. This is evidently intended for *Iya*, since the reference is to the Evil God, not the West Wind.

16. See Walker, *Sun Dance*, p. 99.

17. The reference here is apparently to two different societies, the Brave Hearts and the Silent Eaters. See documents 87 and 88 and Wissler, "Societies and Ceremonial Associations," pp. 25, 75.

18. Short Bull was a Brulé, although he lived among the Oglalas at Pine Ridge. There is no implication, however, that a Brulé would "read the picture" differently from any other Lakota.

19. This document combines two manuscripts, "Piercing the Ears. By Rocky-bear. Feb. 1st, 1905" (before the first asterisks) and "The Lakota Custom of Piercing the Ears. Information by Rocky-bear" (after the first asterisks).

20. Parenthetical comments evidently added by Walker. The reference is to the Kit Fox, or *Tokala*, society.

21. 1805 in the No Ears winter count, to be printed in Walker, *Lakota Society*, forthcoming.

22. Short Bull also made Walker *Hunka*. See Walker, *Sun Dance*, p. 140.

23. In modern Lakota the accent falls on the second syllable of *lowanpi*, not the first.

24. Parenthetical comment by Walker identifying the Man from the Land of the Pines with *Waziya*, although Afraid of Bear seems to be referring instead to a historical personage.

25. The manuscript gives Rattling Shield, obviously a variant translation of Ringing Shield. In document 83 Walker refers to the same man as Running Shield.

26. The No Ears winter count gives 1802 as the year "A good white man came," 1804 as "They bring home curley horses," and 1805 as "They sing with each other using horse tails (*Hunka* Ceremony)."

27. *Skita*, "bound"; see Part II, note 39.

28. Evidently intended for *Hunka tawa*, "his *Hunka*."

29. *Knega* in the manuscript, evidently an error; we have corrected it to *kaniga* to conform with later repetitions of the word in this document. The term is *kaȟniga*, "to choose, select, elect or appoint" (Buechel, *Lakota-English Dictionary*).

30. *Alowanpi*: "they sing in praise of someone," used here for *walowan*, the person who knows the songs and conducts the ceremony.

31. Cf. Walker, *Sun Dance*, pp. 124–25.

32. The wands are illustrated in Densmore, *Teton Sioux Music*, pl. 3, facing p. 72.

33. This is an earlier draft of Walker's description of the *Hunka* ceremony, sent to Wissler on March 21, 1912. Walker intended the material in parentheses to be printed as footnotes. The method was so cumbersome that he abandoned it. Cf. *Sun Dance,* pp. 122–40. Walker later incorporated the symbolic data from myths used in this document in "Secret Instructions for a Shaman," *Sun Dance,* pp. 78–92.

34. In his synthesis Walker gives *Yata* as North Wind and *Eya* as West Wind. Cf. *Sun Dance,* p. 85, which also describes this pipe ceremony. Evidently Walker reached his final understanding of the Winds when he translated Sword's text "When the Directions Were Made on the World," printed as "When the Wizard Came" in *Sun Dance,* pp. 167–68. The original Lakota text for this myth has not been located. In the myth as printed, *Eya* (West Wind) is systematically given as *Iya.* See Walker to Wissler, March 14, 1916.

35. Walker consistently used the English word *fetish* to translate *wašicun.* See *Sun Dance,* p. 87.

36. Cf. Walker, *Sun Dance,* pp. 69–70. Fletcher, "Indian Ceremonies," p. 284, gives the name of the altar, or "mellowed earth," as *u-ma-nee.* Densmore, *Teton Sioux Music,* p. 122, calls it *owanka wakan,* "sacred place."

37. Walker, *Sun Dance,* p. 79, gives this as "*Wakan Kolaya,* the Associate Gods." Relative Gods, or Related Gods, seems closer to the Lakota concept of *kola,* a close ritual friendship considered to be a kin relationship.

38. The myth, told by Left Heron, is printed as "The Buffalo Woman" in Walker, *Sun Dance,* pp. 183–90.

39. Walker means that to the Lakotas a ritual father, *Ate,* functions as a mentor.

40. Evidently the White Owners society. See documents 87 and 88.

41. This is an undated draft of an account of the Buffalo ceremony which presents more data than the version printed in *Sun Dance,* pp. 141–51. The ceremony is also called *Išnati awicalowanpi,* "They sing over the one dwelling alone," a reference to a woman's seclusion during menstruation. See document 44; also see Black Elk's account in Brown, *Sacred Pipe,* pp. 116–26.

42. *Tonwan,* according to Sword, is "something like" a spirit (Walker, *Sun Dance,* p. 152). Also see document 13 and p. 230, above.

43. The word is *išnati,* "lone tipi," the place of seclusion of a menstruating woman.

44. Another example of the use of *Yata* instead of *Eya* for the West Wind.

45. Evidently intended for *Wakan Škanškan;* cf. document 27.

46. Here the shaman speaks as if he were *Tatanka.*

47. A reference to the buffalo skull on the altar. Cf. Walker, *Sun Dance,* p. 146.

Part V. Warfare

1. The major published sources on Lakota men's societies are Wissler, "Societies and Ceremonial Associations," pp. 7–74; Densmore, *Teton Sioux Music,* pp. 311–75; and Amos Bad Heart Bull, *A Pictographic History of the Oglala Sioux* (Lincoln: University of Nebraska Press, 1967), pp. 104–16. Helen H. Blish, *Ethical Conceptions of the Oglala Dakota,* University of Nebraska Studies, vol. 26, nos. 3–4 (1926, pp. 81–93), and Thomas E. Mails, *Dog Soldiers, Bear Men and Buffalo Women* (Englewood Cliffs, N.J.: Prentice-Hall, 1973), pp. 225–68, summarize from the other sources.

2. Here *Iya* is used for the East Wind, which Walker in his synthesis (*Sun Dance,* p. 84) calls *Yanpa.* This is repeated in Wissler, "Societies and Ceremonial Associations," p. 19. This is the only place in all of Walker's material where two of the winds are identified as *Taku Škanškan* and *Inyan.* These inconsistencies suggest that there was not unanimity among Walker's informants as to the classification of the gods.

3. The Sacred Bow was an Oglala men's association. See Helen H. Blish, "The Ceremony of the Sacred Bow of the Oglala Dakota," *American Anthropologist* 36 (1934): 180–87; Sword, "The Holy Bow," manuscript in the Department of Anthropology, AMNH (to appear in the forthcoming edition of Sword's writings). See insignia no. 2, color plate 4.

4. Wissler, "Societies and Ceremonial Associations," pp. 36, 75, differentiates between the Big Bellies, another name for the Chiefs' society, and the Silent Eaters, a feasting association.

5. Tyon entitled this text *Tokala Okolakiciye kin He,* "This is the Kit Fox society."

6. The etymology of the term may be *can* (wood) + *wounyeya* (to have for victim); see Buechel, *Lakota-English Dictionary, "canwowinge"* and *"wounyeya."*

7. Riggs, *Dakota-English Dictionary,* gives for Lakota *wašicun,* "a familiar spirit," and *wotawe,* "armor; weapons conscrated by religious ceremonies; whatever is relied upon in war."

8. Throughout the text Tyon uses the term *xkan (škan,* "to move," in a specific way, evidently indicating movement in a ceremonial manner, as in a dance or procession. We have simply translated it "to act." The implication is that the society regalia (the *canwounye*) function in the capacity of *wotawe* or *wašicun* to empower the members to perform brave deeds in battle. Thus they give the members power to act *(taku yuha škanpi),* "something they have with which to act."

9. The term *wapaha* is used to designate both the warbonnet and the feathered staff (see colored plates 6 and 7); Riggs, *Dakota-English Dictionary,* differentiates the two by placing the accent on the first syllable for the staff and on the second syllable for the warbonnet.

10. The idea expressed here is that a man's generosity is considered a central part of his bravery. With the cessation of warfare, the act of giving became the most important expression of a man's bravery. The text implies that some men disposed of their society regalia in order to avoid these obligations.

11. Drum stakes are used to support the society drum off the ground while it is in use.

12. Tyon also entitled this text *Tokala Okolakiciye kin He*, "This is the Kit Fox society." This text is a fragment of the Cheyenne sacred tradition concerning Sweet Medicine the Prophet, his institution of the Cheyenne warrior societies, and his bringing of the Sacred Arrows to the Cheyenne tribe. Cf. Peter J. Powell, *Sweet Medicine*, 2 vols. (Norman: University of Oklahoma Press, 1969), 2:462, and references cited therein.

13. Wissler used parts of this document in "Societies and Ceremonial Associations," pp. 15, 20.

14. These drawings were commissioned by Clark Wissler. Thunder Bear was paid twenty-eight dollars for the work. See Richard Nines to Wissler, June 12, 1912 (AMNH). For other data on feather symbolism, see Garrick Mallery, *Picture-Writing of the American Indians*, Smithsonian Institution, Bureau of American Ethnology, Annual Report 10 (1893), pp. 433–35.

15. The Lakota word *kte* can mean either "he killed" or "he counted coup."

16. This word is spelled in a variety of ways, probably reflecting different pronunciations; the etymology of the term is unclear.

17. For depictions of Kit Fox society regalia, see Wissler, "Societies and Ceremonial Associations" p. 70, and Bad Heart Bull, *Pictographic History*, p. 114.

18. There seems to be no mention in the literature of an Owl society, although Densmore, *Teton Sioux Music*, pp. 184–88, describes an owl dreamer.

19. The Lakota inscriptions on these drawings, presumably written by Thunder Bear, are difficult to translate and seem to reflect less experience in writing than the texts of Tyon or Sword. Walker's translations of these captions are demonstrably incorrect in many details; we have given a very free translation, which may be checked against the original Lakota on the drawings. Note the expression *Lakota Šahiyela*, literally "Lakota Cheyenne," evidently meaning "Cheyenne Indian" (interpreting *Lakota* in its widest sense), but possibly interpretable as "allied Cheyenne."

20. The manuscript reads "indicates that the enemy was a Cheyenne," an obvious error that we have corrected.

21. There seems to be no mention in the literature of a Beaver society.

22. For depiction of *Sotka* society regalia, see Wissler, "Societies and Ceremonial Associations," p. 71, and Bad Heart Bull, *Pictographic History*, p. 108.

23. There seems to be no mention in the literature of an Otter society.

24. For a depiction of regalia of the Brave Heart society, see Wissler, "Societies and Ceremonial Associations," p. 68, and Bad Heart Bull, *Pictographic History*, p. 104.

25. There are additional colored drawings numbered from 18 to 29 that depict feather ornaments and various ways of cutting and painting feathers as insignia. However, they lack explanatory notes, and since they do not add to the information given here, they have been omitted from this volume. There are also two more drawings of war exploits by Thunder Bear, without captions or explanations of any kind, in the Department of Anthropology, AMNH.

Bibliography

Around Him, John. *Lakota Ceremonial Songs.* Translated by Albert White Hat, Sr. Rosebud. S. Dak.: Sinte Gleska College, 1983.

Bad Heart Bull, Amos. *A Pictographic History of the Oglala Sioux.* Lincoln: University of Nebraska Press, 1967.

Beede, Aaron McGaffey. Family papers. Chester Fritz Library, University of North Dakota, Grand Forks. Other Beede papers, including correspondence with M. R. Gilmore, are in the North Dakota State Historical Society, Bismarck.

Black Elk, Wallace and William S. Lyon. *Black Elk: The Sacred Ways of a Lakota.* San Francisco: Harper & Row, 1990.

Blish, Helen H. *Ethical Conceptions of the Oglala Dakota.* University of Nebraska Studies, vol. 26, nos. 3–4, 1926, pp. 79–123.

———. "The Ceremony of the Sacred Bow of the Oglala Dakota." *American Anthropologist* 36 (1934): 180–87.

Boas, Franz. *The Mind of Primitive Man.* New York: Macmillan, 1911.

———. Introduction. *Handbook of American Indian Languages.* Smithsonian Institution, Bureau of American Ethnology, Bulletin 40, pt. 1, 1911, pp. 1–83.

Boas, Franz, and Ella Deloria. *Dakota Grammar.* Memoirs of the National Academy of Sciences, vol. 23, no. 2, 1941.

Bourke, John G. "Capt. Bourke on the Sun-Dance." In J. Owen Dorsey, *A Study of Siouan Cults.* Smithsonian Institution, Bureau of American Ethnology, Annual Report 11, 1894, pp. 464–66.

Bray, Edmund C., and Martha Coleman Bray, eds. *Joseph N. Nicollet on the Plains and Prairies: The Expeditions of 1838–39 with Journals, Letters, and Notes on the Dakota Indians.* St. Paul: Minnesota Historical Society Press, 1976.

Brennan, John R. Personal papers. South Dakota State Historical Society, Pierre.

Brown, Joseph Epes, ed. *The Sacred Pipe: Black Elk's Account of the Seven Rites of the Oglala Sioux.* Norman: University of Oklahoma Press, 1953.

———. *The Spiritual Legacy of the American Indian.* New York: Crossroad, 1982.

Buechel, Eugene, S.J. *A Dictionary of the Teton Dakota Sioux Language: Lakota-English, English-Lakota.* Edited by Paul Manhart, S.J. Pine Ridge, S. Dak.: Red Cloud Indian School, 1970.

Buechel, Eugene, S.J., et al. *Lakota Tales and Texts.* Edited by Paul Manhart, S.J. Pine Ridge, S. Dak.: Red Cloud Indian School, 1978.

Bushotter, George. Lakota texts. MS 4800, National Anthropological Archives, Smithsonian Institution, Washington, D.C.

Catlin, George. *North American Indians.* 2 vols. 1841. Reprint ed., Edinburgh: John Grant, 1926.

Commissioner of Indian Affairs. *Annual Reports,* 1891–1900. Washington, D.C.: Government Printing Office.

Curtis, Edward S. *The North American Indian.* Vol. 3. 1908. Reprint ed., New York: Johnson Reprint Corporation, 1970.

Curtis, Natalie, ed. *The Indians' Book.* 1907. Reprint ed., New York: Harper and Brothers, 1935.

Deloria, Ella C. *Dakota Texts.* Publications of the American Ethnological Society, vol. 14. New York: G. E. Stechert & Co., 1932.

———. Correspondence with Franz Boas. 1927–34. MS 31, Boas Collection, American Philosophical Society Library, Philadelphia.

———. *Speaking of Indians.* New York: Friendship Press, 1944.

Deloria, Ella C., ed. and trans. Dakota Autobiographies. Ca. 1937. MS 30(X8a.4), Boas Collection, American Philosophical Society Library, Philadelphia.

———. Teton Myths [the George Bushotter collection]. Ca. 1937. MS 30(X8c.3), Boas Collection, American Philosophical Society Library, Philadelphia.

———. Dakota Commentary on Walker's legends. 1937–38. MS 30(X8a.5), Boas Collection, American Philosophical Society Library, Philadelphia.

———. Dakota Texts from the Sword manuscript. 1938. MS 30(X8a.18), Boas Collection, American Philosophical Society Library, Philadelphia.

———. Dakota texts from the Minnesota manuscript [Pond brothers' Santee myths]. 1941. MS 30(X8a.17), Boas Collection, American Philosophical Society Library, Philadelphia.

DeMallie, Raymond J. "A Partial Bibliography of Archival Manuscript Material Relating to the Dakota Indians." In *The Modern Sioux: Social Systems and Reservation Culture,* edited by Ethel Nurge, pp. 312–43. Lincoln: University of Nebraska Press, 1970.

———. "George Bushotter: Teton Sioux, 1864–1892." In *American Indian Intellectuals,* edited by Margot Liberty, pp. 91–102. St. Paul: West Publishing Co., 1978.

DeMallie, Raymond J., ed. *The Sixth Grandfather: Black Elk's Teachings Given to John G. Neihardt.* Lincoln: University of Nebraska Press, 1984.

DeMallie, Raymond J. and Douglas R. Parks, eds. *Sioux Indian Religion: Tradition and Innovation.* Norman: University of Oklahoma Press, 1987.

Densmore, Frances. *Teton Sioux Music.* Smithsonian Institution, Bureau of American Ethnology, Bulletin 61, 1918.

Dixon, Joseph Kossuth. *The Vanishing Race: The Last Great Indian Council.* 3d ed., rev. Philadelphia: National American Indian Memorial Association Press, 1925.

Dooling, D. M., ed. *The Sons of the Wind: The Sacred Stories of the Lakota.* New York: Parabola Books, 1984.

Dooling, D. M. and Paul Jordan-Smith, eds. *I Become Part of It: Sacred Dimensions in Native American Life.* New York: Parabola Books, 1989.

Dorsey, George A. *The Arapahoe Sun Dance; The Ceremony of the Offerings Lodge.* Field Museum Anthropological Series 4, 1903.

———. *The Cheyenne II: The Sun Dance.* Field Museum Anthropological Series 9, no. 2, 1905.

———. "Legend of the Teton Sioux Medicine Pipe." *Journal of American Folk-Lore* 19 (1906): 326–29.

Dorsey, James Owen. *A Study of Siouan Cults.* Smithsonian Institution, Bureau of American Ethnology, Annual Report 11, 1894, pp. 351–544.

Eastman, Charles Alexander. *Indian Boyhood.* New York: McClure, Phillips & Co., 1902.

———. *The Soul of the Indian: An Interpretation.* Boston: Houghton Mifflin, 1911.

———. *The Indian To-day: The Past and Future of the First American.* Garden City, N.Y.: Doubleday, Page & Co., 1915.

———. *From the Deep Woods to Civilization: Chapters in the Autobiography of an Indian.* Boston: Little, Brown, and Company, 1916.

Eastman, Mary. *Dahcotah; or, Life and Legends of the Sioux around Fort Snelling.* New York: John Wiley, 1849.

Feraca, Stephen E. *Wakinyan: Contemporary Teton Dakota Religion.* Studies in Plains Anthropology and History, no. 2. Browning, Mont.: Museum of the Plains Indian, 1963.

Fletcher, Alice C. "The Sun Dance of the Ogalalla Sioux." *Proceedings of the American Association for the Advancement of Science, 1882,* vol. 31 (1883), pp. 580–84.

———. "Indian Ceremonies." Separate reprint from *Report of the Peabody Museum of American Archaeology and Ethnology,* vol. 3, Salem, Mass.: Salem Press, 1884, pp. 260–333.

———. *The Hako: A Pawnee Ceremony.* Smithsonian Institution, Bureau of American Ethnology, Annual Report 22, pt. 2, 1904.

Fugle, Eugene. "The Nature and Function of the Lakota Night Cults." *South Dakota University Museum News* 27 (1966): 1–38.

Gilmore, Melvin Randolph. "Some Native Nebraska Plants with Their

Uses by the Dakota." *Collections* of the Nebraska State Historical Society 17 (1913): 358–70.

———. *Uses of Plants by the Indians of the Missouri River Region*. Smithsonian Institution, Bureau of American Ethnology, Annual Report 33, 1919, pp. 43–154.

Hassrick, Royal B. *The Sioux: Life and Customs of a Warrior Society*. Norman: University of Oklahoma Press, 1964.

Howard, James H. "The Tree Dweller Cults of the Dakota." *Journal of American Folklore* 68 (1955): 169–74.

———. *The Warrior Who Killed Custer: The Personal Narrative of Chief Joseph White Bull*. Lincoln: University of Nebraska Press, 1968.

———. *The Canadian Sioux*. Lincoln: University of Nebraska Press, 1984.

Hyde, George E. *Red Cloud's Folk: A History of the Oglala Sioux Indians*. Norman: University of Oklahoma Press, 1937.

———. *A Sioux Chronicle*. Norman: University of Oklahoma Press, 1956.

———. *Spotted Tail's Folk: A History of the Brulé Sioux*. Norman: University of Oklahoma Press, 1961.

Jahner, Elaine. "The Spiritual Landscape." *Parabola* 2 (1977): 32–38.

Johnson, A. F. "Career of Captain George Sword." *Oglala Light*, 1910, pp. 21–23.

Keating, William H. *Narrative of an Expedition to the Source of St. Peter's River*. 2 vols. 1824. Reprint ed., Minneapolis: Ross & Haines, 1959.

Kemnitzer, Luis. "The Cultural Provenience of Artifacts Used in Yuwipi, a Modern Teton Dakota Healing Ritual." *Ethnos* 35 (1970): 40–75.

———. "Structure, Content, and Cultural Meaning of *Yuwipi*, a Modern Lakota Healing Ritual." *American Ethnologist* 3 (1976): 261–80.

Kroeber, Alfred L. *The Arapaho*. Bulletin of the American Museum of Natural History, vol. 18 (1902–1907), pp. 1–229, 279–454.

Lame Deer, John (Fire) and Richard Erdoes. *Lame Deer, Seeker of Visions*. New York: Simon and Schuster, 1972.

Lewis, Thomas H. *The Medicine Men: Oglala Sioux Ceremony and Healing*. Lincoln: University of Nebraska Press, 1990.

Lincoln, Kenneth with Al Logan Slagle. *The Good Red Road: Passages into Native America*. San Francisco: Harper & Row, 1987.

Lynd, James W. "The Religion of the Dakotas." *Minnesota Historical Collections* 2 (1864): 150–74 (2d ed., 1881).

McGaa, Ed (Eagle Man). *Mother Earth Spirituality: Native American Paths to Healing Ourselves and Our World*. San Francisco: Harper & Row, 1990.

Mails, Thomas E. *Dog Soldiers, Bear Men and Buffalo Women*. Englewood Cliffs, N.J.: Prentice-Hall, 1973.

———. *Sundancing at Rosebud and Pine Ridge*. Sioux Falls, S.Dak.: Augustana College, 1978.

Mallery, Garrick, *Picture-Writing of the American Indians*. Smithsonian Institution, Bureau of American Ethnology, Annual Report 10, 1893.

Mead, Margaret, and Ruth L. Bunzel, eds. *The Golden Age of American Anthropology.* New York: George Braziller, 1960.

Meyer, Roy W. *History of the Santee Sioux: United States Indian Policy on Trial.* Lincoln: University of Nebraska Press, 1967.

Miller, David Reed. "Charles Alexander Eastman, Santee Sioux, 1858–1939." In *American Indian Intellectuals,* edited by Margot Liberty, pp. 61–73. St. Paul: West Publishing Co., 1978.

Mirsky, Jeanette. "The Dakota." In *Cooperation and Competition among Primitive Peoples,* edited by Margaret Mead, pp. 382–427. 1937. New ed., Boston: Beacon Press, 1966.

Mooney, James. *The Ghost-Dance Religion and the Sioux Outbreak of 1890.* Smithsonian Institution, Bureau of American Ethnology, Annual Report 14, pt. 2, 1896.

Neihardt, John G. *Black Elk Speaks: Being the Life Story of a Holy Man of the Ogalala Sioux.* New York: William Morrow & Co., 1932.

————. *When the Tree Flowered: An Authentic Tale of the Old Sioux World.* New York: Macmillan, 1952.

————. Papers. Western Historical Manuscript Collections, University of Missouri, Columbia.

Olden, Sarah Emilia. *The People of Tipi Sapa (The Dakotas).* Milwaukee: Morehouse Publishing Co., 1918.

Olson, James C. *Red Cloud and the Sioux Problem.* Lincoln: University of Nebraska Press, 1965.

Palmer, Ralph S. *The Mammal Guide.* New York: Doubleday & Co., 1954.

Parker, Donald Dean, ed. *The Recollections of Philander Prescott, Frontiersman of the Old Northwest, 1819–1862.* Lincoln: University of Nebraska Press, 1966.

Pearce, Roy Harvey. *The Savages of America: A Study of the Indian and the Idea of Civilization.* 1953. Reprinted as *Savagism and Civilization: A Study of the Indian and the American Mind.* Baltimore: The Johns Hopkins Press, 1965.

Pine Ridge Reservation: A Pictorial Description. Pine Ridge, S.Dak.: Oglala Light, 1909.

Pond, Gideon H. "Power and Influence of Dakota Medicine-Men." In *Information Respecting the History, Conditions and Prospects of the Indian Tribes of the United States,* edited by Henry R. Schoolcraft, vol. 4, pp. 641–51, Philadelphia, 1854.

————. "Dakota Superstitions." *Collections* of the Minnesota Historical Society 2 (1867): 32–62.

Pond, Samuel. "The Dakotas or Sioux in Minnesota as They Were in 1834." *Collections* of the Minnesota Historical Society 12 (1908): 319–501.

Powell, Peter J. *Sweet Medicine: The Continuing Role of the Sacred Arrows, the Sun Dance, and the Sacred Buffalo Hat in Northern Cheyenne History.* 2

vols. Norman: University of Oklahoma Press, 1969.

Powers, William K. *Oglala Religion*. Lincoln: University of Nebraska Press, 1977.

——. *Yuwipi: Vision and Experience in Oglala Ritual*. Lincoln: University of Nebraska Press, 1982.

——. *Sacred Language: The Nature of Supernatural Discourse in Lakota*. Norman: University of Oklahoma Press, 1986.

Prescott, Philander. "Contributions to the History, Customs and Opinions of the Dacota Tribe." In *Information Respecting the History, Condition and Prospects of the Indian Tribes of the United States,* edited by Henry R. Schoolcraft, vol. 2 (1852), pp. 168–99; vol. 3 (1853), pp. 225–46; vol. 4 (1854), pp. 59–72. Philadelphia.

Prucha, Francis Paul, ed. *Documents of United States Indian Policy*. Lincoln: University of Nebraska Press, 1975.

Radin, Paul. *Primitive Man as Philosopher*. 1927. Reprint ed., New York: Dover Publications, 1957.

Rice, Julian. *Lakota Storytelling: Black Elk, Ella Deloria, and Frank Fools Crow*. New York: Peter Lang, 1989.

Ricker, Eli. Interview with James R. Walker, 1906. MS. Tablet 25, Ricker Collection, Nebraska State Historical Society, Lincoln.

Riggs, Stephen R. *Tah̄-koo Wah-kaṅ; or, The Gospel among the Dakotas*. Boston: Congregational Publishing Society, 1869.

——. *A Dakota-English Dictionary*. Edited by J. Owen Dorsey. Contributions to North American Ethnology, vol. 7. Washington, D.C.: Government Printing Office, 1890.

——. *Dakota Grammar, Texts, and Ethnography*. Edited by J. Owen Dorsey. Contributions to North American Ethnology, vol. 9. Washington, D.C.: Government Printing Office, 1893.

Ruby, Robert H. *The Oglala Sioux: Warriors in Transition*. New York: Vantage Press, 1955.

Sapir, Edward. "Time Perspectives in Aboriginal American Culture: A Study in Method." 1916. Reprinted in *Selected Writings of Edward Sapir in Language, Culture and Personality,* edited by David G. Mandelbaum, pp. 389–462. Berkeley: University of California Press, 1949.

Skinner, Alanson. "Notes on the Sun Dance of the Sisseton Dakota." American Museum of Natural History, *Anthropological Papers* 16 (1919): 381–85.

——. "Medicine Ceremony of the Menomini, Iowa, and Wahpeton Dakota with Notes on the Ceremony among the Ponca, Bungi Ojibwa, and Potawatomi." *Indian Notes and Monographs* 4 (1920): 1–357.

Smith, John L. "A Short History of the Sacred Calf Pipe of the Teton Dakota." South Dakota University *Museum News* 28 (1967): 1–37.

——. "The Sacred Calf Pipe Bundle: Its Effect on the Present Teton Dakota." *Plains Anthropologist* 15 (1970): 87–93.

Standing Bear, Luther. *My People the Sioux*. Boston: Houghton Mifflin, 1928.

——. *Land of the Spotted Eagle*. Boston: Houghton Mifflin, 1933.

Steinmetz, Paul, S.J. "Explanation of the Sacred Pipe as a Prayer Instrument." *Pine Ridge Research Bulletin*, no. 10 (1969), pp. 20–25.

——. *Pipe, Bible, and Peyote among the Oglala Lakota: A Study in Religious Identity*. Knoxville: University of Tennessee Press, 1990.

Steltenkamp, Michael F. *The Sacred Vision: Native American Religion and Its Practice Today*. New York: Paulist Press, 1982.

Stewart, Omer C. "Tribal Distributions and Boundaries in the Great Basin." In *The Current Status of Anthropological Research in the Great Basin*, edited by Warren L. d'Azevedo et al. Desert Institute Publications in the Sciences and Humanities, vol. 1, pp. 167–238. Reno, Nev. 1966.

Stocking, George W., Jr. *Race, Culture, and Evolution: Essays in the History of Anthropology*. New York: Free Press, 1968.

Stocking, George W., Jr., ed. *The Shaping of American Anthropology, 1883–1911: A Franz Boas Reader*. New York: Basic Books, 1974.

Stolzman, William, S.J. *The Pipe and Christ: A Christian-Sioux Dialogue*. Pine Ridge, S. Dak.: Red Cloud Indian School, 1986.

Taylor, Allan R. "The Colorado University System for Writing the Lakhóta Language." *American Indian Culture and Research Journal* 1 (1975): 3–12.

Vestal, Stanley. *Warpath: The True Story of the Fighting Sioux Told in a Biography of Chief White Bull*. Boston: Houghton Mifflin, 1934.

Walker, James R. "Sioux Games." *Journal of American Folk-Lore* 18 (1905): 277–90, 19 (1906): 29–36.

——. "Tuberculosis among the Oglala Sioux Indians." *American Journal of Medical Science*, n.s. 132 (1906): 600–605.

——. "Tuberculosis among the Oglala Sioux Indians." *Southern Workman* 35 (1906): 378–84.

——. "Oglala Kinship Terms." *American Anthropologist* 16 (1914): 96–109.

——. "The Sun Dance and Other Ceremonies of the Oglala Division of the Teton Dakota." American Museum of Natural History *Anthropological Papers* 16, pt. 2 (1917): 50–221.

——. *Lakota Society*. Edited by Raymond J. DeMallie. Lincoln: University of Nebraska Press, 1982.

——. *Lakota Myth*. Edited by Elaine A. Jahner. Lincoln: University of Nebraska Press, 1983.

Wallis, Wilson D. "The Sun Dance of the Canadian Dakota." American Museum of Natural History, *Anthropological Papers* 16 (1919): 317–80.

——. "Beliefs and Tales of the Canadian Dakota." *Journal of American Folklore* 36 (1923): 36–101.

————. "The Canadian Dakota." American Museum of Natural History, *Anthropological Papers* 41 (1947): 1–225.

Weygold, Frederick. "Die Hunkazeremonie." *Archiv für Anthropologie* 11 (1912): 145–60.

Williamson, John P. *An English-Dakota Dictionary.* New York: American Tract Society, 1902.

Wissler, Clark. "The Whirlwind and the Elk in the Mythology of the Dakota." *Journal of American Folk-Lore* 18 (1905): 257–68.

————. "Some Dakota Myths." *Journal of American Folk-Lore* 20 (1907): 121–31, 195–206.

————. "Measurements of Dakota Indian Children." *Annals of the New York Academy of Sciences* 20 (1911): 355–64.

————. "Societies and Ceremonial Associations in the Oglala Division of the Teton-Dakota." American Museum of Natural History, *Anthropological Papers* 11, pt. 1 (1912): 1–99.

————. General Introduction. American Museum of Natural History, *Anthropological Papers* 16 (1921): v–ix.

Zimmerly, David. "On Being an Ascetic: Personal Document of a Sioux Medicine Man." *Pine Ridge Research Bulletin,* no. 10 (1969), pp. 46–71.

Index

A-, 96
Adoption, and *Hunka,* 199, 203, 206, 211
Afraid of Bear, 200, 283
Ahinila Iota, Ahinila wota, Ainila wota, Ainila Wotapi. See Silent Eaters
Air, Spirit of the, 114
Akan, 96
Akicita, 80, 81, 96, 141, 181, 223, 235, 281; of supernatural beings, 79, 84, 230
Alcoholic beverages, 5–6
Alowanpi (walowan), 202, 211, 216, 220–21, 222–38, 240
American Anthropologist, 33
American Horse, xiv, 68, 283
American Journal of Medical Science, 12
American Museum of Natural History, xvi, xx, xxi, xxii, 13–14, 300 n9
American Philosophical Society, xxi
Animals, 69, 71, 98, 101, 103, 144; in dreams, 135–36, 157, 160, 161, 184
Anog Ite, 39, 53, 94, 106, 107, 140, 228, 231, 233; and the Buffalo ceremony, 241, 242, 243, 248, 249, 251. *See also* Double Woman; Two-Face
Anp, 52
Anpao, 244, 245
Anpaoluta, 141
Anp-etu, 52
Anpeyoka, 141
Antelope, 184, 274
Anthropometry, xxii, 16, 18–19
Arapahoes, 13, 25, 143, 269
Associate Gods, 35, 50. *See also* Relative Gods
Associations. *See* Societies
Ate, 194, 195, 196, 198, 202, 205, 206, 209, 210, 237. *See also Hunka Ate; Kaniga Ate*
Aurora borealis, 104, 120, 127, 204

Badgers, 169–70
Badger society, 260, 265, 267–68
Bad Heart Bull, 183, 283
Bad Wound, xiv, 93–96, 124, 208–11, 283
Bannocks, 143
Bare Lance society, 178, 260, 265, 267–68, 269; insignia of, 278–79, 280–81
Bats, 125
Bear, The, 50–51, 116, 128, 227, 231, 232. *See also Hunonp*
Bear medicine, 61, 74, 91–93, 105, 136, 157–59, 291 n41
Bears, 101, 121; dreams of, 116, 136, 157–59, 161, 184, 231, 232
Bear society, 157–59
Beasts, spirits of the, 208
Beautiful Woman, the, 94. *See also Wohpe*
Beavers, 101, 121, 263
Beaver society, 277
Beede, Aaron McGaffey, 57–58
Belted kingfishers, 161
Benedict, Ruth, 59
Big Bellies, 101, 263. *See also* Silent Eaters
Bird medicine men, 105, 161
"Biting the Snake," 28, 190
Black (color), 118, 186, 187, 189, 202, 235, 246, 281; in war insignia, 273, 274, 275, 278, 281
Black Elk, 59
Blackfeet, 15, 26
Blackfeet Lakotas, xxv
Black-tailed deer, 167
Blotahunka, blotanhunka, blotohuka, 74, 271, 272, 274
Blue (color), 35, 51, 108, 115, 118; in the Sun Dance, 183, 184, 186; in *Hunka,* 213–14, 215, 216, 217; in

315